RELIGION AND MODERN LITERATURE

Essays in Theory and Criticism

edited by

G. B. TENNYSON

and

EDWARD E. ERICSON, JR.

WILLIAM B. EERDMANS PUBLISHING COMPANY
GRAND RAPIDS, MICHIGAN

Copyright © 1975 William B. Eerdmans Publishing Co.
All Rights Reserved

Printed in the United States of America

Library of Congress Cataloging in Publication Data

Ericson, Edward E., Jr.   comp.
  Religion and modern literature.

  Includes bibliographical references.
  1. Religion and literature—Addresses, essays,
lectures.   I. Tennyson, G. B., joint comp.   II. Title.
PN49.E7   809'.933'1   74-13237
ISBN 0-8028-1578-1 (pbk.)

Contents

5

III   RELIGIOUS DIMENSIONS IN MODERN LITERATURE

Preface

After a long period of being confined to seminaries and denominational schools the study of religion has lately come to be a matter of interest throughout the academic world. Students in large secular state institutions as well as in small private colleges have by their interest in religious questions called forth an academic response in terms of courses and curricula that would have been novel, and to some scandalous, only a decade ago. One of the areas of greatest concern has been that of the relation of religion to literature and especially to modern literature. Accordingly, courses treating these concerns have been appearing with increasing frequency since the sixties. What has not been readily available, however, is reference and study material concerned with the very topic these courses endeavor to explore. The present anthology is designed to help provide such course and reference material for students and teachers.

To offer an anthology like the present one is to raise at once a host of questions. What is the relationship, if any, of religion to literature, especially modern literature? Does it differ, and if so how, from the relationship of religion to other kinds of art or to other kinds of human activity? How does the treatment of the relationship of religion to literature differ from, or relate to, the treatment of the relationship of literature to other activities—to history, biography, economics, sociology, and psychology? Even if some kind of general statement can be made about the relation of religion to literature, how does one proceed from there? How does one discern and analyze the relationship in terms of individual literary works, especially works of the modern age with their often totally divergent views of life and society? And so on. The purpose of this collection is to help answer such questions by offering the thoughts of a wide variety of contemporary scholars and critics on these topics.

Most questions involving the relationship of religion to literature resolve themselves into the theoretical and the practical. The theoretical questions are questions of aesthetics and the philosophy of literature and ultimately questions of theology. The practical questions about analyzing literary works from the point of view of their religious dimensions are questions about procedure and the use of evidence once the principles have been established.

The following selections have been divided into three main sections precisely to facilitate the movement from the general to the particular. The essays of the first section are concerned with such matters as the way religious belief affects what a literary artist creates and the validity of using religious categories to talk about literature. The second section offers essays that bring these larger issues into focus in terms of twentieth-century literature, essays on the philosophic background of modern literature and essays on the religious issues that have gained particular prominence in modern writing. The third section provides essays that are practical examinations of the religious dimensions of particular works and authors, illustrations of the application of religious and theological ideas to the business of criticism. The arrangement of the essays is therefore paradigmatic. The reader should be able first to consider the theoretical foundations for the study of religion and literature and then to see how they operate in given cases.

Readers will note that some variety exists in the style of the essays. Some were originally lectures, others originally parts of larger works. To preserve the original character of the selections the editors have not modified the authors' texts, believing that the context will make the setting clear. Because approaches to the subject of religion and literature vary so widely the editors have also not provided study guides or questions, or theme topics, after each essay or section. Rather, the editors see this work as providing a core of contemporary views around which a variety of courses could be built. A course concerned primarily with the theoretical and aesthetic problems might use this collection to illustrate the various approaches taken to these questions. The emphasis then would fall on sections I and II. A course based on specific modern works could use the present anthology as commentary and insight on those works. Here the emphasis would fall on section III, and instructors might want to select primary texts based on the commentary available in that section. Further, as a library reference work the present collection brings together a large number of essential essays not otherwise readily available. It is the editors' hope that this anthology will prove its versatility both in the classroom and on the reference shelf.

For their aid in helping to make this volume possible the editors are grateful to the following: Mrs. Mary G. Bisgay and Mrs. Janet D. Keyes at UCLA; Mrs. Doris Byron at Westmont College; Marlin Van Elderen and Jon Pott at Eerdmans; and a special debt of gratitude to Elizabeth Tennyson for proofreading and preparation of the index.

GBT
EEE

Introduction

The study of the relationship of literature to religion is at once one of the oldest and one of the newest concerns of criticism. It is one of the oldest because what we call literature arose out of religion and only gradually detached itself into a separate "field." It is one of the newest because only in the past century and a half has literature been so completely detached, not only from religion but from belief and from any notion of didacticism, that the question can have arisen as to what its relationship with religion could be or whether there was any relationship at all. Thus to take up the question of religion and literature is to take up a topic of almost unlimited antiquity and a topic of complete modernity.

To see how a study can be both so old and so new it is necessary to call to mind some of the circumstances of literature and literary criticism in past ages and to look at the circumstances of literature and literary criticism now.

It is easy to forget that the earliest kinds of writing that come down to us from any language are almost invariably religious, for we tend to think of them all loosely as "literature." But when we begin to enumerate the earliest surviving literary works—the Old Testament, the Bhagavad Gita, the Eddas, the myths and legends of Greece or of the Northmen, even Runic inscriptions and funerary epigraphs—we are faced with the fact that, whatever else they may also be, these pieces of writing are in some sense religious. Indeed, there is every reason to suppose that the original composers of these documents and the audiences to which they were directed thought very little, if at all, about what we would call the purely literary dimensions of these works but thought a great deal, if not exclusively, about what we would call their religious dimensions. This is not to say that there are no literary dimensions to the Old Testament or the Norse myths; it is only to say that it is unlikely that they were composed in the first instance or received in the first instance for the sake of those literary dimensions. Rather, these works arose out of the nature of belief and worship. That we perceive many of them, or that some of us perceive all of them, solely as literature tells us a great deal about ourselves but not always as much about the works as we imagine.

9

To be sure, we are here speaking of religion in the broadest sense, in the sense of any kind of concern with a supernature, with ultimate reality, with last things; and religion is more properly understood to be a disciplined body of belief and a pattern of worship that binds (the original meaning of *religion* after all) its adherents to a code of conduct and practice. But that very disciplined body of belief and that very code of conduct are themselves generated by what is held to be ultimate truth. Thus religion in its narrow sense issues from religion in that broad sense of concern for ultimate reality which the earliest literature is about. Moreover, learning has yet to reach back with certainty to a time when man had no religion in either sense. And learning's chief vehicle for investigation after all is the written word, including that word we have come to call early literature. That literature always raises religious considerations.

Even when we move somewhat closer to our own time and begin to be able to associate literary works with particular authors and with demonstrably secular activities, we find that we are not detached from religion all at once. The earliest extant plays of the Greek drama, for example, are held to have arisen out of religious and religio-cultural activities. And truly the gods are participants, and the atmosphere that these works project is one of at least quasi-religious awe. Today it is even quite widely maintained that the possibility of tragedy itself is dependent upon a belief in some supernatural reality and that in a secular age such as our own we can expect nothing more than a somewhat enfeebled domestic tragedy such as *Death of a Salesman*. Whether or not this particular observation is valid is not our concern except as it reminds us of the religious connotations of early writing, even after it has left the anonymous phase and become what is unmistakably literature. When Antigone defies Creon and his decree against burying Polyneices, she berates him for supplanting the "unwritten and unfailing" laws of the gods with his own. The laws of the gods, she says, "always live" and "no one knows their origin in time." For all of Greek drama one can say that the laws of the gods always live and no one knows their origin in time.

Nor is the situation much different outside of the drama. If we turn to Homer we do not find ourselves in a purely secular world: the gods participate as freely in human activities in the *Iliad* as they do in the plays of Aeschylus or Sophocles. And this participation is not some kind of idle fantasy-making. Divine laws are real because divine beings are real. While neither Homer nor the Greek dramatists are writing religion, their works are nevertheless inconceivable without the religious dimension and without an awareness by the reader of the whole issue of belief and its attendant morality and ethics.

All these circumstances are curiously paralleled by later European literatures, those that arose by and large independently centuries after the classical literatures of Greece and Rome had flowered and faded. The literature of the English-speaking world is the most familiar example. Old English literature offers above all two types of writing: stories of war and battle not unlike the Homeric epics—an example would be *Beowulf* with its supernatural forces, or even the Christian God, in the background—and such explicitly Christian poems as "Caedmon's Hymn," the earliest example of literature surviving from the Anglo-Saxon period. In that poem the religious element may seem to be the only element, since half of the poem is composed of kennings for God; certainly the religious element is dominant. But we can still receive the poem as literature as well. The fusion of the two helps us to see the impulse behind so much early literature, the impulse that moved men to literary utterance, that in fact gave birth to literature.

As late as the rise of drama in the Middle Ages, we still find the religious element dominant, for the medieval drama arose in striking parallel with the earlier and independent origin of drama in the Mediterranean. That is, it arose out of the celebration and worship of the Church. The process is even clearer in medieval drama than in Greek, for much of what must have preceded the great Greek dramatists is lost. But the early medieval dramatic tropes, especially the *Quem quaeritis* trope that seems to have determined later forms, still survive. In that celebrated *Quem quaeritis* scene, the spectator is presented with the situation at the sepulchre on Easter day. "Whom are ye seeking?" (*Quem quaeritis?*) says the angel standing at the empty tomb to the three Marys who have gathered there. "Jesus of Nazareth," is their reply. And in the dramatic words of the Vulgate Bible the angel tells them that He is risen. One cannot help noticing that in rendering this situation in dramatic form men of the Middle Ages were perhaps engaged more in religion and worship itself than they were in drama or literature. But it is poised exquisitely on the edge. By presenting the scene at the church door they make the first move towards drama as such. We now can see the playhouse in the distance. But what is most noteworthy is what it is that has impelled them toward literature. Once again it is religion.

Religion, then, was there at the birth of literature. But a skeptic might well point out that what is really striking about these early literary ventures is the speed with which they became secularized. This translation, however, is more apparent than real. It is true that since the waning of the Middle Ages and the dawn of the modern world, literature has become increasingly thisworldly. We are all familiar with the often intensely secular themes of Renaissance poetry and drama. The sonnet cycles of Italy, France, and England that glorify physical love and beauty seem far removed from the mystery plays and miracle plays of the Middle Ages. And even as far as concerns drama directly, one might argue that the Globe Playhouse is quite a long way from the church porch, that Shakespeare's dramas are works in which this world figures more prominently than the next, works in which human action plays a greater role than divine action. But much of this secularity is deceptive. No serious student of post-medieval literature thinks of leaving religion out of account. In fact, religion may in many instances be a more important matter than purely secular concerns—and not only in explicitly religious authors such as Milton, but in Shakespeare and his fellow dramatists as well. The stature of a Hamlet or a Lear is a function of the religious world-view that Shakespeare shared with his audience, for the Elizabethan plays are descendants of the medieval drama of religious inspiration, and the detachment of literature from religion has proved to be a slow and gradual matter. It is not really complete today, if indeed it ever can be.

Even in the seventeenth, eighteenth, and nineteenth centuries with the rise of the novel, that most secular and bourgeois of literary forms, works like *The Pilgrim's Progress* remind us that literature and religion were far from divorced and that many still thought of literature as religion's handmaiden. Not indeed until the nineteenth century do we find literature dominantly secular, and even then the clouds of religious glory that literature trails operate not infrequently to obscure its essentially secular character. But a sign of the times surely resides in the fact that in the nineteenth century the study of literature becomes the dominant academic study in the universities, with "humane letters" (meaning still largely classical literature) replacing the study of theology in popularity in such institutions as Oxford. In literature itself, the enormous increase in popular novels of a secular though intensely moral cast marks the triumph of literature as a wholly nonreligious enterprise. Literature had left the cloister by the end of the Middle Ages; in the Renaissance and through the eighteenth century it operated mainly from the schoolroom (the drama being in these periods a secular exception); by the nineteenth century literature is an activity of the secular world. Most of the novelists of the age were not even university trained, let alone products of the cloister; and religion itself had become another sort of activity, sometimes the subject of literary works, more often not.

Just when the apparently complete detachment of religion from literature occurred is not at the moment important. The important thing is that it did occur. We no longer think of literary persons as especially concerned with religion. We no longer think of literature as an aspect or department of religion. We no longer even think of literature and religion as necessarily compatible. Religion has become simply one of the many possible themes or subjects that literature might happen to treat. Literature has long been its own self, whatever we hold that self to be.

This survey of the development of literature out of religion is not intended as a history of literature; nor is it intended to exhaust the ways of looking at the development of literature. It is intended, however, to remind us that literature has a paternity: its first parents were religion and wonder, and it only gradually evolved into a mode that was dominantly literary. If some would claim today a hostility between literature and religion, it may be because they have forgotten the ancestry of literature or because they wish to deny that ancestry.

Just as literature has a family history, so to speak, so too does criticism, and it is part of the same family. If first there was belief, or at least wonder and awe, there was ultimately reflection and analysis. Before we had literature we had to have a subject matter and a cause for literature; that was found in religion. Before we had criticism we had to have a subject matter and a cause for criticism; that was found in literature. It is not surprising that the first evidences of criticism are found in works which can be read as literature as well as criticism. To abide in this instance with English literature—for its development appears to parallel that of classical literature—we often find earlier critical utterances embedded in literary works and we find those utterances closely tied to religious ideas. Chaucer wrote, paraphrasing St. Paul, that "all that is written is written for our instruction" ("oure doctryne," Chaucer wrote), and that we should "take the fruit and leave the chaff." He meant thereby that everything written even in what is often thought a secular work—for example, his own *Canterbury Tales*—was in fact to be applied to our religious teaching and therefore subordinated to theology. While Chaucer was a consciously Christian poet and consequently had in mind Christian doctrine, his attitude towards literature does not differ markedly from that of the ancients, who held also that literature was above all an instructive and morally uplifting activity. Chaucer and the ancients, we should say, did not believe in art for art's sake.

Not that men of the Middle Ages or of classical times ignored the purely aesthetic aspect of literature. Generally, in fact, they coupled the instructive with the entertaining. The Horatian formula—*dulce et utile* (pleasing and useful)—can be said to have dominated criticism through most of western literary history. At times some writers have stressed one or the other aspect but never one to the exclusion of the other. Thus Christian writers often spoke of the pleasing aspect of literature as constituting the "sweet coating" on the "bitter pill" of morality. But not until quite recent times did literary critics hold that the sweet coating stood alone as literature's excuse for being.

The detachment of criticism from religion was, of course, gradual; and it merely paralleled the detachment of literature itself from religion. Whereas Chaucer subordinated literature to theology, the devout Samuel Johnson in the eighteenth century objected to Milton's *Paradise Lost* for dealing with topics unsuited to literature, topics proper only to theology. Of course, at the same time Johnson never doubted that literature should have a strong moral content. As time went on, however, even that conviction began to come into question among literary critics.

One of the consequences of the Romantic movement of the nineteenth century was an increased concern, first with the character of the artist, and then with the distinctive character of his work, as opposed to the traditional concern with the import and the message of the work of art. The new emphasis on originality, individuality, uniqueness led in one of its lines of development to the twentieth-century New Criticism, especially as this was received in the academy in the second quarter of this century. Although it may be unfair to hold many of the New Critics responsible for the excesses to which their doctrines were put, it is nevertheless the case that the term New Criticism came to be synonymous with the notion that a literary work was a thing unto itself, that it had no reference to matters outside itself, and that it could be understood only on its own terms. A consequence of such a view of literature was a concern with the aesthetic or pleasing aspect to the virtual exclusion of the useful or instructive. Yet a further consequence was that with the casting out of interest in the useful or instructive part of literature came also a casting out of any concern with the ideas, beliefs, or systems of thought that might lie behind the literature or even those that the literature might be designed to reinforce or express.

Religion was not the only casualty of the emphasis on the autonomy of literary works, though it may have been the most serious one. Other systems of ideas and bodies of knowledge were downgraded as well. It might be necessary in certain cases to refer to these "outside" systems of belief or thought but only insofar as they shaped the form or peculiar character of the work itself. Certainly it would not do to ask of ideas expressed in a literary work whether they were true. Thus, to take but one example, literary works of all kinds were found to abound in "Christ figures," but nowhere at the same time was the figure of Christ permitted to play a role in the critic's thinking. Everything was as interesting as everything else, for it was all merely raw material that had no significance except as it was shaped in the work in question.

Criticism, in short, had more than kept pace with literature itself. If men no longer made religion and its doctrines the subject of their literary works, criticism no longer needed to consider the religious dimensions of literature. To some this arrangement seemed both just and convenient. Criticism could forget its paternity just as literature had.

The difficulties with the foregoing position have become increasingly clear in the past decade or so, although there were always those who declined to accept the critical position that literature like all art, as Pater phrased it, aspires to the condition of music. It is with these now evident difficulties that the modern study of the relation of literature to religion begins.

The critical position that the religious dimension of literature is irrelevant is an understandable extension of the doctrine that a work of art has its own structure and harmony and is not merely a piece of propaganda for or against a certain intellectual position. Indeed, 'the overemphasis on the instructive side of literature needs from time to time a corrective in the direction of the aesthetic side. Otherwise we should have to find that the most pedestrian religious tract was superior as literature to, say, *The Divine Comedy* or *Paradise Lost,* if that tract happened to correspond more closely with our own theology. Or, considering *Paradise Lost* alone, we might find that we were judging Milton's poem in terms of our agreement or disagreement with his Arminianism or some other aspect of his theology. Yet we know, if not as a matter of critical principle, then as a matter of aesthetic experience, that *Paradise Lost* is a great work of art whether we share Milton's theology or not; and we know further that it is superior as a work of art to, say, the hymns of Isaac Watts, whether we prefer Watts' morality to Milton's or not. Such aesthetic experience of literature can easily lead to the conviction that Milton's theology (or Dante's or Watts') is irrelevant to his literary work, and further that any author's ideas and beliefs are irrelevant to his work. And it is to such a conviction that much aesthetic experience *has* led.

Yet somehow, just as we know from the experience of *Paradise Lost* or *The Divine Comedy* that these are works of supreme aesthetic achievement, so we also know from the experience of these works that the beliefs that are expressed in them and that lie behind them are not irrelevant to them. What is more, we experience the same awareness in many modern works that are far less obviously religious than works of earlier ages. We may not know in exactly what degree the beliefs impinge upon the works, but we know they impinge. If we want to see these works steadily and whole we know that one of our tasks as reader-critics is to determine just what the relationship of those beliefs to the finished work of art is.

Nor is this a matter of mere sentiment; it is a matter of the nature of words. Simply because a work with which we disagree philosophically (or theologically, or economically, or politically, etc.) is aesthetically superior to one with which we agree, it does not follow that the ideas and beliefs involved are uniformly irrelevant. It follows only that ideas and beliefs are not the only elements of consequence in a literary work. There are those other elements of form and sequence, relation of parts to whole, rhythm, diction, stress, pattern, balance, and so on that rightly must occupy the attention of sensitive readers in trying to understand the peculiar magic of a great work of literature. But these elements in turn relate to the ideas and beliefs that the work projects if for no other reason than that the materials of literature are words, and words, like it or not, persist in having meaning. The efforts of some students of linguistics to demonstrate that words have no real meaning at all have finally foundered on their own absurdity; for if there is no meaning in our words or yours, then neither is there any in those sequences of sounds the linguists have strung together to inform us that words have no meaning. Everyone, nihilists as well as believers, presumes when he speaks that *his* words have meaning. There is no reason to deny the same presumption to a Milton or a Dante, to a T. S. Eliot or a Hemingway.

Literature, then, using the medium of words, cannot escape from meaning, cannot ultimately escape from involving the reader in judgments that are not only aesthetic but also intellectual, moral, and ultimately theological. It is precisely the mixture of the aesthetic and the didactic that makes the study of literature so challenging and that makes it involve our whole being. Today the critical pendulum has started to swing back from the sterile pursuit of form for form's sake. Readers are once again confronting the inescapable fact that literary works have meanings that are somehow bound up with their form. Readers are more and more asking what it is that the sugar coating covers.

The return to an interest in the intellectual import of literary works is, however, by no means a simple return to the days when readers took from their reading the fruit of Christian doctrine and let the chaff fall away. For one thing it can no longer safely be assumed that all that is written is written for our doctrine, that is, for the strengthening of established Christian orthodoxy. Indeed, the most vociferous proponents today of purpose in art are those who espouse some form or other of a Marxist or radical view of art, art as a means of shaping social attitudes, art as an instrument of political propaganda. Such views begin with a contempt for religion and not infrequently end with a contempt for art. But the fact that there is a renewed interest in the didactic element in literature has proved also to be an opportunity for approaches other than the radical socialist ones. Much art, even contemporary art, is either not concerned with political questions or is not concerned solely with political questions. But much contemporary literature, like much earlier literature, does have a religious dimension, and it cannot be understood or perhaps even appreciated fully without serious attention to that religious dimension.

It might seem that we have only come back to the old position of literature as a department of religion, but it is not so. The difference in the critical landscape today from earlier times is not so much that literature is seen to have an intellectual and moral and perhaps at times a religious content—for until our own age, no one doubted it—the difference is that we can no longer take for granted the intellectual and religious position that may be represented in a literary work. The problem today is how to approach the question of literature and religion without doing violence to one or the other. It is no longer possible to ferret out the "message" of a literary work by reference to a catechism. Our literary artists differ too widely in belief one from the other for any kind of received standard interpretation to be imposed upon them. At times it seems that there are almost as many religious positions and as many theologies as there are writers. This is not the case of course, for few writers actually make up whole new theologies and fewer yet are the theologies that can escape all reference to the patterns adumbrated by two thousand years of Christian history; but there is an undeniable variety in contemporary approaches to religious questions in works of literature. They range from an orthodoxy as unswerving as Dante's to total heterodoxy. This is what is new in the study of religion and literature. What is old is that all contemporary literary approaches to religious questions relate to certain enduring questions that religion of any kind has always taken to be its province: what is the purpose of life, what is the meaning of existence, what is the destiny of man? And further, is there a God, if so, what is His nature, what is His aim, how does man relate to Him?

To determine the position of a given author or work toward these and related questions is far from easy. First, it is necessary to have some conception of literature itself that takes into account the relationship in general of literature to religion. Difficult as this is, the practical questions that follow may prove even more difficult. That is, once one has some conception of the relationship of religion to literature—whether it be a general philosophic conception of literature as dealing with "ultimate values" or an intensely theological conception of art as a recapitulation in the finite mind of the eternal creative act, to paraphrase Coleridge—one has then to face the problem of applying such an understanding of literature to concrete cases. This is an enterprise fraught with peril, but one that must be undertaken if one is to understand either contemporary religious thought or contemporary literature. It is also an exciting and illuminating enterprise, one that will help us to respond to literature as such and one that will help us to comprehend individual literary works in their richness and complexity. Finally, it is an enterprise that will help us to know ourselves and lead us to know what we believe and why.

I: RELATIONSHIPS BETWEEN RELIGION AND LITERATURE

RELIGION AND LITERATURE

T. S. Eliot

What I have to say is largely in support of the following propositions: Literary criticism should be completed by criticism from a definite ethical and theological standpoint. In so far as in any age there is common agreement on ethical and theological matters, so far can literary criticism be substantive. In ages like our own, in which there is no such common agreement, it is the more necessary for Christian readers to scrutinize their reading, especially of works of imagination, with explicit ethical and theological standards. The "greatness" of literature cannot be determined solely by literary standards; though we must remember that whether it is literature or not can be determined only by literary standards.[1]

We have tacitly assumed, for some centuries past, that there is *no* relation between literature and theology. This is not to deny that literature—I mean, again, primarily works of imagination—has been, is, and probably always will be judged by some moral standards. But moral judgements of literary works are made only according to the moral code accepted by each generation, whether it lives according to that code or not. In an age which accepts some precise Christian theology, the common code may be fairly orthodox: though even in such periods the common code may exalt such concepts as "honour," "glory" or "revenge" to a position quite intolerable to Christianity. The dramatic ethics of the Elizabethan Age offers an interesting study. But when the common code is detached from its theological background and is consequently more and more merely a matter of habit, it is exposed both to prejudice and to change. At such times morals are open to being altered *by* literature; so that we find in practice that what is "objectionable" in literature is merely what the present generation is not used to. It is a commonplace that what shocks one generation is accepted quite calmly by the next. This adaptability to change of moral standards is sometimes greeted with satisfaction as an evidence of human perfecti-

---

[1] As an example of literary criticism given greater significance by theological interests, I would call attention to Theodor Haecker: *Virgil* (Sheed and Ward).

bility: whereas it is only evidence of what unsubstantial foundations people's moral judgements have.

I am not concerned here with religious literature but with the application of our religion to the criticism of any literature. It may be as well, however, to distinguish first what I consider to be the three senses in which we can speak of "religious literature." The first is that of which we say that it is "religious literature" in the same way that we speak of "historical literature" or of "scientific literature." I mean that we can treat the Authorized translation of the Bible, or the works of Jeremy Taylor, as literature, in the same way that we treat the historical writing of Clarendon or of Gibbon—our two great English historians—as literature; or Bradley's *Logic*, or Buffon's *Natural History*. All of these writers were men who, incidentally to their religious, or historical, or philosophic purpose, had a gift of language which makes them delightful to read to all those who can enjoy language well written, even if they are unconcerned with the objects which the writers had in view. And I would add that though a scientific, or historical, or theological, or philosophic work which is also "literature," may become superannuated as anything but literature, yet it is not likely to be "literature" unless it had its scientific or other value for its own time. While I acknowledge the legitimacy of this enjoyment, I am more acutely aware of its abuse. The persons who enjoy these writings *solely* because of their literary merit are essentially parasites; and we know that parasites, when they become too numerous, are pests. I could easily fulminate for a whole hour against the men of letters who have gone into ecstasies over "the Bible as literature," the Bible as "the noblest monument of English prose." Those who talk of the Bible as a "monument of English prose" are merely admiring it as a monument over the grave of Christianity. I must try to avoid the by-paths of my discourse: it is enough to suggest that just as the work of Clarendon, or Gibbon, or Buffon, or Bradley would be of inferior literary value if it were insignificant as history, science and philosophy respectively, so the Bible has had a *literary* influence upon English literature *not* because it has been considered as literature, but because it has been considered as the report of the Word of God. And the fact that men of letters now discuss it as "literature" probably indicates the *end* of its "literary" influence.

The second kind of relation of religion to literature is that which is found in what is called "religious" or "devotional" poetry. Now what is the usual attitude of the lover of poetry—and I mean the person who is a genuine and first-hand enjoyer and appreciator of poetry, not the person who follows the admirations of others—toward this department of poetry? I believe, all that may be implied in his calling it a *department*. He believes, not always explicitly, that when you qualify poetry as "religious" you are indicating very clear limitations. For the great majority of people who love poetry, *"religious* poetry" is a variety of *minor* poetry: the religious poet is not a poet who is treating the whole subject matter of poetry in a religious spirit, but a poet who is dealing with a confined part of this subject matter: who is leaving out what men consider their major passions, and thereby confessing his ignorance of them. I think that this is the real attitude of most poetry lovers towards such poets as Vaughn, or Southwell, or Crashaw, or George Herbert, or Gerard Hopkins.

But what is more, I am ready to admit that up to a point these critics are right. For there is a kind of poetry, such as most of the work of the authors I have mentioned, which is the product of a special religious awareness, which may exist without the general awareness which we expect of the major poet. In some poets, or in some of their works, this general awareness may have existed; but the preliminary steps which represent it may have been suppressed, and only the end-product presented. Between these, and those in which the religious or devotional genius represents the *special* and limited awareness, it may be very difficult to discriminate. I do not pretend to offer Vaughan, or Southwell, or George Herbert, or Hopkins as major poets: I feel sure that the first three, at least, are poets of this limited awareness. They are not great religious poets in the sense in which Dante, or Corneille, or Racine, even in those of their plays which do not touch upon Christian themes, are great Christian religious poets. Or even in the sense in which Villon and Baudelaire, with all their imperfections and delinquencies, are Christian poets. Since the time of Chaucer, Christian poetry (in the sense in which I shall mean it) has been limited in England almost exclusively to minor poetry.

I repeat that when I am considering Religion and Literature, I speak of these things only to make clear that I am not concerned primarily with Religious Literature. I am concerned with what should be the relation between Religion and all Literature. Therefore the third type of "religious literature" may be more quickly passed over. I mean the literary works of men who are sincerely desirous of forwarding the cause of religion: that which may come under the heading of Propaganda. I am thinking, of course, of such delightful fiction as Mr. Chesterton's *Man Who Was Thursday,* or his *Father Brown.* No one admires and enjoys these things more than I do; I would only remark that when the same effect is aimed at by zealous persons of less talent than Mr. Chesterton the effect is negative. But my point is that such writings do not enter into any serious consideration of the relation of Religion and Literature: because they are conscious operations in a world in which it is assumed that Religion and Literature are not related. It is a conscious and limited relating. What I want is a literature which should be unconsciously, rather than deliberately and defiantly, Christian: because the work of Mr. Chesterton has its point from appearing in a world which is definitely not Christian.

I am convinced that we fail to realize how completely, and yet how irrationally, we separate our literary from our religious judgements. If there could be a complete separation, perhaps it might not matter: but the separation is not, and never can be, complete. If we exemplify literature by the novel—for the novel is the form in which literature affects the greatest number—we may remark this gradual secularization of literature during at least the last three hundred years. Bunyan, and to some extent Defoe, had moral purposes: the former is beyond suspicion, the latter may be suspect. But since Defoe the secularization of the novel has been continuous. There have been three chief phases. In the first, the novel took the Faith, in its contemporary version, for granted, and omitted it from its picture of life. Fielding, Dickens and Thackeray belong to this phase. In the second, it doubted, worried about, or contested the Faith. To this phase belong George Eliot, George Meredith and Thomas Hardy. To the third phase, in which we are living, belong nearly all contemporary novelists except Mr. James Joyce. It is the phase of those who have never heard the Christian Faith spoken of as anything but an anachronism.

Now, do people in general hold a definite opinion, that is to say religious or anti-religious; and do they read novels, or poetry for that matter, with a separate compartment of their minds? The common ground between religion and fiction is behaviour. Our religion imposes our ethics, our judgement and criticism of ourselves, and our behaviour toward our fellow men. The fiction that we read affects our behaviour towards our fellow men, affects our patterns of ourselves. When we read of human beings behaving in certain ways, with the approval of the author, who gives his benediction to this behaviour by his attitude toward the result of the behaviour arranged by himself, we can be influenced towards behaving in the same way.[2] When the contemporary novelist is an individual thinking for himself in isolation, he may have something important to offer to those who are able to receive it. He who is alone may speak to the individual. But the majority of novelists are persons drifting in the stream, only a little faster. They have some sensitiveness, but little intellect.

We are expected to be broadminded about literature, to put aside prejudice or conviction, and to look at fiction as fiction and at drama as drama. With what is inaccurately called "censorship" in this country —with what is much more difficult to cope with than an official censorship, because it represents the opinions of individuals in an irresponsible democracy, I have very little sympathy; partly because it so often

---

[2] Here and later I am indebted to Montgomery Belgion: *The Human Parrot* (chapter on The Irresponsible Propagandist).

suppresses the wrong books, and partly because it is little more effective than Prohibition of Liquor; partly because it is one manifestation of the desire that state control should take the place of decent domestic influence; and wholly because it acts only from custom and habit, not from decided theological and moral principles. Incidentally, it gives people a false sense of security in leading them to believe that books which are *not* suppressed are harmless. Whether there *is* such a thing as a harmless book I am not sure; but there very likely are books so utterly unreadable as to be incapable of injuring anybody. But it is certain that a book is not harmless merely because no one is consciously offended by it. And if we, as readers, keep our religious and moral convictions in one compartment, and take our reading merely for entertainment, or on a higher plane, for aesthetic pleasure, I would point out that the author, whatever his conscious intentions in writing, in practice recognizes no such distinctions. The author of a work of imagination is trying to affect us wholly, as human beings, whether he knows it or not; and we are affected by it, as human beings, whether we intend to be or not. I suppose that everything we eat has some other effect upon us than merely the pleasure of taste and mastication; it affects us during the process of assimilation and digestion; and I believe that exactly the same is true of anything we read.

The fact that what we read does not concern merely something called our *literary taste,* but that it affects directly, though only amongst many other influences, the whole of what we are, is best elicited, I think, by a conscientious examination of the history of our individual literary education. Consider the adolescent reading of any person with some literary sensibility. Everyone, I believe, who is at all sensible to the seductions of poetry, can remember some moment in youth when he or she was completely carried away by the work of one poet. Very likely he was carried away by several poets, one after the other. The reason for this passing infatuation is not merely that our sensibility to poetry is keener in adolescence than in maturity. What happens is a kind of inundation, of invasion of the undeveloped personality, the empty (swept and garnished) room, by the stronger personality of the poet. The same thing may happen at a later age to persons who have not done much reading. One author takes complete possession of us for a time; then another; and finally they begin to affect each other in our mind. We weigh one against another; we see that each has qualities absent from others, and qualities incompatible with the qualities of others; we begin to be, in fact, critical; and it is our growing critical power which protects us from excessive possession by any one literary personality. The good critic—and we should all try to be critics, and not leave criticism to the fellows who write reviews in the papers— is the man who, to a keen and abiding sensibility, joins wide and increasingly discriminating reading. Wide reading is not valuable as a kind of hoarding, an accumulation of knowledge, or what sometimes is meant by the term "a well-stocked mind." It is valuable because in the process of being affected by one powerful personality after another, we cease to be dominated by anyone, or by any small number. The very different views of life, co-habiting in our minds, affect each other, and our own personality asserts itself and gives each a place in some arrangement peculiar to ourself.

It is simply not true that works of fiction, prose or verse, that is to say works depicting the actions, thoughts and words and passions of imaginary human beings, *directly* extend our knowledge of life. Direct knowledge of life is knowledge directly in relation to ourselves, it is our knowledge of *how* people behave in general, of *what* they are like in general, in so far as that part of life in which we ourselves have participated gives us material for generalization. Knowledge of life obtained through fiction is only possible by another stage of self-consciousness. That is to say, it can only be a knowledge of other people's knowledge of life, not of life itself. So far as we are taken up with the happenings in any novel in the same way in which we are taken up with what happens under our eyes, we are acquiring at least as much falsehood as truth. But when we are developed enough to say: "This is the view of life of a person who was a good observer within his limits, Dickens, or Thackeray, or George Eliot, or Balzac; but he looked at it in a different way from me, because he was a different man; he even selected rather different things to look at, or the same things in a different order of importance, because he was a different man; so what I am looking at is the world as seen by a particular mind"—then we are in a position to gain something from reading fiction. We are learning *something* about life from the authors direct, just as we learn something from the reading of history direct; but these authors are only really helping us when we can see, and allow for, their differences from ourselves.

Now what we get, as we gradually grow up and read more and more, and read a greater diversity of authors, is a variety of views of life. But what people commonly assume, I suspect, is that we gain this experience of other men's views of life only by "improving reading." This, it is supposed, is a reward we get by applying ourselves to Shakespeare, and Dante, and Goethe, and Emerson, and Carlyle, and dozens of other respectable writers. The rest of our reading for amusement is merely killing time. But I incline to come to the alarming conclusion that it is just the literature that we read for "amusement," or "purely for pleasure" that may have the greatest and least suspected influence upon us. It is the literature which we read with the least effort that can have the easiest and most insidious influence upon us. Hence it is that the influence of popular novelists, and of popular plays of contemporary life, requires to be scrutinized most closely. And it is chiefly *contemporary* literature that the majority of people ever read in this attitude of "purely for pleasure," of pure passivity.

The relation of what I have been saying to the subject announced for my discourse should now be a little more apparent. Though we may read literature merely for pleasure, of "entertainment" or of "aesthetic enjoyment," this reading never affects simply a sort of special sense: it affects us as entire human beings; it affects our moral and religious existence. And I say that while individual modern writers of eminence can be improving, contemporary literature as a whole tends to be degrading. And that even the effect of the better writers, in an age like ours, may be degrading to some readers; for we must remember that what a writer does to people is not necessarily what he intends to do. It may be only what people are capable of having done to them. People exercise an unconscious selection in being influenced. A writer like D. H. Lawrence may be in his effect either beneficial or pernicious. I am not even sure that I have not had some pernicious influence myself.

At this point I anticipate a rejoinder from the liberal-minded, from all those who are convinced that if everybody says what he thinks, and does what he likes, things will somehow, by some automatic compensation and adjustment, come right in the end. "Let everything be tried," they say, "and if it is a mistake, then we shall learn by experience." This argument might have some value, if we were always the same generation upon earth; or if, as we know to be not the case, people ever learned much from the experience of their elders. These liberals are convinced that only by what is called unrestrained individualism will truth ever emerge. Ideas, views of life, they think, issue distinct from independent heads, and in consequence of their knocking violently against each other, the fittest survive, and truth rises triumphant. Anyone who dissents from this view must be either a mediaevalist, wishful only to set back the clock, or else a fascist, and probably both.

If the mass of contemporary authors were really individualists, every one of them inspired Blakes, each with his separate vision, and if the mass of the contemporary public were really a mass of *individuals* there might be something to be said for this attitude. But this is not, and never has been, and never will be. It is not only that the reading individual today (or at any day) is not enough an individual to be able to absorb all the "views of life" of all the authors pressed upon us by the publishers' advertisements and reviewers, and to be able to arrive at wisdom by considering one against another. It is that the contemporary authors are not individuals enough either. It is not that the world of separate individuals of the liberal democrat is undesirable; it is simply that this world does not exist. For the reader of contemporary literature is not, like the reader of the established great literature of all time, exposing himself to the influence of divers and contradictory personalities; he is exposing himself to a mass movement of writers who, each of them, think that they have something individually to offer, but are really all working together in the same direction. And there never was a time, I believe, when the reading public was so large, or so helplessly exposed to the influences of its own time. There never was a time, I believe, when those who read at all, read so many more books by living authors than books by dead authors; there never was a time so completely parochial, so shut off from the past. There may be too many publishers; there are certainly too many books published; and the journals ever incite the reader to "keep up" with what is being published. Individualistic democracy has come to high tide: and it is more difficult today to be an individual than it ever was before.

Within itself, modern literature has perfectly valid distinctions of good and bad, better and worse: and I do not wish to suggest that I confound Mr. Bernard Shaw with Mr. Noel Coward, Mrs. Woolf with Miss Mannin. On the other hand, I should like it to be clear that I am not defending a "high"-brow against a "low"-brow literature. What I do wish to affirm is that the whole of modern literature is corrupted by what I call Secularism, that it is simply unaware of, simply cannot understand the meaning of, the primacy of the supernatural over the natural life: of something which I assume to be our primary concern.

I do not want to give the impression that I have delivered a mere fretful jeremiad against contemporary literature. Assuming a common attitude between you, or some of you, and myself, the question is not so much, what is to be done about it? as, how should we behave towards it?

I have suggested that the liberal attitude towards literature will not work. Even if the writers who make their attempt to impose their "view of life" upon us were really distinct individuals, even if we as readers were distinct individuals, what would be the result? It would be, surely, that each reader would be impressed, in his reading, merely by what he was previously prepared to be impressed by; he would follow the "line of least resistance," and there would be no assurance that he would be made a better man. For literary judgement we need to be acutely aware of two things at once: of "what we like," and of "what we *ought* to like." Few people are honest enough to know either. The first means knowing what we really feel: very few know that. The second involves understanding our shortcomings; for we do not really know what we ought to like unless we also know why we ought to like it, which involves knowing why we don't yet like it. It is not enough to understand what we ought to be, unless we know what we are; and we do not understand what we are, unless we know what we ought to be. The two forms of self-consciousness, knowing what we are and what we ought to be, must go together.

It is our business, as readers of literature, to know what we like. It is our business, as Christians, *as well as* readers of literature, to know what we ought to like. It is our business as honest men not to assume that whatever we like is what we ought to like; and it is our business as honest Christians not to assume that we do like what we ought to like. And the last thing I would wish for would be the existence of two literatures, one for Christian consumption and the other for the pagan world. What I believe to be incumbent upon all Christians is the duty of maintaining consciously certain standards and criteria of criticism over and above those applied by the rest of the world; and that by these criteria and standards everything that we read must be tested. We must remember that the greater part of our current reading matter is written for us by people who have no real belief in a supernatural order, though some of it may be written by people with individual notions of a supernatural order which are not ours. And the greater part of our reading matter is coming to be written by people who not only have no such belief, but are even ignorant of the fact that there are still people in the world so "backward" or so "eccentric" as to continue to believe. So long as we are conscious of the gulf fixed between ourselves and the greater part of contemporary literature, we are more or less protected from being harmed by it, and are in a position to extract from it what good it has to offer us.

There are a very large number of people in the world today who believe that all ills are fundamentally economic. Some believe that various specific economic changes alone would be enough to set the world right; others demand more or less drastic changes in the social as well, changes chiefly of two opposed types. These changes demanded, and in some places carried out, are alike in one respect, that they hold the assumptions of what I call Secularism: they concern themselves only with changes of a temporal, material, and external nature; they concern themselves with morals only of a collective nature. In an exposition of one such new faith I read the following words:

"In our morality the one single test of any moral question is whether it impedes or destroys in any way the power of the individual to serve the State. [The individual] must answer the questions: 'Does this action injure the nation? Does it injure other members of the nation? Does it injure my ability to serve the nation?' And if the answer is clear on all those questions, the individual has absolute liberty to do as he will."

Now I do not deny that this is a kind of morality, and that it is capable of great good within limits; but I think that we should all repudiate a morality which had no higher ideal to set before us than that. It represents, of course, one of the violent reactions we are witnessing, against the view that the community is solely for the benefit of the individual; but it is equally a gospel of this world, and of this world alone. My complaint against modern literature is of the same kind. It is not that modern literature is in the ordinary sense "immoral" or even "amoral"; and in any case to prefer that charge would not be enough. It is simply that it repudiates, or is wholly ignorant of, our most fundamental and important beliefs; and that in consequence its tendency is to encourage its readers to get what they can out of life while it lasts, to miss no "experience" that presents itself, and to sacrifice themselves, if they make any sacrifice at all, only for the sake of tangible benefits to others in this world either now or in the future. We shall certainly continue to read the best of its kind, of what our time provides; but we must tirelessly criticize it according to our own principles, and not merely according to the principles admitted by the writers and by the critics who discuss it in the public press.

LITERATURE AND RELIGION

J. Hillis Miller

The relations of religion and literature involve methodological problems which may be specified easily enough. To specify them, however, is not to solve them. They constitute one version of that tension between extremes which characterizes all interpretation of literature. One set of these problems has to do with the relation between the critic and the work criticized. Another has to do with the relation between the work and the personal, cultural, or spiritual reality it expresses. I shall discuss the problems in that order.

1

Most students of literature today would agree that the aim of their discipline is elucidation of the intrinsic meanings of poems, plays, and novels. They want to know exactly what a sonnet by Shakespeare, an ode by Keats, or a novel by Trollope *means*. Poetic language, they tend to assume, is self-contained or self-referential. Whatever meanings a poem has are there on the page, shining forth from the words and their relations.

But though the words of a poem may contain its meaning, they do not do this in the way a cigarette package contains its cigarettes, or even in the way a tree contains its sap, a flower its aroma. A poem is not just black marks on the page or sonorous vibrations in the air. It comes into existence as a poem only in the mind and feelings of its reader or auditor. Though its meanings are intrinsic, they are intrinsic to an experience which includes the reader as well as the black marks, the listener as well as the sounds. A poem, unlike a scientific formula or a mathematical proof, cannot even be understood if the reader is too detached from it and regards it with too critical an eye. It exists partly as the emotions inhering in it, and these come into being only when it is read with sympathy. The reader or listener, however, is not a neutral machine for bringing verbal meanings into existence. He has a personality and a history of his own. The inherence of the reader in the poem leads to one of the difficulties involved in the relation of religion and literature.

It is natural for the reader of literature to have religious convictions, however vague or contradictory these may be. Even indifference to religious questions or rejection of them is of course a religious position. On the other hand, many works of literature have religious themes, whether overtly, as in the case of *The Divine Comedy*, the poems of St. John of the Cross, or *Murder in the Cathedral*, or more indirectly, as in the case of the poems of Hölderlin, Keats, or Arnold. The problem arises when a critic, with his own religious convictions, confronts the religious subject matter of a work of literature. Critics have usually chosen one of three characteristic ways of dealing with this problem. Each may lead to its own form of distortion. The critic may tend to assimilate writers to his own religious belief. He may be led to reject writers because they do not agree with his religious views. He may tend to trivialize literature by taking an objective or neutral view towards its religious themes.

Certainly a critic should be granted the right to his religious opinions. The mature man is the committed man, and where is it more important to be committed than in the area of religion? But even though religious faith is not incompatible with the view that God's house has many mansions, nevertheless in practice there is often conflict between the strength of a religious commitment and the historical relativism which the study of literature seems to demand and confirm. An evident fact about literature is the diversity of beliefs which have characterized poets of various times and places, and the knowledge of the way "world views" have varied throughout history is as much a part of present-day assumptions about literature as are the notions of intrinsic meaning and organic form. At one time and place people saw the world in one way and at another time and place in another way, and these endlessly changing views of things are incompatible. Homer, Dante, Shakespeare, Blake, and Wallace Stevens cannot all be equally right about the nature of things. Since this is the case, the first responsibility of the critic, it appears, is to abnegate his own views so that he may re-create with objective sympathy the way things seemed to Homer, Shakespeare, or Stevens. Literary study must be pluralist or relativist because its object is so. The literary critic must be a shape-shifter, a twentieth-century descendant of Keats's poet of negative capability. Having no nature of his own, he must be able to take on the nature of whatever poet he studies, wearing for a time the mask of Shelley, Marlowe, or Chaucer.

And yet to ask the man who holds religious views of his own to give these up when he studies literature is to ask him to become a divided man, keeping two important areas of his life separate. It is not easy, however, to open the frontiers between these areas.

If the critic tries to reconcile his religious belief and his love of literature he may be led to say that the works he reads agree with the insights of his faith, though when viewed with different eyes they do not appear to do so. After all, such a critic says, the world is really as my faith tells me it is, and even those writers who do not know this will testify unwittingly to the truth. Greek and pagan myths, it was once thought, are really distorted versions of Christian revelation. This view, or some modification of it, is still occasionally held. Medieval and Renaissance commentators were able to make Virgil into something like a great Christian poet. In our own day critics both Catholic and Protestant have sometimes argued that the works of a writer like Kafka or Camus are centrally Christian in meaning or at least may be assimilated into a Christian view of things. Another version of this is the anachronism of reading a writer like Coleridge or Shakespeare as a great "existentialist" poet. Such readings may import the categories of a modern religious or quasi-religious philosophy into works of literature to which they are alien. Jean-Paul Sartre, in his book on Baudelaire and in other studies, and Martin Heidegger, in his essays on Hölderlin, have found support for their views in interpretations of earlier works of art or literature, though their studies have been criticized for representing that form of distortion I am discussing.[1] But if Sartre and Heidegger are right about human existence there seems no reason why their insights should not be confirmed by anticipation in earlier poems or paintings. To hold this, however, is implicitly to contradict the notion that there is an intrinsic particularity in the world view of each age or individual, a particularity which may not with impunity be blurred by trans-historical schemes of interpretation.

Even the best of the overtly Christian critics, Jacques Maritain, Allen Tate, or Thomas Gilby among the Catholics, Amos Wilder, Nathan Scott, or W. H. Auden among the Protestants,[2] though they may respect the individuality of non-Christian works, tend to make criticism a

---

[1] See Jean-Paul Sartre, *Baudelaire* (Paris, 1947), and Martin Heidegger, *Erläuterungen zu Hölderlins Dichtung* (Frankfurt am Main, 1951).

[2] See Jacques Maritain, *Art and Scholasticism*, trans. J. F. Scanlan (London: Sheed & Ward, 1930); *Frontières de la poésie et autres essais* (Paris, 1935); with Raïssa Maritain, *Situation de la poésie* (Paris: Bruges, 1938); *Creative Intuition in Art and Poetry* (New York: Pantheon, 1953); Allen Tate, *Reason in Madness* (New York: Putnam, 1941); *On the Limits of Poetry* (New York: Swallow Press, William Morrow & Co., 1948); *The Man of Letters in the Modern World* (New York: Meridian, 1955); *Collected Essays* (Denver, Colo.: Alan Swallow, 1959); Thomas Gilby, *Poetic Experience: An Introduction to Thomist Aesthetic* (London: Sheed & Ward, 1934); Amos Wilder, *The Spiritual Aspects of the New Poetry* (New York, London: Harper & Bros., 1940); *Modern Poetry and the Christian Spirit* (New York: Scribner, 1952); *Theology and Modern Literature* (Cambridge, Mass.: Harvard Univ. Press, 1958); W. H. Auden, *The Enchaféd Flood* (New York: Random House, 1950); *The Dyer's Hand and Other Essays* (New York: Random House, 1962); Nathan A. Scott, Jr., *Rehearsals of Discomposure: Alienation and Reconciliation in Modern Literature* (New York: Columbia Univ., King's Crown Press, 1952); *Modern Literature and the Religious Frontier* (New York: Harper & Bros., 1958); *The Broken Center: Studies in the Theological Horizons of Modern Literature* (New Haven and London: Yale Univ. Press, 1966).

dialogue between their own religious views and the world views of the writers they discuss. They ask in effect: "Of what use is Camus, or Kafka, or Melville to a man who believes as I do?" and their studies often have compound titles which suggest this confrontation: *Modern Literature and the Religious Frontier, The Christian and the World of Unbelief, Christianity and Existentialism, The Tragic Vision and the Christian Faith.*[3]

It is easy to see why it is that the relations of religion and literature are now of special concern. In a time when the power of organized religion has weakened, people have turned, as Matthew Arnold said they would, to poetry as a stay and prop, even as a means of salvation. Many people who are authentically religious in the sense that they seek a supernatural meaning for their lives have made for themselves a religion compounded of a bit of their own inherited faith, a bit of existentialism, a bit of Maritain, a bit of Kafka, a bit of Zen Buddhism, a bit of Rilke, a bit of Ananda K. Coomaraswamy, and so on.

Arnold, however, was wrong, and T. S. Eliot was right. Literature is not a means of salvation. It is the Virgil which can take the pilgrim only so far. Beyond that point only Beatrice can lead the pilgrim farther.[4] Nevertheless, to take a man even so far is in a way a religious service. It may seem unpredictable but scarcely absurd that Paul Claudel should have been converted to Catholicism in part at least by his reading of Rimbaud.[5] Kafka's writings, for example, do have religious themes, as do Rimbaud's, and a critic needs much theological acumen to understand them. It is natural that scholars trained in theology should concern themselves with Kafka's work, or with Shakespeare's, or even with Camus's. Yet such a scholar, if he wishes to remain a literary critic and not become something else, must resist the temptation to grind his own axe.

Nor are critics without explicit religious commitment exempt from this danger. Even a great critic like R. P. Blackmur could, because of his distaste for what seemed to him the weirdly heterodox metaphysics of Yeats's poems, sometimes argue that since the poems are so beautiful the bad metaphysics cannot be an intrinsic part of their meaning,[6]

[3] For *Modern Literature and the Religious Frontier* see n. 2; *The Christian and the World of Unbelief* (New York: Abingdon Press, 1957) is by Libuse Lukas Miller; *Christianity and the Existentialists* is a collection of essays edited by C. Michalson; *The Tragic Vision and the Christian Faith* (New York: Association Press, 1957) is a collection of essays edited by Nathan A. Scott.
[4] See T. S. Eliot, *On Poetry and Poets* (New York: Farrar, Straus and Cudahy, 1957), p. 94.
[5] See Arthur Rimbaud, *Oeuvres,* préface de Paul Claudel (Paris, 1912).
[6] A single sentence cannot do justice to the subtlety of Blackmur's essays on Yeats and to the energy with which he grapples with the problem of belief in Yeats. See, however, p. 97 in "The Later Poetry of W. B. Yeats," *Language as Gesture* (New York: Harcourt, Brace, 1952), where he proposes the following "remedy" for our inability to accept Yeats's "magical mode of thinking": "to accept Yeats's magic literally as a machinery of meaning, to search out the prose parallels and reconstruct the

and some of the early criticism of Gerard Manley Hopkins' work is marred by the assumption that Hopkins' Catholicism must be more or less irrelevant to his poems.[7]

Another case in point is the work of the brilliant French critic Maurice Blanchot. Blanchot is fascinated by a certain conception of the relation between literary creation and a devouring darkness which, for him, underlies language and the human mind. He has written dozens of essays on widely different authors, many of them most impressive in the depth of their penetration. Nevertheless a curious process of assimilation operates in these essays. Whatever Mr. B. reads turns into Mr. B. Though he may begin with objective discussion, his own obsessive ideas are an engulfing whirlpool which sweeps Kafka, Beckett, Joubert, Musil, Rilke, and the rest into an irresistible swirling of language, dissipates their individual contours, and absorbs them into itself, so that each essay can end with another statement of those notions which are, in Blanchot's criticism, repeated again and again in almost the same form. The essays are in their movement a perfect imitation of the conception of literature which they presuppose, but the reader is left wondering whether he should call Blanchot's work literary criticism or give it some other name.[8] Only the wisest and best of men can avoid distorting the writers he studies in the direction of his own beliefs, and this tendency is all the more powerful the more firmly he holds those beliefs.

Suppose, then, we imagine a critic who recognizes this danger and who wishes nevertheless to remain a whole man. He will take a work of literature seriously enough to put in question the truth of its picture of things, and will have the courage to reject those works which seem to him morally or religiously mistaken. What use can a poem have, however beautiful it may be, if it pictures the world falsely? If such a critic finds Wagner salacious, Milton the holder of an inhuman theology, or Yeats's metaphysics absurd, he will not think these elements extrinsic to their art.[9]

---

symbols he uses on their own terms in order to come on the emotional reality, if it is there, actually in the poems—when the machinery may be dispensed with."

[7] See, for one example of this, Vivian de Sola Pinto, *Crisis in English Poetry, 1880-1940* (London: Hutchinson's University Library, 1952), p. 72.

[8] See Maurice Blanchot, *La Part du feu* (Paris, 1949); *Lautréamont et Sade* (Paris, 1949); *L'Espace littéraire* (Paris, 1955); *Le Livre à venir* (Paris, 1959).

[9] See William Empson, *Milton's God* (London: Chatto & Windus, 1961), and Yvor Winters, *The Poetry of W. B. Yeats* (Denver, Colo.: Alan Swallow, 1960). The books of Basil Willey and H. N. Fairchild attempt to combine historical objectivity with judgment based on religious commitment, but in the work of these scholars, particularly in Fairchild's, the religious conviction sometimes enters into the historical description and makes what began as unbiased research turn into polemical judgment. Fairchild's last three volumes, for example, are often an argument against the evil effects of romanticism and science on English poetry. See Basil Willey, *The Seventeenth Century Background* (London: Chatto & Windus, 1934); *The Eighteenth Century Background* (London: Chatto & Windus, 1940); *Nineteenth Century Studies* (London: Chatto & Windus, 1949); *More Nineteenth Century Studies* (London: Chatto & Win-

T. S. Eliot was a man of such courage. He expounds in "Tradition and the Individual Talent" a view of history which sees the literature of Europe from Homer to the present as forming a harmonious whole. If this is the case, then the addition of an authentic new work will alter the meanings of all the works back to *The Iliad*, and the meaning of the new work will lie in its relation to the others, its conformity to them.[10] But what of the work which does not conform? In a sense such a work will not exist at all, as, in Christian theology, evil has only a negative existence. The consequences for analysis and judgment of this view of literature are expressed in *After Strange Gods*, Eliot's most intransigent polemic.[11] Hardy, Lawrence, and Yeats receive the harshest criticism. Because they thought for themselves, or dared, as Yeats said of himself, to make a new religion "of poetic tradition, of a fardel of stories,"[12] they are heretics all. They dwell outside the closed community of European letters and must be condemned for whoring after strange gods. This condemnation follows logically enough from Eliot's religious commitment, and yet his paragraphs on Yeats, Hardy, and Lawrence (as F. R. Leavis has argued for the latter[13]) are hardly satisfactory as criticism, hardly give the reader much sense of the richness and complexity of the work of these writers. Eliot here comes close to substituting censorship for criticism.

The work of Albert Béguin offers another striking example of this. His early book, *L'Ame romantique et le rêve*, is one of the masterpieces of twentieth-century criticism. With great learning, subtlety, and penetration, and above all with an unparalleled power of sympathetic understanding, Béguin re-creates the spiritual itineraries of the major German and French romantic writers. As the years passed, however, his capacity for sympathetic identification gradually narrowed. In the end his full sympathy and approval could go out only to a small group of writers, those representing a certain kind of modern Catholic spirituality: Dostoevski, Georges Bernanos, Léon Bloy, Charles Péguy. Even Pascal, who might be expected to fit Béguin's definition of authentic writing, did not escape his growing tendency to exclusions. Certain pages in one of Béguin's last books, the "Par lui-même" volume on Pascal, describe Pascal as alien to the deepest spiritual experience of today. A remorse-

---

dus, 1956); Hoxie Neale Fairchild, *Religious Trends in English Poetry*, Vol. I: 1700-1740, *Protestantism and the Cult of Sentiment* (1939); Vol. II: 1740-1780, *Religious Sentimentalism in the Age of Johnson* (1942); Vol. III: 1780-1830, *Romantic Faith* (1949); Vol. IV: 1830-1880, *Christianity and Romanticism in the Victorian Era* (1957); Vol. V: 1880-1920, *Gods of a Changing Poetry* (1962) (all published in New York by Columbia Univ. Press).

[10] See T. S. Eliot, *Selected Essays: 1917-1932* (New York: Harcourt, Brace, 1947), pp. 4-11.

[11] New York: Harcourt, Brace, 1934.

[12] *The Autobiography of William Butler Yeats* (New York: Macmillan, 1953), p. 70.

[13] See *D. H. Lawrence, Novelist* (London: Chatto & Windus, 1955).

less logic seems to have led this great critic to narrow more and more the circle of admissible writers.[14]

Suppose then that the critic decides to keep his own views out of his work. Literary study is objective and public, the establishment of the facts about literary history, part of that vast collective body of research which makes up the teamwork of modern scholarship. A man's religious views are his private business and need have nothing to do with his public life as a scholar. Even if literary analysis is to be thought of as the reliving from within of the world view of an author and its creation anew in the words of the critic, still this need have nothing to do with the critic's religious life. He must efface himself before the experience of literature, seek nothing for himself, give his mind and feelings to understanding the work at hand and to helping others to understand it through his analysis.

The problem of the relation between the religiously committed critic and the work of criticism seems to have been solved at one stroke. If this solution is followed rigorously, however, it may turn literary criticism into a trivial pastime. The secret possibility of this triviality undermines the attitude of historicism, as it is present in Nietzsche's thought or in Ortega y Gasset's, or is developed in the criticism of Wilhelm Dilthey, Bernhard Groethuysen, and others, or is present in another form in the work of A. O. Lovejoy and other students of the so-called history of ideas.[15]

Historical relativism has close connections, as Nietzsche's work shows, with that modern form of nihilism which sees all cultural attitudes, all the masquerades that time resumes, as hollow because based on nothing outside man himself. Nietzsche tells man to experiment tirelessly with new life-forms, new world views. This experimentation is a way man can affirm his freedom from any supernatural law and assert his

---

[14] See L'Ame romantique et le rêve, 2 vols. (Marseille, 1937), nouvelle édition (Paris, 1939); La Prière de Péguy (Neuchâtel, 1944); Léon Bloy: Mystique de la douleur (Paris, 1948); Poésie de la présence (Paris, 1957); Bernanos par lui-même (Paris, 1954); Pascal par lui-même (Paris, 1952). For Béguin's reservations about Pascal, see "Pascal sans histoire," in Pascal par lui-même, pp. 59-111.

[15] See W. Dilthey, Gesammelte Schriften, 12 vols. (Leipzig & Berlin, 1923-36); Bernard Groethuysen, Die Entstehung der bürgerlichen Welt- und Lebensanschauung in Frankreich, 2 vols. (Halle/Saale: Niemeyer, 1927, 1930); Philosophische Anthropologie (München & Berlin, 1934), French version: Anthropologie philosophique (Paris, 1952); Mythes et portraits (Paris, 1947); A. O. Lovejoy, Essays in the History of Ideas (Baltimore: Johns Hopkins Press, 1948); The Great Chain of Being (Cambridge, Mass.: Harvard Univ. Press, 1933); The Reason, the Understanding and Time (Baltimore: Johns Hopkins Press, 1961); Reflections on Human Nature (Baltimore: Johns Hopkins Press, 1961); The Thirteen Pragmatisms and Other Essays (Baltimore: Johns Hopkins Press, 1963). For an interesting book on Dilthey's work, see Kurt Müller-Volmer, Towards a Phenomenological Theory of Literature: A Study of Wilhelm Dilthey's "Poetik" (The Hague: Mouton, 1963), and for a recent discussion of Lovejoy's methodology, see Maurice Mandelbaum, "The History of Ideas, Intellectual History, and the History of Philosophy," The Historiography of the History of Philosophy, Beiheft 5 of History and Theory (The Hague: Mouton, 1965), pp. 33-42.

sovereign will to power over the world. What Nietzsche called the "death of God" is the presupposition of his historicism. Dilthey's aim of an exhaustive re-creation of all the types of life-forms leads to admirable works of criticism, but these may leave the reader in the end asking, "Wherefore? If all these forms of life are relative, what value do they have, and why should I bother to relive them?" Dilthey was not unaware of this implication of his work. The conflict between historical relativism and man's need for a universally valid knowledge seemed to him the essential problem raised by historicism.[16] This problem, he felt, could be solved only by pushing the historical sense to its limit. Man can go beyond history only through history. But where would a man be if he were beyond history? To have exhausted all cultural forms, in W. B. Yeats's view at least, is to be face to face with what he calls in "Meru" the "desolation of reality." The vision of all personages of history as relative to their times and places is likely to lead to the world-weariness of Paul Valéry in "La Crise de l'esprit," or to the rage for destruction of Yeats in "Nineteen Hundred and Nineteen."

The negative energy present in a rigorous historicism is especially apparent in the work of A. O. Lovejoy. Lovejoy had immense learning and an indefatigable power to understand the logic of ideas, including religious ones, in their development through history. He also had a great distaste for ambiguities and confusions of thought, and yet he felt that most writers are ambiguous or confused, often expressing conflicting ideas or incongruous feelings on a single page of their writing. Lovejoy's attitude toward Western history was a bit like that of a positivistic anthropologist collecting the strange myths and beliefs of the aborigines. This detachment is apparent in his habit of separating the statement of a "unit-idea" from its living context in the thought of a writer and presenting it in cold isolation where it can be subjected to his merciless power of logical analysis. This analysis puts in question both the idea that there is a unity in the culture of a period and the idea that there is a unity in the thought of an individual man. Examples of this are Lovejoy's fragmentation of romanticism and his discrimination of sixty-six different senses in which the idea of nature was, in antiquity, connected with "norms."[17]

Neither objective description of historical facts nor sympathetic re-creation of the life-forms of the past can be a self-sufficient end in itself. A twentieth-century inheritor of historicism, Wallace Stevens, recognizes this when, in "The Noble Rider and the Sound of Words," he rejects Plato's image of the charioteer of the soul and Verrocchio's splendid

---

[16] See, e.g., the end of his speech on the occasion of his seventieth birthday, in *Die Geistige Welt*, Part 1, *Gesammelte Schriften*, v, 9.

[17] See "On the Discrimination of Romanticisms," *Essays in the History of Ideas*, pp. 228-253, and the Appendix to A. O. Lovejoy and G. Boas, *A Documentary History of Primitivism and Related Ideas* (Baltimore: The Johns Hopkins Press, 1935).

equestrian statue of Bartolomeo Colleoni.[18] They are of little interest to us now, he says, if they are no more than outmoded forms of the past, a stage set which has been taken down and carted away. The study of the supreme fictions of history has value only if it is related to our search for the supreme fictions of today. Dilthey himself, at the end of *Die Einbildungskraft des Dichters,* an essay of 1887, affirms that though there is something universal about the work of the greatest poets, nevertheless even they are creatures of history. This means that the poets of the past can never move us as they did their contemporaries. The poets of most value to us are the poets of today, those who can speak to us of our own experience.[19] The study of literature cannot be justified in the same way as scientific research can. Each new scientific fact builds up man's picture of the universe and may have practical applications in the great technological civilization he is creating. The student of literature, quite properly, wants to know what's in it for him, and a pure historical relativism, to the degree that it answers that there's nothing in it for him, reduces the study of literature to triviality. Homer's work, or Dante's, or Hardy's must be more than just one way of looking at things among innumerable others, and yet the consequences of assuming this involve the difficulties I discussed earlier.

No doubt in practice a good critic can reconcile his religious convictions with catholicity of taste and wide-ranging sympathy for many authors, but still he must be on guard against the dangers of unwittingly making works of literature over in his own image, or of unjustly condemning them, or of failing to take them seriously enough to put in question the authenticity of their religious themes. The tension between dispassionate objectivity and engagement is in the nature of literary study and must be lived by each critic as best he can.

2

Even if the critic interested in the religious aspects of literature makes his peace with this tension, a new set of problems faces him when he considers the external context of a poem or novel. I said at the beginning that a poem embodies its meaning. This is true, but words are not, after all, like notes in music, meaningless except in their relation to one another. They have a complicated cultural history. The notion of intrinsic meaning is not incompatible with the idea that each poem draws into itself all those connections it has with its various contexts. It is often useful to have those connections identified, not only for their own sake, but for the light they may shed on meanings which are there in the words of the work. Such investigations may show how a certain text draws its life

---

[18] See *The Necessary Angel: Essays on Reality and the Imagination* (New York: Alfred A. Knopf, 1951), pp. 7, 9.
[19] *Die Geistige Welt,* Part 2, *Gesammelte Schriften,* VI, 241.

from similar passages in other works by the author, or from books read by the author, or from the social and historical milieu in which it came into existence, or from the tradition to which it belongs.

But where does the context of a poem stop? Its relations to its surroundings radiate outward like concentric circles from a stone dropped in water, and it may be extremely difficult to give a satisfactory inventory of them. Moreover, this investigation tends to disperse the poem into the multiplicity of its associations until it may become little more than a point of focus for the impersonal ideas, images, and motifs which enter into it. Instead of being a self-sufficient entity, it is only a symptom of ideas or images current in the culture which generated it.

If the critic rejects this implication of contextual study and returns to the poem itself, another danger awaits him. The more completely he cuts the poem off from its mesh of defining circumstances, the less, it may be, he can allow himself to say about it. The poem means only itself, and any commentary falsifies it by turning it into something other than itself. Fearing the heresies of paraphrase and explanation, he may be reduced to silence, or to repeating the poem itself as its only adequate commentary.[20]

No doubt there is validity in both these views of literature. Each authentic poem is something altogether individual, and even other poems by the same writer are more or less irrelevant to its self-enclosed integrity. On the other hand, the insights gained by study of a poem's context may help the critic in many ways in his attempt to understand this particularity.

The problem of the proper focus to choose for the interpretation of a given work or author has, however, special difficulties in relation to the study of religious themes in literature. How is the critic to treat these? Is he to hold that each religious poem has a meaning which is peculiar to that poem alone? If this is the case then there is, for example, one religious view of things for Gerard Manley Hopkins' "The Windhover," another for "God's Grandeur," another for "Spelt from Sibyl's Leaves," another for "The Wreck of the Deutschland," and so on. In each case the religious meanings must be developed solely from the words of the particular poem, and this means that each religious poem will have a unique religious meaning. A strict "new critical" approach to Hopkins work would follow this path, and in fact many of the essays on "The Windhover" assume that it can be understood more or less in isolation from the rest of Hopkins' work.

Obviously, however, there are echoes, resemblances, fraternal similarities between one poem by Hopkins and the others. Nor are his letters, notebooks, essays, and devotional writings without relevance to an

[20] Jean Starobinski has eloquently described this paradox of criticism in *L'Oeil-vivant* (Paris: Gallimard, 1961), pp. 24-27.

understanding of his poems. Each poem lives in a context which includes everything Hopkins ever wrote. Should the critic therefore attempt to show how that circumambient milieu is a complex harmony of related themes?[21] But then, once more, the individual poem is in danger of losing its integrity and becoming a node in a web of connections or a moment in a spiritual history which transcends it.

On the other hand, why should the critic stop with Hopkins' own writings? The poet was a nineteenth-century Jesuit and a graduate of Oxford. His reading in Scotus, Ignatius, and Suarez, his knowledge of the Bible and of Catholic liturgy, the influence of his tutor at Oxford, Walter Pater, his readings in Greek philosophy as an undergraduate, his place in the Oxford movement or in the general history of Victorian religious experience—none of these associations is irrelevant, and yet their investigation tends, as it proliferates, to dissolve Hopkins into what influenced him, to make his work no more than a "product" of its time.

Certainly all three focuses of criticism are valid, the study of the individual work, the study of all the works of one author, the study of the ideas or sensibility of an age, but each tends to imply a different notion of the way religious themes are present in literature.

The contextual problems in the interpretation of religious literature are especially apparent in the scholarship on medieval and Renaissance poetry. A complex body of learning—traditional topoi, subtle methods of allegory, many-layered symbols—may be hidden in an apparently simple lyric of these periods. For an educated man of the Middle Ages or Renaissance, it is argued, all literature, philosophy, and theological writing from Greek times to the present form a single tradition which should determine the shape and content of any authentic poem. This tradition was taken for granted by a contemporary reader of Chaucer, Spenser, or Milton, and guided his understanding of their poems. The twentieth-century reader must labor to recover the context permitting a just interpretation of such writers, just as a reader of the twenty-fifth century will no doubt have to labor to recover what he needs to know in order to read Faulkner, Camus, or Beckett, not to speak of Eliot or Joyce. To understand Dante, Chaucer, or Donne, or at least to understand them in relation to the traditions in which their work participates, the scholar must steep himself in these traditions, know Greek and Latin literature, classical philosophy, medieval encyclopedias, Biblical commentaries, and so on. Admirable work has been done in this way by scholars as different in their methods and commitments as E. R. Curtius, Erich Auerbach, D. C. Allen, C. S. Singleton, Morton Bloomfield, and D. W. Robertson, Jr.[22]

---

[21] As, e.g., I have tried to do in my chapter on Hopkins in *The Disappearance of God: Five Nineteenth-Century Writers* (Cambridge, Mass.: Belknap Press of Harvard Univ. Press, 1963).

[22] See E. R. Curtius, *Europäische Literatur und lateinisches Mittelalter* (Bern,

Critics still differ, however, about the proper way of interpreting medieval and Renaissance literature. Their recent disagreements have often had to do with the question of the way religious meanings inhere in secular literature. C. S. Singleton and R. H. Green, to cite one example, have argued about whether *The Divine Comedy* is to be considered allegory of the poets or allegory of the theologians.[23] The question at issue is whether or not it is proper to read Dante's poem strictly on the model of the four-level allegorical interpretation which was applied in the Middle Ages to the Bible. The answer to this question will determine what is meant when *The Divine Comedy* is called a religious poem.

Quarrels about context arise as much or more from disagreement about which is the important context for a given poem as from disagreement about whether or not a given poem can be understood in isolation. Even though all scholars would probably now agree that *Beowulf* is a Christian poem, still the poem changes magically if it is moved from the milieu of the Bible and Latin literature of the Middle Ages to the milieu of Germanic heroic poetry. On the other hand, a secular lyric of the Middle Ages or Renaissance may appear innocent of religious meaning when it is looked at in isolation, but when it is set against texts from the Bible, St. Augustine, St. Gregory, Rhabanus Maurus, and so on, images which seemed realism or decoration take on another meaning and reveal themselves to be symbols of transcendent truths. Who is to say that this symbolism is in the text itself and has not been installed there by the legerdemain of the learned critic? Only the tact born of long immersion in the literature of the period can tell, but the long immersion produces different results in different cases. A consensus among critics in these areas is an ideal to be worked toward rather than a goal yet attained.

1948), English trans. Willard R. Trask (New York: Pantheon, 1953); Erich Auerbach, *Mimesis* (Bern, 1946), 2nd ed. (Bern, 1959), English trans. Willard R. Trask (Princeton, N. J.: Princeton Univ. Press, 1953); *Literatursprache und Publikum in der lateinischen Spätantike und im Mittelalter* (Bern, 1958), English trans. Ralph Manheim (New York: Bollingen Foundation, 1965); "Figura," *Archivum Romanicum,* XXII (1938), 436-489; "Typological Symbolism in Mediaeval Literature," *Yale French Studies,* No. 9 (1952), pp. 5-8; D. C. Allen, *The Harmonious Vision: Studies in Milton's Poetry* (Baltimore: Johns Hopkins Press, 1954); *Image and Meaning: Metaphoric Traditions in Renaissance Poetry* (Baltimore: Johns Hopkins Press, 1960); C. S. Singleton, *An Essay on the Vita Nuova* (Cambridge, Mass.: Harvard Univ. Press, 1949); *Dante Studies* (Cambridge, Mass.: Harvard Univ. Press, 1954—); Morton Bloomfield, *The Seven Deadly Sins* (East Lansing: Michigan State College Press, 1952); *Piers Plowman as a Fourteenth-Century Apocalypse* (New Brunswick, N. J.: Rutgers Univ. Press, 1962); D. W. Robertson, Jr., and B. F. Huppé, *Piers Plowman and Scriptural Tradition* (Princeton, N. J.: Princeton Univ. Press, 1951); D. W. Robertson, Jr., A *Preface to Chaucer: Studies in Medieval Perspectives* (Princeton, N. J.: Princeton Univ. Press, 1963).
[23] See C. S. Singleton, "Dante's Allegory," *Speculum,* XXV (1950), 78-83; "The Other Journey," *Kenyon Review,* XIV (1952), 189-206; "The Irreducible Dove," *Comparative Literature,* IX (1957), 129-135, and Richard Hamilton Green, "Dante's 'Allegory of Poets' and the Mediaeval Theory of Poetic Fiction," *Comparative Literature,* IX (1957), 118-128.

3

The problem of context is associated with another problem, the last of the issues involved in the relation of religion and literature which I shall discuss. Exactly what does it mean to say that religious meanings are present in a poem or a play? It may mean the following: The poet belonged to a certain culture. Among the elements of that culture were religious beliefs. These were part of the world view of his age, and naturally they enter into his poems, since all men are subject to the spirit of their times. To take this view is to accept that historicism which, as I argued earlier, tends to turn religious themes in literature into something other than themselves. Of what religious interest are such themes in Dante's poems, or George Herbert's, or T. S. Eliot's if they are accidents of a certain time and place, determined horizontally, as it were, by the influence of other men and their books? Religious themes in literature are without religious significance unless they spring from a direct relationship between the poet and God, however much they may take a form dictated by the age. If human history is made by men alone, then religious elements in culture have only a human meaning. For Ludwig Feuerbach and other such humanists religious ideas are symptoms of the way men lived together at a certain time. Religion for Feuerbach or for George Eliot is the cement of culture, a collective belief which holds people together.[24]

A similar transmutation of the religious import of literature is implicit in an exclusive commitment to either of the other focuses of criticism I have identified. If, as the structural linguists and some "new critics" tend to assume, the meanings of a work of literature are entirely intrinsic, generated by the interaction among its words, then the symbolizing process predominates over what is symbolized, and literature is in danger of becoming a play of words mirroring one another vacantly. In such a case, religious themes will not be different in kind from any other themes in literature, since poetry on any subject does no more than demonstrate the power of language to develop complex symbolic structures. To such a view of literature a man interested in religious themes in poetry could make the same approach Paul Ricœur directs against the anthropological structuralism of Claude Lévi-Strauss. Ricœur sees in Lévi-Strauss's work "an extreme form of modern agnosticism." "For you," he said to Lévi-Strauss in a public discussion of June 1963, "there is no 'message,' not in the cybernetic sense, but in the 'kerygmatic' sense; you give up meaning in despair; but you save yourself by the notion that if human beings have nothing to say, at least they say it so well that one can subject their discourse to a structural analysis. You save meaning,

---

[24] See Ludwig Feuerbach, *Das Wesen des Christenthums*, Bd. 7 of his *Sämmtliche Werke* (Leipzig, 1849), English translation by George Eliot (London, 1854), also available in Harper Torchbook series.

but it is the meaning of meaninglessness, the admirable syntactic arrangement of a discourse which says nothing. I see you at that point of conjunction of agnosticism and an acute understanding of syntaxes."[25]

The same kind of restriction may limit that form of criticism which takes as its goal the comprehension of the mind of an author as revealed in the ensemble of his works. If each writer's mind is autonomous, the sole originator of the meanings which are expressed in his works, then any seemingly religious themes in those works will have a human rather than a divine meaning. They will be nothing but a part of the pageant of human history.

Any method of criticism which presupposes that meaning in literature is exclusively derived from the interrelations of words, or from the experiences of a self-enclosed mind, or from the living together of a people will be unable to confront religious themes in literature as such. Only if some supernatural reality can be present in a poem, in a mind, or in the cultural expressions of a community can there be an authentic religious dimension in literature. Only if there is such a thing as the spiritual history of a culture or of a person, a history determined in part at least by God himself as well as by man in his attitude toward God, can religious motifs in literature have a properly religious meaning. The scholar's position on this issue will follow from his religious convictions, which returns me to the assertion that the religious commitment of the critic, or lack of it, cannot be considered irrelevant to his work.

In the relation of the critic to the work criticized and in the relation of the work to its context there are methodological problems which take especially difficult forms when the connections of religion and literature are in question. Though there is no easy way to solve these, no golden mean which will allow a happy steering between extremes, there is an attitude toward literary study which will escape some of its dangers. The scholar-critic must be as learned as possible, not only in literature itself, but in history, philosophy, theology, the other arts, and so on. Only in this way can he avoid egregious errors caused by ignorance. Nevertheless, the end of literary study is still elucidation of the intrinsic meanings

[25] *Esprit*, 31ᵉ année, No. 322 (novembre 1963), pp. 652, 653: "Je penserais plutôt que cette philosophie implicite entre dans le champ de votre travail, où je vois une forme extrême de l'agnosticisme moderne; pour vous il n'y a pas de 'message': non au sens de la cybernétique, mais au sens kérygmatique; vous êtes dans le désespoir du sens; mais vous vous sauvez par la pensée que, si les gens n'ont rien à dire, du moins ils le disent si bien qu'on peut soumettre leur discours au structuralisme. Vous sauvez le sens, mais c'est le sens du non-sens, l'admirable arrangement syntactique d'un discours qui ne dit rien. Je vous vois à cette conjonction de l'agnosticisme et d'une hyperintelligence des syntaxes." See also, in the same number of *Esprit*, the essay by Paul Ricœur entitled "Structure et herméneutique" (pp. 596-627). Ricœur's essay is an excellent discussion of the relation between the objectivity proper to structuralism and that form of interpretation from within which he calls, after Dilthey and others, "la compréhension herméneutique." The latter he sees as most appropriate for reaching, by way of sympathetic participation in a tradition, religious meanings in literature and in other cultural forms.

of poems, plays, and novels. In the effort toward such elucidation the proper model for the relation of the critic to the work he studies is not that of scientist to physical objects but that of one man to another in charity. I may love another person and know him as only love can know without in the least abnegating my own beliefs. Love wants the other person to be as he is, in all his recalcitrant particularity. As St. Augustine puts it, the lover says to the loved one, "Volo ut sis!"—"I wish you to be." If the critic approaches the poem with this kind of reverence for its integrity, it will respond to his questioning and take its part in that dialogue between reader and work which is the life of literary study.

The metaphor of lover and beloved will also indicate what tone the critic should take with *his* reader. I may tell you what the man or woman I love is like, but this is no substitute for your direct confrontation with that person. Criticism too is only a preliminary to the reader's own dialogue with the work. In the end criticism must efface itself before the texts, stand back, having done the work of interpretation, to let the works show themselves forth as they are. Only in this way will those religious meanings which are in the work and not in the beholder's eye be made visible.

CHRISTIANITY AND LITERATURE

C. S. Lewis

When I was asked to address this society, I was at first tempted to refuse
because the subject proposed to me, that of Christianity and Literature,
did not seem to admit of any discussion. I knew, of course, that Christian
story and sentiment were among the things on which literature could
be written, and, conversely, that literature was one of the ways in which
Christian sentiment could be expressed and Christian story told; but
there seemed nothing more to be said of Christianity in this connection
than of any of the hundred and one other things that men made books
about. We are familiar, no doubt, with the expression 'Christian Art',
by which people usually mean Art that represents Biblical or hagiologi-
cal scenes, and there is, in this sense, a fair amount of 'Christian Literature'. But I question whether it has any literary qualities peculiar to
itself. The rules for writing a good passion play or a good devotional
lyric are simply the rules for writing tragedy or lyric in general: success in sacred literature depends on the same qualities of structure,
suspense, variety, diction, and the like which secure success in secular
literature. And if we enlarge the idea of Christian Literature to include
not only literature on sacred themes but all that is written by Christians
for Christians to read, then, I think, Christian Literature can exist only
in the same sense in which Christian cookery might exist. It would be
possible, and it might be edifying, to write a Christian cookery book.
Such a book would exclude dishes whose preparation involves unnecessary human labour or animal suffering, and dishes excessively luxurious.
That is to say, its choice of dishes would be Christian. But there could
be nothing specifically Christian about the actual cooking of the dishes
included. Boiling an egg is the same process whether you are a Christian
or a Pagan. In the same way, literature written by Christians for Christians would have to avoid mendacity, cruelty, blasphemy, pornography,
and the like, and it would aim at edification in so far as edification was
proper to the kind of work in hand. But whatever it chose to do would
have to be done by the means common to all literature; it could succeed or fail only by the same excellences and the same faults as all literature; and its literary success or failure would never be the same thing
as its obedience or disobedience to Christian principles.

"Christianity and Literature." From Rehabilitations and Other Essays *by C. S.
Lewis (London: Oxford University Press, 1939). Reprinted by permission of
the Estate of C. S. Lewis.*

I have been speaking so far of Christian Literature *proprement dite*—that is, of writing which is intended to affect us as literature, by its appeal to imagination. But in the visible arts I think we can make a distinction between sacred art, however sacred in theme, and pure iconography—between that which is intended, in the first instance, to affect the imagination and the aesthetic appetite, and that which is meant merely as the starting-point for devotion and meditation. If I were treating the visible arts I should have to work out here a full distinction of the work of art from the icon on the one hand and the toy on the other. The icon and the toy have this in common that their value depends very little on their perfection as artefacts—a shapeless rag may give as much pleasure as the costliest doll, and two sticks tied crosswise may kindle as much devotion as the work of Leonardo. And to make matters more complicated the very same object could often be used in all three ways. But I do not think the icon and the work of art can be so sharply distinguished in literature. I question whether the badness of a really bad hymn can ordinarily be so irrelevant to devotion as the badness of a bad devotional picture. Because the hymn uses words, its badness will, to some degree, consist in confused or erroneous thought and unworthy sentiment. But I mention this difficult question here only to say that I do not propose to treat it. If any literary works exist which have a purely iconographic value and no literary value, they are not what I am talking about. Indeed I could not, for I have not met them.

Of Christian Literature, then, in the sense of 'work aiming at literary value and written by Christians for Christians', you see that I have really nothing to say and believe that nothing can be said. But I think I have something to say about what may be called the Christian approach to literature: about the principles, if you will, of Christian literary theory and criticism. For while I was thinking over the subject you gave me I made what seemed to me a discovery. It is not an easy one to put into words. The nearest I can come to it is to say that I found a disquieting contrast between the whole circle of ideas used in modern criticism and certain ideas recurrent in the New Testament. Let me say at once that it is hardly a question of logical contradiction between clearly defined concepts. It is too vague for that. It is more a repugnance of atmospheres, a discordance of notes, an incompatibility of temperaments.

What are the key-words of modern criticism? *Creative*, with its opposite *derivative; spontaneity,* with its opposite *convention; freedom,* contrasted with *rules. Great* authors are innovators, pioneers, explorers; bad authors bunch in schools and follow models. Or again, great authors are always 'breaking fetters' and 'bursting bonds'. They have personality, they 'are themselves'. I do not know whether we often think out the implication of such language into a consistent philosophy; but we certainly have a general picture of bad work flowing from conformity and discipleship, and of good work bursting out from certain centres of explosive force—apparently self-originating force—which we call men of genius.

Now the New Testament has nothing at all to tell us of literature. I know that there are some who like to think of Our Lord Himself as a poet and cite the parables to support their view. I admit freely that to believe in the Incarnation at all is to believe that every mode of human excellence is implicit in His historical human character: poet-hood, of course, included. But if all had been developed, the limitations of a single human life would have been transcended and He would not have been a man; therefore all excellences save the spiritual remained in varying degrees implicit. If it is claimed that the poetic excellence is more developed than others—say, the intellectual—I think I deny the claim. Some of the parables do work like poetic similes; but then others work like philosophic illustrations. Thus the Unjust Judge is not emo-tionally or imaginatively like God: he corresponds to God as the terms in a proportion correspond, because he is to the Widow (in one highly specialized respect) as God is to man. In that parable Our Lord, if we may so express it, is much more like Socrates than Shakespeare. And I dread an over-emphasis on the poetical element in His words because I think it tends to obscure that quality in His human character which is, in fact, so visible in His irony, His *argumenta ad homines,* and His use of the *a fortiori,* and which I would call the homely, peasant shrewdness. Donne points out that we are never told He laughed; it is difficult in reading the Gospels not to believe, and to tremble in believing, that He smiled.

I repeat, the New Testament has nothing to say of literature; but what it says on other subjects is quite sufficient to strike that note which I find out of tune with the language of modern criticism. I must begin with something that is unpopular. St Paul tells us (1 Cor. xi, 3) that man is the 'head' of woman. We may soften this if we like by saying that he means only man *quâ* man and woman *quâ* woman and that an equality of the sexes as citizens or intellectual beings is not therefore absolutely repugnant to his thought: indeed, that he himself tells us that in another respect, that is 'in the Lord', the sexes cannot be thus separated (*ibid.,* xi, 11). But what concerns me here is to find out what he means by Head. Now in verse 3 he has given us a very remarkable proportion sum: that God is to Christ as Christ is to man and man is to woman, and the rela-tion between each term and the next is that of Head. And in verse 7 we are told that man is God's image and glory, and woman is man's glory. He does not repeat 'image', but I question whether the omission is intentional, and I suggest that we shall have a fairly Pauline picture of this whole series of Head relations running from God to woman if we picture each term as the 'image and glory' of the preceding term.

And I suppose that of which one is the image and glory is that which one glorifies by copying or imitating. Let me once again insist that I am not trying to twist St Paul's metaphors into a logical system. I know well that whatever picture he is building up, he himself will be the first to throw it aside when it has served its turn and to adopt some quite different picture when some new aspect of the truth is present to his · mind. But I want to see clearly the sort of picture implied in this passage—to get it clear however temporary its use or partial its application. And it seems to me a quite clear picture; we are to think of some original divine virtue passing downwards from rung to rung of a hierarchical ladder, and the mode in which each lower rung receives it is, quite frankly, imitation.

What is perhaps most startling in this picture is the apparent equivalence of the woman-man and man-God relation with the relation between Christ and God, or, in Trinitarian language, with the relation between the First and Second Persons of the Trinity. As a layman and a comparatively recently reclaimed apostate I have, of course, no intention of building a theological system—still less of setting up a *catena* of New Testament metaphors as a criticism on the Nicene or the Athanasian creed, documents which I wholly accept. But it is legitimate to notice what kinds of metaphor the New Testament uses; more especially when what we are in search of is not dogma but a kind of flavour or atmosphere. And there is no doubt that this kind of proportion sum—A:B: :B:C—is quite freely used in the New Testament where A and B represent the First and Second Persons of the Trinity. Thus St Paul has already told us earlier in the same epistle that we are 'of Christ' and Christ is 'of God' (iii, 23). Thus again in the Fourth Gospel, Our Lord Himself compares the relation of the Father to the Son with that of the Son to His flock, in respect of knowledge (x, 15) and of love (xv, 9).

I suggest, therefore, that this picture of a hierarchical order in which we are encouraged—though, of course, only from certain points of view and in certain respects—to regard the Second Person Himself as a step, or stage, or degree, is wholly in accord with the spirit of the New Testament. And if we ask how the stages are connected the answer always seems to be something like imitation, reflection, assimilation. Thus in Gal. iv, 19, Christ is to be 'formed' inside each believer—the verb here used (μορφωθῇ) meaning to shape, to figure, or even to draw a sketch. In First Thessalonians (i, 6) Christians are told to imitate St Paul and the Lord, and elsewhere (1 Cor. xi, 1) to imitate St Paul as he in turn imitates Christ—thus giving us another stage of progressive imitation. Changing the metaphor we find that believers are to acquire the fragrance of Christ, *redolere Christum* (2 Cor. ii, 16): that the glory of God has appeared in the face of Christ as, at the creation, light appeared in the universe (2 Cor. iv, 6); and, finally, if my reading of a much disputed passage is correct, that a Christian is to Christ as a mirror to an object (2 Cor. iii, 18).

These passages, you will notice, are all Pauline; but there is a place in the Fourth Gospel which goes much farther—so far that if it were not a Dominical utterance we would not venture to think along such lines. There (v. 19) we are told that the Son does only what He sees the Father doing. He watches the Father's operations and does the same (ὁμοίως ποιεῖ) or 'copies'. The Father, because of His love for the Son, shows Him all that He does. I have already explained that I am not a theologian. What aspect of the Trinitarian reality Our Lord, as God, saw while He spoke these words, I do not venture to define; but I think we have a right and even a duty to notice carefully the earthly image by which He expressed it—to see clearly the picture He puts before us. It is a picture of a boy learning to do things by watching a man at work. I think we may even guess what memory, humanly speaking, was in His mind. It is hard not to imagine that He remembered His boyhood, that He saw Himself as a boy in a carpenter's shop, a boy learning how to do things by watching while St Joseph did them. So taken, the passage does not seem to me to conflict with anything I have learned from the creeds, but greatly to enrich my conception of the Divine sonship.

Now it may be that there is no absolute logical contradiction between the passages I have quoted and the assumptions of modern criticism: but I think there is so great a difference of temper that a man whose mind was at one with the mind of the New Testament would not, and indeed could not, fall into the language which most critics now adopt. In the New Testament the art of life itself is an art of imitation: can we, believing this, believe that literature, which must derive from real life, is to aim at being 'creative', 'original', and 'spontaneous'. 'Originality' in the New Testament is quite plainly the prerogative of God alone; even within the triune being of God it seems to be confined to the Father. The duty and happiness of every other being is placed in being derivative, in reflecting like a mirror. Nothing could be more foreign to the tone of scripture than the language of those who describe a saint as a 'moral genius' or a 'spiritual genius' thus insinuating that his virtue or spirituality is 'creative' or 'original'. If I have read the New Testament aright, it leaves no room for 'creativeness' even in a modified or metaphorical sense. Our whole destiny seems to lie in the opposite direction, in being as little as possible ourselves, in acquiring a fragrance that is not our own but borrowed, in becoming clean mirrors filled with the image of a face that is not ours. I am not here supporting the doctrine of total depravity, and I do not say that the New Testament supports it; I am saying only that the highest good of a creature must be creaturely— that is, derivative or reflective—good. In other words, as St Augustine makes plain (*De Civ. Dei* xii, cap. I), pride does not only go before a fall but is a fall—a fall of the creature's attention from what is better, God, to what is worse, itself.

Applying this principle to literature, in its greatest generality, we should get as the basis of all critical theory the maxim that an author should never conceive himself as bringing into existence beauty or wisdom which did not exist before, but simply and solely as trying to embody in terms of his own art some reflection of eternal Beauty and Wisdom. Our criticism would therefore from the beginning group itself with some existing theories of poetry against others. It would have affinities with the primitive of Homeric theory in which the poet is the mere pensioner of the Muse. It would have affinities with the Platonic doctrine of a transcendent Form partly imitable on earth; and remoter affinities with the Aristotelian doctrine of μίμησις and the Augustan doctrine about the imitation of Nature and the Ancients. It would be opposed to the theory of genius as, perhaps, generally understood; and above all it would be opposed to the idea that literature is self-expression.

But here some distinctions must be made. I spoke just now of the ancient idea that the poet was merely the servant of some god, of Apollo, or the Muse; but let us not forget the highly paradoxical words in which Homer's Phemius asserts his claim to be a poet—

Αὐτοδίδακτος δ᾽ εἰμί, θεὸς δέ μοι ἐν φρεσὶν οἴμας
Παντοίας ἐνέφυσεν. (*Od.* xxii, 347.)

'I am self-taught; a god inspired me with all manner of songs.' It sounds like a direct contradiction. How can he be self-taught if the god has taught him all he knows? Doubtless because the god's instruction is given internally, not through the senses, and is therefore regarded as part of the Self, to be contrasted with such external aids as, say, the example of other poets. And this seems to blur the distinction I am trying to draw between Christian imitation and the 'originality' praised by modern critics. Phemius obviously claims to be original, in the sense of being no other poet's disciple, and in the same breath admits his complete dependence on a supernatural teacher. Does not this let in 'originality' and 'creativeness' of the only kind that have ever been claimed?

If you said: 'The only kind that ought to have been claimed', I would agree; but as things are, I think the distinction remains, though it becomes finer than our first glance suggested. A Christian and an unbelieving poet may both be equally original in the sense that they neglect the example of their poetic forbears and draw on resources peculiar to themselves, but with this difference. The unbeliever may take his own temperament and experience, just as they happen to stand, and consider them worth communicating simply because they are facts or, worse still, because they are his. To the Christian his own temperament and experience, as mere fact, and as merely his, are of no value or importance whatsoever: he will deal with them, if at all, only because they are the medium through which, or the position from which, something universally profitable appeared to him. We can imagine two men seated in different parts of a church or theatre. Both, when they come out, may tell us their experiences, and both may use the first person. But the one is interested in his seat only because it was his—'I was most uncomfortable', he will say. 'You would hardly believe what a draught comes in from the door in that corner. And the people! I had to speak pretty sharply to the woman in front of me.' The other will tell us what could be seen from his seat, choosing to describe this because this is what he knows, and because every seat must give the best view of something. 'Do you know', he will begin, 'the moulding on those pillars goes on round at the back. It looks, too, as if the design on the back were the older of the two.' Here we have the expressionist and the Christian attitudes towards the self or temperament. Thus St. Augustine and Rousseau both write *Confessions;* but to the one his own temperament is a kind of absolute (*au moins je suis autre*), to the other it is 'a narrow house too narrow for Thee to enter—oh make it wide. It is in ruins—oh rebuild it.' And Wordsworth, the romantic who made a good end, has a foot in either world and though he practises both, distinguishes well the two ways in which a man may be said to write about himself. On the one hand he says:

> [For] I must tread on shadowy ground, must sink
> Deep, and aloft ascending breathe in worlds
> To which the heaven of heavens is but a veil.

On the other he craves indulgence if

>   *with this*
> I mix more lowly matter; with the thing
> Contemplated, describe the Mind and Man
> Contemplating; and who and what he was—
> The transitory being that beheld
> This vision.

In this sense, then, the Christian writer may be self-taught or original. He may base his work on the 'transitory being' that he is, not because he thinks it valuable (for he knows that in his flesh dwells no good thing), but solely because of the 'vision' that appeared to it. But he will have no preference for doing this. He will do it if it happens to be the thing he can do best; but if his talents are such that he can produce good work by writing in an established form and dealing with experiences common to all his race, he will do so just as gladly. I even think he will do so more gladly. It is to him an argument not of strength but of weakness that he should respond fully to the vision only 'in his own way'. And always, of every idea and of every method he will ask not 'Is it mine?', but 'Is it good?'

This seems to me the most fundamental difference between the Christian and the unbeliever in their approach to literature. But I think there is another. The Christian will take literature a little less seriously than the cultured Pagan: he will feel less uneasy with a purely hedonistic standard for at least many kinds of work. The unbeliever is always apt to make a kind of religion of his aesthetic experiences; he feels ethically irresponsible, perhaps, but he braces his strength to receive responsibilities of another kind which seem to the Christian quite illusory. He has to be 'creative'; he has to obey a mystical amoral law called his artistic conscience; and he commonly wishes to maintain his superiority to the great mass of mankind who turn to books for mere recreation. But the Christian knows from the outset that the salvation of a single soul is more important than the production or preservation of all the epics and tragedies in the world: and as for superiority, he knows that the vulgar since they include most of the poor probably include most of his superiors. He has no objection to comedies that merely amuse and tales that merely refresh; for he thinks like Thomas Aquinas *ipsa ratio hoc habet ut quandoque rationis usus intercipiatur*. We can play, as we can eat, to the glory of God. It thus may come about that Christian views on literature will strike the world as shallow and flippant; but the world must not misunderstand. When Christian work is done on a serious subject there is no gravity and no sublimity it cannot attain. But they will belong to the theme. That is why they will be real and lasting—mighty nouns with which literature, an adjectival thing, is here united, far over-topping the fussy and ridiculous claims of literature that tries to be important simply as literature. And *a posteriori* it is not hard to argue that all the greatest poems have been made by men who valued something else much more than poetry—even if that something else were only cutting down enemies in a cattle-raid or tumbling a girl in a bed. The real frivolity, the solemn vacuity, is all with those who make literature a self-existent thing to be valued for its own sake. Pater prepared for pleasure as if it were martyrdom.

Now that I see where I have arrived a doubt assails me. It all sounds suspiciously like things I have said before, starting from very different premises. Is it King Charles's Head? Have I mistaken for the 'vision' the same old 'transitory being' who, in some ways, is not nearly transitory enough? It may be so: or I may, after all, be right. I would rather be right if I could; but if not, if I have only been once more following my own footprints, it is the sort of tragi-comedy which, on my own principles, I must try to enjoy. I find a beautiful example proposed in the *Paradiso* (XXVIII) where poor Pope Gregory, arrived in Heaven, discovered that his theory of the hierarchies, on which presumably he had taken pains, was quite wrong. We are told how the redeemed soul behaved; '*di sè medesmo rise*'. It was the funniest thing he'd ever heard.

HOLD ON HARD TO THE HUCKLEBERRY BUSHES

R. W. B. Lewis

The search for religious elements in literature, especially in American literature, has become a phenomenon in recent years that would have startled and bewildered Matthew Arnold, who did not have this sort of thing in mind at all. An increasing number of books address themselves to the subject, courses and symposia are given over to it, and I believe a university department or two have been established to make the undertaking permanent. Some of the work, like some of the workers, displays a high degree of cultural relevance; but in general practice the study of "religion and literature," as the phrase usually is, exhibits several rather disturbing oddities, the first of which is implied by the phrase itself. It is theologically correct but aesthetically perilous: in a way which might ultimately damage the theology. Absolutely speaking, as between religion and literature, religion no doubt comes first; but in the actual study of a particular literary text, it probably ought to follow, and follow naturally and organically and without strain—for the sake of the religion as well as the literature. Or so I shall try to suggest. We may perhaps recall the remark made to Emerson by an old Boston lady who, talking about the extreme religious sensibility of an earlier generation, said about those pious folk that "they had to hold on hard to the huckleberry bushes to hinder themselves from being translated." Their instinct was as sound as their impulse was proper.

1

It was characteristic of Emerson to have quoted those words, for he knew well enough that his own hold tended to slip from time to time. He was articulately dedicated to the actual; he embraced, as he said, the common and explored the low and familiar, both in life and literature. But the Over-Soul drew him like a magnet, and he was regularly prone to premature translation into the vast, unindividuated realm of the One. The atmosphere he found there was invariably sunny and smiling; and it is by stressing the sunshine and disregarding the translatability,

"Hold on Hard to the Huckleberry Bushes." First published in The Sewanee Review, LXVII, 3 (Summer, 1959). © 1959 by the University of the South, Sewanee, Tennessee. Reprinted by permission of The Sewanee Review and the author.

that Randall Stewart, in *American Literature and Christian Doctrine*,[1] is able to condemn Emerson to the sixth circle, the place reserved for the burning tombs of the heresiarchs. "Emerson is the arch-heretic of American literature," says Professor Stewart, "and Emersonism [sic: a foreshortening rhetorically equivalent to the phrase Democrat Party] the greatest heresy. By no dint of sophistry can he be brought within the Christian fold. His doctrine is radically anti-Christian, and has done more than any other doctrine to undermine Christian belief in America." There is a kind of health in the hardness of Professor Stewart's saying. But I confess that it has for me a pointless irrelevance which it would not be easy to measure, though it may be important to define.

Professor Stewart's little book is amiably unambiguous in statement, and engagingly direct in style; it is sprinkled with nice personal reminiscences of a long and honorable academic life for which many of us have cause to be grateful. The book belongs, in its slender way, to the number of studies which have sought to examine the whole of American literature from a single organizing viewpoint; and in this respect it follows a path opposite to the one followed by Frederick I. Carpenter in *American Literature and the Dream*[2]—a neglected work, in which Emerson appears as the high priest and dream purveyor rather than the arch heretic. But Professor Stewart's title is radically misleading, just as his method is revealingly—one is tempted to say, importantly and usefully—ill advised. By Christian doctrine, Professor Stewart means Protestant doctrine; by Protestant doctrine, he means American Puritan doctrine (in a manner that rather confirms than refutes the contention of the great Protestant historian of dogma, Adolph von Harnack, that there can be no such thing as Protestant dogma); by Puritan doctrine, Professor Stewart means very simply the doctrine of Original Sin; and by the doctrine of Original Sin, it is no longer clear what he means, since the matter has grown too small to be visible. He seems to mean even less, so far as one can make out, than T. E. Hulme meant thirty-five years ago, when he said—in a sentence that has done as much harm to the cause of cultural good sense as any that one can rapidly remember— that "dogmas like that of Original Sin . . . are the closest expression of the categories of the religious attitude." Separated from the rich theological framework within which it historically evolved, the concept of Original Sin is not much of a concept at all; it is more an image of unredeemably depraved human nature shivering somewhere in the void. In any case, this is the image that provides the single instrument by which Professor Stewart gauges the value of American writers from Edwards to the present. By the use of it, he denounces the villains, those who seem unaware of Original Sin (Paine, Franklin, Jefferson, Emerson,

[1] Baton Rouge, La., 1958.
[2] New York, 1955.

Whitman, Dreiser, Lewis), and salvages the elect (Edwards, Hawthorne, Melville maybe, James, Eliot, Hemingway, Faulkner, Warren).
But the writings of both heroes and villains suffer a sort of total defeat.
The latter are blown into oblivion by the author's rumbling southern
rhetoric; and the former are blotted out behind an enormous O S, as
Hester Prynne's image was lost behind the gigantic A reflected in the
convex surface of the shining armor.

In Professor Stewart's case, the translation was effected before the
huckleberry bushes were ever taken hold of. The actualities of the
works in question—their actions, their words, their concrete embodiments, their sensuous images, their characters, their incidents—seem to
have evaporated before a single glance descended on them. This is the
likely consequence of the doctrinal approach to literature. If Professor
Stewart had taken a more generous view of Christian doctrine, he might
have composed a more interesting book; but I am not sure that it would
have been a more pointed and purposeful book, or that it would have
done better service to the field of literature or of religion; for the issue
of priority would still remain. This issue is whether one scrutinizes
literature for its univocal formulations of particular historical doctrines
one cherishes or whether one submits for a while to the actual ingredients and the inner movement and growth of a work to see what attitude
and insight, including religious attitude and insight, the work itself
brings into being. Emerson continues to be a valuable case. Proceeding
from Emerson's words as he uttered them, Newton Arvin—who is anything but a sophist, and is on the contrary one of America's most intelligent, tactful, and scholarly critics—has managed to bring Emerson
some slight way "within the Christian fold."[3] Emerson, Mr. Arvin says,
did after all have a knowledge of evil and an awareness of human sin;
his famous cheerfulness was for the most part an achievement, a matter
of discipline and hard intellectual choice. But Emerson could not
convey his conceptions in the theological vocabulary available to him,
because it was not comprehended within that vocabulary; and he was
not in command of the vocabulary which could, in fact, convey it.
He set it forth in tropes and figures, in shadings and insistences, in
asides and repetitions of his own; and he emerged with a view of evil
so profoundly different from that of his contemporaries that of sin itself
he has seemed to have been simply and blissfully unconscious. For
Emerson's sense of the problem was surprisingly similar to the older
and more really traditional Christian attitude: the one that held firm
from St. Augustine to the Reformation: the view of evil as non-being,
as a privation, as a negation and an absence of good. Emerson normally
preferred to talk about something rather than nothing, about being
rather than non-being, and affirmation rather than negation; he lacked

---

[3] "The House of Pain," *Hudson Review*, 12 (1959), 37-53.

the special taste and affection for evil of so many modern intellectuals. But (here I am pushing Mr. Arvin's argument beyond anything he would wish to claim for it) it might be salutary to reflect that, as regards the doctrine of sin, it is Hawthorne who was the heretic and Emerson who was working toward the restoration rather than the undermining of Christian belief in America.

Emerson did not knowingly aim at the restoration of anything: except of the soul's fresh and immediate perception of certain aspects of the universe, getting rid of the linguistic and institutional clutter in which those aspects had gone stale, and relating them anew to the instant of experience. "They only who build on Ideas, build for eternity. . . . The law is only a memorandum. We are superstitious, and esteem the statute somewhat: so much life as it has in the character of living men is its force." That is Emerson's authentic voice, or one of his authentic voices: the voice of a man disentangling the Idea from the historical record of it, and allowing it again to invigorate the present. But it is a suggestive and representative accident that, in pursuit of that aim, Emerson's metaphysical gaze lighted just occasionally and without historical awareness upon the essences of certain moral and religious doctrines that had been given their fullest elaboration in pre-Reformation Christian theology. It is this essential (or, may one say, essentializing) quality in Emerson that should dictate the method and scope of any significant religious inquiry into his writing; and it is this quality that relates him as an American of his time to his most talented contemporaries.

The same faculty for arriving by mistake at the very heart of some ancient doctrine, long since smothered by Calvinism, is observable in the two Henry Jameses, and to a greater or lesser extent in Hawthorne and Poe. The elder James, for example, wrestling in New York with the secret of Swedenborg, emerged with his own version of the Augustinian concept of the *felix culpa,* the notion that the fall of man was a happy and a fortunate event. Not a syllable of James consciously echoes either St. Augustine or the medieval *Exultet* which celebrated the fortunate fall; nor was his statement of the idea (Adam's fall was "an every way upwards step indeed, pregnant with beatific consequences") buttressed by the traditional theological scheme that lent some measure of logic to the paradox. But there he was, driven by his personal intellectual momentum and his private tropes, at the naked center of the old doctrine. Henry James, Jr., is a much more complex and awe-inspiring case, deserving lengthy analysis elsewhere. Here let us say only that either James is a cultural miracle, or else he had devoured (as seems distinctly improbable) almost all of Aristotle, St. Augustine, St. Thomas, St. Bonaventura, and Dante Alighieri. And as to Poe, his root idea, according to the persuasive essay by Allen Tate,[4] the one idea he did not merely "entertain" but which actually pushed and bedeviled him was the grand old heresy of attributing to human beings the intellect and imagination that God had reserved for the angels. It is a heresy, to be sure, but one form of it was indispensable to the scholastic thinking of the twelfth century, and in particular to St. Anselm, of whom Poe is unlikely to have heard. And so on.

The American Protestant analyst, if sufficiently limited in viewpoint, is apt to miss these strange appearances and theological throwbacks. He tends to go at the business wrong way round, looking for unmistakable recurrences of key terms and neglecting the cumulative suggestive power of the terms or images or special private meanings of the individual writers; while the doctrine accidentally echoed or latent in the work inspected may not be a part of the American Protestant stock in trade. Hawthorne tried out *his* version of the fortunate fall by having Kenyon, the sculptor in *The Marble Faun*, broach it to conventionally Protestant Hilda; and "Oh, hush!" she tells him, shrinking away "with an expression of horror," saying that she could weep for him, she is shocked beyond words, his "creed" makes a mockery "of all religious sentiments . . . [and] moral law"—that is, the sentiments and the law drilled into her back in New England. Kenyon hushes.

2

I have probably not escaped, in the preceding few paragraphs, from seeming to honor in Emerson, Hawthorne, and the others their rediscovery of "pieties that are older and more solid than the Puritan ones"; but, much as I respect those older pieties, the pieties of age-old Catholic Christianity, that is not precisely what I am trying to do. It *is* what is attempted in *American Classics Reconsidered,* from which the last quotation above is taken. This book, edited by Harold C. Gardiner, S.J.,[5] brings together essays by ten Roman Catholic writers on the major American men of letters in the early and middle nineteenth century. It is by no means a work of systematic expropriation. The intellectual standards are Catholic ones, and the approach is explicitly theological; but there is a reasonably sustained effort to deal with the writers as writers and as Americans, and very little effort to scold or convert them. "Quite literally, I think," says Michael F. Moloney in a creditable essay on Thoreau, "[Thoreau] went out to Walden Pond to write a book. . . . He went . . . to strike a blow in defense of the poet's right to existence. . . . He must be evaluated primarily as a creative artist rather than as a thinker." Mr. Moloney does so evaluate

---

[4] "The Angelic Imagination," in *The Man of Letters in the Modern World* (New York, 1955), pp. 113-31.
[5] New York, 1958.

him; yet it is a sign of a certain uneasiness, as of one who has muddled a little the right order of the goods, that Mr. Moloney's title is "Christian *malgré lui.*" The phrase luckily has almost nothing to do with the essay's content; for if it were Mr. Moloney's intention to Christianize Thoreau despite himself, it would be a serious misdirection of energy. A similar sense of strain is detectable, or seems to me to be, in most of the other essays; and I shall offer some hints about the possible reasons for it, by looking in some detail at the essay by Joseph Schwartz on Hawthorne.

The latter is not necessarily the best contribution to the book. Although the volume is almost inevitably uneven, the level of critical and scholarly accomplishment strikes me as pretty high. The treatments of Longfellow, Poe, Melville, and "the literary historians" are perfunctory, perhaps because the writers in question are perfunctory themselves, like Longfellow, or because they have been drained of blood, like Melville, by the interminable critical surgery of the past few decades. (I digress to wonder with a certain anxiety how long the relatively small store of American literature is going to survive the writing about it, and especially the writing about the whole of it. Our production has fallen badly behind our consumption, as Henry James foresaw seventy years ago when he told a summer school on "the novel" at Deerfield, Massachusetts, that "We already talk too much about the novel in proportion to the quantity of it having any importance that we produce.") But the long analysis by Robert C. Pollock of Emerson's "single vision," for example, is a work of genuine scholarly composition; it composes something (a view of reality), and it is about the effort to do so. Mr. Pollock makes good overt use of Charles Feidelson's brilliant *Symbolism and American Literature* to clarify Emerson's long struggle "to free men from the delusion of a split universe, which, as he knew, had reduced human life to a fragmented state." Perhaps Mr. Pollock presents Emerson as achieving too completely what Emerson only succeeded in aiming at, and when he says that Emerson "steadfastly refused to recognize any split between the higher and lower worlds," he may have chosen the wrong verbal. What Emerson refused was to accept a split that he did recognize; he remains, in fact, America's most knowing and moving portrayer of the failures of connection in human experience—of the appalling lack of context, in modern times, for action and for judgment.

In addition to the chapters on Emerson, Thoreau, and Hawthorne, several other items in *American Classics Reconsidered* are to be commended. They include Ernest Sandeen's sometimes awkwardly phrased but compassionate and suggestive examination of Whitman ("He must accept even the social and moral outcast because he is himself an outcast asserting his claim to be accepted"); Alvan S. Ryan's intelligent survey of Orestes Brownson and his dialectical involvement with New England idealism; Charles A. Brady's informed and even loving study of the life and writings of James Fenimore Cooper—in my opinion, the most valuable as well as readable essay in the book, rather unexpected considering not Mr. Brady but James Fenimore Cooper, and rising to a poetic evocation of Leather-Stocking as a godlike figure similar to Oberon and Herakles ("Hawkeye and Chingachgook . . . become twin numina, two great *genii loci,* two waiting presences, tutelary deities of the American continent, joining hands in amity over a coil of motives and cross-purposes, the Green Man and the Red Manitou");[6] and Father Gardiner's brief introductory chapter, which establishes the theological perspective and makes up for a debatable salute to Colin Wilson's *The Outsider* by citing the special relevance, for his volume, of Charles Feidelson's book.

Father Gardiner urges, in his introduction, that "modern criticism would do well to minimize somewhat its preoccupation with techniques and return to more theological approaches." With that advice, I am personally very largely in agreement, up to what is for me a crucial point. And it should be added, especially on the evidence of this volume, that *most Catholic* writers, unlike *some* Protestant writers, are aware that in the theological approach some account must be taken of God. There is an extraordinary contemporary intellectual reluctance to utter the name of God, or even to allude to God in any definite way at all: a phenomenon peculiarly notable in books and courses on religion and literature. This is a current characteristic of the highest significance, though it does not, I believe, mean that God is dead in the consciousness of the present time (the report of God's death has been very much exaggerated). It means something rather different, my main suggestion about which I shall shortly and belatedly come round to. But in much of the purportedly "religious writing" of the day, God is treated, if at all, in the manner dramatized time and again by Graham Greene (who is, I am aware, a Catholic of sorts)—as a married man's mistress, someone who must never be mentioned openly, is only thought about with a far corner of the mind, and is met briefly and on occasion in dark and hidden places, for illicit reasons. God, in short, is associated primarily with the sometimes titillating modern sense of sin and guilt. Hence it is that the entire range of Christian doctrine can be narrowed down to a belief in Original Sin, and Emerson, who had a more sublime view of the universe and its creator, dismissed as a corruptive influence on young minds and one who made the better cause appear the

---

[6] Like Henry Bamford Parkes, in an extremely valuable essay published in *Modern Writing* No. 3 (New York, 1956), Mr. Brady emphasizes the organic continuity between Leather-Stocking and the hard-eyed private detective of recent years, affirming the claims of morality in the midst of cross-purposes more frightful and treacherous than any Leather-Stocking knew of.

better. Even certain American forms of Roman Catholicism, I am told, are not always free of this bleak reductive tendency. But Father Gardiner's volume of essays is. When Michael F. Moloney wants to distinguish between Thoreau's humanistic mysticism and that of an authentically Christian religious mystic, he says rightly and flatly, "Man is Thoreau's primary concern, not God"; and Father Gardiner's own list of the great issues that he regards as central to the theological approach includes "the indwelling of God in the soul" as well as "the nature of sin and responsibility and the role of free will in responsibility." It also includes "[God's] Providence and salvific will . . . detachment from created goods, the communion of saints . . . and the real and proper 'divinity of man.'"

Those terms (especially "salvific," which I had to look up, and which means "tending to save" and is listed as obsolete) are not ones that an outsider in the non-Wilsonian sense can feel very easy with. But that they partake of a comprehensive and unmistakably theological vocabulary is hardly open to doubt. What is open to doubt is not the value of a theological approach to literature, but the value of approaching this particular body of literature with any set of terms and doctrines that has been fully and finally elaborated, historically, once and for all. That is just the question perhaps unwittingly pushed into prominence by Joseph Schwartz, in his essay on Hawthorne: an essay in this case appropriately titled "God and Man in New England."

Mr. Schwartz begins with the proposition that "the history of literature has been an attempt to put such abstractions ["free will, the natural desire for God, fatalism, and providence"] into concrete statements for the benefit of mankind"; and hence that it is proper to seek out in Hawthorne his concept of "the moral and religious character of man." The crux of the problem may be right there. Mr. Schwartz's principle runs counter, of course, to the most influential critical convictions and prejudices of the past few decades, according to which literature does not "put abstractions into concrete statement," but, rather, generates a special kind of idea by the special processes of the creative imagination. The basis of those critical convictions has been the observation that modern literature, at least, can be shown to be doing just that: which has led to the suspicion that maybe the greatest literature in all ages has been up to the same poetic business. Hawthorne is an uncommonly tangled and contradictory case. From time to time, he most certainly did put abstractions into concrete form, and his notebooks let us watch him as he does so. But at other moments, he seems rather to have begun with a particular image or incident and to have allowed it to expand in his mind till it reached its maximum suggestiveness.[7]

---

[7] Ronald Gray's little book on Kafka (Cambridge, 1958) traces in scrupulous detail an analogous development in the composition of *The Castle,* and manages thereby to

Similarly, while the conclusion of "The Artist of the Beautiful," published in 1844, declares that the symbol which makes beauty perceptible becomes at last of little value for the artist who has "possessed himself . . . of the reality," the conclusion of "The Antique Ring," published a year earlier, argues that the artist "can never separate the idea from the symbol in which it manifests itself." The two statements have different contexts, and they are not strict opposites in any case. But they illustrate the magnificent hedging of which Hawthorne was a master, and which was radically necessary under the cultural circumstances in which he found himself. The same thing shows up still more revealingly in his habit of dramatizing a humane resistance to the metaphysical and theological concepts he has at the same time splendidly acknowledged. So, at least, I read tales like "The Birthmark" and "Ethan Brand," neither of which would readily yield their full and echoing discordance to the critic who searches for the abstractions made concrete in them.

Mr. Schwartz knows, at any rate, the right abstractions to look for: the conception of God and of God's relation to man. As he attempts to make these things visible, he (I think persuasively) disengages Hawthorne from the legend of an uninterruptedly Puritan ancestry. Militant orthodoxy seems to have vanished from the Hawthorne family by the mid-eighteenth century; Nathaniel's mother, who had exclusive charge of him from the time he was four, was an unemphatic Unitarian; Hawthorne was never, on the evidence, indoctrinated or proselytized; and when he arrived at Bowdoin, he gravitated instinctively toward persons "of the same noncommittal temperament." Mr. Schwartz draws the picture of a man with a strong religious impulse and an intense religious curiosity who yet had the opportunity of choosing the forms in which his sense of religious experience might get itself articulated and who disliked and distrusted all the forms available to a nineteenth-century New Englander—all the gradations of orthodoxy and the varieties of "liberal Christianity." He then makes too little of the form Hawthorne finally did choose for his purposes: the form of the narrative art.

If he slights that eventuality, it is probably because the art of narrative does not appear to Mr. Schwartz as one of the forms accessible to the religious impulse. For a person to whom none of the modes of Protestant Christianity in the nineteenth century were satisfying, only one other religious mode—Mr. Schwartz seems, not unnaturally, to assume—could be possible. He becomes explicit only at the moment when he relates Hawthorne's account of Donatello's "way to the Lord" to a sermon by St. Thomas Aquinas for "The Feast of Saint Martin," and expresses "amaze[ment] at Hawthorne's knowledge of Catholicism

demonstrate the relative unsoundness of the Christian or Jewish doctrinal attack on that novel.

as it affected a character drawn from that tradition." The religious pattern which Hawthorne is here found to be slowly fulfilling is the pattern of traditional Catholicism. Central to that pattern and to Hawthorne's fiction as studied by Mr. Schwartz is the image of a God of love and of hope.

It is a useful counterbalance to the occasional description of Hawthorne as presenting a hopelessly depraved human nature cowering away beneath the imminent chastisement of a coldly angry deity. And for about half of his essay, Mr. Schwartz holds on pretty hard to Hawthorne's huckleberries, to the human and artistic elements sensibly at work in the notebooks and some of the earlier stories: but then the process of translation sets in, and nothing further hinders it. The remainder of Hawthorne's writings, including *The Scarlet Letter* and *The Marble Faun,* are translated out of their unique existence into the (for those writings) deforming emphases of Catholic Christianity. An entire interpretation of *The Scarlet Letter* rests on the theory that "Dimmesdale's fundamental weakness . . . is his failure to recognize that God is a God of love"—an excellent notion for a psychoanalytically trained confessor to try to inculcate into a real-life Dimmesdale, but not the one central to the realized stress and strain of the novel itself. And a bundle of quotations about "the promises of a blessed eternity" and "O beautiful world! O beneficent God!" leads Mr. Schwartz to identify Hilda, who sometimes does talk like that in *The Marble Faun,* as "winningly virtuous." Hilda comes at us in fact, from the fictional context she inhabits, as a girl so bloodlessly virtuous as to be well-nigh terrifying, and partly because of the way she talks. That Hawthorne, or a part of him, thought of Hilda as such is indicated by his references elsewhere to his belief that the words " 'genteel' and 'lady-like' are terrible ones," and to "the pure, modest, sensitive and shrinking woman of America—shrinking when no evil is intended, and sensitive like diseased flesh that thrills if you but point at it."

This is not to say merely that Hawthorne reveals more fertile contradictions in his work than Mr. Schwartz acknowledges; it is to say, rather, that the contradictions that give Hawthorne's work its particular mood and movement are not entirely translatable into traditional Christian terms—because they are moving away from rather than toward a demonstration of the relevance of those terms. Like Emerson, Hawthorne was largely free of the exact religious formulas of his own time (though he regarded them more closely, and always with a fascinated and creative skepticism). Hawthorne's gaze, too, in its curious range and freedom, rested betimes upon the essence of some central pre-Puritanical piety—an image of God, perhaps, a deep conviction about human responsibility. But those elements remained unrelated except in the quick of Hawthorne's imagination; they were unfortified by anything like a theology, much less a definitely Christian theology. There is no dramatic use (I do not say, no mention) in Hawthorne of the determining items in such a theology—no use whatever of the idea of an intermediary between man and God: of Mary, of the Holy Ghost, and, most crucial of all, of the figure and role of Jesus Christ. There is an important sense in which Hawthorne was not a Christian writer at all.

Hawthorne's view of religious experience is to be found only by following the actual evolution, in each work and from one work to the next, of his persistent images and patterns of relationship. I am not making one more pedantic defense of the absolute integrity of literature; I am trying rather to say something about American and modern literature and the forms of religious expression in our times. As regards Catholic *or* Protestant Christianity, as in his relation to any other major historical development, Hawthorne was neither an outsider nor an insider: he was an in-betweener. His writings and his habitual concerns and responses lie somewhere in between the Christian epoch and an epoch (our own) which, with due modifications, we have to call post-Christian; and Hawthorne's imaginative energies bent forward, not backward. The direction in which he was bending is made clearer by his logical successor, Henry James; for James is probably the representative or at least the introductory figure in the post-Christian epoch.

James was post-Christian in somewhat the way that Virgil seems to us pre-Christian—James could dimly remember about as much of the substance of Christianity as Virgil could dimly foresee. The two men stand at opposite ends of the most enormous cultural curve in Western history, and almost everything they wrote had to do with their sense of where they stood. Each was beautifully shaken by premonitions of some gigantic disaster and by opaque hopes of an eventual transformation scene in the affairs of the cosmos. James's fiction, R. P. Blackmur once remarked in a singularly tantalizing sentence, was his reaction to "the predicament of the sensitive mind during what may be called the interregnum between the effective dominance of the old Christian-classical ideal through old European institutions and the rise to rule of the succeeding ideal, whatever history comes to call it." To the phrase "sensitive mind" in Mr. Blackmur's remark, I should like to add "religious imagination"; for James was, I believe, a religious writer, and his fiction was increasingly caught up in the web of circumstances investing and indeed creating the relationship between man and God.

James never put it that way: he was American and modern. Both the human and the literary problem of the present epoch was summed up by Merton Densher in *The Wings of the Dove*, when, trying to make good his lie to Maude Massingham about having been on his way to church on Christmas morning, he asked himself miserably, "To what church was he going, to what church . . . *could* he go?" He went, finally, to the Oratory on Brompton Road, but we must not make too much of that decision, any more than Merton did. It was no more than a transient effort to find a traditional Christian form in which to acknowledge what Merton had long before realized was nothing less than a religious experience. That realization was compounded altogether of Merton's sense of Milly Theale and of the course and meaning of his relationship with *her*. It was this that was "too sacred to describe," just as it was the genuine sacredness of the relationship that James had spent some seven-hundred odd pages in describing: or, rather, in creating. The creation is achieved while carefully avoiding any direct utterance of the name of God; we have instead the names of Milly Theale, Merton Densher, and the others. This is the point of a reverent witticism made by a friend of mine who, when asked whether he thought that Milly Theale is a Christ-figure, replied, "No, but perhaps Christ is a Milly-figure."

It was, in short, characteristic of James, as representative of the post-Christian epoch, to have conveyed his religious sense by intensifying the human drama to the moment where it gave off intimations of the sacred. And it was characteristic of him to have done so almost exclusively by the resources of the narrative art, generating the "vision" *within* the developing work of art, and with almost no help from and perhaps very little knowledge or recollection of the traditional Christian doctrines. (Hence, by the way, the strange and baffling quality—strange and baffling, at least, for those who probe them from a systematic theological viewpoint—of James's mainly self-begotten symbols.) It was toward the Jamesian position and method that Hawthorne and his contemporaries were heading in an earlier generation. Perry Miller was luminously right when he claimed, in his introduction to *The Transcendentalists,* that Emersonian transcendentalism was "a religious demonstration" in which, however, the persons concerned put their cause into the language of literature rather than of theology. But it must always be added that when that is done, as I have suggested elsewhere, something happens to the cause as well as to the language. There is a deep propriety in searching for religious elements in works of literature, since that is where they often appear with greatest urgency in the modern epoch; but there is a certain impropriety and perhaps an irrelevance in searching for historically grounded doctrinal elements. Christianity itself may very likely *not* be a historical phenomenon, or at least not in any decisive manner a purely historical phenomenon. But its institutions and its vocabulary are historical phenomena, and they may in some instances become as unusable for our present religious purposes as Anglo-Saxon is to our linguistic ones. The analogy is intended to be reasonably precise, for in both cases some very important use yet remains. James is representative in this respect as well, for he is post-Christian in the sense of coming after and making scant dramatic use of the finished frames of doctrine: while various essences of Christianity continue to work in his prose and to color and flavor the forms he finds and the forms he creates in human experience.

NOVELIST AND BELIEVER

Flannery O'Connor

Being a novelist and not a philosopher or theologian, I shall have to enter this discussion at a much lower level and proceed along a much narrower course than that held up to us here as desirable. It has been suggested that for the purposes of this symposium, we conceive religion broadly as an expression of man's ultimate concern rather than identify it with institutional Judaism or Christianity or with "going to church."

I see the utility of this. It's an attempt to enlarge your ideas of what religion is and of how the religious need may be expressed in the art of our time; but there is always the danger that in trying to enlarge the ideas of students, we will evaporate them instead, and I think nothing in this world lends itself to quick vaporization so much as the religious concern.

As a novelist, the major part of my task is to make everything, even an ultimate concern, as solid, as concrete, as specific as possible. The novelist begins his work where human knowledge begins—with the senses; he works through the limitations of matter, and unless he is writing fantasy, he has to stay within the concrete possibilities of his culture. He is bound by his particular past and by those institutions and traditions that this past has left to his society. The Judaeo-Christian tradition has formed us in the west; we are bound to it by ties which may often be invisible, but which are there nevertheless. It has formed the shape of our secularism; it has formed even the shape of modern atheism. For my part, I shall have to remain well within the Judaeo-Christian tradition. I shall have to speak, without apology, of the Church, even when the Church is absent; of Christ, even when Christ is not recognized.

If one spoke as a scientist, I believe it would be possible to disregard large parts of the personality and speak simply as a scientist, but when one speaks as a novelist, he must speak as he writes—with the whole personality. Many contend that the job of the novelist is to show us how man feels, and they say that this is an operation in which his own

"Novelist and Believer." First given as an address at Sweetbriar College, Virginia, in March, 1963. Reprinted from Mystery and Manners: Occasional Prose, *ed. Sally and Robert Fitzgerald (New York: Farrar, Straus and Giroux, 1969). Copyright 1969 by Flannery O'Connor. Reprinted by permission of Farrar, Straus and Giroux. Also reprinted by permission of Harold Matson Co. Inc.*

commitments intrude not at all. The novelist, we are told, is looking for a symbol to express feeling, and whether he be Jew or Christian or Buddhist or whatever makes no difference to the aptness of the symbol. Pain is pain, joy is joy, love is love, and these human emotions are stronger than any mere religious belief; they are what they are and the novelist shows them as they are. This is all well and good so far as it goes, but it just does not go as far as the novel goes. Great fiction involves the whole range of human judgment; it is not simply an imitation of feeling. The good novelist not only finds a symbol for feeling, he finds a symbol and a way of lodging it which tells the intelligent reader whether this feeling is adequate or inadequate, whether it is moral or immoral, whether it is good or evil. And his theology, even in its most remote reaches, will have a direct bearing on this.

It makes a great difference to the look of a novel whether its author believes that the world came late into being and continues to come by a creative act of God, or whether he believes that the world and ourselves are the product of a cosmic accident. It makes a great difference to his novel whether he believes that we are created in God's image, or whether he believes we create God in our own. It makes a great difference whether he believes that our wills are free, or bound like those of the other animals.

St. Augustine wrote that the things of the world pour forth from God in a double way: intellectually into the minds of the angels and physically into the world of things. To the person who believes this—as the western world did up until a few centuries ago—this physical, sensible world is good because it proceeds from a divine source. The artist usually knows this by instinct; his senses, which are used to penetrating the concrete, tell him so. When Conrad said that his aim as an artist was to render the highest possible justice to the visible universe, he was speaking with the novelist's surest instinct. The artist penetrates the concrete world in order to find at its depths the image of its source, the image of ultimate reality. This in no way hinders his perception of evil but rather sharpens it, for only when the natural world is seen as good does evil become intelligible as a destructive force and a necessary result of our freedom.

For the last few centuries we have lived in a world which has been increasingly convinced that the reaches of reality end very close to the surface, that there is no ultimate divine source, that the things of the world do not pour forth from God in a double way, or at all. For nearly two centuries the popular spirit of each succeeding generation has tended more and more to the view that the mysteries of life will eventually fall before the mind of man. Many modern novelists have been more concerned with the processes of consciousness than with the objective world outside the mind. In twentieth-century fiction it increasingly happens that a meaningless, absurd world impinges upon the sacred consciousness of author or character; author and character seldom now go out to explore and penetrate a world in which the sacred is reflected.

Nevertheless, the novelist always has to create a world and a believable one. The virtues of art, like the virtues of faith, are such that they reach beyond the limitations of the intellect, beyond any mere theory that a writer may entertain. If the novelist is doing what as an artist he is bound to do, he will inevitably suggest that image of ultimate reality as it can be glimpsed in some aspect of the human situation. In this sense, art reveals, and the theologian has learned that he can't ignore it. In many universities, you will find departments of theology vigorously courting departments of English. The theologian is interested specifically in the modern novel because there he sees reflected the man of our time, the unbeliever, who is nevertheless grappling in a desperate and usually honest way with intense problems of the spirit.

We live in an unbelieving age but one which is markedly and lopsidedly spiritual. There is one type of modern man who recognizes spirit in himself but who fails to recognize a being outside himself whom he can adore as Creator and Lord; consequently he has become his own ultimate concern. He says with Swinburne, "Glory to man in the highest, for he is the master of things," or with Steinbeck, "In the end was the word and the word was with men." For him, man has his own natural spirit of courage and dignity and pride and must consider it a point of honor to be satisfied with this.

There is another type of modern man who recognizes a divine being not himself, but who does not believe that this being can be known anagogically or defined dogmatically or received sacramentally. Spirit and matter are separated for him. Man wanders about, caught in a maze of guilt he can't identify, trying to reach a God he can't approach, a God powerless to approach him.

And there is another type of modern man who can neither believe nor contain himself in unbelief and who searches desperately, feeling about in all experience for the lost God.

At its best our age is an age of searchers and discoverers, and at its worst, an age that has domesticated despair and learned to live with it happily. The fiction which celebrates this last state will be the least likely to transcend its limitations, for when the religious need is banished successfully, it usually atrophies, even in the novelist. The sense of mystery vanishes. A kind of reverse evolution takes place, and the whole range of feeling is dulled.

The searchers are another matter. Pascal wrote in his notebook, "If I had not known you, I would not have found you." These unbelieving searchers have their effect even upon those of us who do believe. We begin to examine our own religious notions, to sound them for genuineness, to purify them in the heat of our unbelieving neighbor's anguish. What Christian novelist could compare his concern to Camus'? We have to look in much of the fiction of our time for a kind of sub-religion which expresses its ultimate concern in images that have not yet broken through to show any recognition of a God who has revealed himself. As great as much of this fiction is, as much as it reveals a wholehearted effort to find the only true ultimate concern, as much as in many cases it represents religious values of a high order, I do not believe that it can adequately represent in fiction the central religious experience. That, after all, concerns a relationship with a supreme being recognized through faith. It is the experience of an encounter, of a kind of knowledge which affects the believer's every action. It is Pascal's experience after his conversion and not before.

What I say here would be much more in line with the spirit of our times if I could speak to you about the experience of such novelists as Hemingway and Kafka and Gide and Camus, but all my own experience has been that of the writer who believes, again in Pascal's words, in the "God of Abraham, Isaac, and Jacob and not of the philosophers and scholars." This is an unlimited God and one who has revealed himself specifically. It is one who became man and rose from the dead. It is one who confounds the senses and the sensibilities, one known early on as a stumbling block. There is no way to gloss over this specification or to make it more acceptable to modern thought. This God is the object of ultimate concern and he has a name.

The problem of the novelist who wishes to write about a man's encounter with this God is how he shall make the experience—which is both natural and supernatural—understandable, and credible, to his reader. In any age this would be a problem, but in our own, it is a well-nigh insurmountable one. Today's audience is one in which religious feeling has become, if not atrophied, at least vaporous and sentimental. When Emerson decided, in 1832, that he could no longer celebrate the Lord's Supper unless the bread and wine were removed, an important step in the vaporization of religion in America was taken, and the spirit of that step has continued apace. When the physical fact is separated from the spiritual reality, the dissolution of belief is eventually inevitable.

The novelist doesn't write to express himself, he doesn't write simply to render a vision he believes true, rather he renders his vision so that it can be transferred, as nearly whole as possible, to his reader. You can safely ignore the reader's taste, but you can't ignore his nature, you can't ignore his limited patience. Your problem is going to be difficult in direct proportion as your beliefs depart from his.

When I write a novel in which the central action is a baptism, I am very well aware that for a majority of my readers, baptism is a meaning-less rite, and so in my novel I have to see that this baptism carries enough awe and mystery to jar the reader into some kind of emotional recognition of its significance. To this end I have to bend the whole novel—its language, its structure, its action. I have to make the reader feel, in his bones if nowhere else, that something is going on here that counts. Distortion in this case is an instrument; exaggeration has a pur-pose, and the whole structure of the story or novel has been made what it is because of belief. This is not the kind of distortion that destroys; it is the kind that reveals, or should reveal.

Students often have the idea that the process at work here is one which hinders honesty. They think that inevitably the writer, instead of seeing what is, will see only what he believes. It is perfectly possible, of course, that this will happen. Ever since there have been such things as novels, the world has been flooded with bad fiction for which the religious impulse has been responsible. The sorry religious novel comes about when the writer supposes that because of his belief, he is some-how dispensed from the obligation to penetrate concrete reality. He will think that the eyes of the Church or of the Bible or of his particular theology have already done the seeing for him, and that his business is to rearrange this essential vision into satisfying patterns, getting himself as little dirty in the process as possible. His feeling about this may have been made more definite by one of those Manichean-type theologies which sees the natural world as unworthy of penetration. But the real novelist, the one with an instinct for what he is about, knows that he cannot approach the infinite directly, that he must pene-trate the natural human world as it is. The more sacramental his theol-ogy, the more encouragement he will get from it to do just that.

The supernatural is an embarrassment today even to many of the churches. The naturalistic bias has so well saturated our society that the reader doesn't realize that he has to shift his sights to read fiction which treats of an encounter with God. Let me leave the novelist and talk for a moment about his reader.

This reader has first to get rid of a purely sociological point of view. In the thirties we passed through a period in American letters when social criticism and social realism were considered by many to be the most important aspects of fiction. We still suffer with a hangover from that period. I launched a character, Hazel Motes, whose presiding passion was to rid himself of a conviction that Jesus had redeemed him. Southern degeneracy never entered my head, but Hazel said "I seen" and "I taken" and he was from East Tennessee, and so the general reader's explanation for him was that he must represent some social problem peculiar to that part of the benighted South.

Ten years, however, have made some difference in our attitude toward fiction. The sociological tendency has abated in that particular form and survived in another just as bad. This is the notion that the fiction writer is after the typical. I don't know how many letters I have received telling me that the South is not at all the way I depict it; some tell me that Protestantism in the South is not at all the way I portray it, that a Southern Protestant would never be concerned, as Hazel Motes is, with penitential practices. Of course, as a novelist I've never wanted to characterize the typical South or typical Protestantism. The South and the religion found there are extremely fluid and offer enough variety to give the novelist the widest range of possibilities imaginable, for the novelist is bound by the reasonable possibilities, not the probabilities, of his culture.

There is an even worse bias than these two, and that is the clinical bias, the prejudice that sees everything strange as a case study in the abnormal. Freud brought to light many truths, but his psychology is not an adequate instrument for understanding the religious encounter or the fiction that describes it. Any psychological or cultural or economic determination may be useful up to a point; indeed, such facts can't be ignored, but the novelist will be interested in them only as he is able to go through them to give us a sense of something beyond them. The more we learn about ourselves, the deeper into the unknown we push the frontiers of fiction.

I have observed that most of the best religious fiction of our time is most shocking precisely to those readers who claim to have an intense interest in finding more "spiritual purpose"—as they like to put it—in modern novels than they can at present detect in them. Today's reader, if he believes in grace at all, sees it as something which can be separated from nature and served to him raw as Instant Uplift. This reader's favorite word is compassion. I don't wish to defame the word. There is a better sense in which it can be used but seldom is—the sense of being in travail with and for creation in its subjection to vanity. This is a sense which implies a recognition of sin; this is a suffering-with, but one which blunts no edges and makes no excuses. When infused into novels, it is often forbidding. Our age doesn't go for it.

I have said a great deal about the religious sense that the modern audience lacks, and by way of objection to this, you may point out to me that there is a real return of intellectuals in our time to an interest in and a respect for religion. I believe that this is true. What this interest in religion will result in for the future remains to be seen. It may, together with the new spirit of ecumenism that we see everywhere around us, herald a new religious age, or it may simply be that religion will suffer the ultimate degradation and become, for a little time, fashionable. Whatever it means for the future, I don't believe that our present society is one whose basic beliefs are religious, except in the

South. In any case, you can't have effective allegory in times when people are swept this way and that by momentary convictions, because everyone will read it differently. You can't indicate moral values when morality changes with what is being done, because there is no accepted basis of judgment. And you cannot show the operation of grace when grace is cut off from nature or when the very possibility of grace is denied, because no one will have the least idea of what you are about.

The serious writer has always taken the flaw in human nature for his starting point, usually the flaw in an otherwise admirable character. Drama usually bases itself on the bedrock of original sin, whether the writer thinks in theological terms or not. Then, too, any character in a serious novel is supposed to carry a burden of meaning larger than himself. The novelist doesn't write about people in a vacuum; he writes about people in a world where something is obviously lacking, where there is the general mystery of incompleteness and the particular tragedy of our own times to be demonstrated, and the novelist tries to give you, within the form of the book, a total experience of human nature at any time. For this reason the greatest dramas naturally involve the salvation or loss of the soul. Where there is no belief in the soul, there is very little drama. The Christian novelist is distinguished from his pagan colleagues by recognizing sin as sin. According to his heritage he sees if not as sickness or an accident of environment, but as a responsible choice of offense against God which involves his eternal future. Either one is serious about salvation or one is not. And it is well to realize that the maximum amount of seriousness admits the maximum amount of comedy. Only if we are secure in our beliefs can we see the comical side of the universe. One reason a great deal of our contemporary fiction is humorless is because so many of these writers are relativists and have to be continually justifying the actions of their characters on a sliding scale of values.

Our salvation is a drama played out with the devil, a devil who is not simply generalized evil, but an evil intelligence determined on its own supremacy. I think that if writers with a religious view of the world excel these days in the depiction of evil, it is because they have to make its nature unmistakable to their particular audience.

The novelist and the believer, when they are not the same man, yet have many traits in common—a distrust of the abstract, a respect for boundaries, a desire to penetrate the surface of reality and to find in each thing the spirit which makes it itself and holds the world together. But I don't believe that we shall have great religious fiction until we have again that happy combination of believing artist and believing society. Until that time, the novelist will have to do the best he can in travail with the world he has. He may find in the end that instead of reflecting the image at the heart of things, he has only reflected our broken condition and, through it, the face of the devil we are possessed by. This is a modest achievement, but perhaps a necessary one.

LITERATURE AND BELIEF

David Daiches

1

One aspect of the relation between *Dichtung* and *Wahrheit*, between imaginative literature and literal truth, continues to trouble the critics—indeed, it troubles them today perhaps more than it ever has. What is to be our attitude toward a poet whose beliefs differ radically from ours, who is working in a tradition which for us is invalid or meaningless? Can we really enjoy Dante if we are shocked by the idea that errors of faith deserve an eternity of punishment? Can we fully appreciate *Paradise Lost* if we feel that it has not in fact justified the ways of God to men? Or, to put the problem in a more typically modern form, can we appreciate the poems of Ezra Pound if he was a fascist? What are we to do with the fantastic mystical systems of Yeats? At what point, in short, does our disagreement with a writer's ideas interfere with our appreciation of his work as imaginative literature? Does what a poet believes *matter?*

If literary value consisted merely in the patterning of ideas or images or both, such questions could be easily dismissed. We could say at once that content is irrelevant and that all that matters is the way in which that content is arranged. And in a sense this would be true, for literary quality emerges from the way in which a work is ordered, not from any paraphrasable content. But, as we have emphasized, such an ordering serves a purpose; it does not exist for its own sake, though it is often possible to appreciate it for its own sake. Literature is that ordering of the expression which expands the meaning to the point where it pro-duces cumulatively the maximum amount of insight into man's fate. But few works of literature are ostensibly written to serve such a purely literary purpose; many great writers, in fact, would refuse to recognize such a purpose as valid. And in any case all works of literature bear the marks of their author's beliefs and of the tradition in which he wrote. Often the proper significance of an image or an incident can only be appreciated with reference to those beliefs. Must we believe in marriage as an institution before we can accept the marriage of the hero and

"Literature and Belief." From New Literary Values: Studies in Modern Litera-ture *by David Daiches (Edinburgh: Oliver and Boyd, 1936). Reprinted by per-mission of David Higham Associates, Inc., acting for the author.*

heroine at the end of a Shakespearean comedy or a Victorian novel as a satisfactory resolution of the plot? If the full expansion of meaning can often occur only with reference to the context of beliefs within which the writer operated, what happens when that context is shattered and the reader approaches the work without its assistance?

There are several points involved here. Insofar as the images, references, allusions, symbols employed by a writer derive their significance, either wholly or in part, from a particular context of beliefs and attitudes, knowledge of that context becomes as important for the reader as knowledge of the language in which the work is written—and it is important in the same kind of way. We cannot even see the "bare text" for what it is unless we have some knowledge of the cultural framework with reference to which the words have their full meaning. But this does not mean that we must agree with the beliefs shared by those who operated within that framework, any more than when we understand the word "civil" in its modern sense of "polite" we have to agree with its etymological implication that politeness is a necessary characteristic of citizens. We must know what gives meaning to expressions without necessarily agreeing with the beliefs which originally gave them that meaning. This is an aspect of all language and presents no very great problem. In works of imaginative literature (and especially in poetry), where meanings are made to reverberate into ever wider implications, we must know the frames of reference which enable the writer to achieve those reverberations, or remain with only a partial knowledge of his language. Some frames of reference are historical, and can be learned by study; others, however, depend on less objective factors and can be understood only through continued experience in reading. A poet uses language with reference to what men believe, what men know, and how men feel. Beliefs and knowledge change, and though the basic pattern in human emotions seems to have remained fairly stable throughout recorded history, there are minor variations even there.

It is not therefore a simple matter to see the work of literature in itself as it really is. We have to learn our poet's language, through developing an awareness of and a sensitivity to the kinds of richness of implication which he utilizes. It is not enough to say, particularly in dealing with a work of the past, that the reader must take the work as he finds it and that by looking at it simply as a self-existent poem or play or piece of fiction he can adequately appreciate it. This would be as logical as to say that a reader ignorant of Greek could take an ode of Pindar as he finds it and appreciate it as a collection of meaningless marks on paper. For the only completely objective existence a work of literature possesses is as a series of marks on paper. So-called "ontological" criticism can never really be practiced, and those who consider that their critical method is ontological are deceiving themselves. To understand a work of literature we must know the meaning of the text, but we cannot know that meaning fully unless we appreciate that it lies in the relation of what is written to what certain men have thought, felt, and known.

One need not share a writer's beliefs, therefore, before appreciating how they operate in enriching the meaning of the words he employs, but sometimes it is necessary to be aware of them. (It is not necessary to be aware of them when the reader unconsciously shares them: when Burns compares his love to a red rose we do not require any information about Burns's attitude to redness and to roses, for in the experience of most men the two words stand for beauty and freshness in nature. This illustrates how the purely semantic aspect of words shades imperceptibly into the meanings they acquire from particular beliefs.) The same situation arises in larger units of plot. Marriage of hero and heroine as a symbol of the resolution of the action can be accepted even by readers who do not believe that marriage provides a stable and satisfactory relationship if in terms of the working out of the plot such a solution becomes a symbol of such a relationship. If we did not know what marriage was, or if we never knew that men had at a certain period of civilization regarded it as the only satisfactory relationship between a man and a woman who loved each other, we would require some background information before we could fully understand and appreciate the ending of the story. With that information, if the work were well constructed, we should be in a position to appreciate the resolution of the plot whatever our personal beliefs about the relation between the sexes.

There would, however, be certain exceptions to this. A reader who felt violently that the whole idea of marriage involved a complete distortion of the facts of human nature, that marriage was essentially something false, ugly, and dishonest, would perhaps find himself unable to accept the ending as satisfactory however adequate the construction and however much information he had acquired about the beliefs of the author and of the society in which he moved. In situations of this kind it must be admitted that a reader's differences of belief from those of the author would affect his appreciation. Such situations do occur, and most readers have individual blind spots or sensitive areas which prevent them from understanding or appreciating certain works. Of course, a novel which is not a genuine work of imaginative literature but simply a fable designed to advocate a certain attitude or course of action will always fail to appeal to readers whose beliefs differ radically from those of the author. But this is a quite different problem. The interesting question concerns those who, whatever their intentions, have produced works of literature in the fullest sense.

But what are we to do when the very fabric of the work is constructed out of beliefs which we may repudiate? The answer to this question is not really as complicated as it may seem. All great works of literature contain more than their ostensible subject: starting from a particular set of beliefs, a story such as the biblical story of the temptation of Adam and Eve or a journey through the underworld, the true poet, in presenting his material, keeps reaching out at every point to touch aspects of the human situation which are real and recognizable whatever our beliefs may be. By turns of phrase, imagery, the simultaneous use of the musical and the semantic aspects of words, the deft ordering of words and events, the poet turns his story and his creed into a technical device for shedding light on man. The combined knowledge of man's nobility and his weaknesses, the sense of man's looking back or forward to a golden age coupled with the knowledge that, partly because of the very characteristics of man as man, such a golden age can only be envisioned but never realized, the sense that man's life is governed by change and linked always with the movements of the day to night and back to day, with the passing of the seasons, with resolutions that fluctuate and moods that alter, but a sense, too, that only a determination to do what can be done at the moment of decision can ever get man anywhere—all this and a thousand more such archetypical ideas are carried alive and passionately into the mind of the reader by Milton's *Paradise Lost;* and this is achieved, not in the pallid discursive way represented by the description just given, but implicitly, cumulatively, insistently, as the work flowers before the reader's eyes. We may feel that the debate in Heaven represents bad metaphysics and that God is in fact responsible for Satan and his activities; but though this attitude would be contrary to what Milton intended us to believe, he does not rest on his belief, for he has carried the meaning of his work infinitely further, so that, if as a theological work *Paradise Lost* is inadequate, as a *poem* it is completely adequate. As a poem its subject is not the justification of the ways of God to men but the essential and tragic ambiguity of the human animal. Expanding his meaning, by means of images, similes, and sheer choice of vocabulary, to include all that Western man had thought and felt, pivoting the action on a scene which, as Milton describes it in the poem, illuminates immediately the paradox of man's ambition (at once good because noble and bad because arrogant) and human love (both bad because selfish and because passion clouds the judgment and good because unselfish and self-sacrificing), linking the grandiose action at every point to images suggestive of man in his daily elemental activities in fields, cities, and on the ocean, developing, as in his picture of ideal nature in the early scenes in Eden, all the implications of man's perennial desire for a better world with the continuous awareness of man's tendency to trip himself up and turn his very virtues into snares—achieving all this in spite of the plot, as it were, by placing an image where it will sing most eloquently and by linking each unit to others so that the chorus of implication grows ever richer, reverberates ever more widely, Milton, by operating as a poet rather than as a theologian and moralist, in spite of himself probes deeper into man's fate than his formal scheme would seem to allow and in the magnificent close sums up in one climactic image all that has ever been said about man's capacity to hope in spite of despair, about loneliness and companionship, about the healing effects of time and the possibility of combining bewilderment with a sense of purpose, giving us, in fact, his final echoing statement about man's place in the world:

> Some natural tears they dropped, but wiped them soon;
> The world was all before them, where to choose
> Their place of rest, and Providence their guide:
> They hand in hand with wandering steps and slow,
> Through Eden took their solitary way.

That final couplet, read in the light of all the previous action, is Milton's last word on man, and, read in its context, it reaches out far beyond any agreement or disagreement with his conception of God's justice or man's responsibility for his fall. We see now that Milton's theological purpose and plot were, in a sense, as much a part of his *technique* as his language, and that the modern reader can regard them in that light.

Some modern critics have tried to make Dante and Milton acceptable to us by arguing that their literal beliefs are not absurd and can—and indeed should—be held by modern man. But this is to make appreciation of imaginative literature dependent on one's literal acceptance of the author's creed, and it is a dangerous activity for a literary critic. What are we to do with the Greek dramatists, with Lucretius and Virgil and innumerable other earlier writers, if we have to make their theology acceptable before we can justify them? A critic is, of course, perfectly free to defend Dante's or Milton's theology, but in doing so he is not acting in his capacity of literary critic. Moreover, it can be argued with some plausibility that the reader who is in literal agreement with such a writer as Dante or Milton or Bunyan is apt to interpret what he reads too narrowly and see it as a much less comprehensive and exciting work than it is in the eyes of the reader who comes to the author in order to read a work of imaginative literature. The history of Dante criticism, or of the criticism of any religious poet, tends to confirm the view that *literary* appreciation not only does not depend on complete agreement with the author's beliefs but often does not fully develop until the question of agreement or disagreement has been ruled out as irrelevant.

It is only possible, however, to consider an author's beliefs as part of his language or his technique when he does in fact use them as such—that is, when he is a poet (in the widest sense of the term) and uses his material poetically. If he does not use his material poetically, then the question of the rightness or wrongness of his framework of beliefs will be very relevant, for the value of the work will be as a contribution to ethical theory or religious thought or some similar category.

There are also occasions where a writer's beliefs are so narrow or corrupting or so at variance with anything that civilized man can tolerate that it becomes impossible to regard them as merely part of his technique. However, an interesting natural law of genius comes into operation here: if a man holds such narrow or corrupting beliefs, he will not in fact be able to handle them poetically, he will not be able to use his material in such a way that it becomes recognizable as an illumination of human experience. Technique must have something to base itself on, and as far as beliefs go, they may be right or wrong but they must be capable of leading the reader to man as he is, of reflecting genuine light on the human situation. A wholly preposterous view of man would, from a purely technical point of view, be incapable of being used poetically. This is not to say, of course, that every reasonable view of man can always be employed poetically, but it *is* true that a wholly ridiculous or corrupt view can never be so used.

This brings up the much debated question of art and fascism. Can a fascist (using the term to denote an attitude toward man and his destiny wholly abhorrent to civilized and thoughtful people) be a good artist? The first answer to this question would be on the lines of the preceding paragraph. A corrupt view of man can never be an adequate basis for art. (One must distinguish between a corrupt view and a wrong view: the former is always the latter, but the latter is not necessarily the former.) But there are occasions when people have, through ignorance or naïveté or self-deception, associated themselves with movements which discerning observers know to be the deliberate creation of corrupt minds, yet do not themselves share in that corruption. Political ignorance or naïveté will not necessarily prevent a writer from producing some kinds of effective literature. A poet could write a good imagist poem whatever his political or moral confusion. The degree to which such confusion would show itself in his art would depend on the scope of his art. Mere craftsmanship is independent of all beliefs, but, as we have seen, art is more than mere craftsmanship. Ezra Pound supported Italian fascism because he was confused and self-deceived, not because he was corrupt and malicious. His early poems, limited in scope and confining themselves largely to carefully etched pictures of individual scenes or situations, are excellent of their kind; his *Cantos* are confused and inartistic because in them he was attempting to do more than present specific images or perceptions, and the same self-deception and confusion which led him to support Italian fascism rendered him incapable of writing a coherent or significant long poem.

Literature of any scope can never be independent of beliefs, for the devices the writer uses in order to expand the implications of his statements until they achieve that continuously reverberating significance that is one of the marks of successful art depend at every point on the relation between object, situation, or incident and the place they hold in human attitudes and creeds. When attitudes and creeds change, that relation will change, and the reader will have to recapture that attitude artificially if he wishes to appreciate the work fully. When literature is produced in an age which, like the present, has no common background of belief with reference to which objects, situations, and incidents can be given literary meaning by the writer, a problem arises of which every artist is all too aware. Poets—for whom this problem is particularly acute—are driven to try to create their own body of beliefs and present it (as Yeats did) to their readers as guides to the understanding of their works; or they are led to depend on purely private associations or personal reading, which has led to so much obscurity in modern poetry. The more able and sensitive the poet, the more he will be driven to try to find some sort of solution to this problem, by a private mystical system, as in Yeats; by dependence on a personal reading list, as Eliot did in *The Waste Land;* by autobiographical devices whose significance cannot be fully known to the reader, as in some of the early poems of Auden; or by other methods. It is a fault in poetry to be obscure to contemporaries (to be obscure is not the same as to be difficult, which is sometimes a virtue), but the better the poet the more likely he is to have that fault today. For the modern poet has, in fact, no contemporaries, in the sense that Virgil or Dante or Milton or even Tennyson had: he cannot speak to men living under the same curtain of beliefs for in our time such a curtain has almost disappeared; he can speak with reference only to his own personal universe. If we have to reconstruct the world of Milton in order to appreciate fully the significance of each phrase and image of *Paradise Lost* (though that poem is intelligible and fascinating without *full* appreciation), we have no less to reconstruct the world of Eliot in order to appreciate fully the significance of each phrase and image in *The Waste Land.* And Milton's world he shared with his age; Eliot's is his own. Clearly a poet loses something by treating his contemporaries as posterity; it leads him to combine autobiographical with pontifical gestures, and they do not sort well together. Only Yeats, who knew how to season his personal symbolism with irony and sometimes with pure play, could, at his best, avoid the modern dilemma. This is not to say that there are no good modern poets or poems; but too few of them can be judged by the reader without preparation. We should not have to do that kind of homework in order to enjoy the work of our contemporaries; that we often have to do so is the fault not of the poet but of his age.

It would be an oversimplification to say that all good poets must today be obscure: certain kinds of poetry are less dependent on the poet's relation to a community of belief and can therefore be produced effectively whatever the state of public attitudes. But the fullest use of the characteristically poetic method demands the achievement of an expansion of meaning possible only when each unit of expression is set within a context of belief from which it derives continuous enrichment. Public belief becomes a matter of technique, and when it ceases to exist writers have often to find new technical devices to compensate for the loss of a device no longer available. To convey the individual sensibility of the writer directly and impressively to the reader, without first referring it to common notions which link reader and writer and in terms of which the meaning can be objectified and universalized, demands new kinds of subtlety in expression, which we find in, for example, the novels of Virginia Woolf. The reason for the great spate of technical experimentation and innovation in both poetry and prose in the last fifty years is precisely that the writers have been looking for ways of compensating by new technical devices for the loss of public belief. Public belief is an aspect of language, and when it fails language loses a dimension.

2

If the literary artist uses public belief as part of his technique, it means that often the results are apparent in his work without our having to reconstruct those beliefs for ourselves. That is one reason why, even though a complete appreciation of all the implications of a past work may demand some scholarship, great works of the past can nevertheless generally be understood and enjoyed without such preparation. The appreciation of past literature is, indeed, often easier than the proper appraisal of contemporary writing. It is easy to see the value of books which have been winnowed by time and which the diverse voices of succeeding generations have acclaimed as great. Knowing that they must be great, we actively look for their impressive qualities and in doing so train ourselves to read them. The judging of contemporary literature is much more difficult. There is no unanimous voice of the generations to tell us which are good, no long array of critics to point us to their virtues. We must make up our own minds. And it is not always easy to assess the value of new works, for it sometimes means dissociating ourselves from our contemporary feelings about the situations described and looking at the work as a whole as an effective artistic illumination of experience. The situations must be considered aesthetically, according to how they are integrated into a rich and significant pattern. But ultimately aesthetic significance is a human significance, a way of presenting insights into the human situation, so that there is no simple and mechanical means of divorcing one's attitude as contemporary human being from one's attitude as reader of a work of art. A situation might have tragic implications in view of what we know and feel about it today without those implications really deriving from anything in the book as written, and in such a case we might consider the book an effective tragedy because of our inability to see that those implications exist only for us in the circumstances in which we find ourselves and are not really effectively brought out in the book. We all make mistakes in judging contemporary literature; the most "objective" critic is not immune. It is perhaps easiest to go astray in poetry, for in the adequate reading of poetry we must actively give so much of ourselves that we are always in danger of giving too much, of contributing to the poem an emotional experience which derives solely from our own autobiography and for which there is no real warrant in the poem. The more experience we have of reading great works of literature, the more likely we shall be to avoid such mistakes, but in appraising new works we shall always make some. This may be why some critics prefer to confine their reading to older literature; but that is the coward's way out. We do no permanent harm to ourselves or our civilization if we occasionally make a judgment on a book which later generations, freed from the particular situation that misled us, will have to reverse. But we do harm if we avoid taking the risk.

There is another kind of error that is hard to avoid in estimating new works. It is often difficult to see new techniques for what they really are: imagining that they are intended for old techniques, we may misread them and so consider confused or awkward what is really highly effective if approached in the proper way. Here experience with older literature will not necessarily help us—it may in fact lead us astray by conditioning us to expect a conventional technique when the writer has used a new one. To distinguish a genuine new technique from a fraudulent one, and to find a standard for making such a distinction, are among the most difficult tasks of criticism. Here again the "innocent eye" will help more than an elaborate scholarly apparatus: we must learn to see the work for what it is, not for what we might have expected it to be. There is the further danger, once we have learned to appreciate the new technique, of refusing any merit to the old. There is a kind of snobbery to be found among modern criticism which is really less forgivable than the inability to appreciate the new, for it is less likely to be honest. Not to appreciate Auden because we have been brought up on Keats is understandable if not laudable, but to refuse all merit to, say, Arnold's "Dover Beach" because we have come to like Hopkins suggests simply a desire to be "advanced." There are all sorts of affectations threatening the integrity of criticism, and the desire for modernity is not the least of them. We must learn to steer a middle path between a critical hardening of the arteries, which comes from too long dwelling in one area of past literature, and the enthusiasm for what is new and different for its own sake to which the desire to avoid the former fault sometimes leads.

THE RELATION OF THEOLOGY TO LITERARY CRITICISM

Roy W. Battenhouse

It has been said lately by D. A. Stauffer that the "most vexing" and probably the "most vital" problem for literary criticism today is that of the relation of belief to criticism.[1] The question concerns whether and to what extent a critic can judge a work of art without at some point bringing in his own convictions. Can the critic of Shelley, for example, discuss adequately the greatness of Shelley's poetry without involving himself in an estimate of Shelley's faith? Can the critic of Dante, to use another example, gain a full appreciation of *The Divine Comedy* if he comes to its reading as one who does not share Dante's faith? Does the having of a faith hamper or help an author? Specifically, will a holding of the Christian faith make one a better or a poorer writer or critic than one might otherwise be? These are important questions; and I shall be able in this paper to do no more than tentatively set forth some preliminary lines of reasoning on a few of the issues involved.

1

Admittedly, poetry is not to be evaluated as if it were metaphysics or religion. The poet's task as poet is neither to pursue truth nor to save man but to imitate or make something. If he has no skill in craftsmanship he is a poor poet, however true his ideas or philanthropic his motives. Yet it would seem difficult to deny that the work of art when completed always implies an order of metaphysical or religious valuation. The finished poem has an organization of symbol and a structure of myth which no merely esthetic reasons can account for. And commonly this symbolic and mythical element in a poem has a great deal to do with the attraction or aversion which readers feel. Some readers will regard as immature or incoherent the very pattern of imagery and sequence of event which certain other readers consider splendid and wise. Crucial examples from modern poetry are Eliot's *The Waste Land* and its "refutation," Hart Crane's *The Bridge;* both works have ardent admirers and

---

[1] *The Intent of the Critic* (Princeton University Press, 1941), p. 29.

judicial detractors. How are we to explain this diversity? What is it that makes a poem's symbolism legitimate and its myth valid? Faith, it would seem, enters into the answer. Why else should some readers prefer Crane's symbols of subway and bridge to Eliot's symbols of wasteland and rain? Key symbols have a way of being tests of belief as well as means of communication. They indicate an author's "way of seeing things," which, no less than his mastery of language, is what gives him his "style." The extent to which we can sympathize with a particular poet's way of seeing conditions our enjoyment of his style.

Contributing to the confusion of esthetic response in our own day is the fact that we lack an established tradition in matters of belief. Our age has no common "way of seeing things," at least beyond their surface aspects, because there is no common stand in reason or revelation from which it can be assumed people will look out on life. As a result there is very little common folklore. Any one of a variety of myths, springing from the most diverse traditions, may be drawn on today by the man who is attempting to account for an area of human experience. This poses a problem for the artist. What mythology shall he adopt? What tradition shall he appeal to? In an age unstable in its vision he cannot rely on the age but must rely on himself to find his way to a focus of vision which will display pattern and meaning in the flow of daily perception.

When we review such modern authors as D. H. Lawrence, W. B. Yeats, and T. S. Eliot, we discover that they have been conscious seekers after myth.[2] Lawrence, reacting violently against Puritanism, has followed his Inner Light to the dark myths of Mexico. Yeats, attracted by mysticism, has jumbled together the traditions of pagan Ireland and of theosophic Byzantium. Eliot, seeing with Ezekiel the possibilities of Christianity's dry bones, has sought a resurrection of the body of Christian myth and symbol. With each of these writers the question of a working tradition is plainly central to the problem of composition and of communication. Each realizes that unless some key to order is adopted and some scheme of myth embraced, no significant patterns can be discerned in experience and no symbol will have other than purely imagist value.

The artist's need for myth, then, is not only a need for a frame, like a weaver's frame, by which he may give order and proportion to his insights as he weaves them; more fundamentally, it is a need for a key by which to unlock insight, a stand from which to view experience, a selected and given story by which to approach human events with a

---

[2] For a development of this point, see T. S. Eliot, *After Strange Gods: A Primer of Modern Heresy* (New York, 1934); David Daiches, *Poetry and the Modern World* (University of Chicago Press, 1940); and Cleanth Brooks, *Modern Poetry and the Tradition* (University of North Carolina Press, 1939).

view to reading their story. Myths serve the artist as first principles by which both to explore and to explain. They enable a poet to make a beginning and to make toward an end. They determine his plot or fable. They define his logic. Without myth the effort at poetry cannot rise above indiscriminate sensibility, or blind reporting, or a hesitant groping amid winds of doctrine toward the ever elusive story of man.

One must recognize, of course, that myth alone does not make poetry. The ability to manipulate words, a power of sympathy, a delicacy of sensibility, and a capacity for synthesizing poetic experience on the level aimed at are factors more important in enchanting us than is the pattern of a story's logic. Even the wisest of fables, if it is not set forth in the garb of fresh and immediate experience, no more constitutes poetry than discarnate logic makes up speech. Yet it is true that whenever speech is spoken, or poetry written, the logic or myth is that for and around which attention is chiefly aroused. If the logic is feeble, the most skillful excitements in its expression will not hold us permanently. When a poem's myth turns out to be silly, shallow, perverse, or radically at odds with myths already treasured by the reader, the poem is to an important degree crippled. Our conclusion, then, must be this: that, other qualities being equal (which is possible, of course, only in a hypothetical comparison), the poem having the truer myth will always be the greater poem.

But how shall we measure the truth of a myth? At least three tests can be applied: does the myth account adequately for the facts of experience it pretends to organize? does it have internal coherence? does it have richness or scope—what some critics would call "greatness" or "significance"?[3] These are very difficult questions to answer. Indeed, I am disposed to think they cannot be accurately answered without recourse to philosophy and theology, the two disciplines proper to the areas of reason and revelation from which myths arise.

I should not wish to argue that the two disciplines of philosophy and theology are necessary adjuncts of all literary criticism. Even without them much valuable comment can be made, if one is at home in the sciences of prosody and rhetoric. Still, one is measuring the poem's form rather than its content in applying these sciences. If one is to measure the poem's content he must always ask the question: how faithful is it in "holding the mirror up to nature?" If Aristotle is right, says Norman Foerster,[4] in thinking of imaginative literature as not only an art giving pleasure or delight but as a reasonable imitation of human action and human nature, then "the ethical or philosophic aspect of literature is not only a legitimate but an indispensable concern of the

---

[3] B. C. Heyl, *New Bearings in Esthetics and Art Criticism* (Yale University Press, 1943) discusses in order these and other definitions of "truth" in art.

[4] "The Esthetic Judgment and the Ethical Judgment," in *The Intent of the Critic*, ed. Stauffer, p. 74.

literary critic." An attempt must be made to judge the wisdom inherent in literature, the firmness and range of its imitation of life. And here the critic can answer, I think, only as he himself assumes as his standard an interpretation of nature arising from given principles. These principles extend beyond ethics and philosophy, as mentioned by Foerster, to include also theology. The issue is well stated in its full perspective by S. L. Bethell, a British lecturer and critic:

> When it comes to a judgment of value [he writes], the Marxist critic will say one thing, the Christian another, and the critic who is "nothing in particular" will be the least reliable of all, a prey to his own prejudices. Thus criticism, if it is to issue in evaluation—and what use is it otherwise?—cannot be an independent art. It must always depend upon and function within the context of a specific philosophy or religion. While there are Marxists there will be a Marxist criticism; and, what is more immediately important, if the Church is to fulfil its obligations to every aspect of the social order, it must maintain, not only its theology, its sociology, and so forth, but also a body of sound and respected Christian criticism.[5]

Bethell's point is carefully made. He is not claiming that literary criticism is an aspect of philosophy or theology. He is saying, rather, that these two disciplines furnish its context. They set the stage for esthetic judgment by clarifying those matters with which esthetics is inextricably related. W. H. Auden has lately warned critics of the necessity of co-ordinating esthetic values with values in other spheres of life. The pitfall of the Renaissance, he says, was that it "broke the subordination of all other intellectual fields to that of theology and assumed the autonomy of each."[6]

What happens when literary criticism denies its relatedness to theology? Some remarks of John Henry Newman in his lectures *On the Idea of a University* are here pertinent. Without theology, says Newman, the total field of experience cannot be explored and assessed. Still more importantly, even those areas which can be assessed without theology cannot rightly be assessed without its guidance, since the lesser sciences lose the right sense of proportion in their own fields of investigation as soon as they part company with theology.[7] In other words the lesser sciences, which can give at best only truncated results, begin to give untrustworthy results when exercised in strict isolation. If Newman is right, it follows that a literary criticism divorced from theology is not only incomplete criticism but also a criticism constantly inclining to inexactitude in purely esthetic judgments by reason of its refusal to allow for principles of discrimination arising outside itself.

---

[5] *The Literary Outlook* (London, 1943: The Christian News-Letter Books, No. 17), p. 9.

[6] "Criticism in a Mass Society," in *The Intent of the Critic*, ed. Stauffer, pp. 137, 142.

[7] See especially his Lecture IV.

2

It can be argued that the conclusion we have reached must be true of literary criticism, since it is demonstrably true of the literary works which criticism evaluates. What is most fundamentally wrong, for example, with Ezra Pound's *Draft of XXX Cantos?* T. S. Eliot gives, I think, the right answer: the human beings in these cantos are unreal and vaporous. Why? Is it because Pound lacks mastery of techniques in his art? No, indeed; it is, more radically, because his techniques are not guided by a proper principle for discriminating good and evil— he lacks an understanding, says Eliot, of the doctrine of Original Sin![8]

An equally serviceable illustration, though from a far better poet, is Archibald MacLeish's *Conquistador.* Technically, this poem is superb, but it fails to touch the deepest areas, the most distinctively human areas, of human experience. It treats man as if he were a wondrously sensitive participant in an environment of sun, wind, rain, reverie and disaster. But the reverie never rises into thought, nor the disaster into tragedy. MacLeish seems to have plenty of art but not enough scope (cf. Shakespeare's "Desiring this man's art and that man's scope"); and since art and scope are necessarily interrelated, even the art is reduced to a bordering on preciosity by the lack of scope. "The poem," says Allen Tate, "is one of the examples of our modern sensibility at its best; it has the defect of its qualities." It is too purely "literary." "The refinement of its craftsmanship hovers over a void." There being "no objective design to uphold the sensibility of the narrator-hero," his melancholy is necessarily meaningless and obscure.[9]

Still another example, to cite a nineteenth-century instance, is Shelley's *Queen Mab.* In the techniques of versification and in brilliance of imagery *Queen Mab* undoubtedly excels. Yet it has flaws both in local texture and in grand design. They stem from the fact that Shelley, while attempting a history of man more all-embracing than MacLeish's epic-history, nevertheless does not include God in his scope—except as a shadow-being. The result is a shadow quality in the art itself; the pageant is insubstantial and its characters hardly plausible. The whole action is flimsy. Undisciplined by an adequate myth, the sentiment of the poem lapses into sentimentality, abundantly justifying F. R. Leavis's observation that "Shelley's pathos is corrupt," apparently justifying also a dictum of W. H. Auden's, that "False beliefs in fact lead to bad poetry."[10]

But the term "bad poetry" calls perhaps for closer explanation. By bad poetry I do not mean "weak poetry," which is sheer absence of literary

[8] *After Strange Gods,* pp. 45-46.
[9] See "MacLeish's Conquistador," in *Reactionary Essays on Poetry and Ideas* (New York, 1936).
[10] *Op. cit.,* p. 141.

talent. Neither do I mean, of course, poetry about bad people or bad situations. Shakespeare has these in his plays and makes them the occasion of his best poetry. Poetry must continually deal with the follies, sins, imperfections and hardships which characterize experience in the present world. Bad poetry occurs, however, when these flaws and imperfections are not rightly seen and correctly assessed, when the finite and concrete character of actual events is infirmly or fantastically grasped. An aspect is taken for the whole, or shadow is mistaken for substance. The poetic response then becomes disproportionate to the cognitive element in the experience. The poet, as we would say, simply does not know what he is talking about, and hence he offends us by saying either too much or too little.

Let me illustrate. Ezra Pound's cantos on Hell, I have already indicated, strike me as bad. Their badness consists, however, not in the laboriously accumulated filth with which Pound has surrounded the "damned," but in his total ignorance of what damnation really is, with the result that poetic emotion is abused and misplaced. Shelley's flaw in *Queen Mab* is similar. What disappoints us is not his having strong feelings against tyranny but his having so blurred an apprehension of the actual lineaments of tyranny. MacLeish's offense in *Conquistador* is that he tells us so little of the why and wherefore of conquest. He dallies disproportionately with the fringes of experience. Refusing to take hold of action at its center, he has left us an epic which is a brilliant *tour de force,* a sentimental rather than a substantial history. From these examples it would seem that "bad poetry" can result (among other reasons of a technical nature, which I do not discuss here) from one of two flaws: either, as MacLeish illustrates, from a poet's failure to appreciate the matrix of experience from which he has dissociated a segment or element; or, as Shelley and Pound illustrate, from an attempt to eliminate or deny principles of interpretation necessary to an integrated understanding of the subject treated.

"Good poetry," on the other hand, is (among other things) poetry which is fair to the complexity and mystery of real experience. This demands accurate vision, and as much light as possible. It demands that the myth which a poet uses to integrate a selected experience be the right one for the limits of that experience and either imply or permit of integration in a larger body of myth. In other words, the good poet should be able, like Adam in the Garden, to name every creature correctly. Apprehending the form of each thing that is brought before him, he should be able to assign it its proper place. If this is nowadays achieved by poets only rarely or approximately, it may be because they have lost the perspicacity of original innocence and can regain it only by grace.

Just here, it seems to me, is where Christian revelation can come to the poet's aid. It can restore his vision. Its fables can furnish him a completely adequate world of myth within which all things can be assigned their peculiar place in the total realm of experience and accorded their proportionate and proper value. This need not rule out pagan myths, which may still form the basis of truly excellent poetry, but within limits which only Christian insight can fairly establish. Christian dogma will aid the artist not by giving him a privileged and special subject-matter but rather by defining for him a perspective from which "full light" can be had on all subject matters. Christian revelation will not endow him with poetic talent when by nature he has none, nor will it give him good eyes when by nature he has poor ones, but it will offer him the important benefit of "full light." And if it is true that the light with which an artist sees inclines to affect the justness of his observations, the presence of full light cannot but clarify the issues of proportion and order. With inadequate lighting, the artist will not see certain things he ought to see; it will be all too easy for him to draw disproportionately what he does see. To put it another way, the artist who takes up his location in Plato's cave has not the same chance as he who sets up shop by Christ's open tomb. Or, as Stanley R. Hopper has expressed the same truth: "It is only at the point of the crossing of the arms upon the Cross that one sees well. From this point of vantage we see things *sub specie Christi*—from the vantage point of the Eternal in time."[11]

Of course, if an artist is careful to draw only what he sees and nothing more, his art can be good art (though not the greatest), even if his light is poor—just as in philosophy the Positivist's approach can be profitable, though limited. But the non-Christian will always find it difficult to be completely fair to reality even within narrow areas. When certain aspects of things come to him with fierce vividness he will find it easy to treat these aspects as the whole, instead of as parts; when he is in ignorance of features of reality needed to complete a canvas of ambitious scope, he will incline to fill in with superstition what he would need to get from revelation. For further comment on this point may I cite, once again, from S. L. Bethell, who seems to me to have put the problem in its proper doctrinal framework:

> I should expect the total *oeuvre* of the Christian [says Bethell] to pro-
> vide a more adequate synthesis of experience than the non-Christian, *if
> Christianity is true* (which, of course, as a Christian, I believe to be es-
> tablished). Ideally the non-Christian synthesis ought itself to be Christian,
> since Christianity is true and the experiencing human being ought to per-
> ceive the truth through the ordering of his experience. Such conditions
> unfortunately passed out of existence with the Fall, and the possession of
> the Christian revelation is a necessary pre-condition (as natural law is

---

[11] *The Crisis of Faith* (New York, 1944), p. 183.

properly understood only by a mind working within the context of revealed religion).[12]

3

The proposition to which we are here driven is, of course, not strictly
provable; it is based on faith. If we accept it we do so because without
it art, and the proper judgment of art by literary criticism, appear handicapped. The appeal to an absolute can be justified only finally in terms
of the results it produces—namely, a more adequate and discriminating
handling of experience.

The decision to invoke a revelational standard assumes that transcendental and supernatural matters do come within the range of man's
experience. It assumes, further, that when art holds the mirror up to
nature it is challenged by nature to mirror the mystery of origins and
ends, to catch those references and overtones by which nature witnesses
to an immanental and transcendental *logos*. This witness of nature, it
would seem, abides in any of its small parts: mere leaves of grass were
to Whitman "the handkerchief of the Lord" and to Carlyle "a God made
visible." In some events of history—so the Bible testifies—the witness
to a supernatural meaning is terrifyingly powerful and clear. We may
safely say that whatever the segment of experience depicted in a poem,
some aspect of transcendental logic is present to it; some "word within
the word" is being spoken, and this "word" requires for its thorough
evaluation not philosophy but theology. "Words! book-words! what are
you?" Whitman once asked, and offered as his reply, "all words are
spiritual—nothing is more spiritual than words."[13]

This means simply that the art of using words cannot, in the last
analysis, be divorced from the science of exploring truth. Many an
earnest philologist has found himself driven by the problems of his
own science to the study of Christian theology. Justin Martyr, it will be
recalled, makes the account of his conversion to Christianity turn on that
discovery. In our own day a like development is illustrated in the careers
of C. S. Lewis and T. S. Eliot. Eliot, who is probably our age's most
sensitive handler of words, has advised poets to perfect their talent for
words by grounding it in tradition, and to perfect tradition by grounding
it in orthodoxy.[14] He has advised critics, similarly, that "Literary criticism should be completed by criticism from a definite ethical and

---

[12] "Poetry and Theology," in *Christendom* (British), XIII (Dec., 1943), 113.

[13] See F. O. Matthiessen, *American Renaissance* (Oxford University Press, 1941),
p. 521. Cf. Jacques Maritain, "Poetry and Religion," *The New Criterion*, V (1927),
15, where Maritain defines poetry as the "divination of the spiritual in the sensible,
which will itself express itself in the sensible."

[14] See his "Tradition and the Individual Talent," in *Selected Essays*; and his *After
Strange Gods*.

theological standpoint," since "the 'greatness' of literature cannot be determined solely by literary standards."[15]

We are brought finally, then, to a conclusion quite different from Matthew Arnold's notion that the critic can gain simply from a reading of the world's "classics" all the norms needed for evaluating literature. Literature can never take the place of dogma, for dogma is what gives ultimate character to a piece of literature by furnishing its latent presuppositions. These presuppositions may be absorbed uncritically by a writer from his own cultural matrix, or they may be embraced consciously after intellectual exploration and discovery. Yet, whether rudimentary and naive, or sophisticated and explicit, dogmas are present to a writer's creative acts of perception and expression.

Norman Foerster has lately argued that literary criticism can give a rounded estimate of a work of art only by restoring to a frequent alternation between two kinds of estimate, the esthetic and the ethical. He calls the two tasks inseparable and interpenetrating.[16] I myself hesitate over the term "interpenetrating" and prefer to say "interrelated." For I am impressed by John Crowe Ransom's distinction between a mechanical mixture like lemonade, where the sugar and the lemon juice interpenetrate, and an organic compound like table salt, where the original elements coexist in a higher synthesis.[17] If good poetry has the single effect of a compound, its elements ought to be treated as if correlating and combining rather than interpenetrating. Poetry at its best, I believe, is not so much an interfusion of sensibility, skill, and moral idealism, as it is a genuine synthesis of these in a creative act of representation. Indeed, I should like to transfer Ransom's figure from the physical to the metaphysical plane and speak of the compound poetry in terms of "substance" and "accidents." Its "substance," I would then suggest, is its myth; its "accidents" the verbal beauties, rhythms, and other literary circumstances under which we apprehend the poem. A complete criticism of the "substance" would seem to require philosophy and theology, while a description of the "accidents" can be dealt with by esthetics alone. When taken as a whole the poem challenges an array of sciences, each in its proper province.

In conclusion may I offer one more theoretical suggestion. Why not describe the true relation between theology and literature in terms of an old ecclesiastical formula used in another connection: "distinct yet inseparable; not to be confused or to be divided"? It was Matthew Arnold's error to confuse theology and literature, blurring the distinction between them. To separate them is the error of the modern Occamist.

---

[15] "Religion and Literature," in *Faith that Illuminates*, ed. V. A. Demant (London, 1935), p. 31.
[16] *Op. cit.*, p. 76.
[17] *The World's Body* (New York, 1938), p. 74.

One group commits the folly of viewing literature as a substitute for dogma. The other group would make of esthetics a wholly autonomous science, unregulated in any way by theology. This is to imitate Occam's doctrine of a "double truth" and to emerge, like Occam, with half-truths.

But literary criticism, I believe, can find a middle practice between the two dangers. It need neither forego all independence to become a mere department of religion, nor yet set up sovereignty as an isolated and self-sufficient province. For it is a plain fact of experience that what we read as literary critics "does not concern merely something called our *literary taste*"; it affects directly "the whole of what we are."[18] Likewise, what we accept as theologians does not affect merely an aspect of life called "religion" but the whole ordering of our habits in judging and enjoying. A literary critic will therefore increase the competence of his pronouncements on esthetic matters as he recognizes this interrelationship of disciplines. If we are, as Christianity teaches, dwellers in two worlds, nevertheless our lives need to be integral, not schizophrenic. The Christian critic can relate the two interests of theology and literature by following a suggestion given by M. B. Reckitt to another group of craftsmen, the politicians: "at least," says Reckitt, "we should step into the natural world with the mood of the supernatural and strive to correct the astigmatism of our fallen natures by looking out upon the world in the light of the theological virtues."[19]

---

[18] T. S. Eliot, "Religion and Literature," p. 42.
[19] "The Christian Virtues and Politics," *Christendom* (British), XIII (Dec., 1943), 99.

THE MORAL EVALUATION OF LITERATURE

Frederick Pottle

For some time I have been led to examine the relations between the theories of general linguistic science and literary criticism, and the more I ponder those relations, the more convinced I become that we have here a fresher and surer guide than is to be found in any other philosophical approach. The great virtue of the linguistic approach is that it confines the problem sharply to the art of linguistic expression, and enables one to come to much more specific and practical assumptions than is possible if one insists on principles that are applicable to the whole field of the arts.

The first assumption that I ask you to consider is that literature is merely human speech, and that all specifically aesthetic problems in the field of literature are linguistic problems. When a man composes an elaborate fiction by writing on paper or by using a typewriter, and then has that fiction printed and sold, he is engaged in the same kind of activity as a man who tells a story in a club room or in an after-dinner speech. When a poet, by choice of words, by rhyme and meter, by assonance and alliteration, strives to transmit to unknown readers the tone and quality of some experience, he is doing the same kind of thing that you did yesterday when you tried to convey to your neighbor the enjoyment you had in an afternoon walk. There is a great difference, of course, but it is a difference of degree, not of kind. The poet or novelist is simply doing more skillfully and on a larger scale what we all do after a fashion. Elaborate form (and under this heading I include not merely rhyme, alliteration, meter, and rhythm but also plot or design) does not make poetry, though it does make particular poems: it reinforces, concentrates, and complicates the purely expressive qualities of language so as to produce a product that is more valuable and memorable than the fleeting and atomic poetry of ordinary speech.

We must therefore not confine our thinking to books if we really want to get at the heart of our problem. Books represent only the tiniest fraction of literary art. The art of books is continuous with the art of magazines and newspapers; finally, with the whole expanse of unrecorded speech. The Puritanical censor has far too narrow a view of his task.

If he could sweep all printed books out of existence, he would still have a large, flourishing, and absolutely ubiquitous expanse of literary art, most of it completely beyond the control of public censorship. Critics talk feelingly of "universal art," and imagine that there are great books which appeal to all men of all times. They forget or ignore the fact that throughout human history the majority of mankind have been illiterate, and that of those who can read, the majority have never looked into the books that are supposed to be universal. It is safe to conclude that the one *really* universal kind of literary art is, and to all appearances always has been, smutty stories.

My second assumption is that there is no necessary connection between literary power and moral virtue. When we see a man of extraordinary physical strength or dexterity—say a prize fighter or a champion swimmer—we do not conclude that he is necessarily a good man. We ought to assume exactly the same attitude toward literary artists. The power of expression is one which some men have to an extraordinary degree, but this brilliant power of expression can coexist with a quite ordinary degree of private virtue. We all know this and admit it practically when we say that so-and-so is a scoundrel but a very amusing man, or again when we deprecate frank biographies of poets on the ground that "it is the poetry that matters." The power to express virtue in words is a linguistic or aesthetic power; it implies a knowledge of virtue but not the practical will to do good deeds. The literary artist is a man gifted in one particular direction: he has the gift of speech.

Men in general have rebelled against this conclusion, and have set up definitions of aesthetic value which include moral goodness or "rightness" of subject matter as an essential constituent. Mystical aesthetic (which is usually fathered on Plato but seems to have been the invention of Plotinus) assumes that the poet is a kind of seer, and that the form he imposes on his materials is a reflection of higher reality.

Another theory which is being eloquently developed by Christian apologists in our own day admits that a man can possess literary *talent* of a higher order without being morally good (for an artist is a sinner, like every one else) or without having a practical conviction of the truth of a traditional theology, but insists nevertheless that the lack of true belief imposes a definite aesthetic limitation in the product, for without the insight afforded by an adequate "myth" the poet cannot make sense of the experience with which he is dealing. His myth does not so much enable him to *select* images as to *see* them. The aesthetic and ethical judgments are inextricably related, and the judgment from the standpoints of philosophy and theology is primary. A specifically aesthetic judgment is legitimate only when it is recognized as part of a larger evaluation which begins with a consideration of the moral worth of the subject matter.

In spite of the enormous vogue that mystical aesthetic has enjoyed, I am convinced that as general theory it leads to sophistries of little utility. Poets by and large are obviously not superior to other men in either virtue or wisdom unless one redefines morality and wisdom so as to make them so. It is one of the flagrant injustices of history that Plato should be charged with this view, for he expressly repudiated it, and exiled all but a few well-disciplined poets from his ideal commonwealth on the ground that poets as a class are too irresponsible to be tolerated in a wholly reasonable community. Tolstoi in his demand for rigorous censorship comes to exactly the same conclusion, though not by the same metaphysical route. It should surely give us pause to find that the two greatest literary geniuses who ever wrote on theory of poetry declined to subscribe to the flattering theory that poets are necessarily seers.

The theory that poetry can have genuine aesthetic value only as it has sound moral content, or, to put it differently, that the images of the poet are vitiated of significance in the extent to which they are not perceived and expressed in the light of a true theology, is much more compelling. I am aware of course of the impossibility in any ultimate sense of separating the form of poetry from its content: when we do separate them, we are only considering the same entity by turns within certain limited and exclusive assumptions. I am also aware of the importance of the beliefs of the poet, not merely in framing and directing his poem, but also in making clear to him what he is trying to express. The last lecture in my Messenger series is an extended demonstration of this principle. Wordsworth's images at the beginning of *Tintern Abbey* are not the full reporting by some unselective machine of all the disturbances a perfectly receptive machine might be supposed to record (the analogy is imperfect, but never mind); they are rather images expressive of the perception of a landscape in terms of a particular religious philosophy. I should not, as a teacher, devote so much time to the study of Wordsworth's thought if I did not think that such study was something more than an evaluation of his doctrines; was, in fact, an aid to the aesthetic appreciation of his poetry. My difficulty is not with the contention that what we conceive to be the soundness or lack of soundness of the poet's beliefs and attitudes will, and should, be a part of our total judgment of his poem; nor is it with the contention that his beliefs and attitudes have the most intimate possible kind of relationship with his images. It is rather with the doctrine that a particular poet with a particular historically limited sensibility will be not only more wise *but also more expressive* in the precise degree to which he subscribes to a right tradition. I should like to believe that, but I find the evidence of history very strongly against it.

History, as I read it, does not support the theory that the relation between expressive power and wisdom is direct and quantitative. Poets not infrequently grow less poetical as they become wiser and more orthodox. I have no doubt that Wordsworth after 1815 had a sounder theology than he had in 1798, and no doubt that he wrote weaker poetry. Mr. T. S. Eliot has reminded us that a poet cannot always write poetry directly expressive of his beliefs. If he wishes to write genuine poetry, he must remain within the limits of his sensibility, and there may be a permanent cleavage between his sensibility and his faith. Consequently, as in Mr. Eliot's own case, his poetry may be a great deal less positive in its statements of belief than his prose. Or, to put it differently, a man can employ for the purpose of poetry only that portion of his beliefs that he can *feel*, the portion that comes to him in terms of quality.

It does not look as though genuine poets start with "myths," with theological and philosophical systems which they proceed to embody in verse. They begin with a sensibility, with an irresistible urgency towards expression which starts them composing before they have much of anything to say. Their search thereafter, so far as they are poets, is not so much for truth and wisdom in an abstract sense as for sanctions for their sensibility, for a body of ideas which will justify their expressive urgency. If they are fortunate as artists (fortunate as *men* is a different matter), they will arrive at just such a body of sanctions as will enable their sensibility to work freely and confidently, and no more. History does not show that unlimited capacity for the poetic absorption of sound belief which this theory demands. It can be maintained that the comparative failure of Wordsworth's later poetry was due more to a waning of natural energy than to the stubborn forcing of an orthodoxy on a historically limited sensibility which could not give poetic body to it, but such evidence as we actually have rather suggests that if Wordsworth had arrived at a complete Christian orthodoxy in 1797 and had insisted on trying to give full expression to it in his poetry, he would have written weaker poetry than he did. His heresies, such as they were, were the necessary condition for the full exploitation of his poetic gift.

Now I know what the reply of the theological critics would be: sin. Cleavage between sensibility and sound belief is, they would assert, evidence of the fallen nature of man. In a state of innocence such a thing could not occur. That is highly theoretical, but it sounds reasonable. If the theological critics will admit that their definition of poetry does not describe the actual poetry of this actual world, but applies only to the poetry of the Garden of Eden, all our differences will be at an end. I think I understand now what Mr. T. S. Eliot meant when he said with reference to Matthew Arnold's dictum that poetry is at bottom a criticism of life, "At bottom: that is a great way down; the bottom is the bottom." He was not, as I thought when I first read the passage, being weakly facetious. He was giving expression to a conviction that a literary history based on ultimate theological principles is not very rewarding. In the light of eternity and with reference to the day of judgment there is probably not much that anybody wants to say about the poetry of William Wordsworth. But in the light of nature there is a great deal.

My own experience has led me to believe that the fullest and most satisfactory results can be obtained by applying both a naturalistic and a theological technique, and by making the aesthetic judgment wholly within naturalistic (which means relativistic) assumptions. I find it better to see linguistic art as something ubiquitous and primary, something to be judged without fixed moral reference: the direct expression of the qualities of experience without regard to its uses. This involves a separation of the aesthetic judgment (whether a thing is good *art*) from the moral judgment (whether a thing is *good* art).

The position too often taken by those who find the mystical synthesis unsatisfactory is that of the hedonist, of "art for art's sake." According to this school, it is profanation of literary criticism so much as to hint the question of morals. This view, which, in modern times at least, rose as a reaction from strongly moralistic criticism, errs as much on one side as moralistic criticism does on the other. Hedonistic criticism is quite right in maintaining that the criticism of literature, as an activity distinct from other activities of the mind, concerns itself with aesthetic value and not with moral utility. The critics of this school have right on their side when they maintain that the moralistic critic, in his eagerness to answer the question, "Is this good for me?" is ignoring the basic question, "Is this a powerful work of art?" And to confine our analysis of things to their practical utility is certainly a narrow and inhumane limitation. It is as though we should restrict our concern with trees to the edibility of their fruit: to say of the yew tree that its berries are poisonous, and dismiss as irrelevant or dangerous any admission that it is beautiful.

But the hedonist errs in forgetting that, as literature is speech, it is the whole of speech, and that as speech has been evolved to express and communicate the whole nature of man, including his moral nature, it is impossible to use speech in such a way that it will have practical meaning without either stating or implying moral concepts. The concept of pure poetry (art whose significance could be exhausted by a strictly aesthetic judgment) is useful and necessary in theory, but no pure poetry exists in practice. Poetry has a special way of saying things, and that way of saying things is what makes it uniquely interesting, but the things it says cannot be held to be empty of moral significance. The dilemma is easily solved if we will agree to maintain both points of view and protect our judgment on the one side from being encroached upon by our judgment on the other. The first of our judgments is purely and specifically literary; the other merges with our other practical decisions.

This being so, we should expect the concept of greatness or supremacy in literature to be in the long run a practical compromise between the claims of the aesthetic and the moral. Common sense prefers two values to one if the two may be had without getting in each other's way. We must sometimes admit that in the perfection of their expressive technique there seems to be little to choose between two given books. But if one of them proceeds from a frivolous, shoddy, or perverse mind and the other from one that is deep, serious, and intense, students of literature (who are merely people who give themselves opportunities to meet literature in its full range) will in the long run find themselves better pleased with the second. But we must repeat again: it was not the moral value of the subject matter which made either book literature in the first place. It was the unusual degree of expressive power possessed by their authors, a power dependent in no certain way on the soundness of their ideas.

I have now granted the reasonableness—indeed, the necessity—of moral judgments in literature, but I do not find myself very well pleased with the history of such judgments. Moralistic criticism of the past too often seems pompous and fussy. It is probable, in the first place, that moralistic critics have reprobated as immoral what was merely revolutionary in technique; and, in the second place, that they were too simple and direct in their conclusions as to the effect of literature on conduct.

I can think of no surer guard against the first error than serious study of the history of language. We are all familiar now with the two views as to "correctness" in speech: on the one hand, the purist view, which maintains the notion of an inherent and absolute correctness in language, fixed by grammars and dictionaries, and sees actual speech as in a deplorable state of decay; on the other hand, the historical view, which regards the statements of grammars and dictionaries as merely descriptive of what has once been the accepted pattern of language for the more elevated forms of discourse. The historical student of language believes that the contemporary vernacular is not in a state of decay but in a state of vigorous and healthy growth. Since language is art and creation, it must change as each individual mind and each society sets itself to express a changing world. This sort of change is neither moral nor immoral, yet it excites more passion than genuine moral turpitude. Most of us can get on quite pleasantly with a libertine, but we hate and despise a man who uses "contact" as a verb. It is a great pity that moral fervor should thus be wasted, and the situation is one that could certainly be improved by better public education in language. It would be better for us to be informed and dispassionate students of the vernacular, eager to observe its variations and novelties, seriously striving to discern the pattern and tone of the emerging idiom. For we can be quite certain that many of those novelties will establish themselves as part of the standard speech which purists of the future will in their turn defend as "correct."

It requires no long historical study of criticism to see that a great deal— I was going to say nine-tenths—of the passionate moral disapproval which has been visited on contemporary literature at all times has really been roused by the style of the work and not by its moral content. It is only human to suspect that innovators are up to no good. It is natural to feel that the world is going to the dogs, and in no way so clearly and certainly as in the arts. But education, if it has any function at all, should aim at training men's minds to distinguish between prejudices; and it is very discouraging to see a large group of men who speak with easy scorn of the critics who failed to discern the greatness of Wordsworth or Keats adopting toward their own contemporaries the attitudes that they condemn in Jeffrey and Lockhart. There is little virtue in recognizing greatness that is already established. The admirable thing is to recognize and describe emerging greatness, even (as will frequently happen) when you cannot bring yourself to care much for it.

Style or expression in itself is not a moral matter. It is to be judged simply and solely for its *adequacy*, its power to record and communicate what the author chose to record and communicate. You cannot decide in advance—you cannot decide, indeed, without prolonged and serious study—that any new departure in style is bad. You must satisfy yourself that you understand what the author wanted to do. If he succeeded in doing that with precision and economy, then he is an artist to be reckoned with. But of course you do not have to give your approval to the subject matter which he chose to express. If it seems to you— again on mature consideration—to be trifling or vicious, your judgment will not be complete until you say so. But do not make the mistake of saying that an author is a bungler when you mean that you find the content of his mind disgusting. A man can be an artist in obscenity and blasphemy no less than in matter of positive moral worth.

The demand that literature shall be moral cannot be narrowed to a demand that it shall explicitly inculcate Christian principles. Literature for a long time now has been overwhelmingly secular, and I do not see how we can expect that it should be anything else. For literature is a sensitive and faithful reflection of the general temper of its age, and the world itself must change before the artist does. Our own age, by and large, is one of moral uncertainty, self-distrust, and violence, and if the artist pictures it so, provided he does it with seriousness and largeness of mind, we ought not to accuse him of depravity. A demand at the present moment for a literature that shall generally avoid coarseness, brutality, and moral deliquescence is a demand for second- and third-rate authors who follow the excellent but outworn formulas of writers of the past.

I shall now, with the diffidence and uncertainty which always accompanies the application of any abstract principle to particular cases, try to illustrate by reference to three important books by modern authors. I do not write the moralistic part with pleasure, because I do not think that I have any special aptitude for it. My standard of morality is that of Christian orthodoxy. It is important to mention this, not that any one who has read me thus far would have any doubt about it, but because I ought to indicate my awareness that the choice of a particular tradition is not inevitable. Within naturalistic assumptions general agreement is ideally possible. All theologies, on the contrary, are a matter of faith, and appear to me to be outside the area in which general agreement can be demanded on logical grounds. The modern world being decidedly divided and pluralistic in its moral systems, many readers of this book will have to take my moral analysis merely as the demonstration of a questionable method. My three books are Somerset Maugham's *Of Human Bondage,* D. H. Lawrence's *Lady Chatterley's Lover,* and Ernest Hemingway's *For Whom the Bell Tolls.* I hope that my reason for choosing each will become apparent as I proceed.

The stylistic novelty of Maugham's book would have been more obvious if he had published it in 1897, when it was first drafted, instead of in 1915, when it actually appeared. What he realized (and it was a necessary thing for a modern author to realize) was that the reigning style of elaborate and figured prose had become artificial and meretricious. The modern temper demands greater simplicity and austerity, a much closer approximation to the direct, uninvolved order and unpretentious phrasing of colloquial speech. He realized this ideal with a firmness and integrity that cannot be too much admired, but with the tact which must always be the possession of any author who wishes to be popular, not merely to help other writers to be popular. That is, though he made conscious innovations, he did not go so far beyond the linguistic conventions of well-bred mixed society as to rouse suspicion and resentment. It is hard to believe that *Of Human Bondage* ran much risk of rousing misdirected moral judgments by novelties of style. Indeed, the tactfulness of its style probably preserved it from moral criticism that could justly have been made. Lawrence and Hemingway, however, have both suffered from mistaken stylistic criticism, but for rather different reasons.

Lawrence, who was the greatest genius of the three and probably one of the most gifted men of modern times, made a frontal attack on the linguistic taboo which rules that the simple and direct names for certain bodily functions and parts of the body cannot be used publicly; indeed, can hardly be used at all without an impression of obscenity. The taboo was revolting to him as an artist, and it must be admitted that all the circumlocutions for the forbidden words which standard English sanctions are too elegant and self-conscious to satisfy any one with a feeling for honest style. It was revolting to him also as a moralist: he believed that the taboo was a symptom of social ill-health. Consequently he used all the words liberally, with the result of course that he ran foul of censorship, both official and private. The unexpurgated text of his novel is still not too easy to come by.

It may be that I have not pondered deeply enough the moral implications of taboo, but it seems to me that this problem is much less one of morals than it is one of tact and taste. The determination to use subject matter that he did use certainly involved a moral choice, but given that subject matter, Lawrence as an artist had a right to draw on all the resources of language to express it. But if he had not been self-willed and fanatical—in short, if he had had more common sense— he would have seen and admitted that linguistic taboo is far too powerful to be overthrown by a single author, be he ever so gifted. The medium of words has a decorum, like the medium of any other of the arts: there is a great area in which change can be attempted with hope of success, but limits beyond which change—or at any rate sudden change—is impossible. Significant authors are always trying to raise the ordinary homely words of the vernacular to the level of standard English, but this was not the same thing. These words are under some degree of taboo at all levels, not merely in the drawing-room; and because of their immemorial associations of covertness and slyness are not plastic even in the hands of a master of language. What he aimed at was naturalness, but the effect was to make the speech of his characters strained and unnatural. The experiment was a linguistic failure, and so far his book can be condemned on purely aesthetic grounds, though I should of course add that this judgment applies to only one feature of his style, which is uneven but as a whole extremely competent.

The stylistic experimentation of *For Whom the Bell Tolls* is of a particularly massive and resourceful kind. It is much more audacious than Maugham's but much more tactful than Lawrence's. Hemingway is not interested in reshaping the sexual mores of the community. There is nothing defiant in his use of unconventional language. He simply wants to write about people—a band of guerrilla soldiers and a gypsy woman—who naturally and habitually use unconventional language, and he wants to express the actual quality of this speech. He is aided by the fact that all the conversation in the book is supposed to be in Spanish, and that the indecencies are therefore not identical with ours. By thinking the speeches in Spanish and then translating them literally into English (at least by using this technique often enough to give a prevailing cast to the style), he keeps the reader constantly aware of a foreign setting and a foreign mentality whose forbidden words, when seen in print, are not so shocking as ours. Some of the indecencies he can leave in Spanish, but this device must be employed sparingly, for comparatively few of his readers can be expected to be fluent in that language. The foreign words, by and large, must be those which an intelligent English-speaking reader can guess accurately enough from the context or from their similarity to words he does know. But for the great majority of the indecencies he prints the English word *obscenity*, a mere counter which we can accept as such (and most of the indecencies of vulgar speech are mere counters or expletives) or convert silently into English coin. The failure or success of the experiment can be judged only by those who have read the book carefully and without impatience. My own conclusion is that it is a successful device but probably a *tour de force*. Hemingway has accomplished something that has hitherto baffled the literary artist, but it is doubtful whether the device can become generally useful.

It seems to me, then, that any man who professes to care for literature can read all three of these books with lively appreciation, analyzing the linguistic problem that faced each author and estimating the degree of his success in solving it. We ought to be able to be interested in craftsmanship considered purely as such. Let us not mistake: there are great values to be had from the patient and calm contemplation of linguistic expression without the intrusion of moral judgment. And those values are the specifically literary ones; the ones, that is, that distinguish literary criticism from other activities of the mind.

But there are other values that a serious mind must consider, and other loyalties more important than that to art. For art (as I have said elsewhere) is experience, and man as a moral being is surely under the necessity of subjecting *all* his experiences to moral evaluation.

I hope I have indicated sufficiently my admiration for Mr. Maugham as a literary craftsman. I feel more complete sympathy with his methods than with those of Lawrence or Hemingway, because his style is less advanced and more like what I can imagine myself as being capable of attaining. I do not find myself in sympathy with his philosophical ideas or the cast of his morality. *Of Human Bondage* may well turn out to be the most important English novel of the first quarter of the twentieth century. If it fails of so high a rating, it will be because of its moral shortcomings. It is, if not a deliberately low-principled book, at least one whose principles waver between a facile cynicism and an equally facile sentimentalism. Much of the objection could have been obviated if Mr. Maugham had expressly made all the philosophical and moral speculation that of his hero and had kept himself clear, but he does not do so. The book is tendentious. The direction of its serious purpose is to discredit the Christian religion and the human conscience, but remnants of both are revived at the end for literary effect. I do not object that Maugham has attacked institutional Christianity, for institutional Christianity is fair game; I do object that he has done it with so little candor. *Of Human Bondage* reduces the complex and noble matter of traditional Christian morality to a cold gentlemanly code of selfishness and irresponsibility and then dissolves in a warm bath of benevolence and self-sacrifice which is equally selfish.

It seems to me not too harsh to call Mr. Maugham's moral relaxation ignoble, but no such term can be applied to Lawrence. Lawrence was an intense moralist, a man of tremendous purpose, who sacrificed himself unhesitatingly to an end which he believed good. He was a fanatic and a heretic, trusting in an intense personal intuition rather than a historical tradition. He broke with Christian morality as completely as Maugham, but there is this important difference: Maugham is sensitive to the Christian tradition and is well aware of its reflection in ordinary social morality though his interpretation of its operation is consistently cynical. Lawrence writes as though he were utterly unaware that it existed as anything but a speculative position. For this reason every one of the characters in *Lady Chatterley's Lover* is an animal deviating from the normal type, a monster. There can be no doubt that his mind was pure and that he was filled with passionate tenderness: it was in fact the shamefaced and prurient reticence of traditional writing and speaking about sexual relations that impelled him to write as he did. But he seems to have had no sense of humor whatever, and is consequently always in danger of lapsing into the ridiculous. In matters of style reference to the standards of older authors is unfair, but in matters of morality such reference is legitimate. Put Lawrence's sexual philosophy beside Fielding's and the comparison is very hard on Lawrence. Fielding is virile and robust to the point of coarseness; he is perfectly frank, and his attitude toward sexual license in young men is pretty easygoing. But he has no doubt that such behavior *is* licentious, and his attitude, though stemming fundamentally from his Christian principles, is strongly reinforced by a sense of humor, which is only a sense of proportion. *Fanny Hill* he would have considered just a dirty book which, as a magistrate, he ought perhaps to suppress; if he sent the author to jail it would have been merely to teach him manners. He would not, I think, have considered *Lady Chatterley's Lover* a dirty book, but he would have thought it a ridiculous and possibly a mad book. He would, that is, have seen in it strong signs of obsession and morbidity, and he might have felt it his duty to make inquiries as to whether its author displayed sufficient social responsibility to make it safe to leave him at large. I have, by a fiction, put the onus of this verdict on Fielding's shoulders, but I am willing to assume it myself. It seems to me, as it seems to

Mr. T. S. Eliot, that *Lady Chatterley's Lover*, though a remarkable work of art, is the work of a very sick man.

For Whom the Bell Tolls, on the contrary, seems to me in its total effect wholesome and even noble. As I have insisted before, the linguistic audacities must be treated as such, not as moral lapse. In the subject matter to be expressed, Hemingway's grasp of moral principle is large, serious, and patient. The book is remarkably full-blooded and remarkably healthy. Political issues are treated fairly and objectively; if Hemingway is a partisan, it is as a partisan of humanity, to whom the death of every man, whether Loyalist or Fascist, is a loss. The love of Robert Jordan and Maria, though handled with greater intimacy than would have been permitted in the last century, is a relationship of tenderness and responsibility: in the canonical practice that obtained before the Council of Trent it would (I guess) have been rated a clandestine but a valid marriage. I do not see how any one who comes to grips with the story can fail to find positive moral value in it.

As to the others, what shall one say? Is a man necessarily the worse for having read *Of Human Bondage* and *Lady Chatterley's Lover?* It would be much more comfortable to be able to give a direct and categorical answer, but I am not encouraged by history to think that such questions can be answered absolutely. The direct Puritan course of branding all secular literature as not convenient is simply impossible for societies which do not segregate themselves from the world; and the experiment, where it has been tried by secular bodies, cannot be said to commend itself to general acceptance. The Puritan retained the Bible because it was the word of God, but the Bible is a fairly extensive library of books and contains some pretty strong stuff. It is, I suggest, no accident that the Puritan, cut off from secular literature and given a special indulgence as to the Bible, developed a fondness for the harshest and most violent parts of it. His reason was aesthetic (for the violent portions of the Bible, e.g., the minatory Psalms, are especially fine as literature), but the result was moral, and moral in a most unfortunate way. When the ordinary man (I do not speak of saints) restricts his aesthetic experiences, he runs the risk of moral unbalance.

This warns us that the relation between aesthetic experience and moral behavior is by no means so simple as is assumed by the Puritan, whether Christian or humanist. Our moral natures need food to grow on, and the mysterious chemistry of digestion can convert very unlikely substances to good. The analogy might profitably be extended. The Puritans are very like those pure-food fanatics, who having found out that the human body needs proteins, carbohydrates, and fats for its sustenance, drew the direct conclusion that if a man got them pure in concentrated form and ate nothing else, he would be healthier. Now science has discovered the vitamins, substances which are apparently not digested themselves, but whose presence is necessary if the chemistry of digestion is to be complete. Live on pure proteins, carbohydrates, and fats, and you get scurvy, beriberi, pellagra, and rickets. I think I perceive in some of the sternly moralistic critics of my acquaintance a condition of inflamed nerves similar to beriberi, and I conclude that they would profit by more roughage in their diet.

The potential harmfulness of literature is a highly relative matter, and must in the long run be left pretty much to the individual conscience. Modern thinking, in its effort to find a plausible substitute for dogmatic theology, has put upon literature a greater moral burden than it is actually fitted to bear. We place a pathetic trust in the power of good books to make people good, and we assign to works of literature greater power for public evil than is really justified. Moral character is formed by acts, and the direct training of home, church, and society is, in the long run, infinitely more powerful. When a character is still unformed, we are justified in being overcautious, in excluding books which might be unsettling. Those of us who thrive on coarse food must be sympathetic and respectful toward those whose stomachs really are more delicate; we should not taunt them with infirmity, and they should be very slow to set up prohibitions for us. We must be perfectly honest in our reading, alert to recognize and obviate evil as we would in any other kind of experience. But I think the conclusion can be put more directly: we should strive constantly, and by disciplines more active than reading, to make ourselves good men. The Church would do well to worry less about the demoralizing effect of contemporary literature and more about the sincerity, persistence, and competence of its training of the young. To a man of good will, a man of Christian conscience with a habit of self-examination, the problem of reading can be trusted to take care of itself.

CHRISTIAN LITERARY SCHOLARS

Joseph H. Summers

> *Il faut un travail pour exprimer le vrai. Aussi pour le recevoir. On exprime et on reçoit le faux, ou du moins le superficiel, sans travail.*
>
> *Quand le vrai semble au moins aussi vrai que le faux, c'est le triomphe de la sainteté ou du génie; ainsi saint François faisait pleurer ses auditeurs tout comme un prédicateur vulgaire et théâtral.*
>
> SIMONE WEIL, *Cahiers*, I (1951), 191.
>
> *Il n'y a pas le point de vue chrétien et les autres, mais la vérité et l'erreur. Non pas: ce qui n'est pas chrétien est faux, mais: tout ce qui est vrai est chrétien.*
>
> SIMONE WEIL, *La Connaissance Surnaturelle* (1950), 24.

1

As Christian literary scholars we have taken a more or less definite position in relation to life and experience. It is inevitable that a good deal of our scholarship should be concerned with the patterns and meanings that are most significant to our own lives. This is not, I believe, a real limitation of our scholarly roles; we have the advantage of being conscious of our position and our traditions, and we should therefore more easily avoid the usual scholarly pitfall: the unconscious projection of an individual's private obsessions and desires upon the literary evidence.

But there are dangers in our position or, perhaps more accurately, dangers that we may misunderstand or distort or discredit our position. Ever since Matthew Arnold, intelligent men have confused literature with religion; by this time all of us should know better. A more serious danger is that, concerned with our particular vision of orthodoxy, we may forget that our first duty as scholars is the discovery and communication of truth, and, instead, spend our chief energies as religious and moral cops and judges, rapping knuckles and heads, assigning sentences. Whether this results in official or unofficial indexes of books or men, it is a distortion of our primary responsibility. Another extreme

"Christian Literary Scholars." From The Christian Scholar, *XLVII (Summer 1964). Reprinted by permission of* Soundings *and the author.*

seems a more real danger today: in an attempt to prove our tolerance (and our equality with our secular colleagues), we may attempt to approve *all* "creative writers," to find hidden Christian meanings in the most unlikely places, and to appropriate forcibly for religious purposes all the currently fashionable literature. (One sometimes glimpses an image of the professional atheist being inexorably hauled, kicking and screaming, to the baptismal font.) The result of such scholarship and teaching is that some students can discover eucharistic symbols in any liquid in any context and Christ symbols under the bed, but can recognize neither the obvious subject of a poem nor traditional Christian stories or doctrines.

These last extreme positions have in common the assumption that the role of the scholar is nearer that of propagandist than that of "seeker" or even "teacher." Scholars from both groups tend to assume that works of literature can and should be manipulated (or even murdered) for special, practical ends. We may need to remember Milton's warning: "As good almost kill a man as kill a good book." I do not mean to imply that propaganda is always bad or that, as individuals, we can afford to be concerned only with contemplative knowledge and never with emotional commitment and action. We should, however, recognize our prime duty to be as informed and as intelligent and as honest as we can and to make (and communicate) fairly subtle discriminations. As convinced Christians, we should not find any contradiction between our scholarly commitment to truth and our religious aims. We do not, surely, believe that God requires us to tell lies for Him. We are committed to the discovery, the preservation, and the communication of truth, and we have faith that the truth will make us free.

2

For most of us, an additional primary duty is to try to make evident and available to those living in our own age the achievements of the Christian literature of the past. Only a little investigation in that vast area will probably lead us to a few elementary and salutary insights: Christianity is larger than we are; it is a religion rather than a philosophy, and, in nineteen hundred years, it has proved more or less compatible with an astonishing number of philosophies; God has indeed in historical times worked in mysterious ways; the gifts of the Spirit are various and can be manifest in surprising forms. If we have fully realized those insights, we may be able to resist the temptation to present one style or genre or historical period (often the one we happen to like best) as *the* Christian one. We should be able to avoid the much more dangerous assumption that large periods of history were simply "mistakes" to be lamented (the Middle Ages, the Renaissance or the

Reformation, the eighteenth or the nineteenth centuries). It is, surely, a serious religious error to believe that God has abandoned the world for large periods of time. We might, in our scholarship and criticism, either eliminate or carefully qualify the word "orthodox," since that word has been applied to various beliefs and practices within the past four hundred years, and we can rarely be sure of the precise meanings which our readers or hearers will attach to it. (In some American literary scholarship, for example, the word is restricted to the theological system of a small group of seventeenth-century Calvinists in Massachusetts; since that system is often considered repellent in some respects and unbelievable in others, the "scholarly" implication may be that "orthodox" Christianity is irrelevant today.) For, when we attempt to deal with an authentic work of religious literature from the past, our first responsibility is not to "correct" its doctrine, however fragmentary, strange, or imperfect we may find it. It is, rather, to attempt to answer accurately a few questions: what does it say? how does it "work"? Perhaps other questions will follow: how was it possible for intelligent and creative men to believe such doctrines? what did the doctrines *mean* for the life of the individual and the community? what was the relation between the doctrines and that literary creation which can still speak to other men? We may, of course, wish to continue with more stringent criticism of the work and its limitations, but we should reverence the life that we find within it. It is possible to identify and condemn the dehumanizing, the deadening, the evil within any civilization or literary work of man, and still to recognize that, insofar as each truly "exists," the work and the will of God live within it.

However historical our interests, we are inevitably concerned with the life and the literature of our own time. But when, as consciously Christian scholars, we attempt to deal with the literature of the modern period (and 1789 may be considered a convenient date for the beginning of the "modern"), we are forced to recognize the fact that many of the most talented writers have been either extremely vague about religious issues or have been consciously non-Christian or anti-Christian. In our desire to show the relevance of Christianity today, we must be careful that we distort neither Christianity nor the specific literary works. However fashionable, or even artistically successful, a work may be, we should not pretend to like it or understand it unless we really do so; and we should not fool ourselves into thinking that all of our responses or "likings" are inevitably religious or Christian. (The parish sermon in the form of a review and "religious analysis" of the latest sensational book or play is likely to confuse the parishioners and to provide additional evidence of bad faith—or intellectual naïveté—to the unbelieving.) As Christian scholars we believe that we have apprehended some values deeper than fashion and deeper than some vague consensus of "the modern." We betray them if we approve of works merely because we know that the authors may be, privately, Christians; and we betray them if we try to present popular non-Christian works as "essentially Christian" merely because we want Christianity, too, to be popular.

3

With a literary work from the modern (as from any other) period, we must first work at understanding. For scholars, such an attempt will probably eventually involve an effort to determine the relationships between the work and the aims and beliefs of the writer. Such relationships are difficult (sometimes almost impossible) to be sure about. Very few writers, Christian or non-Christian, are always conscious of philosophical or religious commitments; if they were, they would probably be formal philosophers or theologians instead of writers of poetry or drama or verse. The only claim that many lyrics make, for example, is that they represent possible and believable ways for fictitious individuals, in specific situations at single moments, to act or feel or respond. But the larger works of major writers do reflect something of a world view. It may be that the full understanding of a significant work by a consciously non-Christian artist will be easier for a scholar who shares something of the writer's general views than for a Christian scholar— just as it is probable that an informed Christian reader can gain a quicker insight into Dante or Milton than an equally informed non-Christian can. But, with patient labor and imagination, it is surely possible for each to understand what is, to some extent, alien to his own experience and belief. It is only after a careful attempt at understanding—after an effort to enter the world of the writer and to "feel" what it would be like to be, in the imaginative situation, a naturalist, an idealist, an atheist existentialist, or whatever—that the scholar may proceed to an attempt at evaluation. Only then the Christian scholar may, if he wishes, show how the particular work fits into the Christian scheme of things, how it may exemplify one or another of the Christian insights or experiences, how the conscious philosophy of the writer may not be so alien to Christian values as the author himself assumes. The scholar may find it necessary or desirable to point out the limitations of the work, or of the author's position; but if he has responded to an authentic imaginative creation, he will probably discover that the shared values are more important than the differences. Authentic human insights are not confined to Christians; certain traditional Christian insights and experiences have in our time been given their most impressive literary form by writers who would reject the name of Christian.

A few modern writers may be fully Christian without knowing it

(Edwin Muir's late discovery comes to mind)—but such an observation takes us quickly into perilous realms of conjecture and judgment. We should respect the serious intellectual formulations of serious men. Still, it is possible to wonder whether certain false notions about the nature of Christianity may not, occasionally, have something to do with individual rejections. Some serious writers today may reject the idea of Christianity because they associate it with fundamentalism, or with the authoritarianism or the lethargy or the simple mindlessness of some of the churches; or because they identify it with an insensitive and oppressive social "establishment"; not merely because they cannot imagine or believe in a providential God. A few may even reject Christianity because they think it fully mirrored by some contemporary "religious" literature and art and criticism. If to some observers of the recent literary scene, Christianity has seemed a desperate stratagem of retreat, associated with personal defeat, social hopelessness, and political reaction, that impression has not been wholly favorable for the encouragement of conversions. Certain modern works of literature may sometimes have given the impression that Original Sin was almost the only Christian doctrine. It is, as I understand it, a central and profound doctrine; but there are also the doctrines of the Incarnation, and Redemption, and Grace. We should, as Christians, never fail to remember the Crucifixion; but we must never forget the Resurrection. To think of Christianity as concerned only with suffering and death and the defeat of personal desires (as to think of a "modern world" totally without value) is to distort almost beyond recognition Christ's "Good News."

It is absurd, of course, to fuss at serious writers or to try to tell them what and how they should write. Significant writers at their best, I believe, write what they must, not what they may wish to—or think they wish to; from their experiences, not merely from their wills. When not quite at their best, they may, like other men, be too much influenced by fashionable conventions. (I have sometimes been amused to catch glimpses of how much certain prophets of gloom, both religious and secular, enjoy themselves and their friends privately.) But these are problems which the writers must largely work out for themselves. Preaching from the scholars and critics is usually irrelevant or worse.

But as scholars we are concerned with the continuing life of civilizations. As both scholars and teachers we must, occasionally at least, face the question of what would be worth doing and reading should we and our civilization suddenly die. We should see our students both as living parts of a continuing civilization and as the possible initiators of a civilization which may have to be created from very few fragments. Part of our duty as Christian scholars is to attempt to keep alive and potentially available certain obvious Christian insights: that life is, with all its sufferings and frustrations and inevitable physical death, good;

that there is a "Christian warfare," concerned with fulfilling rather than destroying life, and that it is worth fighting, however seemingly inevitable our unaided defeat; that heroism is possible, and that, in any society and at any time, it is likely to prove disturbing to the *status quo;* that we die a bit when we are indifferent either to truth or to the lives of those around us; that God is both Love and the Creator; that joy, however much attended with suffering, is a mark of the Christian life.

In our day by day work, however, most of these beliefs (and others) will probably emerge as implications. Unless we aspire to the role of preacher or philosopher or aesthetician, we do not usually need to make them obvious or to erect theoretical systems based upon them. We can afford simply to be "realists," or, to some extent, "empiricists"; and we can afford these roles with a better conscience than some of our colleagues because we are convinced that reality does have meaning, and that individual experiences and creations may have value—both apart from our observations of them or any scheme we may impose upon them. We do not have to "create our own worlds." As Christian scholars we must work as carefully and as sceptically as we can in order to discover and to communicate all the truths which we are capable of perceiving.

POSTSCRIPT: CHRISTIANITY AND ART

W. H. Auden

Art is compatible with polytheism and with Christianity, but not with philosophical materialism; science is compatible with philosophical materialism and with Christianity, but not with polytheism. No artist or scientist, however, can feel comfortable as a Christian; every artist who happens also to be a Christian wishes he could be a polytheist; every scientist in the same position that he could be a philosophical materialist. And with good reason. In a polytheist society, the artists are its theologians; in a materialist society, its theologians are the scientists. To a Christian, unfortunately, both art and science are secular activities, that is to say, small beer.

No artist, qua artist, can understand what is meant by *God is Love* or *Thou shalt love thy neighbor* because he doesn't care whether God and men are loving or unloving; no scientist, qua scientist, can understand what is meant because he doesn't care whether to-be-loving is a matter of choice or a matter of compulsion.

To the imagination, the sacred is self-evident. It is as meaningless to ask whether one believes or disbelieves in Aphrodite or Ares as to ask whether one believes in a character in a novel; one can only say that one finds them true or untrue to life. To believe in Aphrodite and Ares merely means that one believes that the poetic myths about them do justice to the forces of sex and aggression as human beings experience them in nature and their own lives. That is why it is possible for an archaeologist who digs up a statuette of a god or goddess to say with fair certainty what kind of divinity it represents.

Similarly, to the imagination, the godlike or heroic man is self-evident. He does extraordinary deeds that the ordinary man cannot do, or extraordinary things happen to him.

The Incarnation, the coming of Christ in the form of a servant who cannot be recognized by the eye of flesh and blood, but only by the eye of faith, puts an end to all claims of the imagination to be the faculty which decides what is truly sacred and what is profane. A pagan god can appear on earth in disguise but, so long as he wears his disguise, no man is expected to recognize him nor can. But Christ appears looking just like any other man, yet claims that He is the Way, the Truth and the Life, and that no man can come to God the Father except through Him. The contradiction between the profane appearance and the sacred assertion is impassible to the imagination.

It is impossible to represent Christ on the stage. If he is made dramatically interesting, he ceases to be Christ and turns into a Hercules or a Svengali. Nor is it really possible to represent him in the visual arts for, if he were visually recognizable, he would be a god of the pagan kind. The best the painter can do is to paint either the Bambino with the Madonna or the dead Christ on the cross, for every baby and every corpse seem to be both individual and universal, *the* baby, *the* corpse. But neither a baby nor a corpse can say *I am the Way*, etc.

To a Christian, the godlike man is not the hero who does extraordinary deeds, but the holy man, the saint, who does good deeds. But the gospel defines a good deed as one done in secret, hidden, so far as it is possible, even from the doer, and forbids private prayer and fasting in public. This means that art, which by its nature can only deal with what can and should be manifested, cannot portray a saint.

There can no more be a "Christian" art than there can be a Christian science or a Christian diet. There can only be a Christian spirit in which an artist, a scientist, works or does not work. A painting of the Crucifixion is not necessarily more Christian in spirit than a still life, and may very well be less.

I sometimes wonder if there is not something a bit questionable, from a Christian point of view, about all works of art which make overt Christian references. They seem to assert that there is such a thing as a Christian culture, which there cannot be. Culture is one of Caesar's things. One cannot help noticing that the great period of "religious" painting coincided with the period when the Church was a great temporal power.

The only kind of literature which has gospel authority is the parable, and parables are secular stories with no overt religious reference.

There are many hymns I like as one likes old song hits, because, for me, they have sentimental associations, but the only hymns I find poetically tolerable are either versified dogma or Biblical ballads.

Poems, like many of Donne's and Hopkins', which express a poet's personal feelings of religious devotion or penitence, make me uneasy. It is quite in order that a poet should write a sonnet expressing his devotion to Miss Smith because the poet, Miss Smith, and all his readers know perfectly well that, had he chanced to fall in love with Miss Jones instead, his feelings would be exactly the same. But if he writes a sonnet expressing his devotion to Christ, the important point, surely, is that his devotion is felt for Christ and not for, say, Buddha or Mahomet, and this point cannot be made in poetry; the Proper Name proves nothing. A penitential poem is even more questionable. A poet must intend his poem to be a good one, that is to say, an enduring object for other people to admire. Is there not something a little odd, to say the least, about making an admirable public object out of one's feelings of guilt and penitence before God?

A poet who calls himself a Christian cannot but feel uncomfortable when he realizes that the New Testament contains no verse (except in the apocryphal, and gnostic, *Acts of John*), only prose. As Rudolf Kassner has pointed out:

> The difficulty about the God-man for the poet lies in the Word being made Flesh. This means that reason and imagination are one. But does not Poetry, as such, live from there being a gulf between them?
>
> What gives us so clear a notion of this as metre, verse measures? In the magical-mythical world, metre was sacred, so was the strophe, the line, the words in the line, the letters. The poets were prophets.
>
> That the God-man did not write down his words himself or show the slightest concern that they should be written down in letters, brings us back to the Word made Flesh.
>
> Over against the metrical structures of the poets stand the Gospel parables in prose, over against magic a freedom which finds its limits within itself, is itself limit, over against poetic fiction (*Dichtung*), pointing to and interpreting fact (*Deutung*). (*Die Geburt Christi.*)

I hope there is an answer to this objection, but I don't know what it is.

The imagination is a natural human faculty and therefore retains the same character whatever a man believes. The only difference can be in the way that he interprets its data. At all times and in all places, certain objects, beings and events arouse in his imagination a feeling of sacred awe, while other objects, beings and events leave his imagination unmoved. But a Christian cannot say, as a polytheist can: "All before which my imagination feels sacred awe is sacred-in-itself, and all which leaves it unmoved is profane-in-itself." There are two possible interpretations a Christian can make, both of them, I believe, orthodox, but each leaning towards a heresy. Either he can say, leaning towards Neoplatonism: "That which arouses in me a feeling of sacred awe is a channel through which, to me as an individual and as a member of a certain culture, the sacred which I cannot perceive directly is revealed to me." Or he can say, leaning towards pantheism: "All objects, beings and events are sacred but, because of my individual and cultural limitations, my imagination can only recognize these ones." Speaking for myself, I would rather, if I must be a heretic, be condemned as a pantheist than as a Neoplatonist.

In our urbanized industrial society, nearly everything we see and hear is so aggressively ugly or emphatically banal that it is difficult for a modern artist, unless he can flee to the depths of the country and never open a newspaper, to prevent his imagination from acquiring a Manichaean cast, from *feeling*, whatever his religious convictions to the contrary, that the physical world is utterly profane or the abode of demons. However sternly he reminds himself that the material universe is the creation of God and found good by Him, his mind is haunted by images of physical disgust, cigarette butts in a half-finished sardine can, a toilet that won't flush, etc.

Still, things might be worse. If an artist can no longer put on sacred airs, he has gained his personal artistic liberty instead. So long as an activity is regarded as being of sacred importance, it is controlled by notions of orthodoxy. When art is sacred, not only are there orthodox subjects which every artist is expected to treat and unorthodox subjects which no artist may treat, but also orthodox styles of treatment which must not be violated. But, once art becomes a secular activity, every artist is free to treat whatever subject excites his imagination, and in any stylistic manner which he feels appropriate.

We cannot have any liberty without license to abuse it. The secularization of art enables the really gifted artist to develop his talents to the full; it also permits those with little or no talent to produce vast quantities of phony or vulgar trash. When one looks into the window of a store which sells devotional art objects, one can't help wishing the iconoclasts had won.

For artists, things may very well get worse and, in large areas of the world, already have.

So long as science regards itself as a secular activity, materialism is not a doctrine but a useful empirical hypothesis. A scientist, qua scientist, does not need, when investigating physical nature, to bother his head with ontological or teleological questions any more than an artist, qua artist, has to bother about what his feelings of sacred awe may ultimately signify.

As soon, however, as materialism comes to be regarded as sacred truth, the distinction between the things of God and the things of Caesar is re-abolished. But the world of sacred materialism is very different from the world of sacred polytheism. Under polytheism, everything in life was, ultimately, frivolous, so that the pagan world was a morally tolerant world—far too tolerant, for it tolerated many evils, like slavery and the exposure of infants, which should not be tolerated. It tolerated them, not because it did not know that they were evil, but because it did not believe that the gods were necessarily good. (No Greek, for example, ever defended slavery, as slave owners in the Southern States defended it, on the grounds that their slaves were happier as slaves than they would be as free-men. On the contrary, they argued that the slave must be subhuman because, otherwise, he would have killed himself rather than endure life as a slave.)

But, under religious materialism, everything in life is, ultimately, serious, and therefore subject to moral policing. It will not tolerate what it knows to be evil with a heartless shrug—that is how life is, always has been and always will be—but it will do something which the pagan world never did; it will do what it knows to be evil for a moral purpose, do it deliberately now so that good may come in the future.

Under religious materialism, the artist loses his personal artistic liberty again, but he does not recover his sacred importance, for now it is not artists who collectively decide what is sacred truth, but scientists, or rather the scientific politicians, who are responsible for keeping mankind in the true faith. Under them, an artist becomes a mere technician, an expert in effective expression, who is hired to express effectively what the scientific politician requires to be said.

II: RELIGIOUS BACKGROUNDS OF MODERN LITERATURE

THE NAME AND NATURE OF
OUR PERIOD-STYLE

Nathan A. Scott, Jr.

One of the characters in the late Richard Chase's brilliant dialogue, *The Democratic Vista*, gives me a kind of text for this first chapter when he remarks, "It seems that the greatest writers of the first half of the twentieth century lived in a high, tense world of strenuous and difficult metaphysics, moral doctrine, political ideology, and religious feeling."[1] The young man who says this is a graduate student of literature who, together with his wife and two children, is spending a late summer week-end on the Massachusetts coast in the home of a professor at his university, and it is to his senior friend that he offers his observation. He is perhaps being characteristic of his generation when he argues that "it is no longer possible to share" the intellectual and spiritual preoccupation of the great heroes of the modern tradition, of people like Eliot and Joyce and Pound. But though his foreclosure may be too narrow and too premature, he does identify accurately the most important distinguishing feature of the great classic tradition of modern letters, for that is most certainly a tradition that posits "a high, tense world of strenuous and difficult metaphysics . . . and religious feeling."

When we think, for example, of Mann and Lawrence and Kafka and Faulkner, it becomes immediately apparent, of course, that all of these writers cannot easily be sheltered under the same umbrella: their methods of practicing the arts of fiction and the various gestures they make toward reality represent enormous diversity and the amazing differentiation of attitude and language that is a chief hallmark of literary art in our period. But, despite this multifariousness of creative technique and fundamental point of view, they are writers whom we feel impelled to regard as constituting in some sense a genuine community and a unitary tradition. We take this view, I believe, because these are writers whose most emphatic insistence has been upon the fact of their being unsustained by any vital and helpful traditions: the commu-

---

[1] Richard Chase, *The Democratic Vista: A Dialogue on Life and Letters in Contemporary America* (Garden City, Doubleday, 1958), p. 16.

nity which they have formed has been rooted in their common awareness of their isolation. And this is an isolation which has not been primarily an affair of the artist's tenuous position in the polity of modern
society: to be sure, that has been something uncertain and problematic,
and the artist's social marginality has undoubtedly at times greatly
added to his unease; but what has most fundamentally given his life
the aspect of crisis has been that recession of faith and that erosion of
the religious terrain announced by Nietzsche in the nineteenth century,
and, in our own time, by Sartre.

In an age when all is in doubt and when, as Yeats says, "Things fall
apart" and "the center cannot hold," the philosopher may not be utterly
crippled if he is willing to have his vocation confined to the analysis of
nothing more than the structure of sentences; and the social critic can
always be kept busy in notating the tics and the spasms that are the signs
of our distress. In similar reduced ways the other custodians of cultural
life may in some manner continue to function when overtaken by a late
bad time. But when the traditional premises regarding the radical significance of things have collapsed and when, therefore, there is no longer
any robust common faith to orient the imaginative faculties of men with
respect to the ultimate mysteries of existence—when, in other words, the
basic presuppositions of a culture have become just yawning question
marks—then the literary artist is thrust upon a most desolate frontier
indeed. For, though his role is sometimes spoken of as though it involved
presiding over an act of *communication,* this is a vulgar version of it
which could pass muster only in an age of television and of what is
called the mass-audience. The writer may, to be sure, take his stand
before a microphone and speak to a crowd in whose fate he is not at all
implicated; and, when he does this, he may perhaps play a part in
something that might be called a process of communication. But, when
this is his position, surely it is impossible for anything to be "shared, in
a new and illuminating intensity of awareness," as Allen Tate has
reminded us. Indeed, the very concept of literature as communication
may well, in its currency, betoken a tragic victory of modern secularism
over the human spirit. "Our unexamined theory of literature as communication could not," he says,

> have appeared in an age in which communication was still possible for any
> appreciable majority of persons. The word communication presupposes the
> victory of the secularized society of means without ends. The poet, on
> the one hand, shouts to the public, on the other (some distance away),
> not the rediscovery of the common experience, but a certain pitch of
> sound to which the well-conditioned adrenals of humanity obligingly
> respond.[2]

No, says Mr. Tate, the language of communication may be the lan-

[2] Allen Tate, *The Forlorn Demon* (Chicago, Regnery, 1953), pp. 13, 12.

guage of radio and television; but the language which the artist seeks sensitively to supervise is the language not of communication but of *communion;* it is that language into which an effort has been made to put a deep and authentic knowledge of what is involved in the life together of free men, and it is, therefore, a language which invites us to reenter what Martin Buber calls "the world of *I* and *Thou.*"

This is, of course, to say that the language of imaginative literature is not the ethically and spiritually neutral jargon of any science: it is, rather, a language which, if it is to do its proper work, needs to be heavily weighted with the beliefs, sentiments, and valuations that are the deep source in a culture of its "hum and buzz of implication"[3] and that bind its people together with ties that separate them from the people of other cultures. Only when the artist's language bears this kind of freight can it be something more than a vehicle of communication. Only then can it become an instrument of communion and—what all art is ultimately intended to be—a servant of love.

We are now brought back to that desolate frontier on which I have said the modern writer has found himself, for what has made his position as an artist so insecure has been precisely the very great difficulty he has had in making contact with any significant body of belief that, having vital authority in our period, might furnish his imagination with the premises of its functioning and facilitate the transaction between himself and his reader. "In the profoundest human sense," said Kenneth Burke in one of his early books, "one communicates in a *weighted* vocabulary in which the weightings are shared by [one's] group as a whole."[4] But it is just at this point that modern culture has presented great privation. There is, in fact, little of profound significance that is widely shared by modern men. The dominant dispensation has, of course, been of a scientific character, but, as Max Planck once reminded us, "there is scarcely [even] a scientific axiom that is not now-a-days denied by somebody."[5] And, outside the realm of our scientific culture, the resistant pressure that has been offered to the relativizing tendencies of our time has been negligible indeed.

In his important book *Diagnosis of Our Time,* the late Karl Mannheim proposes the interesting and cogent hypothesis that the despiritualization of modern life is best understood in terms of the gradual evaporation in our period of authentic "paradigmatic experience" and of those great "primordial images or archetypes" which, being formed out of this kind of experience, have directed the human enterprise in the most genuinely

---

[3] Lionel Trilling, *The Liberal Imagination* (New York, Viking, 1950), p. 206.
[4] Quoted in Herbert Muller, *Modern Fiction* (New York, Funk and Wagnalls, 1937), p. 10.
[5] Quoted in Harry Slochower, *No Voice Is Wholly Lost* (New York, Creative Age, 1945), p. vii.

creative moments of cultural history. By the term paradigmatic experience, Mannheim refers to those "basic experiences which carry more weight than others, and which are unforgettable in comparison with others that are merely passing sensations." Without experiences of this kind, he says,

> no consistent conduct, no character formation and no real human co-existence and co-operation are possible. Without them our universe of discourse loses its articulation, conduct falls to pieces, and only disconnected bits of successful behaviour patterns and fragments of adjustment to an ever-changing environment remain.[6]

And his contention is that paradigmatic experience, insofar as it yields some conviction as to what is radically significant, also, in effect, yields a kind of "ontological hierarchy" in accordance with which we say, "This is bad, this is good, this is better." But, of course, the whole drive of the positivistically oriented secularism of modern culture has been towards such "a neutralization of that ontological hierarchy in the world of experience" as encourages the belief that one experience is as important as any other and that the question of right or wrong is merely one concerning the most efficient environmental adjustments. So the result has been the evaporation of those primordial images which objectify a people's faith and provide the moral imagination with its basic premises. And when there are no paradigmatic experiences, then nothing is any longer revealed as having decisive importance, and men are ruled, said Mannheim, by a kind of kaleidoscopic concept of life which, in giving equal significance to everything, does, in effect, attribute no radical significance to anything. In such an age, the individual is condemned to the awful prison of his own individuality, since nothing means the same thing to any broad segment of people—the primary fact about the human community is disclosed as being the complete collapse of anything resembling genuine community.

This is a fact which has been dramatized by much recent social criticism in its notation of the astonishing lack of drama in modern society. The life of the average megalopolitan today is ungraced by any rituals which strengthen the ties of sympathy and fellow-feeling that bind him to his neighbors. Nor is the civic scene complicated and enlivened by any round of celebrations and festivities comparable to the religious liturgies or the secular rites which figured so largely in the common life of earlier times. In the great cities of our day we are cave-dwellers, scurrying about the urban wilderness from one vast compound to another, like "bits of paper, whirled by the cold wind," says T. S. Eliot in "Burnt Norton." Like the members of Captain Ahab's crew, we are, in Melville's words, "nearly all Islanders," none "acknowledging the

---

[6] Karl Mannheim, *Diagnosis of Our Time* (New York, Oxford, 1944), pp. 146-48.

common continent of men, but each *Isolato* living on a separate continent of his own."

This, then, is the intractable and unpromising reality which the modern writer has been up against. Mr. Burke says that the artist's task is to supervise a weighted language whose weightings are shared by the commonalty. But it has been the fate of the modern artist to live in a time when the commonalty, as anything more than a statistical assemblage of unrelated atoms, is something remembered only by the historical imagination. And this is why the problem of understanding modern literature so largely involves the problem of understanding the stratagems that become inevitable for the artist when history commits him to the practice of his vocation in a vacuum of belief.

What the modern artist has most deeply needed are systems of value, appropriate to the experience of the age, in which his art could find a principle of order and unity. This is, indeed, what the artist has always needed; and, when the circumstances of his culture have afforded a good soil for art, the ethos of his community has provided him with coordinating analogies, key-metaphors, myths, and symbols which, in flowing out of the funded memories and experience of his people, could well serve him as instruments for the full evocation of the human communion. Surely it is no merely willful or sentimental nostalgia that leads us, when we roam back through the tradition, to account in these terms for the greatness of the achievement of Sophocles and Dante, of Shakespeare and Racine, or, on a far less exalted level, of, say, Madame de Lafayette or Jane Austen. In the older writers we feel a freedom and a security of reference that strike us as being a consequence of their having had the good fortune to live in cultures which, having a vital unity, could liberally provide them with those primordial images and archetypes which centralize and order the poetic imagination. These older writers were the lucky ones, for they did not have to invent for themselves ways of construing or making sense of experience: they were fortunate, because the writer who has to expend energy on philosophical and theological enterprises before he can get his literary project underway will have squandered reserves of imaginative power that, in more favorable circumstances, would be used up in the practice of his art. And when one thinks, say, of Jane Austen in relation to the woman of our own time who wrote such a book as *Nightwood*, we cannot help but feel that the older writer was more fortunate because, in receiving her ultimate terms of reference from her culture, she was relieved of any uncertainty about how to establish contact with her readers and was, therefore, enabled in her fundamental terms of speech to make the kinds of assumptions that facilitate the poetic transaction.

This is precisely the kind of good fortune that the writer in the modern period has not enjoyed. He has inherited no traditional and widely accepted frame of values from his culture. Before his art could be steadied by some executive principle of valuation, it has been necessary for the artist to try to construct some viable system of belief for himself by an effort of personal vision: he has had to become, in a sense, his own priest, his own guide, his own Vergil. He has been condemned by the cultural circumstances of his time to draw from himself everything that forms and orders his art. The waters in which he has swum have been the deep waters of his own mind into which he has descended to search for a clue to the principles by which the anarchy of experience might be controlled and given a shape and a significance. This is why it might be said that the reigning law of the modern movement in the arts has been that of the *principium individuationis*.

Indeed, much of the great literature of the modern period might be said to be a literature of metaphysical isolation, for the modern artist—and this is perhaps the fundamental truth about him—has experienced a great loneliness, the kind of loneliness known by the soul when, unaided by ministries either of Church or of culture, it undertakes the adventure of discovering the fundamental principles of meaning. And this is unquestionably the reason for the obscurity of so many great modern texts—of Rimbaud's *A Season in Hell*, of Rilke's *Duino Elegies*, of Joyce's *Finnegans Wake*, of Malcolm Lowry's *Under the Volcano*. For, amid the confusion of values of this age, the artist is attempting to invent a system of attitudes and beliefs that will give meaning to his world. And it is this idiosyncrasy, this extreme individuality, of modern poetic vision that has often made our finest literature so difficult to penetrate. What has been most distinctive of the great heroes of the modern tradition is, as Stephen Spender says, that they assumed the task "of re-experiencing everything as though it had never been experienced before, and then expressing it not in terms with which traditions and education have made us familiar but in new ones minted out"[7] of their separate sensibilities. In a time when

> *So various*
> *And multifoliate are our breeds of faith*
> *That we could furnish a herbarium*
> *With the American specimens alone*[8]

the writer has felt himself to be without a common background of reference by which his own imaginative faculties and those of his readers might be oriented and brought into profound rapport with one another. So he has turned inward, pursuing a system of values or beliefs in the world of his own subjectivity. The result is that "it becomes

---

[7] Stephen Spender, *The Creative Element* (London, Hamish Hamilton, 1953), p. 176.

[8] Karl Shapiro, *Essay on Rime* (New York, Reynal and Hitchcock, 1945), p. 63.

increasingly difficult for the reader to understand the significance of the writer's symbols and language, without his having experienced the process of the writer's experiencing. . . . Hence a vast literature explaining texts and the circumstances of each writer's life has grown up around the modern movement."[9] This development has tended to institutionalize the originally unique experimentations of the great modern pioneers and to make them, indeed, a staple of the new academic tradition—as is indicated, for example, by the statement on the jacket of William York Tindall's book, *James Joyce,* that Mr. Tindall "is a member of the James Joyce Society, and has made the pilgrimage of Dublin." Yet this is precisely what the appropriation of Joyce's work demands—membership in scholarly societies devoted to its study and foundation-sponsored tours to Dublin in search of scraps of information that may assist in unraveling the bafflements of Joyce's incredibly complex art. For this writer does in himself constitute a cosmos and a culture and a total mythology. And the necessity we confront, when we tackle a book like *Finnegans Wake,* is that of trying to make some coherent sense out of a vast chaotic array of notes toward what its author heroically strove to make the great modern novel.

Indeed, the Joycean experiment, however stillborn it may in part have been, does at least succeed in stating significant questions and in drawing attention to what has been a fundamental dilemma of the artist in our period. We may say the lesson of Joyce's career teaches us that, though the artist cannot by fiat produce adequate surrogates for traditions of faith and culture that are no longer available to him, he may, in attempting to do so, vividly dramatize what it is that makes his task difficult in the modern period. And that is what Joyce succeeded in doing. As T. S. Eliot put the issue in his famous review of *Ulysses* in 1923:

> In using the myth, in manipulating a continuous parallel between contemporaneity and antiquity, Mr. Joyce is pursuing a method which others must pursue after him. . . . It is simply a way of controlling, or ordering, of giving a shape and a significance to the immense panorama of futility and anarchy which is contemporary history.[10]

The radicalism of his effort to find this shape and this significance makes Joyce the great exemplar of the literary artist in the modern age: he gives the age away—he puts us in mind of how much "the greatest writers of the first half of the twentieth century lived in a high, tense world of strenuous and difficult metaphysics . . . and religious feeling." When we think not only of Joyce but also of Proust, Kafka, Lawrence, and Gide, we immediately remember how much these artists, amid the

---

[9] Spender, pp. 176-77.

[10] T. S. Eliot, "*Ulysses,* Order and Myth," in *Critiques and Essays on Modern Fiction,* ed. John V. Aldridge (New York, Ronald Press, 1952), p. 426.

disintegration and incoherence of our intellectual systems, in the quest for a viable body of beliefs or first principles expended energies that in a more fortunate age could have been directed into the labor of composition. These are all writers who, in various ways, were handicapped in not having been given by their culture an adequately objective framework of religious commitments and metaphysical beliefs. But these writers, like many other great artists of our period, are also notable by reason of the ardor with which they sought to compensate for this disability by religious and philosophic improvisations whose virtuosity is perhaps without previous parallel in literary history. Indeed, the real religious power and greatness we feel in the great classic tradition of modern literature is, I believe, a direct consequence of the immense courage with which the chief protagonists of this tradition have steered their lonely, separate courses through the spiritual void of our time.

Now it is precisely the extreme self-reliance in the quest for first principles that I have been positing as the inescapable necessity facing the modern writer—it is precisely this that makes evident his descendance from the great Romantics of the nineteenth century and also makes evident the fact that the literature of the age of Joyce and Kafka is essentially a late development of the Romantic movement. Here we must not be misled by the vigorous anti-Romanticism that informs so much of twentieth-century literature. It is true, of course, that men like Valéry and Eliot and Pound in poetry, and Joyce and Proust in the novel, have sponsored programs of one sort or another whose aim has been to encourage a rejection of the legacy of Romanticism—its inspirationist aesthetic, its cult of sincerity, its artlessness, and its confusions of art and religion. But, steady as this quarrel with the Romantic movement has been in our time, it is a family quarrel, and the fact remains that the great tradition of twentieth-century literature is, fundamentally, a product of the Romantic dispensation. Robert Langbaum has observed:

> Whatever the difference between the literary movements of the nineteenth and twentieth centuries, they are connected . . . by their response to the same wilderness. That wilderness is the legacy of the Enlightenment, of the scientific and critical effort of the Enlightenment which, in its desire to separate fact from the values of a crumbling tradition, separated fact from all values—bequeathing a world in which fact is measurable quantity while value is man-made and illusory. Such a world offers no objective verification for just the perceptions by which men live, perceptions of beauty, goodness, and spirit. It was as literature began in the latter eighteenth century to realize the dangerous implications of the scientific world-view that Romanticism was born. It was born anew in at least three generations thereafter as men of genius arrived intellectually at the dead-end of the eighteenth century and then, often through a total crisis of personality, broke intellectually into the nineteenth. As literature's reaction to the eighteenth century's scientific world-view, Romanticism

connects the literary movement of the nineteenth and twentieth centuries.[11]

This recognition of the havoc wrought by Enlightenment iconoclasm did not, in the great English Romantics, lead to an exacerbation of spirit so extreme as that which is often noticeable in their French and German contemporaries, but we can, nevertheless, detect the signs of this unrest in Coleridge and Wordsworth and in Keats and Shelley. They all make us feel that for them the traditional archetypes and systems of faith had ceased to be effective and that they, as a result, in their dealings with the world were thrown back upon their own private resources. They had all felt what Keats in "Lamia" called "the touch of cold philosophy," and they knew themselves, as a consequence, to be deprived of that mythical machinery for ordering experience which writers in earlier periods of the tradition had been blessed in having: they knew themselves to be fated by the logic of their culture to bear, alone and unassisted, what Wordsworth called "the weight of all this unintelligible world." So, in works like "Tintern Abbey," the "Immortality" ode, "The Rime of the Ancient Mariner," "Adonais," the "Ode to the West Wind," and the "Ode to a Nightingale," these men attempted to perform what Coleridge believed to be the poet's task "of spreading the tone, the *atmosphere,* and with it the depth and height of the ideal world around forms, incidents, and situations, of which, for the common view, customs had bedimmed all the lustre, had dried up the sparkle and the dew drops."[12]

When we turn, however, to continental Romanticism, particularly in France, and here not to such relatively early figures as Rousseau, Chateaubriand, and Lamartine but to such later writers of this Romantic tradition as Baudelaire, Rimbaud, and Lautréamont, then we leave the elegiac temper of the English school and come to a new kind of intensity and violence that point directly towards the *Angst*-ridden literature of the twentieth century. It was with this tradition in mind that the distinguished French critic Jacques Rivière remarked in his essay, "La Crise du concept de littérature," that "with Romanticism . . . the literary act began to be conceived as a kind of assault on the absolute, and its result as a revelation," the writer becoming a kind of priest. Indeed, said Rivière, this whole literature is "a vast incantation toward the miracle."[13] But not only does the artist working under the dispensation of Baudelaire and Lautréamont become a priest, he also becomes a kind of scientist: for, wanting to rescue himself from the metaphysical void of

---

[11] Robert Langbaum, *The Poetry of Experience* (New York, Random House, 1957), pp. 11-12.

[12] S. T. Coleridge, *Biographia Literaria*, ed. J. Shawcross (London, Oxford, 1907; Impression of 1954), 1, 59.

[13] Jacques Rivière, "La Crise du concept de littérature," *Nouvelle Revue Française* (Feb. 1, 1924).

his culture, he is so much in the grip of a great passion for knowledge
that the poetic process itself becomes not primarily a process of the
artist's *making* but rather a process of the artist's *discovering* the ultimate frontiers of human existence and of there staking out his claim
to dominion. Rimbaud, for example, in a letter to his friend, Paul
Demeny, says:

> The first study for a man who wants to be a poet is the knowledge of
> himself, entire. He looks for his soul, inspects it, learns it. As soon as he
> knows it, he cultivates it: it seems simple. . . . But the soul has to be made
> monstrous, that's the point. . . .
> One must, I say, be a *seer*, make oneself a *seer*.
> The poet makes himself a *seer* through a long, a prodigious and ra-
> tional disordering of *all* the senses. Every form of love, of suffering, of
> madness; he searches himself, he consumes all the poisons in him, keep-
> ing only their quintessences. Ineffable torture in which he will need all his
> faith and superhuman strength, the great criminal, the great sickman, the
> utterly damned, and the supreme Savant! For he arrives at the unknown!
> Since he has cultivated his soul—richer to begin with than any other! He
> arrives at the unknown: and even if, half crazed, in the end, he loses the
> understanding of his visions, he has seen them! Let him croak in his leap
> into these unutterable and innumerable things: there will come other hor-
> rible workers: they will begin at the horizons where he has succumbed.[14]

Here we have an inner dislocation which this particular poet called a
sacred disorder, but it is clear that what it really signified was his having
yielded to "an invasion of vertigo" and lost his footing. Therefore, it is
not surprising that he abandoned poetry in 1873 at the age of nineteen
to spend the rest of his brief life in exotic adventure and in angry
defiance of bourgeois Philistinism. But, despite Rimbaud's abdication
from literature, his prophecy was borne out, and other laborers did come
after him, "who began," as Jacques Maritain says, "at the horizons where
he had collapsed."[15] A horizon, of course, is the place where the extremes
of earth and sky meet, and the particular horizon where Rimbaud collapsed was the point at which his own desperate need, as an artist and
as a man, for metaphysical and religious order collided with the spiritual
void of the nineteenth century. And this is the precise horizon on which
we may locate that great modern procession that includes, in addition to
Baudelaire, Rimbaud, and Lautréamont, such earlier writers as Hölderlin, Leopardi, and Vigny as well as such later writers as Mallarmé,
Valéry, Joyce, Hart Crane, André Gide, André Malraux, St.-John Perse,
and many others. For all these, in the sense that I am claiming for the
term, are Romantics: that is, they are writers bent upon *improvising*
perspectives and principles in terms of which a shape and a significance

---

[14] Arthur Rimbaud, *Prose Poems from the Illuminations,* trans. Louise Varèse (New
York, New Directions, 1946), pp. xxvi-xxvii.
[15] Jacques Maritain, *Creative Intuition in Art and Poetry* (New York, Pantheon
Books, 1953), p. 186.

may be given to the immense panorama of modern experience, thus making it accessible to art. This is their passion and their chosen task; and such a dedication makes them candidates for the special kind of sainthood that the avant-garde has tended to produce in the modern period. That is, in a way they have been martyrized by the dislocations of the time, in having to bear upon their own souls the stigmata of the bent and broken world to which they were committed by modern history.

This, it seems to me, is the first major observation to be made about the great classic tradition of contemporary letters: we must say that in its tone and style and outlook it incorrigibly follows in the Romantic tradition. This is seen, for example, even in apparently so non-Romantic a figure as T. S. Eliot, who, to be sure, made his way back to a classical tradition of religious faith and found in Christian history the deepest inspiration for the work of his last thirty-five years. But the particular tradition of Christian faith in which Eliot chose to live—the tradition, say, of Origen and Dame Julian of Norwich and Jacob Boehme and St. John of the Cross—is hardly one which strikes us as belonging to the great central tradition of Christian culture: it is very special and irregular, and its reclamation by a contemporary Christian poet suggests that even his "orthodoxy" did, in its attainment, represent something of the improvisation that has tended generally to characterize the modern artist's philosophic and religious stratagems.

But, now, a second major specification must be made of the modern tradition in literature, for we shall not fully comprehend it until we recognize it as a tradition which represents that particular late development of the Romantic movement that comprises the whole experiment of Existentialism. Not only must we say that this is a Romantic literature: we must say that it is an Existentialist literature as well. Of course, when I denominate the central tradition in our literature as Existentialist, it must be apparent that I do not refer merely to certain recent writers, particularly in France, who have found a theoretical sanction for their vision in the doctrines of Existentialist philosophy. I use the term in a much broader sense and intend it to define the literature of the past hundred years in which we find reflected an experience of existence as fundamentally and, perhaps even, essentially problematic.

It will doubtless be our first impulse to regard this experience as having been occasioned by those ultimate exigencies in the history of the modern spirit to which Nietzsche called attention in his announcement of the death of God. But the death of God, as a cultural fact of the modern age, is itself something whose fundamental cause is to be sought in the "death of man" in our time, for this is the really primary fact in modern experience. What we confront, throughout the whole polity of modern society, is a tragic devitalization of the very concept of the person. That special sort of life en masse, so distinctive of our period, has been made possible by a system whose inner logic has necessitated a high degree of specialization in all fields of man's labor. And this, in turn, by a dreadful kind of inexorability has accomplished what might even be said to be a mutation in human nature itself, insofar as the habit of requiring a man to justify himself by his ability to perform a special task has weakened in us the capacity to make the crucial distinction between the function and the human being who performs it. Not only has the distinction become difficult to make but the human act by which a man transcends his various social and economic functions has, under the pressures of a commercialized culture, also become an act that it is increasingly more difficult to perform. Many of the most thoughtful observers of modern life have noticed how the logic of a technocratic culture reduces the concrete particularity of the unique individual to a purely abstract and functional identity; and they also have noticed the gray anonymity of life that this reduction accomplishes. What every reporter on the present human condition has, indeed, to take into account is the sense that men have today of being thrust into the nudity of their own isolated individual existence. Though "huddled together" in the great metropolises of the contemporary world "like dust in a heap," that which figures most prominently in their awareness is a sense of the world's vacancy, and the loss of which they are most acutely conscious is the loss of the real *proximity* of friends and neighbors. Life seems, Karl Jaspers says, to have grown "indefinitely vast"; it no longer has that "interlinkage" which holds it together, "so that it is not frittered away" and disintegrated into "the brief perspective of the [immediate] present."[16] A man has the function that he performs for eight hours a day, and he has his bit of breathing-space somewhere in the urban or the suburban wilderness. But, as we are told in one of the choruses in T. S. Eliot's *The Rock:*

> *The desert is squeezed in the tube-train next to you,*
> *The desert is in the heart of your brother.*

So, though all the time we live closer and closer together in our great urban compounds, we find it more and more difficult to recognize one another or even to retain a sense of our own identities. Amid this gray, dreary anonymity, we know that we live in a world from which all the gracious marks of "presence" have been banished.

"Just as primitive man believed himself to stand face to face with demons and believed that could he but know their names he would become their master," so too, says Karl Jaspers, contemporary man is faced by something that is "incomprehensible, which disorders his cal-

16 Karl Jaspers, *Man in the Modern Age*, trans. Eden and Cedar Paul (Garden City, Doubleday Anchor, 1957), pp. 209, 202, 210.

culations. . . . the nameless powers of Nothingness are, in our world whence the gods have been driven forth, the analogy of the demons that confronted primitive man."[17] I believe this is why men in the modern period have believed God to be silent and absent and even dead. This has been their conclusion, because they have not lived out their days in real nearness to one another; and, not having known the gracious reality of presence in their relations with their neighbors, their imaginations have been unable to grasp the possibility of the world itself being grounded in a transcendent Presence.

In a world where the human communion has been destroyed and man's condemnation is to an empty and unfertile solitude, what Gabriel Marcel calls *Présence*[18] appears to be, irretrievably, a thing of the past: not only does it appear that God is dead but also that an obituary notice is to be written that will memorialize the disappearance of man as well. In this "place of disaffection" (to use T. S. Eliot's phrase), the only available dispensation seems to be that of loneliness and exile. And the sober acceptance of this icy alienation as the inescapable ground of human existence constitutes that special modern sensibility which the Existentialist movement has brought most sharply into focus.

The "existentialist experience" is not, of course, the sole property of those contemporary theorists whose program goes under the name of Existentialism. Their nineteenth-century predecessors were, to be sure, among the first to give it emphatic definition. It first became a public fact in the Berlin lectures of Schelling (*Die Philosophie der Mythologie und der Offenbarung*) during the Winter of 1841-42, and in later writings of men like Kierkegaard and Marx and Feuerbach and Nietzsche and Max Weber. But the existentialist experience may also be dated from that morning when Baudelaire looked out upon the Paris landscape—"that vast cemetery that is called a great city"— and felt an immense disgust. We find it in such writers as Baudelaire, Rimbaud, Dostoievski, and Strindberg, and also in artists like Cézanne, Van Gogh, and the American, Albert Pinkham Ryder. These were all men who belonged to that nineteenth-century vanguard of revolutionaries who were distinguished by the clarity and courage with which they acknowledged the bitter facts of alienation and estrangement as the central facts of modern existence. And when, as Paul Tillich says in *The Courage to Be*, "the nineteenth century came to an end" on the thirty-first of July, 1914, the existentialist experience ceased to be the experience of a sensitive minority and became the dominant experience of the age. In this century it has furnished the perspectives of the philosophic tradition that has been established by such thinkers as Berdyaev, Chestov,

---

[17] *Ibid.*, p. 191.
[18] See Gabriel Marcel, *The Mystery of Being* (Chicago, Regnery, 1951), *1*, Chs. 9, 10 (trans. O. S. Fraser); *2*, Ch. 1 (trans. René Hogue).

Heidegger, Jaspers, Sartre, and Marcel; it is the experience that one feels in Stravinsky's *Petrouchka*, in Schoenberg's *Pierrot Lunaire*, in Alban Berg's *Wozzeck*, in Bartók's second *Quartet,* and in much of the great music of our time. It is also the experience that has been painted into many canvases of such classic moderns as Picasso and Rouault and the early de Chirico or of such recent artists as Willem de Kooning and Jackson Pollock and Hans Hofmann.

This strain of sensibility is central in much of twentieth-century literature: we recognize it in such poets as Rainer Maria Rilke, Hart Crane, Robert Penn Warren, and Gottfried Benn, and in such poets of the novel as Conrad, Kafka, Faulkner, and Malraux. Indeed, as Lionel Trilling has remarked, "There is scarcely a great writer of our own day who has not addressed himself to the ontological crisis, who has not conceived of life as a struggle to be—not to live, but to be."[19] What one feels to be formative in much representative literature of our period is the profound need for a deep restoration of confidence in the stoutness, reliability, and essential healthiness of the things of earth. The trauma that has been suffered is the trauma inflicted upon the imagination when it appears that both God and man are dead.

Thus the narrative at the center of our literature is a narrative of estrangement and alienation: the story told is a tale of our abandonment "in some blind lobby," "or corridor of Time." "And in that dark," says Robert Penn Warren, "no thread."[20] No thread! We are given some measure of how emphatic is the insistence upon our lostness by the apocalypticism and hyperesthesia of the modern literary imagination, "its feeling," as Richard Chase says, "that no thought is permissible except an extreme thought: that every idea must be directly emblematic of concentration camps, alienation, madness, hell," "that every word must bristle and explode with the magic potency of our plight."[21]

In our American tradition, the figure of William Dean Howells as a novelist has suffered a very considerable eclipse. We may be helped at least in part to understand the decline of his prestige by remembering the observation made many years ago by Henry James when he said of Howells, "He is animated by a love of the common, the immediate, the familiar, and the vulgar elements of life, and holds that in proportion as we move into the rare and strange we become vague and arbitrary."[22] And, when today we reread books like *The Rise and Fall of Silas Lapham* and *A Hazard of New Fortunes* and *A Modern Instance,* we realize that, with his customary acuteness, James put his finger exactly

---

[19] Lionel Trilling, *The Opposing Self* (New York, Viking, 1955), p. 140.

[20] Robert Penn Warren, *Brother to Dragons* (London, Eyre & Spottiswoode, 1953), p. 7.

[21] Richard Chase, "Christian Ideologue," in *The Nation* (April 8, 1950), p. 330.

[22] Henry James, *The American Essays* (New York, Vintage Books, 1956), p. 152.

on one of Howells' primary qualities. Thus it is not surprising that the contemporary reader finds it so difficult to enter into a happy and reciprocal relation with his work, for, as Mr. Trilling has reminded us, "We consent to the commonplace [only] as it verges upon and becomes the rare and the strange": we "want something that has affinity with the common, the immediate, the familiar," but "we like them represented in their extremity to serve as a sort of outer limit of the possibility of our daily lives, as a kind of mundane hell."[23]

All the great charismatic seers of modern literature from Baudelaire to Kafka and from Pirandello to Faulkner, in one way or another, have wanted us to understand that we are lost in a dark wood and that, in this maze, what is least trustworthy is the common, the immediate, the familiar. Therefore, the motion that the modern artist has very often performed before the revolving universe has been one of recoil. Sometimes, like Rimbaud, he has fallen in love with what Jacques Maritain calls "the blind glitter of nothingness" and made of his art a kind of incantatory magic. Or, like the author of *Finnegans Wake*, sometimes he himself has decided to be God and to create *ex nihilo* a universe of his own. On occasion, his retreat, like Mallarmé's, has been into *la poésie pure*—or, like the early Hemingway or the Dos Passos of the *U.S.A.* trilogy, it has been into the neutral factuality of naturalistic documentation. The recoil has also been expressed in the subjectivistic perspectives of a Proust or a Virginia Woolf, or as that distress which provokes the belch of disgust, say, in Jean-Paul Sartre's *La Nausée*. Various as the configurations are, it can, nevertheless, be said that many major literary artists of our time, whether they knew it or not, have had as their patron saint not St. Athanasius but Dionysius the Areopagite, for, in their dealings with the body of this world, their Way has been not the Way of Affirmation but the Way of Rejection. That is, they have not known the kind of confidence in the world and in temporal reality that was managed in happier moments in the literary tradition.

Those Roman Catholic apologists who explain this attrition in terms of the anti-sacramentalism of a Protestant ethos are doubtless right in part—but they are right only in part, for the authentic sacramentalism of Christian faith has also been obscured by what has often been the theological and cultural obscurantism of post-Tridentine Romanism. Nor can we forget the role that has been played in this development by the deep fears generated by the continual expansion of the universe being mapped out by modern science and modern cosmology. In the seventeenth century, Pascal was already conscious of the anxiety caused by contemplating "the infinite immensity of spaces" being revealed by the new science, and, in what is one of the great expressions of

---

[23] Trilling, *The Opposing Self*, p. 88.

modern consciousness, he said, "The eternal silence of these infinite spaces frightens me."[24] Of course, even far more frightening than the universes of modern physics have been the perils of modern historical existence itself which have tended increasingly to involve a global insecurity unexperienced in previous times. But by far the deepest cause of the despondency and sense of alienation in modern literature is to be found in the collapse of any real certainty that what is Radically and Ultimately Significant is not absolutely secluded from that which is only provisionally significant in nature and in history. To the men of our age, God seems, as Heidegger says, to be "withholding" Himself: he seems to be absent and perhaps even dead. As a consequence, our journey through the world seems to be a terribly uncertain and perilous journey: as Stanley Hopper puts it, "the familiar trails to reality are swallowed up in thickets of confusion: the spoors are thickly overlaid,"[25] and the artist's recoil before this dark and threatening wood is but type and example of the deep mistrust with which modern man faces today the indigence and privation of the world of finite, historical existence.

W. H. Auden tells us that Kafka bears to our own age the kind of relation that Dante bore to his, and, I am certain, a part of what he means is that, whereas the hero of Dante's poem is a pilgrim and the movement of the poem is from an initial darkness to a final light, the hero of the Kafkan fable, at the end of his journeying, is no nearer the Castle than he was at the beginning and remains forever quavering in the dungeon of his dereliction. In the one case, we have the Christian drama of rebirth and redemption; in the other, we have a story of the soul's exclusion from the Courts of the Most High and of the despair which overtakes the soul in its abandonment and isolation—the story, in other words, that embodies the characteristic judgment of the human condition that is rendered by the Existentialist imagination in modern literature.

Ours is, then, an "extreme" literature which plunges us into "extreme" situations. Conrad's Decoud, Kafka's K., Gide's Lafcadio, Malraux's Kyo, Faulkner's Joe Christmas, and Penn Warren's Jeremiah Beaumont are all men who have been cast into a world that offers no place of safety or security. Their lives have to be lived at a great distance from whatever are the sources of ultimate meaning, and, as a consequence, the salient stigmata of the modern hero are to be seen in his scepticism and in his despondency and alienation. However, the miracle that occurs in the existentialist universe of a Conrad or a Kafka or a Malraux or a

<hr/>

[24] Blaise Pascal, *Pensées*, trans. W. F. Trotter, Fragment 206 (New York, Dutton, 1943), p. 61.
[25] Stanley R. Hopper, "On the Naming of the Gods in Hölderlin and Rilke," in *Christianity and the Existentialists*, ed. Carl Michalson (New York, Scribner's, 1956), p. 156.

Faulkner is that, through the grace of some power that is unnamed and perhaps unknown, this scepticism and this despondency are prevented from so completely encircling the hero as to undo his humanity, so that he, in his great moments, has had what Tillich calls "the courage of despair"—the courage, despite everything problematic and uncertain in his world, to affirm his humanity. And since, despite all the nihilism in modern literature, this courage is an expression of a kind of faith— faith, as Dr. Tillich says, is simply "the state of being grasped by the power of being-itself"[26]—it is not surprising that the redefinition in our time of classical traditions of faith has often been deeply informed by this whole body of testimony. The Orthodox thinker Nicolas Berdyaev, the Roman Catholics Romano Guardini and Jacques Maritain, and the Protestant theologian Paul Tillich are representative of many other leading strategists of contemporary religious thought who have been alert to the fact that, if the high forms of faith are once again to appear at least *possible* for us, their reinterpretation must be informed by the kind of awareness that comes from facing the distresses of life without any of the supports and consolations of religious faith. And so, in the attentiveness with which the religious community today often listens to our poets and novelists and dramatists, we may discern some earnest of the reconstructive role that may yet be played by modern negation and denial.

---

[26] Paul Tillich, *The Courage To Be* (New Haven, Yale University Press), p. 172.

MODERN LITERATURE AND THE DEATH OF GOD

Charles I. Glicksberg

Have you heard of that madman who lit his lantern in bright daylight, ran into the marketplace, and cried continuously: "I am looking for God!" . . . Since many happened to be gathered about who did not believe in God there arose a great laughter. "Has he gone astray?" one asked. "Has he lost his way like a child?," said another. "Or is He hiding? Is He afraid of us?" "Has He boarded some boat, perhaps emigrated?" Thus the cries and laughter went. The madman leaped into their midst and pierced them with his eyes. "What has become of God?," he cried, "I will tell you! *We have murdered Him*, you and I. All of us are murderers. But how did we do it? How were we able to drink up the ocean? Who gave us the sponge to wipe out the horizon? What did we do when we unchained the earth from its sun? Whereto is it moving now? Whither are we moving? Away from every sun? Are we not continuously falling? And backwards, sidewards, forward to all sides? Is there still an up and down? Are we not wandering aimlessly through an infinite void? Does not an empty space breathe upon us? Has it not grown colder? Isn't night and always more night approaching? Must not lanterns be lighted in the forenoon? Do we as yet hear nothing of the gravediggers who are burying God? Do we as yet notice nothing of the divine decay?—Gods also decay! God is dead! God will remain dead! And we have killed Him! The most sacred and the most mighty that the world has hitherto possessed has bled to death from our knives—who will wipe his blood from us? With what waters can we be cleansed? What feasts of atonement, what sacred games will we have to invent? Is not the magnitude of this deed too much for us? Will we not ourselves have to turn into gods merely to seem worthy of it? There never was a greater deed—and whoever is born after us because of this will belong to a higher age than all history has been thus far!"
Friedrich Nietzsche, The Gay Science, quoted in Otto Manthey-Zorn, Dionysus: The Tragedy of Nietzsche. Amherst: Amherst College Press, 1956, p. 77.

The growing realization in the twentieth century that God is dead was bound to bring about a transformation in consciousness, sensibility, and ontological values more revolutionary than that which took place when Copernicus overthrew the Ptolemaic system or when Newtonian physics triumphed and the laws of Nature supplanted the laws of God. In the pre-Copernican view of the universe, man was accorded a central place; all the spheres revolved around the earth. What made this planet important was not the central position it occupied but the fact that it was inhabited by rational creatures whose destiny hung in the balance, that it was the object of Heavenly solicitude. God might dwell in solitary and self-sufficient splendor up above, but he was not unmindful of man and his affairs. But the astronomical systems of Copernicus and Kepler pushed back the boundaries of the medieval universe so that the physical universe was infinite in space, infinite in the number of solar systems it contained. In the light of these discoveries Christian theology would in some of its details have to be revised and brought up to date.[1] And now the twentieth century ushered in an age which acknowledged the death of the God of Abraham, Isaac, and Jacob, the end of the moving myth of the Incarnation and Redemption.

Without the presence of God, even if only immanent in the heart of creation, without the horizon of the absolute, the dimension of the eternal, the writer beholds a world no longer held together and transfigured by the sense of the divine. It is changed, alas, into a bare, alien, desolate universe of sense data and quantum mechanics. By eliminating the realm of the supernatural, science intensified the perception of the absurd. For the image of Nature red in tooth and claw that nineteenth-century biological science projected was utterly indifferent to the passion of subjectivity, the inveterate human longing for immortality, the desire of man to become like God. With the relentless logic of a Kirillov, Michael Bakunin, the Russian anarchist, argued in *God and the State* that if God exists, then man is deprived of freedom. But man must be free and he has the power to win his freedom; "then, God does not exist."[2] Yet the syllogism, though it serves to make man free, thrusts upon him a burden of responsibility that is the source of his intense existential anguish. It is this counterpointed theme of Promethean defiance and Sisyphean torment that we shall attempt to analyze as it makes itself felt in the literature, chiefly, of the twentieth century.

Man is free to choose, but of what importance is the choice he finally makes in a world infected with absurdity? Nietzsche had taken pride in his role as the murderer of God, but his blasphemous rejoicing could not dispel the terror of the infinite. How would humankind bear up under the inevitable and always imminent threat of death now that it had been deprived of the promise of salvation? If God is dead and the old supernatural sanctions are but superstitious myths of the infancy of the race, then there is no transcendent goal toward which mankind must move and no answer which the mind can provide for its metaphysical questioning. Henceforth godless man, despite all his soul-searching and

[1] Arthur O. Lovejoy, *The Great Chain of Being*. Cambridge: Harvard University Press, 1948, pp. 102-108.
[2] Michael Bakunin, *God and the State*. New York: Mother Earth Publishing Association, n. d., p. 25.

desperate conflicts of conscience, could discover neither meaning nor purpose in Nature. As Theodore Dreiser confesses:

> As I see him, the unutterably infinitesimal individual weaves among the mysteries a floss-like and wholly meaningless course—if course it be. In short, I catch no meaning from all I have seen, and pass quite as I came, confused and dismayed.[3]

Having caught a glimpse of the night of nothingness which swallows up all human ideals and aspirations, Nietzsche, the forerunner of modern consciousness, sought to view life and the world as an aesthetic spectacle that required no further justification. In *The Birth of Tragedy*, as we shall see in a subsequent chapter, he exalts the rebel who recognizes only aesthetic values, and his Dionysian cry of abandonment won him a host of disciples. There was, he saw, no goal for humanity, no cosmic support for moral aspirations. Men must chart their own course and create their own gods, so that they may be led to believe in god. Men are in need of sustaining illusions. Truth is but a means to a desirable end. With an élan of fanaticism that was "religious" in its ultimate concern, even though this took the form of a radical negativity, he pursued the quest for meaning without the benefit of the divine. This was the mark of his extraordinary courage as an existential thinker: he was resolved to find out whether values could be affirmed without dependence on God. If he celebrated the Greeks and their capacity for giving birth to tragedy, it was because they possessed the moral strength to look horror in the face and still say yes to life.

The modern writer, distrusting like Nietzsche the validity of the truth his intelligence wrests from the mysterious universe, resigns himself with a bad grace to a purely aesthetic resolution of the problem of existence. He begins to doubt, too, the value of his dedication to art. For he has come to feel that he has lost the tragic sense of life. His metaphysical passion has become self-conscious, critical, and destructive as it fights in vain the fatality of the myth of nothingness. But, as Kierkegaard declared more than a century ago, "when the age loses the tragic it gains despair. There lies a sadness and a healing power in the tragic, which one truly should not despise...."[4]

Dostoevski had faced the same problem but after his encounter with death before a firing squad, the execution that was called off at the last moment, and his period of exile in "the house of the dead" in Siberia, he came to the conviction that nihilism represented the greatest menace to mankind. It had to be combated, and the fiction he produced is the testament of his struggle against the demonic, the plague of the

---

[3] Theodore Dreiser, "What I Believe," *The Forum*, LXXXII (November 1929), p. 320.

[4] Sören Kierkegaard, *Either/Or*. Translated by David F. Swenson and Lillian Marvin Swenson. Princeton: Princeton University Press, 1946, I, 118.

meaningless, the curse of dwelling in a universe that is without the light of God. He was too honest and too profound a novelist not to reveal "the truth" that supported the Devil's argument; he knew in his own mind and flesh and conscience the singular force of the temptation that resides in nihilism. Dostoevski and Kierkegaard as opposed to Nietzsche — these are the vital figures in whose name the conflict is fought in the literary consciousness of the modern age. When Dostoevski prepared to compose a long novel entitled *Atheism,* later called *The Brothers Karamazov,* he decided — and that was, as we shall point out in a later section, characteristic of his method and the complexity of his tragic vision — to wade through a whole library of atheistic works. In his original conception of the novel, he had planned to present a character who suddenly loses his belief in God, a theme that would be thoroughly Russian in treatment. It would portray the disastrous effect this loss of faith has on the hero, but at the end he would find salvation in the Russian Savior and the Russian God. The fundamental idea of the novel, as Dostoevski explained in one of his letters, "is one that has tormented me, consciously and unconsciously, all my life long; it is the question of the existence of God."[5] That is why he chose a hero who would be an atheist. According to an apocryphal tradition in the family, Dostoevski pictured himself in the character of Ivan Karamazov.

Dostoevski's resolute struggle, on a conscious level, against the virulent disease of nihilism, availed him naught in the construction of this epic novel. Father Zossima is overshadowed by the figure of the Grand Inquisitor, Ivan is a more dynamic and compelling character than the saintly Alyosha, just as in *The Possessed* it is not Shatov, a tormented religious seeker, who chiefly engages our attention but Kirillov and Stavrogin. Pitting reason against life, Dostoevski in *Notes from the Underground* fiercely espoused the side of life. By refusing to accept the limitations of the rational, he preserved in his fiction the tensions that are basic to the tragic vision, so that, though he clung to the Christian faith which is beyond proof, no writer is more obsessed with the voice of the Tempter, the Devil who contemptuously denies all that the heart passionately affirms. Dostoevski is scrupulously faithful to the creative logic of his material and to the seductive power of atheism even when he portrays his nihilistic heroes as driven to the point of madness or suicide. One is reminded in this context of an entry Kierkegaard made in his *Journals* in 1837, when he was only twenty-four years old: "A man wishes to write a novel in which one of the charac-

---

[5] *Letters of Fyodor Michailovitch Dostoevsky to his Family and Friends.* Translated by Ethel Colburn Mayne. New York: The Macmillan Company, n.d., p. 190.

ters goes mad; while working on it he himself goes mad by degrees, and finishes it in the first person."[6]

The evangel of redemption from the tyranny of God that both Nietzsche and Bakunin sounded so challengingly brought man a freedom for which he was unprepared and which proved a curse rather than a blessing. A Kirillov was "mad" enough to kill himself as a means of proving that God did not exist, but the intellectuals had no desire to do away with themselves, though the theme of suicide plays a prominent part, as we intend to show, in the work of a number of twentieth-century writers. Freedom in a godless world was at first an exhilarating and then a truly frightening experience, but suicide was, after all, a futile, self-defeating gesture since it rendered impossible the human protest against the absurdity of existence. The modern hero was free, but for what earthly purpose would he use his freedom? Can the writer in our time give birth to a tragic literature that is not borne up by the passionately cherished hope of transcendence? On what grounds and with what justification can he continue to create in a universe that is unutterably absurd?

He has lost even the crusading passion that inflamed the nineteenth-century atheist in his war against what he considered the infamous lies of religion. No longer can he take up arms against the foe and dash off epics in the vein of *Prometheus Unbound,* envisioning a golden age of freedom to be established in the future in which all the man-made evils on earth would be abolished. Increasingly, in an age of crematoria and atomic extermination, he has had to surrender his faith not only in God but also in man. What was there, after all, to bind him in sacred solidarity to his kind, what moral obligation, what categorical imperative? Did not the Nazis act on the assumption that God was dead and therefore everything was permitted? Pity was weakness; the race was to the swift; Caesar reigned instead of Christ. But if the writer also lacked this vital faith in man and the ultimate meaning of life which man embodied, how could he fulfill himself creatively? The source of his spontaneity and productivity dried up. In the name of what ideal was the literary enterprise to be undertaken? What truth is he seeking to justify in his modern version of *Paradise Lost?* It was as absurd to go on writing as it was to go on living.

Sartrean Existentialism is a philosophy dedicated to the proposition that man is doomed but not damned. The distinction is important. If man were damned he would be suffering from a sense of guilt, and thus there would be ideals to strive for, bliss to attain, just as hell, by the law of polarity, presupposes the existence of heaven. Sartre puts an end to all such illusions. There is neither heaven nor hell, neither

---

[6] *The Journals of Sören Kierkegaard.* Translated by Alexander Dru. London and New York: Oxford University Press, 1927, p. 16.

sin nor guilt, neither God nor Devil. Man is doomed in a universe that is indifferent to his needs. Once the gods created him they ceased to have power over him. The one thing neither God nor Nature can take away from him is this freedom of choice, and if man exercises that freedom he need not be tormented any longer by the furies of remorse. His doom constitutes his tragic grandeur. Alone of all living creatures he knows his end and can face it with fortitude. Existentialism, like Dada but on a higher plane, expresses the spiritually orphaned state of modern man, his incapacity to make any meaningful affirmation.

Existentialism has drawn the necessary conclusion: if God is dead, then the moral laws that man had hitherto obeyed unquestioningly must be abandoned. Man shapes his own values and must depend on his own resources. Heidegger had formulated a metaphysic which showed how man could escape the coils of inauthentic existence by taking on his own shoulders the burden of responsibility for his destiny, and that meant freely acknowledging the terminus of death toward which he is inexorably driven. Out of this awareness of the contingency of existence, his final indenture to death, springs the overwhelming feeling of "dread." Caught in the trap of time, man reaches out eagerly to the future, fleeing from nothingness and yet rushing headlong toward the death that is nothingness. Heidegger's philosophy, oriented toward atheism, is congenial to those people who find it impossible to believe in God. Man must face his loneliness in the universe and the prospect of annihilation, without the narcotic comforts of religion.

This is the condition of alienation and revolt André Gorz, a disciple of Sartre, describes so poignantly in *The Traitor*. Here is a confession which, as Sartre points out in his foreword, is not concerned about the requirements of art but interested solely in exposing the nothingness in which the self is hopelessly situated. Gorz wrote in order "to get rid of his existence."[7] Once he decided to stay alive, he had to find a meaning for his life, but what could that be? His life, he concluded, could have only one meaning, "that of not having any. When you cannot keep from crying out though you know you will not be heard, you may as well decide that this cry which has no meaning has a meaning insofar as it has none—that it is in itself its own absurd meaning."[8] Finding that life has no meaning for him, Gorz is actually writing about the non-meaning of life, trying to demonstrate "that all roads are blocked save this one—this demonstration itself, and the remedy it provides against the experience it contradicts."[9] Logic defeats itself: if nothing is of any importance, "then the consciousness that nothing has any im-

[7] André Gorz, *The Traitor*. Translated by Richard Howard. New York: Simon and Schuster, 1959, p. 184.

[8] *Ibid.*, p. 188.

[9] *Ibid.*, pp. 37-38.

portance, has no importance."[10] Here, then, is a literature which, like
the fiction and the plays of Samuel Beckett, is dedicated to the God of
Nothingness. In composing this metaphysical soliloquy, *The Traitor,*
Gorz is seeking to objectify the absurdity of the universe, since he knew
that God, the universal, did not exist.

Though *The Traitor* ends on a note that glorifies the authenticity
of the work of art and sounds a spirited call for the creation of a new
and better world, this resolution, in view of all that has gone before, is
not particularly convincing. For the vast systems of social engineering
on which modern man centered his utopian hopes—Comtism, Marxism,
science—failed to materialize or, if they did, they failed to satisfy his
metaphysical longing. Science could not serve as a surrogate for the
death of God. Henceforth man would live not in the shadow of eternity
but in the confines of history. And how could creative man adjust himself to this loss of the Absolute? He did so at first by deifying Reason.
Now he is situated in the matrix of a culture that has thrown off the
myth of the supernatural. As André Malraux points out in *The Voices
of Silence:* "The art of living religion is not an insurance against death
but man's defence against the iron hand of destiny by means of a vast
communion. . . . Our culture is the first to have lost all sense of it, and it
has also lost its trust in Reason. . . ."[11] When man loses God, he is nailed
on a cross of despair from which he feels he will never be taken down.
Time will not redeem him nor history justify the passion of his existence. Once he sees himself as only a part of Nature and yet somehow
alien to it, he ceases to be "heroic."

Since he is no longer a son of God, he feels himself alienated in the
universe. The religious struggle of our time as it works itself out in the
context of literature, is essentially a struggle over the soul of man. Just
as the naturalistic interpretation of character as the product of the
combined forces of heredity and environment fails to do justice to man
in his subjectivity, his life of spirit and striving, so the social delineation
of character gives but a limited picture of his inner potentialities. For
there is in man a vertical as well as horizontal dynamism, an upward
reach of vision, an existential involvement in becoming, a craving not
to be denied for transcendence. But how can he possibly fulfill this
craving in a universe that has been stripped of the supernatural?
Nevertheless, this aspect of his being continues to haunt him and will
not let him go. Whatever science may disclose about the structure of
the physical world he still persists in his search for meaning; he will
not abandon his effort to know, if he can, the ultimate truth about
himself. Not satisfied with the limitations of his socioeconomic role

[10] *Ibid.,* p. 180.
[11] André Malraux, *The Voices of Silence.* Translated by Stuart Gilbert. New York:
Doubleday and Company, 1953, p. 496.

he engages, in ways peculiar to himself, in this defeated quest for a God in whom he does not believe. Dylan Thomas declared that his aim was to produce "poems in praise of God's world by a man who doesn't believe in God."[12]

In short, it is not God but God's world that is to be praised, whereas with Ivan Karamazov the situation was reversed: it was not God he rejected but the world he created, a world based on suffering and injustice. The decline of religion in our age has thus wrought a profound change in the creative vision of the writer. As T. S. Eliot, a poet and critic who is sensitively aware of these traumatic changes in the spiritual climate of the twentieth century, says in *On Poetry and Poets:*

> The trouble of the modern age is not merely the inability to believe certain things about God and man which our forefathers believed, but the inability to feel towards God and man as they did. A belief in which you no longer believe is something which to some extent you can still understand; but when religious feeling disappears, the words in which men have struggled to express it become meaningless.[13]

In this perceptive analysis of the spiritual dilemma of the modern writer, Eliot, a devoutly orthodox Anglo-Catholic, employs distinctions that are characteristic of this age of doubt: a belief in which one can no longer believe; a belief that can be grasped by the understanding but that is cut off from the deep sources of religious feeling; the desiccation of the precious symbols that were once spontaneous and universal carriers of meaning.

That is exactly what happened: the advance of atheism transformed not only the consciousness of the writer but also the language that is his medium of communication. He cannot simply liquidate God and accept the liberating gospel of scientific rationalism. He is not even a blasphemer, for he lacks the energy to *believe* in his disbelief; his denial of God does not culminate in a desire to elevate man to the vacated throne. Unlike Shelley, who was inspired by the Promethean myth, he cannot denounce Jupiter, the tyrant of the world; he cannot rejoice that the painted veil of life is torn aside and that the loathsome mask of religion has fallen; the intense inane that Shelley contemplated with such Platonic rapture has become the source of extreme spiritual despair, as modern man beholds the specter of nothingness.

There is the paradox that strikes an ambiguous note right at the start of our investigation, for the God over whose murdered body the Zarathustrian Nietzsche rejoiced is very much alive in the cultural tradition of Western Europe and the United States. There is the blind

---

[12] John Malcolm Brinnin, *Dylan Thomas in America.* Boston and Toronto: Little Brown and Company, 1955, p. 128.

[13] T. S. Eliot, *On Poetry and Poets.* New York: Farrar, Straus and Cudahy, 1957, p. 15.

alley in which a number of writers are caught. Like H. G. Wells, the apostle of redemption for mankind through the use of intelligence and the instrumentalities of science and technology, they have come to the realization that the world is at the end of its tether. If the race is to be saved from collective suicide, it is the heart of man that must be transformed, but how is that transformation to be effected? In the name of what transcendent principle? What moral order shall modern man affirm, what high purpose shall he strive to carry out, what faith is to sustain him in his quarrel with God and the universe? And if God is dead, then the problem of bringing the theme of transcendence with aesthetic "rightness" into the design of fiction or drama becomes stupendously complex. The resolution of the tragic conflict cannot be imposed from without, by resorting to some *deus ex machina*. Oppressed by the terrors of history, the contemporary hero cannot plunge out of time into the kingdom of eternity. All literature today which deals with the spiritual dimension (and how can it be left out?) must be a dialectical struggle between affirmation and denial, the divine and the human, the Absolute and Nothingness.

In contemporary fiction God often appears as a quality of blackness, a source of ontological emptiness. Whereas Camus, in *The Stranger*, delineates a new Ivan Karamazov, a "hero" who has abandoned all faith in the future, all belief in immortality or conventional moral values, Joyce's fiction is instinct with elements of blasphemy. Stephen Dedalus, the apostate who prefers to worship the truth rather than the divinity of Christ, forsakes Catholicism for the religion of art. For him the artist supplants the function of God; he "remains within or behind or beyond or above his handiwork, invisible, refined out of existence, indifferent, paring his fingernails."[14] The hero of *A Portrait of the Artist as a Young Man* has chosen to become an artist rather than a priest. Or if he remains a priest at heart, it is as "a priest of the eternal imagination, transmuting the daily bread of experience into the radiant body of everlasting life."[15] But even his aesthetic heresy is charged with the metaphor of the faith he has abandoned; the sacrament of the Eucharist still haunts his imagination. For he is still afraid of the unknown and esoteric symbols in which mankind in the past projected the image of God. He neither believes nor disbelieves in the Eucharist, and yet, as Cranly points out dispassionately, it is a curious thing how his mind is supersaturated with the religion in which he says he disbelieves.[16]

It is his integrity as an artist that Dedalus is resolved to maintain at

---

[14] James Joyce, *A Portrait of the Artist as a Young Man*. New York: The Modern Library, 1916, p. 252.

[15] *Ibid.*, p. 260.

[16] *Ibid.*, p. 282.

all costs. It is not the God of the Roman Catholic Church he fears if he were guilty of making a sacrilegious communion. "I fear more than that the chemical action which would be set up in my soul by a false homage to a symbol behind which are massed twenty centuries of authority and veneration."[17] He has no intention, of course, of becoming a Protestant. What kind of liberation would that be, he asks, to forsake "an absurdity which is logical and coherent and to embrace one which is illogical and incoherent?"[18] It is freedom he craves, and he is not afraid of making a mistake, even if he will suffer for it for the rest of eternity. Though he refuses to kneel in prayer at the bedside of his dying mother, Stephen Dedalus has not yet thrown off the Catholic faith in which he says he disbelieves.

In his debauchery at Bella Cohen's brothel, the ghost of his mother rises from the grave and urges him to repent. At first he is frightened, but his proud intellect asserts itself and he asks her to tell him the worst. Her pious rehearsal of the ancient orthodox formula of faith repels him. He will have no part of God. Here is the blasphemer whose cry is "*Non serviam!*"[19] He is determined not to be "saved," not to be shaken in spirit by the fear of death or the fear of hell. His positive act is not to yield to the power of institutionalized superstition or authority but to proceed always from the known to the unknown, to affirm himself as a conscious and therefore autonomous and sovereign being.

Camus's hero, Meursault, has gone much further than Stephen Dedalus; he is through with the spooks and goblins of theology, the abstractions born of the supernatural. There is only this life in the present, the eternal that is fulfilled in immediacy or not at all. In a secularized universe of the absurd, the only thing man can be sure of is his life now. Hence Meursault rejects all moral and spiritual absolutes; he will make no effort to justify his action in killing the Egyptian on the beach. He is sentenced to die not because of the murder he committed but because he displayed no sign of grief at the funeral of his mother. It is this evidence of perverse impiety which leads to his conviction. Meursault is the absurd man who is filled with amazement at the strange spectacle of life on earth.

Camus is nevertheless a "religious" writer[20] in his search for an authentically human faith. If he turned against the Christian mythos it was because, like Ivan Karamazov, he could not accept a God who permitted the innocent to suffer. Camus does not reject Christianity on intellectual grounds alone; he is not a fanatical rationalist. In his case,

---

[17] *Ibid.*, p. 287.
[18] *Ibid.*
[19] James Joyce, *Ulysses*. Paris: Shakespeare and Company, 1926, p. 545.
[20] See Charles I. Glicksberg, "Camus's Quest for God," in *Literature and Religion*. Dallas: Southern Methodist University Press, 1960, pp. 212-222.

it is not science that has conditioned man to give up his faith in the supernatural. "In fact," says Camus, "modern unbelief is no longer based on science as it was at the end of the last century. It denies the faith of science as much as that of religion."[21] Modern unbelief, he contends, has reached a point of passionate intensity. While this may be true of Camus, it is emphatically not true of the unbelieving generation of writers in our time. For them unbelief is not a passion but a metaphysical disease.

Even fiction that is avowedly naturalistic in content and method betrays this persistent concern with the numinous, with what lies behind the veil of appearances. In the twenties, *The Sun Also Rises*, the novel which became the testament of the lost generation, stresses Hemingway's obsession with time, the inexorable march of the years toward the bourne of death. Jake Barnes is filled with a sense of religious wonder but his capacity for responding to the experience as he feels he should is totally lacking. He cannot pray, and not because he feels particularly sinful. Neither his words nor his soul is able to soar, for his thoughts remain below. When he tries to pray, all sorts of irrelevant associations thrust themselves into consciousness. He prays for his friends, for himself, for the bullfights and the fiesta, but all he can say about Catholicism is "that anyway it was a grand religion, and I only wished I felt religious. . . ."[22] The wish is enough to indicate that this Catholic hero with the wound that incapacitates him for the act of love, has lost his religious feeling.

The motif of alienation from God comes through clearly and consistently developed in *A Farewell to Arms*. When Lieutenant Henry is wounded, he makes no religious appeal. When the priest comes to visit him in the hospital, they talk about God. The priest declares that in his country it is understood that a man may love God. The Lieutenant replies: "I don't love."[23] Though the hero respects the religious issue as a species of illusion, it is very much alive in his consciousness. He is tormented by the fears that come surging forth in the dark of night, the progression of time, the terror of death. These are the matters of ultimate concern that are touched upon, in characteristic Hemingway style, by indirection.

These examples furnish incidental evidence of the collapse of the Absolute in the twentieth century. Western man, alone in the universe, has to face the knowledge, the pain of which is not to be eased by any metaphysical or mystical doctrine of transcendence, that he is doomed

---

[21] Quoted in Philip Thody, *Albert Camus*. London: Hamish Hamilton, 1957, p. 140.

[22] Ernest Hemingway, *The Sun Also Rises*. New York: The Modern Library, 1926, p. 100.

[23] Ernest Hemingway, *A Farewell to Arms*. New York: The Modern Library, 1929, p. 76.

to die. Not even the gods can save him from this fatality. Under Christian as well as secular and scientific auspices, this is the mortal element in his being that drives him to seek avenues of escape, and the art he produces is one expression of his revolt against this iron hand of destiny.

Through the long centuries of civilization man has struggled to wrest from chaos and render imperishable those images which will affirm his dignity and worth as a human being and bear witness to his grandeur. That is how, through the mediation of art, he makes the repeated effort, gallant even if abortive, to rise above the indignity of death. His work will at least outlive the envious erosion of time. Even in the face of death he keeps faith with his creative mission and composes a message that will reach down to posterity and pierce to the heart of the mystery that is life.

The realization that God was dead, as this book will try to demonstrate, meant more than the relinquishment, however painful, of a life-sustaining concept. In the past religious belief had entered actively and fairly completely into the process of shaping the forms of life. What was taken away from twentieth-century man as he absorbed the lessons taught by such sciences as geology, biology, astronomy, and anthropology, was not an abstraction, *an idea* of the divine; his whole universe of consciousness was transformed, and henceforth his vision of life on earth would be drastically altered. From the moment he ceased to believe in the miracle of the Incarnation and the equally necessary myth of the Resurrection he could expect no privileged treatment, no special dispensation; he knew at last that he was at the mercy of natural forces that had no concern whatsoever for his anthropomorphic illusions.

Alone in the time-space continuum he knows now of a certainty that none of his subjective wishes can ever influence the course of events. He is a part of Nature, and yet Nature is indifferent to his moods and cravings, not caring which species survived in the furious struggle for existence. Unlike the animal, however, he is a victim of time, sensible of the passage of the years and, cut off forever from the divine source, aware of the nothingness of the grave. And the writers of today are afflicted with this metaphysical nausea. God is, as in *Waiting for Godot*, a shadow of desire, an empty word, a promise of hope that will never be kept. Nevertheless, modern writers, even as they repudiate God, wrestle with the religious problem, but the image of God they invoke is compounded of negation. Or else they indulge, like Joyce, in the dialectics of blasphemy. In either event, what they give utterance to is the desolateness of the despair they feel in a world abandoned by God. God is dead but the "religious" impulse persists: the quest for the Transcendent that is beyond all reason and beyond all proof. Not that the figure of God ever enters constitutively into the body of literature. Since God remains invisible and unknowable, the writer must of necessity confine himself to the universe of the human, the realm of the sensuous, the temporal, the finite.

Nevertheless, the knowledge of the absence of God makes a tremendous difference in the way a writer responds to the challenge of existence and interprets the nature of man. As Paul Tillich cogently states the problem: "Whatever the subject matter which an artist chooses, however strong or weak his artistic form, he cannot help but betray by his style his own ultimate concern, as well as that of his group, and his period. He cannot escape religion even if he rejects religion, for religion is that state of being ultimately concerned. And in every style the ultimate concern of a human group is manifest."[24] If this interpretation is correct, then religion, the state of being ultimately concerned, pervades every sphere of experience and expression. Even negative reflections of life, the outcropping of the demonic, are essentially religious in their confrontation of reality. All that matters is the degree of courage and honesty with which the writer faces the mighty challenge of being. "He who can bear and express meaninglessness," according to Tillich, "shows that he experiences meaning within his desert of meaninglessness."[25] Tillich and André Gorz, though they begin with radically different premises, arrive at substantially the same conclusion.

This is the challenge to which modern man must somehow respond: how to bear and express meaninglessness in a universe that seemingly functions efficiently as a machine, without the presence of God. He confronts a cosmos which appears to be inexplicably absurd, and how shall he make his peace with the myth of absurdity? He has given up the vain desire to merge with the Wholly Other, this futile nostalgia for the Absolute, but he cannot give up the quest for identity. As man conceives of the world, so he conceives of himself. The equation is reversible: as he interprets himself and his relation to God, so in large measure he interprets the world.

---

[24] Paul Tillich, *Theology of Culture*. New York: Oxford University Press, 1959, p. 70.
[25] *Ibid.*, p. 75.

THREE IMAGES OF MAN

Edmund Fuller

Our time has been described variously as an age of anxiety, an age of schism in the soul, a time when man suffers not only from war, persecution, famine, and ruin but from inner problems fully as terrible: despair, a conviction of isolation, randomness, meaninglessness in his very existence. The despair, strangely, and the conviction of meaninglessness, appear to afflict him most not under condition of war, persecution, famine, and ruin but under circumstances of material prosperity and plenty.

There were times, in this century and the previous one, when the disintegration of society was a major theme of the writer. Today it is the disintegration of the individual creature himself—of man. There is no doubt that in much of our violent, distorted, degraded fiction a vast, pity-compelling pain and agony are reflected, but the reality of the torment or confusion from which these creations spring does not insure the reality of the images of life which they project. The pity, the compassion, we may feel for either the external or internal sources of these wretched portrayals of life cannot lead us to accept them as valid. Neither can the sincerity of emotion and idea, or the authentic artistic talent that may accompany them, lend validity to partial or distorted images of man and his life.

It is strange how many of the contemporary portrayals of man's suffering are loveless. In many of our novels man's plight and condition are viewed with a chilling detachment. The writers are standing back and looking on either morbidly or indifferently, without either involvement or intervention, after the manner of crowds on a city curb when an accident has happened.

Sometimes actual and active horror are present, sometimes the vestigial traces of a moral revulsion are seen. These are easily repressed, however, in the absence of an authentically responsive love for the human species. Much of the picture of man projected in our fiction is the obvious product of despairing self-hatred, extended from the individual self to the whole race of man, with its accompanying will to degradation and humiliation. It is a clinical condition.

It is obvious, natural, and valuable that the characteristic conditions of an era find reflection in its arts. But that generalization is not enough to explain the form or channels through which the reflection is projected. This chapter is concerned with a theory of origin, or root, for some of our most conspicuous literary symptoms. It is a necessary prologue, by way of definition, to the further examination of characteristics in current fiction with which the rest of the book is occupied.

In the channels .of criticism and review there is a good deal of talk, pro or con, about our novelists' preoccupation with despair, brutality, violence, sadism, degeneracy, or merely old-fashioned lust (which is almost considered naïve, now), but there have not been enough attempts to evaluate the precise sources or conditions out of which these strong streams in contemporary writing flow.

Our fiction, in the novels of some of its most touted practitioners, has made a distinct break with the great literary tradition, a break which scarcely has been noted amid the flurry of sales, suppressions, and awards. The question best calculated to place the writer of fiction in one or another of the camps of thought that are so numerous and at such odds today is "What is your view of man?" The answer will place a writer in one of two major folds which are distinct from one another, although within each of them there are numerous subdivisions or secondary categories.

This division which I am seeking to establish certainly has been discernible throughout the long history of human culture, but I think it has never existed on a more critical and decisive scale than in the last century, and especially the last half-century. This division is not clearly recognized in most contemporary criticism, yet I think it holds the key to the comprehension of many phenomena which perplex, pain, or offend the reader of modern fiction.

From some answers to the question "What is your view of man?" certainly come clues to the cults of violence, brutality, and sexuality, the moods of morbid self-hate, the ache of anxiety and the smothering conviction of isolation and meaninglessness. Man always is the subject of the storyteller, even when he pretends to be writing about imaginary beings or non-humans, as in animal fables, fairy tales, or science fiction. It is on the nature of man that the world stands divided, for it is out of conflicting views of man and the resultant implications as to how he may be dealt with that radical divisions of a political and economic order arise. On this question men are separated into factions involving politics, ideas, art, science, religion, or any other of the various areas in which we observe that man is divided against himself.

Fundamentally, notwithstanding all the other aspects involved, this is a religious division, for it simply is not possible to express a doctrine about the nature of man without a religious implication of one sort or another.

This world division, of course, does not line up on a simple pattern of countries arrayed against one another. Actually, it cuts across all other lines, and there are specific divisions about the nature of man within the United States, just as there is a general division on this subject between the United States and Russia.

One side of the great division, however subdivided as to creed, sect, or other special premise, holds a view of man that conforms to one expression or another of an unbroken tradition in Western man's history. The other side is singular in the fact that although now of great force and numbers, it takes a position which never before has been accepted as a conscious view by such large numbers of people, even though it has been held by individuals and groups here and there.

Inescapably our literature and other arts reflect these divisions about the nature of man, and where they are not understood, there is difficulty or bewilderment in appraising the reflections in fiction of these conflicts in the minds of men about themselves, their nature, their potentialities, their limitations, their origins, their objectives, and, perhaps above all, their obligations.

All fiction is a comment upon the life and nature of man—though not necessarily consciously so. It cannot help being such inasmuch as varying concepts and projections of the nature of man are the subject of all literature. The writer cannot be wholly coherent, as artist, unless he possesses a wholly coherent view of man to inform, illuminate, and integrate his work.

In other words, every man's novel may not have a *thesis*, but it must have a *premise*—whether declared or tacit, whether conscious or unconscious, it cannot help having a premise. That premise is susceptible to being found out even, as it were, over the author's dead body, and identification of the premise is essential to an evaluation of the work. Explicitly or implicitly, every novel reflects an opinion about the nature of man, even if the author hadn't known he had one.

With exceptions so rare as to be noteworthy, always representing some highly special phenomenon, the vast body of literature from the Hebrews and Homer down to the early part of the present century, or the latter part of the nineteenth century, has been based upon the tacit or declared premise that there is a God. Sometimes it has been gods—a whole pantheon—as in the pagan tradition. It may have been the God of the Jews, or the Trinitarian God of the Christians, or the Allah of Islam, or the gods of Asia, or those of the Teutons and the Nordics. But whatever, or wherever, or however—this vast, centuries-old accretion of our literary heritage is based on the premise that there is a God.

The attitudes of individual writers in relation to God have been infinitely various, even within Holy Scripture. He has been adored, revered, loved, feared, hated, denounced, defied, or denied in the special sense that is in itself religious. He may have been criticized, concepts of Him set at variance with other concepts, but the persistent concept of God dominates the great heritage of our culture.

The appearance of individual strains of thought tending to challenge the very existence of God goes back a long way. But such a challenge has not attempted to dominate an entire culture until quite recent times. Our present generations now practicing the art of fiction are the first generations in which there have been large, influential, and admired groups of novelists working, in many instances quite unconsciously, on the tacit or declared premise that there is no God, basing the patterns of their work on the implications, again often unconscious, that arise out of that premise.

Now how does this involve one's view of man? It is possible to forget that the question of whether or not there is a God, with further questions of man's possible relationship with Him, carry incalculable implications about the nature of man and the condition of his life. Also, the writer who does not believe in God, or is indifferent to the question of His existence, may subscribe to the classic Western tradition of man without reflecting upon the premise which is the foundation of this conception. More seriously, the writer who has dismissed or overlooked the relationship between man and God, may find himself projecting an image of the human creature drastically at variance with Western tradition, while either conscious or unconscious that the altered image is the consequence of an altered premise.

In both the Judeo-Christian and Hellenic traditions there is a basic view of man which for all the religiously crucial differences of creed involved still can be reduced to certain premises common to these traditions. In effect, in Western culture they have fused into one tradition.

Within this Western historical-literary tradition, then, man is seen as, or tacitly understood to be, a created being, with an actual or potential relationship to his Creator. Each man is a unique person. Man is seen as inherently imperfect, but with immense possibilities for redemption and reconciliation with his Creator. On the one hand, he is not able to perfect himself through his own works, and the theme of tragedy frequently is his fall through pride in attempting to do so. On the other hand, he is never deterministically fixed in any one state or condition—a point which sufficiently deep reading will substantiate even within the concept of Fate in Greek tragedy. Man is not portrayed as *either* good *or* bad, but as *both* good *and* bad. He inhabits an orderly universe. His fundamental moral laws are commands of his Creator, not just social contracts between himself and his fellows; they are fixed obligations to his God. Thus man, so seen within this vast, varied, but basically consistent tradition, is individual, responsible, guilty, redeemable. Happily, some of the best novels of today still are being written within this great tradition and view of man.

By contrast, we began to find in the last part of the nineteenth century, and then in our own, in great quantity with considerable weight of prestige attached to it, a type of novel the counterpart of which is not to be found, in any significant numbers, earlier than late nineteenth century. It is the work, in many instances, of writers who do not know the implications of what they have written, who are not the architects of their own idea-structures, who are not consciously the mouthpieces of the thesis to which their work is linked.

I speak of the novel of MAN—in capital letters. It is based on the concept of man as a being who is any or all of the following: biologically accidental, self-sufficient, inherently good, ever-progressing, self-perfectible, morally answerable only to his social contracts. He inhabits a morally neutral universe created by random forces. You should recognize this man, for he walks through the pages of many twentieth-century novels and plays. Shaw and Wells were among those who got the movement started. In the most advanced cases, again with some still current, man is identified with God Himself—either collectively in a pantheism, or in the Shavian-Bergsonian view of an emergent, creative-evolutionary God, in whose development man is the growing tip.

But this view already is obsolete and now is overshadowed by a corollary, or reverse face of the same coin. The last twenty-five years have not been kind to the "better-and-better," inherently good, self-sufficient, emergent-God concepts of man. These have been hard-pushed, even though they are persistent. But some wings of their adherents have broken and given ground. When that optimistic concept of self-generating and progressing man becomes disillusioned or gives way to despair, often an ugly and sinister image emerges which is recognizably from the same root.

From this disillusionment we get that terrible spate of novels now current in which man is seen specifically and insistently as an ironic biological accident, inadequate, aimless, meaningless, isolated, inherently evil, thwarted, self-corrupting, morally answerable to no one, clasped in the vise of determinisms economic or biological. His uniqueness as a person is denied or suppressed. He inhabits a hostile universe which is the creation of irrational and possibly malignant forces. The themes of these novels, to borrow some words from Lewis Carroll, are *ambition, distraction, uglification,* and *derision.* Unlike the great tradition of man as individual, responsible, guilty, but redeemable, this despairing disillusionment sees man as collective, irresponsible, morally neuter, and beyond help.

This creature is substantially *less* than true man, *less* than a person. A prime example, Meursault, in Camus' *The Stranger*, is essentially subhuman, whether Camus conceives him as inherently such, or as reduced to such. The same can be said of Nelson Algren's Dove Linkhorn, in *A Walk on the Wild Side*, and a host of figures in other recent American novels.

James Jones' second novel, *Some Came Running*, is characteristic of those that offer us the Yahoo as social arbiter. When Swift created his Yahoos he loathed them as a projection of the subhuman in man. Jones creates Yahoos and has an abiding tenderness for them. One of them he passes off as the type of the artist-writer. His Dave Hirsh, vulgar, often sullen, lecherous, semi-literate as presented to us although supposed to be sensitive and gifted to the point of near genius, is a specimen of the Yahoo-hero of the tough novelists. This person's values, credos, standards, and tastes are generalized into those of the writer in the abstract. His are the social and human-value judgments in which this novel and so many like it see the world. He is moderator of the Jonesian Forum.

Through this mouthpiece, Jones states an aim for the writer and a specific view of man. Dave aspires to

> force the human race for once to take an unvarnished unsugarcoated look at itself for a change. . . . They would recoil in such shock and horror at themselves that foreverafter never again would the name of D. HIRSH be mentioned in polite society.

Dave reflects upon Thoreau's "Most men lead lives of quiet desperation," and amends it to "Most men lead lives of desperate crappiness." Pursuing this theme, with his familiar grace of style, he broods:

> There had been so much crap written about the greatness of humanity and love for the human race it like to turned your stomach. It was about time somebody did a little exposing. . . . He wanted to write the truth about life. The real truth. Not all that crap that sentimental jerks crammed together into novels and tried to pretend was literature. The *real* truth about life as it was *really* lived.

We are asked by such literary levelers (always leveling *down*, as Johnson observed) to accept this alleged truth, these judgments, standards, and visions of life, either in the name of a pseudo compassion or of a pseudo democracy. We must accept the spreading cult of semi-literacy of which Dave is a voice. Man is a failure and a fraud. The Yahoo must prevail. To resist him is to be a snob.

There is a substantial body of modern fiction representing this view of man. It is part of what C. S. Lewis has called *The Abolition of Man* in the brilliant little book of that name. This view is either still spreading, or else at best has only stopped expanding but is holding its own. What is more, it has the full cry of whole schools of literary critics who have established a canon and an esthetic for it. It includes the atheistical wing of the existentialists, the less consciously intellectual, mere "tough guy," writers, and a few "arty" pornographers.

It is no slight matter when we are asked to give our literary accolades, uncritical of the conceptual contents of the books, to works and writers who tacitly or explicitly deny the freedom and responsibility—in short, the essential manhood—of man. The literary merits of many such touted books are not so extraordinary as to carry them alone—we must assume unless assured otherwise that the total package, implications and all, is being bought by the juries or critics involved. Particularly open to attack on this count are National Book Award juries. In their eight years, so far, they have passed over many titles to demonstrate that you must (almost in alternate years) be either sufficiently degraded in your image of man or sufficiently obscure in style to pull down the award.

Naturally, as in all attempts at general formulation, there are some writers who fall astraddle of the categories I have enumerated, or who oscillate, from book to book or even within the same book, back and forth across their dividing lines. We can recognize a category of what might be called the "God-residue" novel. Some of our ablest craftsmen write it. They may be considered the spokesmen of T. S. Eliot's "decent, Godless people, whose only monuments are asphalt roads and a thousand lost golf balls."

I think the term "God-residue" is quite precise. In general such writers are sensitive, gifted, ethical humanists. They think that the only thing wrong with religion is the naïve idea of God. They think, reluctantly, that God does not exist but that it would be well for men to live as if He did. But "as if" is not a sound foundation for construction or creation. The literature which these writers produce may be competent, but often is singularly impotent. They are at their best, inevitably, with the presently outdated social or sociological novel, the "liberal" novel, or the "case-history" novel. There are able storytellers among the "God-residue" people, yet much of their literature is withering on the vine, often portraying a waning political effectiveness, or crumbling psychic structures, in the present arena of clashing ideas. I fear that they are dry bones in the valley of decision. They are marooned on "maybe so" while "yes" and "no" are at war about the basic nature of man.

A writer cannot be required to believe in God, or to accept a specific theology if he does believe. We may rejoice when a writer emerges who is intelligently affirmative about the human enterprise, but we cannot demand affirmation, like the prophets of "positive thinking." We are limited to analyzing and appraising the vision each writer offers us.

Whether believing or disbelieving in a God standing in a personal relationship to man, there have been some writers, always, speaking as a minority voice within the great Western tradition of man. The function of such writers—and it is a valuable one—is to ask the anguished questions which life ever demands of the thinking man, believer or skeptic. Many such writers are peculiarly conscious of the gap between human pretension and reality. Not offering a view of man counter to, or in challenge of, the Judeo-Christian Western tradition, nevertheless they are compelled to probe and test unsparingly the validity of that tradition. They are disquieting, and it is needful for man to be disquieted, particularly in periods when complacency, or conformity, produces stagnation at one extreme wing of our culture, while repudiation of the whole human enterprise is aggressively vocal at the other.

I believe the late George Orwell was such a prober, who felt the dilemma of his position with a peculiar intensity. He was firm in what he rejected but uncertain of what he accepted. He wished to preserve, but had become profoundly skeptical of, the Western tradition of man. His skepticism had driven him close to the Marxist image of man. The depth of his pessimism in *1984* lay in the fact that if man is as the Marxist contends him to be, the equivalent of the society of *1984* is logical and inevitable in his future. He hoped to warn us away from such a future, but was not greatly hopeful that the warning could avert it.

A deep skepticism about the human enterprise pervades James Gould Cozzens' *By Love Possessed*. I think the relief of receiving this brilliantly controlled, mature work of craftsmanship in the midst of the deluge of fictional slop may have caused many readers to fail to perceive its reservations about the human creature. This element markedly defines or limits the kind of impact the novel has. *By Love Possessed* interests intellectually, fascinates, and evokes admiration for its mastery of technique, but it does not move us deeply or stir the emotions powerfully. We are not intimately involved. It is written with detachment and read with detachment.

The atheistical wing of the existentialists asserts the meaninglessness of life and the primacy of death. Nicholas Berdyaev answers this with the affirmation that "Deeper truth lies in the fact that the world is not meaningless and absurd, but is in a meaningless state." The definition of that state, the tragedy of it, the origin of it, and the refusal of it are the greatest themes available to the writer today.

Paul Tillich has said that "Man is that being who asks the question of being." This is the true existentialism, for whatever that dismal term is worth. The irony is that the atheistical existentialists, vainly trying to ask the question of being while engaged in negating it, should think that a creature capable of conceiving and attacking so awesome and self-conscious a question could be a creature of random origin and meaningless life.

In the chapters that follow, I am criticizing, in terms of the image of man, a number of contemporary books and their writers. Even in doing so, I recognize that there is no use in inveighing against the artist for what he sees. The writer can only portray the world he sees, and so *must* portray it. Yet we can ask profitably what sometimes causes him to see only a distorted world, or a debased human image. The critical appraisal of his stature and validity as an artist is immediately involved. The possible sickness, lostness, or purblindness of the writer himself are qualifiers of his worth. Yet they do not negate his worth entirely—the nature of man being what it is.

The honest writer should recognize what some writers in some eras have refused to face—that any degradation is possible to a free creature of God. He should recognize also what some of our present writers refuse to face—that no degradation can be ultimate or definitive for this same creature. There is no path down without a path up, there is also no height without its inviting abyss. The path may sometimes be the same, with up or down a question of direction of travel.

My own conception of the image of man, and of the writer's great theme, is well expressed in some words of Stephen F. Bayne, to whom the great sense of writing and reading alike is "that we may see man as he is, single and whole, reasoning and choosing and believing, half of this world and half of some other, the only animal who must decide what kind of animal he will be, the only beast it is shameful to call a beast, whose soul, as Boethius said, 'albeit in a cloudy memory, yet seeks back his own good, but like a drunken man knows not the way home.' "

I believe that all the strands of contemporary fiction can be subsumed and understood in their origin and motivation under the above views of man. Most important, I believe that in the curdled disillusionment of the worship of the creature instead of the Creator we find the source of the ugliest, most loveless and despairing, veins of modern writing. I think, too, that the prevailing trend is shifting, and that a renewed literature in the great tradition of man as a rational, free, responsible, purposeful—even though fallible and imperfect—creature of God is emerging. Evil in all its range will not disappear from his portrayal, for this very man is inextricably compounded of elements of good and evil, but we will no longer be given the illusion that the seamy aspect of man is the sum total of man, which is the distortion in so much current writing. We are restoring the vitally dramatic picture of what Martin Buber has called "the hell-tormented and heaven-storming generations of men."

AN AWARENESS OF SOLITUDE

Stuart Barton Babbage

I shall be a fugitive and a wanderer on the earth.
(Genesis 4:14)

Henri Bergson says that in the soul of the desperate criminal there is always a feeling of remorse, arising from a desire, not so much to evade punishment as to wipe out the past, "to arrange things just as though the crime had never been committed." That is why a criminal will often seek someone to whom he can confess:

> By thus putting himself right, if not in the eyes of all, at least in some-body's eyes, he re-attaches himself to society at a single point, by a thread: even if he does not reinstate himself in it, at least he is near it, close to it; he no longer remains alienated from it; in any case he is no longer in complete rupture with it, nor with that element of it which is part of himself.[1]

Alienation is always a consequence of sin. Ernest Hemingway illustrates this fact in his novel *For Whom the Bell Tolls*. The story is set in the context of the Spanish Civil War. Pablo, who is the leader of a small Republican band operating behind the Fascist lines, is guilty of an act of calculated treachery and betrayal. He is, by nature, a shifty, unreliable opportunist. He deserts, taking with him the dynamite they need to blow up the bridge. His wife, Pilar, is a woman of astonishing determination. She is as resolute as her husband is weak. She is under no illusions about her husband's duplicity. Pablo, after an interval of some days, unexpectedly returns. Pilar regards him with mocking contempt. He shamefacedly blurts out: "Having done such a thing there is a loneliness which cannot be borne."[2]

He has come back, he tells her, because he cannot endure the loneliness, the sense of being cut off, the experience of alienation.

It is the tragic theme of alienation and estrangement which provides

---

[1] *The Two Sources of Morality and Religion* (Doubleday Anchor Books, New York, n.d.), p. 18.
[2] *For Whom the Bell Tolls* (Jonathan Cape, London, 1942), p. 367.

the subject matter of much twentieth-century existentialist literature. Nathan Scott draws attention to the fact that the image of man which recurs most frequently today is man in his isolation and loneliness, and he quotes Melville's description of the Islanders in the Pequod as aptly descriptive of man in contemporary society: "*Isolatoes,* I call such, not acknowledging the common continent of men, but each *Isolato* living in a separate continent of his own."[3] In this twentieth century we are all, in our loneliness and guilt, "displaced persons." We are both restless and rootless. William Faulkner, in *Light in August,* says of Joe Christmas, the hunted mulatto, "there was something rootless about him, as though no town or city was his, no street, no walls, no square of earth his home."[4] It is an apt description of alienated man in the fractured world of today.

Within the neurotic life of modern, urbanized society, we are being increasingly made aware of the problem of human loneliness. David Riesman gives his sociological study of contemporary society the descriptive title *The Lonely Crowd.* According to Rabbinic tradition Cain was the first builder of cities, and it is the city itself which is today pre-eminently the symbol of despair. Shelley says prophetically,

> *Hell is a city much like London—*
> *A populous and smoky city.*[5]

Lewis Mumford, in *The Culture of Cities,* entitles one of his most penetrating chapters, "A Brief Outline of Hell." In hell no community is possible, no meaningful fellowship, no personal relationships.

Jean-Paul Sartre makes this point, with impressive power, in his one-act play *No Exit.* The setting is the seedy living room of a second-rate hotel with hideous Second Empire furniture. There are no windows and no mirrors: there is only a glaring electric light bulb which never goes out. There are three characters, and they are doomed to eternal wakefulness: Garcin, a military coward who has been shot; Inez, a lesbian; and Estelle, a nymphomaniac, who has murdered her child. They realize they are in hell. They are surprised at first to find none of the proverbial fires nor instruments of torture. They soon discover, however, that they are to be their own tormentors. They desperately seek to hide the unedifying facts about themselves from each other. It is Inez who compels them to face the horrid truth.

> INEZ: Look here! What's the point of play-acting, trying to throw dust in each other's eyes? We're all tarred with the same brush.

---

[3] Quoted, *Modern Literature and the Religious Frontier* (Harper, New York, 1958), p. 72.

[4] Quoted, *ibid.*

[5] *Peter Bell the Third,* pt. 3, Hell, i.

ESTELLE (*indignantly*): How dare you!

INEZ: Yes, we are criminals—murderers—all three of us. We're in hell, my
   pets; they never make mistakes, and people aren't damned for nothing.

ESTELLE: Stop! For heaven's sake—

INEZ: In hell! Damned souls—that's us all three!

ESTELLE: Keep quiet! I forbid you to use such disgusting words.

INEZ: A damned soul—that's you, my little plaster saint. And ditto our
   friend there, the noble pacifist. We've had our hour of pleasure, haven't
   we? There have been people who burned their lives out for our sakes—
   and we chuckled over it. So now we have to pay the reckoning.

GARCIN (*raising his fist*): Will you keep your mouth shut, damn it!

INEZ (*confronting him fearlessly, but with a look of vast surprise*): Well,
   well! (*A pause.*) Ah, I understand now. I know why they've put us
   three together.

GARCIN: I advise you to—to think twice before you say any more.

INEZ: Wait! You'll see how simple it is. Childishly simple. Obviously
   there aren't any physical torments—you agree, don't you? And yet we're
   in hell. And no one else will come here. We'll stay in this room together, the three of us, forever and ever. . . . In short, there's someone
   absent here, the official torturer.

GARCIN (*sotto voce*): I'd noticed that.

INEZ: It's obvious what they're after—an economy of manpower—or devil-
   power, if you prefer. The same idea as in the cafeteria, where customers serve themselves.

ESTELLE: What ever do you mean?

INEZ: I mean that each of us will act as torturer of the two others.[6]

They realize that their condition is infernal. There is no escape from
this hell of being eternally together and yet eternally alienated. The
male member of the trio sums up the unpleasant reality of the situation:
"Hell is — other people."

In hell there are no personal relationships, there is no community.
What is hell? Dostoevsky asks, and he makes the profound reply: "It
is the suffering of being unable to love."[7] In hell, each is isolated from
the other, each is an island, an island of egocentricity, an island of
tormenting loneliness and guilt. George Macdonald says: "The one
principle of hell is — 'I am my own.' "[8] Edward Chamberlayne, in *The
Cocktail Party*, says:

> Hell is oneself
> Hell is alone, the other figures in it
> Merely projections. There is nothing to escape from
> And nothing to escape to. One is always alone.[9]

[6] *No Exit and Three Other Plays* (Vintage Books, New York, 1955), p. 17.

[7] *The Brothers Karamazov*, translated by Constance Garnett (Modern Library, New York, n.d.), p. 400.

[8] Quoted, *George Macdonald: An Anthology*, edited, C. S. Lewis (Geoffrey Bles, London, 1946), p. 85.

[9] T. S. Eliot, *The Complete Poems and Plays 1909-1950* (Harcourt, Brace, New York, 1952), p. 342.

It is the problem of loneliness which Sartre further explores in his philosophical novel *Nausea*. It is written in the form of the diary of one Antoine Roquentin, who is working on the biography of the Marquis de Rollebon. Antoine has no commitments, no family responsibilities, no financial anxieties. And yet he is unutterably depressed: he has intermittent spasms of nausea, vertigo, acute anxiety, and other forms of nervous tension which, in the Sartrean universe, says Maurice Cranston, "are not so much symptoms of psychological disorder as intimations of metaphysical reality."[10]

Antoine contemplates his face in a mirror, and confides to his diary:

> I can understand nothing of this face. The faces of others have some sense, some direction. Not mine. I cannot even decide whether it is handsome or ugly. I think it is ugly because I have been told so. But it doesn't strike me.

Later, in the same entry, Roquentin writes:

> Perhaps it is impossible to understand one's own face. Or perhaps it is because I am a single man? People who live in society have learned how to see themselves in mirrors as they appear to their friends. I have no friends. Is that why my flesh is so naked?[11]

His feelings (which he cannot explicate) culminate in an overwhelming and all-pervading sense of nausea. He begins to realize that the problems from which he suffers are not so much external to himself as within himself: "It holds me . . . the nausea is not inside me. . . . I am the one who is within *it*."[12] Finally, he comes to the conclusion that freedom is not to be found in running away from engagement and commitment. He goes to Paris to see his former mistress, Anny, who has invited him to visit her. She is now living with an Egyptian. They talk together of their past life together. She protests that she has outlived herself. Roquentin wonders what to say to her. He finally tells himself: "I can do nothing for her; she is as solitary as I."[13]

Sartre is preoccupied with the problem of human freedom. How can a man achieve authentic existence? How can a man break out of the iron circle of his own egocentricity? The problem, as Sartre appreciates, is not simply moral but also metaphysical. Christianity says the same. It insists that the tragedy of human existence is not only that man is a stranger on earth but also that he is an exile from heaven. "Your iniquities," says the prophet Isaiah, "have made a separation between you and your God, and your sins have hid his face from

---

[10] *Sartre* (Oliver & Boyd, Edinburgh, 1962), p. 14.

[11] *Nausea,* translated by Lloyd Alexander (New Directions Books, Norfolk, Conn., 1959), pp. 27, 29.

[12] *Ibid.,* p. 170.

[13] *Ibid.,* p. 203.

you so that he does not hear" (Isaiah 59:2). Man, in his alienation, is cut off from God. It is this which adds the dimension of terror.

Can a man scale the ramparts of heaven and win acceptance? Is there a bridgehead into the presence of God? Is it possible, in the language of the New Testament, to break down "the dividing wall of hostility" (Ephesians 2:14)? Is there a way back? Can the past be undone?

T. S. Eliot explores the deeper implications of alienation in his sophisticated verse play *The Cocktail Party*. Celia Coplestone visits the psychiatrist, Harcourt-Reilly, and tells him that she has two symptoms. She explains that, in the first place, she has "an awareness of solitude." She admits that this expression of the situation sounds flat. She attempts to be more explicit.

> *I mean that what has happened has made me aware*
> *That I've always been alone. That one is always alone.*
> *Not simply the ending of one relationship,*
> *Not even simply finding that it never existed—*
> *But a revelation about my relationship*
> *With everybody. Do you know—*
> *It no longer seems worthwhile to speak to anyone!*

Reilly asks whether she really doesn't want to see anybody any more, and she replies:

> *No . . . it isn't that I want to be alone,*
> *But that everyone's alone—or so it seems to me.*
> *They make noises, and think they are talking to each other;*
> *They make faces, and think they understand each other.*
> *And I'm sure that they don't.*

Reilly asks about her other symptoms. Celia replies:

> *That's stranger still.*
> *It sounds ridiculous—but the only word for it*
> *That I can find, is a sense of sin.*
> REILLY: *You suffer from a sense of sin, Miss Coplestone?*
> *This is most unusual.*
> CELIA: *It seemed to me abnormal.*
> REILLY: *Tell me what you mean by a sense of sin.*
> CELIA: *It's much easier to tell you what I don't mean: I don't*
> *mean sin in the ordinary sense.*

She is asked to be more precise. She continues:

> *Well, my bringing up was pretty conventional—*
> *I had always been taught to disbelieve in sin.*
> *Oh, I don't mean that it was ever mentioned!*
> *But anything wrong, from our point of view,*

Was either bad form, or was psychological.
And bad form always led to disaster
Because the people one knew disapproved of it.
I don't worry much about form, myself—
But when everything's bad form, or mental kinks,
You either become bad form, and cease to care,
Or else, if you care, you must be kinky.[14]

She is deeply convinced that her feeling of guilt is not a "kink." She speculates for a moment whether perhaps it is some kind of hallucination, but she immediately dismisses the idea: "I'm frightened by the fear that it is more real than anything I believed in." She can neither evade it nor ignore it. She says that she has a feeling "of emptiness, of failure towards some one, or something, outside of myself"; and then she says: "I feel I must . . . *atone* — is that the word?"

Celia Coplestone is aware of her lonely alienation and guilt. She knows that she needs, and needs desperately, absolution and atonement.

Kafka explores these themes in his frightening and disturbing novels, *The Trial* and *The Castle*. According to W. H. Auden, Kafka is the representative writer of the twentieth century, in the same way that Dante is the representative writer of the fourteenth century, and Shakespeare of the sixteenth century, and Goethe of the nineteenth century. Kafka, he insists, is *the* representative writer of the twentieth century.[15]

Kafka's writing is essentially autobiographical. He projects and universalizes his own poignant personal experiences. His attitude to his father was, we learn, ambivalent. Towards his father he felt the contrary and contradictory emotions of both love and loathing, gratitude and resentment. Writing to his father, he confesses: "My writings were about you, in them I merely poured out the lamentations I could not pour out on your breast." In the presence of his father he felt, he says, "an infinite sense of guilt."[16]

In Kafka's relationship to his father we have a symbolic picture, a paradigm, of guilty man's fear in relation to God. In the presence of God we all tend to feel, as Kafka felt in relation to his father, an infinite sense of guilt. At one moment we desire to find God, at the next to flee from Him. We protest vehemently that we want to be left alone, and yet the very thing we most fear is the dread possibility of being left alone. Our deep ambivalence is reflected in Cain's explosive anger in relation to God. "In Cain," writes Oliver Quick, "there appears for the first time that perennial conflict in the soul of fallen man, the conflict between the passionate claim to be left alone, the

---

[14] Eliot, *op. cit.*, pp. 360-1.
[15] Quoted, W. B. J. Martin, "Significant Modern Writers: Franz Kafka," *The Expository Times* (T. & T. Clark, Edinburgh), July 1960, p. 309.
[16] Quoted, Max Brod, *Franz Kafka* (Schocken, New York, 1960), p. 24.

assertion of independence, and the no less passionate terror of being left alone, the obscure foreboding of the hell to which independence leads. The first produces the indignant question, 'Am I my brother's keeper?' the second, the bitter complaint, 'Behold, thou hast driven me out this day from the face of the earth, and from thy face I shall be hid.' "[17]

Like Cain, we are conscious at one and the same time of defiance and desire. According to Helmut Thielicke "the wish to be free of God is the deepest yearning of man. It is greater than his yearning for God."[18] Francis Thompson, in his strangely haunting poem, tells the story of how he sought to flee from God, and of how he found himself relentlessly pursued by the "Hound of Heaven."

> I fled Him, down the nights and down the days;
>   I fled Him, down the arches of the years;
> I fled Him, down the labyrinthine ways
>   Of my own mind; and in the midst of tears
> I hid from Him, and under running laughter.
>   Up vistaed hopes I sped;
>   And shot, precipitated,
> Adown Titanic glooms of chasmed fear,
>   From those strong Feet that followed, followed after.
>
> But with unhurrying chase,
>   And unperturbèd pace,
> Deliberate speed, majestic instancy,
>   They beat—and a Voice beat,
>   More instant than the Feet—
> "All things betray thee, who betrayeth Me."

C. S. Lewis has described his reluctant confrontation with Christ. That night, in Magdalen College, Oxford, he was conscious, he says, "of the steady, unrelenting approach of Him whom I so earnestly desired not to meet." "That which I greatly feared had at last come upon me. . . . I gave in, and admitted that God was God and knelt and prayed: perhaps, that night, the most dejected and reluctant convert in all England. . . . The hardness of God is kinder than the softness of men, and His compulsion is our liberation."[19]

Edwin Muir, through whose enterprise and industry the works of Kafka have been made available to English readers, describes the experiences of the anonymous person who is the subject matter of Kafka's tormented novels.

He looks ahead and sees, perhaps on a distant hill, a shape which he has often seen before in his journey, but always far away, and apparently inac-

[17] *The Gospel of the New World* (Nisbet, London, 1944), p. 40.
[18] *Nihilism* (Harper & Row, New York, 1961).
[19]*Surprised by Joy* (Geoffrey Bles, London, 1955), p. 215.

cessible; that shape is justice, grace, truth, final reconciliation, father, God. As he gazes at it he wonders whether he is moving towards it while it is receding from him, or flying from it while it is pursuing him. He is tormented by this question, for it is insoluble by human reasoning. He feels irresistibly drawn towards that distant shape, and yet cannot overcome his dread of it.

According to Edwin Muir, Kafka, in *The Castle*, describes the struggle to reach it, and in *The Trial*, the flight from it. But the hero can neither reach it nor escape it.[20]

The Trial opens with the words: "Someone must have been telling lies about Joseph K., for without having done anything wrong he was arrested one fine morning." The hero is chief clerk in a bank, and is referred to throughout the book by his initial, as though he was deficient in personality, in family background and status — as indeed he proves to be, for he is the typical uprooted displaced person. The "arrest" takes place on the morning of his thirtieth birthday. Albert Camus says that the age of thirty is a crucial period in a man's life, when it becomes impossible for a man to ignore the threat of time or to fool himself about his achievements.[21] It is clear that Kafka intends this startling event to stand for the middle point in human life, an abrupt jolt into crisis. But at no point in the story is K. told the nature of his crime, nor does he ever come face to face with the judge, nor does his arrest ever take him right out of the familiar workaday world, to which, however, he now sustains a new and bizarre relationship.

At first K. tries to deal with the situation along familiar lines: he supposes it must be a practical joke played upon him by his office friends. Then he tries another tack: it is all a mistake, a blunder committed at headquarters (wherever that is!). He asks the two men sent to apprehend him for their credentials, but they only laugh; he tries to produce his own, but they have mysteriously disappeared. Pulling himself together, he thinks, "It will be all right if I can see someone in authority, not these ignorant menials." But the situation gets worse instead of better. The more rational he strives to be, the more irrational the situation becomes. As the case proceeds, he begins to brood over his past, to analyse his relationships with other people, to analyse himself lest some secret flaw, some unconscious betrayal, has landed him in this plight. "To ask questions is surely the main thing," he says, but what questions? That in itself now becomes a problem. Finally, after many disconcerting, nightmare experiences, during which clichés he has used a hundred times fall to

---

[20] *Essays on Literature and Society* (Hogarth Press, London, 1949), p. 121.

[21] *The Myth of Sisyphus and Other Essays* (Vintage Books, New York, 1959). Quoted, W. R. Mueller, *The Prophetic Voice in Modern Fiction*, p. 103.

pieces on his lips, he is carried off, stabbed to the heart by his warder, "like a dog." Nevertheless, just before the fatal stab he sees a human figure leaning out of a high and distant window toward him and stretching out both arms. K. responds by raising his hands and spreading out all his fingers.

W. B. J. Martin quotes John Middleton Murry's memorable saying: "A truly great novel is a tale to the simple, a parable to the wise, and a direct revelation of reality to the man who has made it a part of his being," and adds these suggestive comments:

> On one level, *The Trial* is a tale, almost a satire on the growingly familiar world of bureaucracy, with its tortuous ramifications and frustrations, a sort of Czechoslovakian *Little Dorrit*, complete with its Circumlocution Office and its maddening delays and buck-passing. Kafka's experience in the Workers' Accident Insurance Office in Prague undoubtedly provided him with rich material here. This world is one in which paper has ousted people, and statistics are more important than souls, a world where the Little Man's life is ruled by powers known only by name, never in face-to-face contact.
>
> But the tale is certainly not for the simple. It only begins to cohere when it is regarded as a parable of the human situation. It declares that man lives on two levels, in two worlds, which have the strange power of mocking and mystifying one another. So Joseph K. suddenly finds the safe, substantial framework of his daily life, the world of the bank in which he was at home, capable and confident, becoming unreal and hostile. When he is transported to the other world, the world of the Court, his mind, which was such a reliable instrument in dealing with finance, accounts, industrial problems, only flounders when it has to deal with the problems presented by the Law Court; not only does he fail to find the answers, he is unable even to understand the questions or to frame questions that will make sense. "Somebody has been telling lies about Joseph K." But were they lies after all? Gradually, Joseph ceases to ponder the question of guilt and innocence; now the question becomes, "Guilty or innocent, how do I satisfy the Law?" On this level the book might be read as a commentary on the doctrine of Justification by Faith. It deals with precisely the same problem that haunted the Apostle Paul, but it only poses the problem in a specially modern manner, it does not come up with a solution.[22]

Kafka wrote in his *Diaries*, "Sometimes I feel I understand the Fall of Man better than anyone," and, again, "The state in which we find ourselves is sinful, quite independent of guilt."[23] It is with this problem that his books deal; and it is this problem which Kafka remorselessly seeks to explore. As W. B. J. Martin further comments:

> *The Trial* can be read on the third level as "a direct revelation of reality to the man who has made it a part of his being." The writings of Kafka

---

[22] "Significant Modern Writers: Franz Kafka," *The Expository Times* (T. & T. Clark, Edinburgh), July 1960, pp. 309-11.
[23] Franz Kafka, *The Great Wall of China* (Schocken, New York, 1960), p. 298.

everywhere show evidence that they were "a part of his being". He himself took to writing as a way of salvation. "My writing", he wrote, "is a form of prayer"; it was his attempt to externalize the nightmare of alienation and to win some measure of control over it.

The section of the novel in which Kafka comes closest to a religious solution is that entitled "In the Cathedral". . . . Joseph K. finds himself in the cathedral, having been sent there by the Bank to meet a client who never appears. As he is on the point of leaving, a strong voice calls his name from the pulpit of the darkened building, and a young priest proceeds to offer him advice on his plight. Among other things he says that K. is depending too much on outside help, the wrong kind of help, whereupon K. turns away in a huff, but is recalled by an agonized shriek. The priest cries out, "Can't you see one step before you!", as if addressing a man walking to his doom. So K., startled and impressed, begs the priest to come down from the pulpit to give him personal advice. . . .

When they are both seated, the priest embarks on a long and very detailed parable, one of the greatest parables in modern literature. . . . The parable concerns a man from the country who seeks admission to the Law. Before the Law stands a doorkeeper on guard, who keeps him there for days, months, years, until finally the man, aged and frail, dies on the radiant threshold. Before he dies, he asks the doorkeeper how it is that through all the years of waiting he has seen no other applicant for admission, whereupon the doorman replies: "No one but you could gain admittance through this door, since the door was intended only for you. I am now going to shut it."

K.'s immediate reaction is to analyse the parable, but every attempt he makes is dismissed by the priest, who tells him that he is like so many commentators in Scripture, who advance theories but refuse to confront the facts. He compares K. to the man in the parable who spent his life examining theories and was too exhausted and wasted to make direct contact with reality.[24]

The meaning of the parable, comments William Mueller, is that salvation is absolutely beyond the power of man. It is futile to argue an innocence which does not exist and to look to oneself or any other human being for an acquittal which it is not his to give. Nevertheless, however inaccessible it may seem, there *is* a "radiance that streams inextinguishably from the door of the Law." Man cannot save himself but there is a radiance which has the power of salvation.[25]

The problems which Kafka attributes to his pseudonymous character K. were also the problems of his own life. "I was an outcast," he confesses to his father, "condemned, defeated, and although I struggled my utmost to flee elsewhere, it was labor in vain, because I was trying to do something that was impossible, that was beyond my strength."[26]

Kafka, according to Max Brod, disputes with God as Job once did.

---

[24] W. B. J. Martin, *op. cit.*, pp. 309-11.
[25] *The Prophetic Voice in Modern Fiction* (Association Press, New York, 1959), p. 109.
[26] Max Brod, *op. cit.*, p. 25.

How can a man find God? In his desperate anguish, Job is moved to protest:

> For he is not a man, as I am, that I might answer him,
>   that we should come to trial together.
> There is no umpire between us,
>   who might lay his hand upon us both (Job 9:32-33).

This is Kafka's problem: how can he win an acquittal? Who will intercede for him? Is there a savior? At the end of *The Trial* K. becomes aware that there *is* a faraway, unknown, indistinct person:

> His glance fell on the top story of the house adjoining the quarry. With a flicker as of a light going up, the casements of a window there suddenly flew open; a human figure, faint and insubstantial at that distance and that height, leaned abruptly forward and stretched both arms still farther. Who was it? A friend? A good man? Someone who sympathised? Someone who wanted to help? Was it one person only? Or were they all there? Was help at hand?[27]

Kafka insists that a man cannot live without "permanent faith." But how is a man to get faith—faith which is "like a guillotine, as heavy and as light"? Kafka says that there is a chariot by which a man can be saved. In one of his meditations, Kafka writes: "Hold fast! . . . then you too will see the unchangeable, dark distance, out of which nothing can come except one day the chariot; it rolls out, gets bigger and bigger, fills the whole world at the moment it reaches you—and you sink into it like a child sinking into the upholstery of a carriage that drives through storm and night."[28] These words are strangely reminiscent of the haunting words of the Negro spiritual with its suggestion of divine rescue and redemption: "Swing low, sweet chariot, coming for to carry me home."

The Trial is an exploration of the problem of guilt. K. comes to a sudden conviction of sin. His feeling of unrest is caused by a sudden awareness of uncleanness, not growing out of any specific identifiable crime, but out of his first shattering apprehension of the human condition. He marks his discovery by breakfasting on "a fine apple." The Biblical overtones cannot be ignored. K., conscious of his guilt, desires to plead his case before the court in the tenement attic of the city. He errs, however, in thinking that any human court can grant him an acquittal. "The Court wants nothing from you," the priest says. "It receives you when you come and it dismisses you when you go."

Again, it is the problem of loneliness which Kafka explores in *The*

---

[27] *The Trial* (Penguin Books, Harmondsworth, Middx., 1953), p. 250.
[28] Max Brod, *op. cit.*, pp. 172-3.

Castle. The hero, who is simply called K., in autobiographical fashion, passes through life alone. A surveyor by profession, he seeks to settle in a village, but to do this, he needs the permission of the castle. He finds the castle barred against him, and he also finds that the peasants are hostile to him and turn their backs: "Nobody can be the companion of anyone here," he is told. The castle, in the symbolism of the novel, stands for divine guidance, and the peasants for mother earth. He discovers that he is not only an exile from heaven but a stranger on the earth. "I have been here quite a long time and am already feeling a little deserted," he complains to the schoolmaster. "To the peasants I don't belong and to the castle I don't either, I suppose." "Between the peasants and the castle there is no difference," the schoolmaster replies.

St. Paul reminds the Ephesians that there was a time when they were "separated from Christ, alienated from the commonwealth of Israel, and strangers to the covenants of promise, having no hope and without God in the world" (Ephesians 2:12). Writing to the Colossians the Apostle repeats the charge: "You [were] once estranged and hostile in mind, doing evil deeds" (Colossians 1:21). Every unregenerate man is in a state of alienation which speaks, with grim foreboding, of a more dreadful alienation yet to come. In hell, Jesus says, in words of awful solemnity, their worm does not die and the fire is not quenched. "The great cries of the soul in literature and in life," says John A. Hutton, "are the cries of those who are afraid of that loneliness"—that loneliness which is a consequence of the averted face of God—"or who are already tasting the bitterness of it."[29]

[29] *Ancestral Voices* (Hodder & Stoughton, London, 1915), p. 238.

THE DECLINE OF THE NOVEL

Edwin Muir

When one tries to define the difference between the position of the novelist fifty or a hundred years ago and his position to-day one finds that, though far-reaching, it can be put in simple terms. To the novelist fifty or a hundred years ago life obediently fell into the mould of a story; to the novelist to-day it refuses to do so. This recalcitrance of the subject-matter is not absolute; the novelist still manages to tell a story: *Ulysses* is a story. But it is a story without an ending, and the characteristic modern novel is a story without an ending. At the start the novelist finds that his theme moulds itself obediently enough into a story, and the impetus carries him along for a while; but then it weakens, and when it has weakened to vanishing point the story has to stop, for it has no fixed destination. The modern novel is like a sentence that sets out confidently; the grammatical construction is ingenious; we admire the writer's skill in insinuating explanatory and qualifying clauses and all sorts of parentheses; but the sentence remains hanging in the air. This is another way of saying that the contemporary novelist has an imaginative grasp of origins but not of ends. There was a time when the novelist (and the poet and everybody) had a grasp of both. To have this is a mark of that order of thought and imagination which is generally called classical. Our own order is not a classical order; we have a grasp of origins but not of ends; our existence, like our works, is an unfinished sentence. And the novel describing the life we live is a symptom of the order in which we live; its incompleteness is a reflection of the incompleteness of a whole region of thought and belief.

This is obvious enough; but our position in time makes it difficult for us to acknowledge it. We look upon the contemporary novel as one thing, and the order out of which it springs as another, and regard their problems as separate problems. We do not make this mistake when we think of the eighteenth-century novel; for when we read Fielding or Sterne we are conscious of the general body of sentiment, belief and thought that went into their work and belonged

to the eighteenth century and to no other. Standing outside the
eighteenth century, we can see it whole. But we cannot stand outside
our own century, for we are part of it, and so the contemporary novel
is a special and technical problem to us, one among many problems.
Yet really there is perhaps only the problem caused by the lack of
a normal and complete order in which existence would have unity
and meaning.

Before going further it would be best to show what I mean by a
story with and without an ending:

(A) Joseph remains blest with his Fanny, whom he doats on with
the utmost tenderness, which is all returned on her side. The
happiness of this couple is a perpetual fountain of pleasure to
their fond parents; and, what is particularly remarkable, he declares he will imitate them in their retirement, nor will he be
prevailed on by any booksellers, or their authors, to make his
appearance in high life.

(B) I lingered round them [the graves], under that benign sky:
watched the moths fluttering among the heath and harebells,
listened to the soft wind breathing through the grass, and
wondered how anyone could ever imagine unquiet slumbers for
the sleepers in that quiet earth.

(C) She ran forward, always forward, into a faint streak of light.
The darkness unfolded before her. There was joy in the
running and with every step she took she achieved a new
sense of escape. A delicious notion came into her mind. As
she ran she thought the light under her feet became more
distinct. It was, she thought, as though the darkness had
grown afraid of her presence and sprang aside, out of her path.
There was a sensation of boldness. She had herself become
something that within itself contained light. She was a creator
of light. At her approach darkness grew afraid and fled away
into the distance. When that thought came she found herself
able to run without stopping to rest and half wished she might
run on for ever, through the land, through towns and cities,
driving darkness away with her presence.

(D) Quickly, as ·if she were recalled by something over there, she
turned to her canvas. There it was—her picture. Yes, with all
its greens and blues, its lines running up and across, its attempt at something. It would be hung in the attic, she thought;
it would be destroyed. But what did that matter? she asked
herself, taking up her brush again. She looked at the steps;
they were empty; she looked at her canvas; it was blurred.
With a sudden intensity, as if she saw it clear for a second,
she drew a line there, in the centre. It was done; it was finished.
Yes, she thought, laying down her brush in extreme fatigue,
I have had my vision.

These four passages, in their order, are the last paragraphs of *Joseph Andrews, Wuthering Heights,* Sherwood Anderson's *Out of Nowhere into Nothing,* and Virginia Woolf's *To the Lighthouse.* The thing which strikes us most strongly now about the end of *Joseph Andrews* is its banality; indeed the end of the traditional novel, when it is not tragic as in *Wuthering Heights,* is generally banal, for it is expected. The last words in the stories by Sherwood Anderson and Virginia Woolf are far more interesting and more worthy of the mind's attention, for they show a deeper concern with the problem of experience, and can therefore be taken more seriously than Fielding's, which are purely conventional, a mere ceremonious good-bye to the chief characters. But though they are more interesting, and even significant, they are not entirely convincing; or rather they convince us only of the authors' search for a new kind of experience, not of the reality and ultimate significance of that experience as attributed to the characters. The significance of the traditional novel, whether comic like *Joseph Andrews,* or tragic like *Wuthering Heights,* lies within it, and the conclusion is merely a conclusion. In *Out of Nowhere into Nothing* and *To the Lighthouse,* the writer is still struggling to seize the full significance when the story ends. After Joseph is married and Heathcliff is buried, we feel there is nothing more to say. But after reading the last words of Sherwood Anderson and Virginia Woolf we feel that there is still something of the greatest importance to say, and that the ending is really a sort of beginning, the beginning of a quite different story. Something should have followed; but what that something is we do not know, because we live by an unfinished conception of life, exist in a circle which is never closed. Such endings are expressions of a hope of completion, arrows shot into the irresponsive future. Lawrence's *Sons and Lovers* ends with Paul striding back towards the lights of the town with his fists clenched; Joyce's *Portrait of the Artist as a Young Man,* with Stephen's solemn proclamation of his creed as a writer. Fifty or a hundred years ago a novelist would have asked: What next? What will happen when Paul is back in the town and has to unclench his fists? What will happen to Stephen's creed as a writer? Will it have changed in five or ten years' time? But our imagination stops short at a certain point and cannot go farther, for Paul and Stephen are launched into a world where neither their creators nor we can follow them. They stand at the beginning of a story which is never told.

A story without an ending describes a mode of existence which has not been thought out and stops short of meaning. The vision or the illumination is an acknowledgment of that lack of meaning, an attempt to fill up a void with a personal and mystical hope. A comprehensive and widely accepted conception of human life produces good imaginative art; a tentative and partially accepted conception of life, unsatisfactory imaginative art. In an age when such a conception prevails the subject-matter of the artist will not mould itself into a form; every image of human existence will have the mark of organic imperfection.

Is there any universal mark by which we can recognise a conception of human life that is complete and in a high sense normal to mankind? I shall hazard the assertion that all such conceptions postulate a transcendent reality and recognise man's relation to it, and that human life must always stop short of meaning if we seek its meaning merely in itself. To seek its meaning in itself is to seek its meaning in time; and the conception of life which prevails to-day is a conception of life purely in time. The contemporary novel is a story of time against a background of time. The traditional novel is a story of time against a permanent pattern. This does not mean that Fielding or Jane Austen were religious in any sense, or that when describing Tom Jones or Elizabeth Bennet they were concerned with eternal truths. But they lived in an order in which everybody possessed without thinking about it much the feeling for a permanence above the permanence of one human existence, and believed that the ceaseless flux of life passed against an unchangeable background. Men still felt this whether they were Christians or not. They felt also that there was a relation between the brief story of man and that unchangeable order; and this sentiment, in whatever terms it was held, was the final earnest of the completeness of their conception of life.

To return to the novel: it may be advanced that without this permanent background there can be no whole picture of life. Seen against eternity the life of man is a complete story. Seen against time it is an unfinished one, a part of endless change, a fleeting picture on an unstable substance. The traditional recognition of a permanence beyond the duration of the happenings told in one story belongs to a certain mode of thinking and feeling which has prevailed during the known past of European civilisation; it now prevails effectually no longer. That mode was auspicious to imaginative literature; and originally it was the creation of religion. So that in a sense imaginative literature is, if not the child, at least the grandchild or great-grandchild of religion. It may be that in its early stages the decay of religion encourages the production of imaginative literature, and the one thrives at the expense of the other, as during the Renaissance; but the complete decay of the religious sense would bring with it the atrophy of the creative imagination, which needs as a working hypothesis something more durable than the immediate subject-matter on which it works. It may be (if we can put reliance on contemporary theorists who think in terms of thousands of years, future years) that poetical and imaginative production is merely a passing human activity made possible by certain historical conditions and fated to disappear with them. This is the complement of another theory: that we are witnessing in our time the definitive liquidation of religion, and that in a few centuries the religious sense will have vanished for good. If that were so, it would be easy to believe that poetry and imagination in all its forms would disappear too. But the question is whether the religious sense can ever disappear. If it cannot, then neither can poetry and the various other forms of imaginative art.

The norm of human existence remains. There are certain beliefs which are natural to man, for they satisfy his mind and heart better than any alternative ones. The mark of such beliefs is their completeness; they close the circle. In a state of irremediable imperfection such as man's, the circle can be closed only by calling on something beyond man; by postulating a transcendent reality. So the belief in eternity is natural to man; and all the arts, all the forms of imaginative literature, since they depend on that belief, are equally natural to him. When that belief partially fails, imagination suffers an eclipse, and art becomes a problem instead of a function. If that belief were to fail completely and for good, there would be no imaginative art with a significance beyond its own time. But it is inconceivable that it should fail, for it is native to man.

THE CHANGING PATTERN: CONTRASTS IN MEDIEVAL AND MODERN POETRY

Martin Turnell

On 30th October 1929 André Gide finished reading Claudel's *Satin Slipper* and recorded his opinion of it in his diary.

> 'I am filled with dismay,' he wrote. 'I find it difficult to believe that in any other religion Claudel's weaknesses would have flourished with the same ease as in Catholicism.'

This pungent observation focuses our attention sharply on the problem of literature and religious belief. There are two strongly conflicting views. No one supposes that belief can be a substitute for talent; but given the talent, Christians have argued that a writer's creative ability will be nourished and strengthened, his range broadened and deepened by a firmly grounded system of beliefs. Unbelievers have maintained, with equal tenacity, that any form of belief is a hindrance to the writer, that so far from nourishing his creative ability it has to reverse effect: it warps and stunts his talent, acts as blinkers which restrict or obliterate his vision.

Some thirty years ago Professor I. A. Richards congratulated Mr. T. S. Eliot on effecting, in *The Waste Land,* what he described as 'a complete severance between his poetry and *all* beliefs'. Mr. Eliot replied, tartly, that he found the statement 'incomprehensible'. Whatever the opinions of the theorists, imaginative writers have seldom accepted the view that belief is inimical to creative writing. It is a matter of historical fact that in ages of settled belief men have tended to write well, and that in ages of declining belief they have gone out of their way to discover some system of belief, or some philosophy, which would provide them with a framework and give unity and shape to their artistic experience. We can add, parenthetically, that one of the difficulties about contemporary literature, one of the things that often makes it look fragmentary and confused, is precisely the fact that the writer is obliged to expend his energies in creating the conditions in which literature becomes possible instead of putting the whole of his talent into his books.

"The Changing Pattern: Contrasts in Medieval and Modern Poetry." From Modern Literature and Christian Faith *by Martin Turnell (London: Darton, Longman and Todd, Ltd., 1961). Reprinted by permission.*

The problem of literature and belief is a complex one. The writer tries to give his reader an imaginative interpretation of the world as he sees it, or what is often called his 'vision'. The core of the problem is the relation between beliefs intellectually held and the writer's sensibility, or mode of feeling. We only get a truly Christian work of literature when the writer's whole outlook is informed by his beliefs, when we do not feel (as we do with so many contemporary Catholic writers) that intellectually held beliefs are either being imposed on experience from without, or are only very imperfectly assimilated into the experience.

While I take it as axiomatic that belief can never be a substitute for talent, I am not primarily concerned in this work to prove that one kind of literature or one writer is better than another. I simply want to describe the effect on writers of changes in belief which have taken place during the past four hundred years.

I think the period can be divided into five phases.

In the first the writer is living in a society which generally speaking is Christian. This does not mean, of course, that everyone is living an exemplary Christian life. It simply means that the writer is a member of a community which accepts the Christian faith even if individuals do not always practise it, that his work is a reflection of the communal outlook even if he is not dealing with a specifically Christian subject, that his conception of the nature of man is basically Christian.

In the second phase there is a break in the pattern. The community is divided into a large number of warring factions and conflicting outlooks. The Church is replaced by the churches; Theology by the theologies; Philosophy by the philosophies; Science by the sciences. The literature of this phase is dominated by a feeling of unrest, by the writer's sense of living in an age of crisis.

A third phase might be called the Age of Compromise. It is, as we shall see, the period of the Counter-Reformation and Baroque art. The Christian artist tries to come to terms with the new experience and new insights released by the upheavals of the previous century.

In the fourth phase literature divides into two main classes: religious and secular. The Christian writer, so far from feeling himself a member of a homogeneous society, is very clearly a member of a minority, and his work is coloured by his isolation.

In the final phase, the sense of belonging to a minority is transformed into the sense of belonging to the opposition. It is in this phase, as I shall try to show, that an internal conflict seems to arise between the writer's artistic experience and a religion which is held intellectually.

I have never cared for abstractions. I have never been able to feel much enthusiasm for the sort of abstract debate which raged with such fury in France a quarter of a century ago about 'the purity of the source' and 'the sanctity of truth'. It seems to me that the discussion of the problem of literature and belief can only serve any useful purpose if it is firmly based on concrete examples. In this first chapter, I give a broad and necessarily simplified picture of some of the main changes that have taken place between the sixteenth and the twentieth centuries illustrated by quotations from six poets. In chapter two I examine the effect of the absence of belief on the work of three twentieth-century novelists. In the final chapter I look at the work of three contemporary Catholic writers. I shall then try to draw some general conclusions.

I shall begin by comparing passages from representative medieval and modern poems. The first passage comes from Chaucer's *Prologue*, the second from Eliot's *Waste Land*.

This is Chaucer:

> *Whan that Aprillë with his shourës sote*
> *The droghte of Marche hath percèd to the rote,*
> *And bathèd every veyne in swich licour,*
> *Of which vertu engendrèd is the flour;*
> *Whan Zephirus eek with his swetë breeth*
> *Inspirèd hath in every holt and heeth*
> *The tendre croppès and the yongë sonne*
> *Hath in the Ram his halfë cours y-ronne,*
> *And smalë fowlës maken melodye,*
> *That slepen al the night with open yë,*
> *(So priketh hem nature in hir corages):*
> *Than longen folk to goon on pilgrimages*
> *(And palmers for to seken straungë strondes)*
> *To fernë halwës, couthe in sondry londes;*
> *And specially, from every shirës end*
> *Of Engelond, to Caunterbury they wende,*
> *The holy blisful martir for to seke,*
> *That hem hath holpen, whan that they were seke.*

This is Eliot:

> *April is the cruellest month, breeding*
> *Lilacs out of the dead land, mixing*
> *Memory and desire, stirring*
> *Dull roots with spring rain.*
> *Winter kept us warm, covering*
> *Earth in a forgetful snow, feeding*
> *A little life with dried tubers.*

The first difference is the contrast between Chaucer's spontaneous joy in the created world—we remember the gorgeous Wife of Bath's enthusiastic plea for 'octogamye'—and the mixture of horror and disgust with which Eliot regards it. In one, harmony and stability: in the other immense uncertainty and unrest; Chaucer rejoicing in something possessed, Eliot overwhelmed by a sense of something irrevocably lost. This is apparent in the details of the passages. Both writers are describing changes that occur in nature with the coming of spring. It is a time of awakening, and for the medieval poet awakening means an increase of life, a joyful release from the bondage of winter. April showers are 'sweet', and their virtue is to break up the winter-bound earth; they bring flowers and the fruits of the earth; the crops are 'tender', the sun 'young'. For Eliot, on the contrary, April is 'the cruellest month' precisely because it is the end of winter and the beginning of change from insensibility to awakening. Winter is not, as it was for Chaucer, a time of death but of pleasant numbness and insensibility. It is an awakening from which the poet would gladly escape. All that the earth produces is a few lilacs whose pale fragility is thrown into relief by the neutral background of the wilderness. The roots are 'dull', unwilling to grow. Chaucer is sensitive enough to the effects of the spring. Birds sing and cannot sleep. Men are revived by the stimulus of the season, are restless and feel the need to travel after being shut up all winter. In Eliot the effects of spring are narrowly sexual. It brings memories which stir sluggish desires, but there is, none of the gaiety suggested by Chaucer's singing birds: it is an unhappy, morbid state. While Chaucer's is a poetry of acceptance, Eliot's by comparison is a poetry of refusal and as such represents the modern outlook as Chaucer's represents the medieval.

Perhaps the most striking thing about the two passages is the difference of focus. The medieval poet is interested primarily in *things*, and his poem is a record of his reactions to them. The balance of the poem comes from the close correspondence between emotion and the object which evokes it. In the modern poet the process is reversed. The poem is an analysis of a state of mind and the connection with spring, and the use of a vocabulary drawn from spring, in a way fortuitous and subjective. In other words, the poet is not describing spring or even his sensations in spring: he is equating spring awakening with a particular mood, and simply uses images drawn from spring to exteriorise certain very personal feelings.

I must emphasise again that I am not concerned with the relative merits of the two passages. I am not saying that Chaucer is better than Eliot, or Eliot better than Chaucer. I am not saying that Eliot is not a great poet, or is an 'escapist'. I think he is a great poet, and that his greatness is apparent in the unflinching honesty with which he faces a tragic situation. It is this honesty, or so it seems to me, that gives his finest verse its peculiar toughness and resilience. All that I am concerned with is the contrasting attitudes of the two poets towards their world. It is evident that Chaucer's work is the product of a young civilisation. This explains the simplicity and directness of his reactions. The simplicity and uncomplicated reactions are reflected in the straightforward syntax and the number of active verbs: 'percèd', 'bathèd', 'inspirèd', 'wende'. They are also reflected in the difference between Chaucer's 'longen' and Eliot's 'memory'. The pilgrims' 'longing' to take to the road is prompted by memories, but they are pleasant memories which lead to action, lead them to plunge lightheartedly once again into the active, open-air life: there is none of the *passive* nostalgia that is evident in Eliot's 'memory'. There is a marked difference, too, between Chaucer's fondness for the active verb and Eliot's reliance on present participles—there are five of them in seven lines—on those dragging, wistful present participles which paradoxically have the effect of binding the passage together, giving it its personal tautness and strength, while at the same time conveying an almost suffocating sense of resignation.

This brings me to a final point. For Chaucer's bawdy pilgrims the expedition to Canterbury was no doubt an excuse for a 'jaunt', and certainly piety plays little part in the tales that they exchange. Nevertheless, they are on a pilgrimage. In this sense, the poem can be regarded as an allegory of the Christian life. For the Christian life is essentially a pilgrimage; all Chaucer's characters are moving towards a known goal. It is this which distinguishes them from the characters in modern poems. Travel bulks large in the literature written during the past century, but the pilgrim of Chaucer or Bunyan has been replaced by the tourist who has no fixed goal and travels for the fun of the journey, in the hope of running into adventures or simply because he cannot sit still. In nineteenth-century France the traveller is always looking wistfully backwards over his shoulder towards the 'lost paradise' of childhood which had become the symbol of unity and security: a vanished unity and a security that had gone. The travellers in Baudelaire's poem *Le Voyage* find themselves pursuing a moving goal, a mirage which leads them on and gets them nowhere, while in Eliot's poem the journey is a circular tour of the Waste Land, a spiritual stocktaking which ends with a depressing balance sheet where everything is in the red, and there is only a mark of interrogation beyond.

I think that we can say that the value of medieval poetry, the value of Dante or Chaucer or Langland, different as they are in outlook and stature, lies to a very considerable degree in the feeling of stability and confidence, in the belief in a fixed unchanging order, a world with a heaven above and a hell beneath, which they succeed in communicating to the reader. I am going to suggest that the appeal of later poets lies in something which is the opposite of this, that it lies in a sense of the dissolution of the old world, in the loss of unity.

For at the Renaissance the stability which pervades almost every line written by Dante or Chaucer was destroyed for a large section of European society. The old world had come to an end: a new world was beginning. It is true that the Renaissance made discoveries about man, about the external world, but its enormous delight in nature and in man involved a sundering of God and man who had been joined in the Incarnation, of nature and the supernatural. There is a feeling that nature and man are both independent of anything outside them, and in consequence a failure to relate experience to unchanging principles which had been natural to the medieval mind.

This view has been stated in a striking article by George Santayana called 'The Absence of Religion in Shakespeare'. He finds that Shakespeare is 'remarkable among the greater poets for being without a philosophy and without a religion'. 'In his drama', he goes on, 'there is no fixed conception of any forces, natural or moral, dominating our mortal energies.' He concludes from this that 'we can hardly find in Shakespeare all that the highest poet could give'.

I doubt whether contemporary Shakespearean critics would accept this view without considerable qualifications, but as a general account of what occurred after the break-up of the medieval synthesis it seems to me to be valid. I do not propose to discuss Shakespeare: he is too big to serve as an example. I propose instead to look at another poet. A great poet certainly, but not a poet of the calibre of Shakespeare. I mean John Donne.

If Donne was one of the most important poets of his century, it was because he was at once the last scholastic and the first of the moderns. In his work two worlds meet with a difference. For Donne lived in an age of transition from the medieval to the modern worlds. It is a change from a state of spiritual unity to the dualism of the contemporary world. One critic has spoken of his poetry as 'the battle-ground of the difficulty of belief and the reluctance to doubt'.

This puts the matter extremely well. Donne was one of the first poets to find himself obliged to choose between conflicting outlooks, for whom a choice of outlook was a major issue. There had been differences of opinion in the Middle Ages, but differences within a single philosophy. From Donne onwards a difference of opinion means a complete difference of outlook. He was born a Catholic and became an Anglican. He had Catholicism in his blood and did not find it easy to throw over the inherited habits of mind and ways of feeling of innumerable generations. He himself was very conscious of the difficulty. In 1615, only a few months after his ordination, he said in a remarkable letter to Sir Henry Godere:

> 'You shall seldom see a coyne, upon which the stamp were removed, though to imprint a better, but it looks awry and squint. And so, for the most part, do minds which have received divers impressions. I will not, nor need you, compare the Religions. The channels of Gods mercies run through both fields; and they are sister teats of his graces, yet both diseased and infected, but not both alike.'

From this we can turn to the famous sonnet written three years later:

> Show me deare Christ, thy Spouse, so bright and clear,
> What! is it She, which on the other shore
> Goes richly painted? or which rob'd and tore
> Laments and mournes in Germany and here?
> Sleepes she a thousand, then peepes up one year?
> Is she selfe truth and errs? now new, now outwore?
> Doth she, and did she, and shall she evermore
> On one, on seaven, or on no hill appeare?
> Dwells she with us, or like adventuring knights
> First travaile we to seeke and then make Love?
> Betray kind husband thy spouse to our sights,
> And let myne amorous soule court thy mild Dove,
> Who is most trew, and most pleasing to thee, then
> When she is embrac'd and open to most men.

This is not by any means among the best of Donne's religious poems. There is an element of frivolity in the comparison between the believer and 'adventuring knights' pursuing a reluctant mistress, which recalls some of the more cynical of the *Songs and Sonnets*. But it does reflect, as surely as the letter to Sir Henry Godere, the perplexity of the man of goodwill in the seventeenth century who is trying to discover the source of truth. What is notable about both letter and sonnet is not so much the attitude of moderation and toleration, as the implication that there is no one church which is the repository of truth, that each of them has its points, but that each is in some degree 'diseased and infected'.

It should now be possible to draw some tentative conclusions. When I said that the value of medieval literature lies in its power of communicating a feeling of stability and confidence, I was not forgetting that Dante lived in a politically divided world, or that Langland was Chaucer's contemporary. There was tension enough in the Middle Ages and an instance nearer home—Gerard Manley Hopkins—shows that Catholicism does not exclude tension. We have to distinguish between writers who are outside the tension and those who are inside it. Beneath the clash recorded by Dante, beneath Villon's lament for lost beauty, beneath the apparent disunity of Hopkins, there is an underlying unity. Their unrest is related to a background of harmony as Donne's is not. With Donne we meet, perhaps for the first time, that divided self which is characteristic of modern poetry. He expresses for the first time the writer's awareness of living in an age of spiritual crisis, and it is this awareness which dominates a great deal of the most significant poetry written since his day. The scene shifts, there are variations, apparent changes of emphasis, but at bottom the crisis is the same. Donne's work is the more intense because he was at the point at which the break took place. The unity which was destroyed was real for him, not simply an inherited memory, a lost paradise as it is for the contemporary poet.

The change from a theocentric to an anthropocentric world, the tendency of man to regard himself and his world as self-subsistent and self-sufficient, the wholesale glorification of the visible world, which were among the results of the Renaissance, clearly presented religious people with a problem. What in fact was the attitude of the Christian to be towards the new humanism? He naturally disapproved of it in so far as it was pagan, but he could not be blind to its positive virtues. The Church has always claimed that she can assimilate anything that is good or true in other systems. That is what the artists of the Age of Baroque attempted to do. They tried to harness the vitality released by the Renaissance, and it does indeed become almost tangible in the immense angels of Baroque sculpture and the flying draperies which envelop its saints.

The readiness to accept, to assimilate, to transform is reflected in the differences between medieval and Baroque art. In a medieval work like the carvings at Chartres the emphasis falls on two themes: Creation and Incarnation. The men who made them could not of course omit all reference to the 'sorrowful mysteries', but it is confined to a glimpse of the foot of the Cross and a couple of Nails on one of the porticoes. It is not until the seventeenth century that the Crucifixion becomes the centre of religious art, that poetry and painting drip with the Blood of Christ and the martyrs. Now the Counter-Reformation made one distinctive contribution to religious art. The brilliant ornate churches, the statues of saints swooning in ecstasy with distorted features and writhing limbs, the poetry where an immense exuberance threatens to burst through language, was the last conscious attempt to hold the balance between spirit and flesh. It was intended not merely to startle and impress, not merely as a protest against the gloomy iconoclasm of the Protestant north; it was intended to attract the unbeliever into the gay fantastic churches to marvel in the hope that he would remain to pray. It was an extraordinary performance certainly, but it was the product of a divided Europe.

We feel already that the artist had an axe to grind, that he was trying to prove something.

He was trying to prove something, but not by argument or the methods of the schoolmen. He was trying to put across an experience which would *compete* with the humanists on their own ground. He was also using them as allies in the struggle against Protestantism and the Lutheran view of the consequences of the Fall of Man. In its discovery of the Natural Man, the Renaissance had insisted on the pleasures of the eye and ear, the senses of touch, taste and smell. It wanted to satisfy the senses which seemed to have been starved by medieval asceticism. The Baroque artist tried to do the same thing through religion, tried to create a Religious Man who was far nearer to the Natural Man of the Renaissance than to the medieval ascetic.

It is not surprising that men living in a period of religious upheaval should have been preoccupied with sin and suffering, that their minds should have been dominated by the figure of the suffering Christ rather than by that of the glorious or the triumphant Christ. Yet it would clearly be untrue to say that the seventeenth century was exclusively preoccupied with suffering, and the paintings and statues of saints in ecstasy are there to prove the contrary. The answer lies deeper than that. The artists discovered that representations of suffering, ecstasy, and death were much better calculated to serve their purpose. They could be made to appeal to the senses. They could be represented not merely in words, but in paint and stone. The first result was the tendency of the different arts to merge into one another, to approximate to the visual arts. In the Middle Ages sculpture had been formal: it had shown the Christian Saint rather than a particular saint. In the seventeenth century it became highly realistic. The sculptor tried to represent movement, to probe into man's deepest and most intimate experiences, to catch and hold the actual instant of ecstasy or death, as Bernini did in his St. Teresa or his Blessed Ludovica Albertoni, as El Greco did in his painting of Pentecost.

All this is true of the poetry of the period, particularly of Crashaw's. It is extremely rich in visual, concrete, physical images. Not merely one, but all five senses are solicited on every page, almost in every line. In his rendering of Aquinas's *Adoro te devote*, for example, we read:

> *O soft self-wounding Pelican!*
> *Whose breast weepes Balm for wounded man.*
> *Ah this way bend thy benign floud*
> *To'a bleeding Heart that gaspes for blood:*
> *That blood, whose least drops soveraign be*
> *To wash my worlds of sins from me.*

Aquinas's *Pie pellicane* is transformed into a 'soft self-wounding Pelican' which does not merely bleed, but 'weepes' blood for another wounded, bleeding heart which 'gaspes' for still more blood.

The Divine Epigram on the text 'Blessed be the paps which Thou hast sucked' is much more startling:

> *Suppose He had been tabled at thy teats,*
> *Thy hunger feels not what He eats;*
> *He'll have His teat ere long, a bloody one,*
> *The mother then must suck the son.*

Small wonder that Mr. Aldous Huxley once remarked that some Baroque art makes us feel that we have walked into a room at the wrong moment.

I think that the Baroque artists must have known that they could not communicate the actual vision of the saint in ecstasy, or describe what happens at the moment of death. They also knew that ecstasy and death had marked physiological repercussions. They tried by a realistic representation of the physiological aspects to get as close as possible to the content of experience. In the end this involved a more and more determined appeal to the senses in the attempt—the impossible attempt—to reach through the senses something which lay outside the field of sense-perception.

I want to make a jump now of two hundred years and glance briefly at a much more extreme example of compromise. I want to describe what happens when the attempt to assimilate is pushed to the point at which the thing assimilated becomes the true substance of the poem, and is simply covered with a veneer of religion.

Coventry Patmore is one of the more curious figures among English nineteenth-century poets. He married three times. He is said by his grandson to have fallen physically in love with Alice Meynell when he was over seventy. In addition to a handsomely bound edition of the works of Aquinas, a complete set of a work called the *Eroticon Biblion* was among the treasures of his library. He tried, in a sequence of poems called *To the Unknown Eros*, to work out a sort of parallel between the union of God and His Church and the union of two people in marriage. This has won for him considerable favour among Catholic writers as a mystical poet.

His pre-conversion poem on married love, *The Angel in the House*, is of small literary value, but it provides one or two good laughs. Opening the poem at random, we come across this gem of Victorian complacency which occurs in a conversation between the hero of the piece and his future father-in-law who is an Anglican dean. The young man has just asked the dean for his daughter's hand:

> *He gave*
> *His glad consent, if I could get*
> *Her love. A dear, good Girl! she'd have*
> *Only three thousand pounds as yet;*
> *More bye and bye.*

'His writings are never dull', remarks the editor of the Oxford edition in an introduction which must rank as one of the curiosities of modern criticism. Superficially, the versification of *To the Unknown Eros* may appear more virile. Yet if we compare it with the genuine vitality of the mature Hopkins we see at once that the appearance of tautness, which is seldom maintained, depends not on rhythm, but on a harsh, awkward syntax, and on irritating habits of inversion and elision. It reveals the same prolixity that we find in nearly all Victorian verse, and the same poetic clichés. Nor can we be impressed by the alleged profundity of the psychology of love. When we come to the end of an ode, we cannot help remarking how very little has in fact been said. And nothing can compensate us for the ugly, gritty syntax.

In *Eros and Psyche* we read:

> *O, heavenly Lover true,*
> *Is this thy mouth upon my forehead press'd?*
> *Are these thine arms about my bosom link'd?*
> *Are these thy hands that tremble near my heart?*
> *Where join two hearts, for juncture more distinct?*
> *By thee and by my maiden zone caress'd,*
> *What dim, waste tracts of life shine sudden, like moonbeams*
> *On windless ocean shaken by sweet dreams!*

The construction of the last three lines defeats me, but I am in no doubt about the significance of 'my maiden zone caress'd', or of the 'juncture more distinct'. What is curious is the mixture of these crudely sexual images and the tiresome poetic jargon of the time: the 'bosom', 'moonbeams', 'sweet dreams', and the rest. The poem goes on:

> *Ah, stir not to depart!*
> *Kiss me again, thy Wife and Virgin too!*
> *O love, that, like a rose,*
> *Deckest my breast with beautiful repose,*
> *Kiss me again, and clasp me round the heart,*
> *Till filled with thee am I*
> *As the cocoon is with the butterfly!*

We know that Patmore purported to establish some sort of relation or parallel between the union of God with the soul and the union of man and woman in marriage. His theory is proudly produced by his apologists with suitably fulsome commendation. Clearly the odes can be read in this way, but the crucial point is where the emphasis lies. For myself, I can only say that Patmore's religious allegory has a very sexual underneath. His 'Virgin' is singularly out of place with that very phallic rose, and the still more phallic butterfly.

In *Aureas of Delight* he wrote:

> *I, with heart-quake*
> *Dreaming or thinking of that realm of Love*
> *See, oft, a dove*
> *Tangled in frightful nuptials with a snake . . .*

This throws an essential light on his failure and on the failure of his age. Underneath the tiresome clichés and the conventional sentiments there was both ability and vision. But there was something badly wrong with their minds, and the result was not poetry but a mess. For the 'frightful nuptials with a snake' and 'the tortur'd knot' of the next line belong to the Victorian nightmare. It was a very Freudian nightmare, but it seems best to recognise it for what it was instead of trying to hide poetic failure by fanciful theories of divine and human love. It is at least a possible view that rather than being 'a great Catholic poet' his principal characteristic was obsession with sexuality.

It is commonly but mistakenly assumed that the primary function of religious poetry is to provide the reader with some form of transcendental experience, and literary critics have contracted the bad habit of describing almost any poetry with a religious theme as 'mystical'. Poetry is a human activity. We expect religious poetry to interpret life in terms of religion certainly, but we also expect religion to *conserve* the natural human instincts. Now one of the most disquieting things about modern religious poetry is the failure of the poet's religion to do precisely that. Patmore is one example. Francis Thompson is another. Thompson, one feels, was a man whose best instincts had collapsed. His religion was a temptation instead of a discipline. It encouraged him to import into his verse the worst and shoddiest emotional clichés of the day, and was in the last analysis indistinguishable from a decadent religiosity which was fashionable in the eighties and nineties.

Hopkins was a great poet because his religion did enable him to resist the disintegrating forces of his time. It was responsible for the freshness and vitality of his language which relate him to Shakespeare and distinguish him from his Victorian contemporaries. Nearly all his critics have commented on the sensuous element in his work, but there is something essentially vital and alive about his descriptions of nature: a sense of things living and growing which is the opposite of the hot-house blooms of Thompson or Patmore's queer, drooping, sexy azaleas. I have quoted some examples of Patmore's contorted syntax. When we turn to Hopkins's we find by contrast that it possesses a genuine, sinewy tautness:

> *No worst, there is none. Pitched past pitch of grief,*
> *More pangs will, schooled at forepangs, wilder wring . . .*

In these lines the words are literally wrung out of the poet by the intensity of his agony. The alliteration in the first line is immensely effective in giving the language its extraordinary density: 'Pitched past pitch of grief . . . ', while the inserted clause in the second line, separating the auxiliary from its infinitive, produces the sense of flexibility and vigour.

Consider again this description of the nun on board the sinking *Deutschland:*

> *The rash smart sloggering brine*
> *Blinds her . . .*

There is nothing 'poetic' in the derogatory sense about the unexpected adjectives 'rash' and 'smart', or the immensely effective 'sloggering' with its obvious Anglo-Saxon antecedents. We have an acute physical sensation of the cold, biting water violently hurled against the solitary figure, which is heightened by the alliteration—another ancient device—and the enjambment.

Hopkins was a great poet who made no concessions to the age, but his work nevertheless does not entirely escape the general limitation that we find in nearly all post-Reformation religious poetry. We can say, with Dante and Chaucer and Villon in mind, that in the Middle Ages religious poetry was not a special department of poetry: religion extended instead of limiting the poet's range. In the modern world religious poetry tends more and more to become a special branch of poetry, and the poet thinks of himself as an isolated figure. He thinks of himself as the spokesman either of a particular religious body as Crashaw and Herbert—the Catholic and the Anglican did—, or as the champion of Christianity waging a lonely war against the forces of secularism. *Paradise Regained* is not a Christian epic: it is the epic of Protestant modernism and the voice is the strident voice of a president of the Modern Churchman's Union. Racine's *Athalie* is the drama of the Jansenist fighting a losing battle on two fronts against political despotism and the machinations of the Society of Jesus. There is a third group—the group which includes Donne's *Holy Sonnets,* the best of Hopkins and a poem like Eliot's *Little*

Gidding—in which the poet is concerned less with the interpretation of life in terms of a universal religion than with the expression of a personal religious drama.

THE LOSS OF THE HISTRIONIC AND THE MODERN QUANDARY OF THEOLOGY

Tom F. Driver

We live at a time when the dramatic imagination and the histrionic sensibility do not flourish. As a drama critic whose love of the theater goes back to his earliest memories, it pains me to say such a thing, but it is true nevertheless. The theater does not yield today our major artistic statements.

Which of us, to pose the matter rhetorically, would not rather have been the author of *The Sound and the Fury* than *A Streetcar Named Desire?* Who would not rather have written *Sunday Morning* than *Death of a Salesman?* Who would prefer to be instructed in the life of the mind by Eugene O'Neill, Arthur Miller, Tennessee Williams, Edward Albee rather than by Nathaniel Hawthorne, Herman Melville, Mark Twain, Henry James, Faulkner, Frost, Aiken, Stevens, Robert Penn Warren, or any number of other poets and novelists we might mention?

The greater degree of admiration we hold for the latter group does not mean simply that our best men of letters happen not to be writing plays. It means that the dramatic form does not at this time afford them a means of saying what they wish to say. The dramatic imagination is somehow at odds with our experience. That is why, when an Archibald MacLeish, a William Faulkner, a Saul Bellow, or a Robert Lowell writes a play, he produces something inferior to his other work.

Drama requires, for its maximum fulfillment, a high degree of social cohesion with regard to values, symbols, and myths. Drama must be predicated upon certain understandings of life and its processes held in common by the audience. Above all other arts, drama is the art of shared response. (At least, above all other arts of the spoken or written word, though perhaps not more than music or dance.) In a theater, one's feeling of solidarity with the audience is the prerequisite of his becoming involved with what happens on the stage. Without the former, the latter cannot be very great.

It does not follow that the main function of drama is to perpetuate or increase the cohesion of society. In fact, the history of drama shows the opposite to be true. Most major dramatists attack the solidarity of the audience, by attacking the values and received opinions the audience holds and which hold the audience together. It has been said, notably by Ferdinand Brunetière, that the "law of the theater" is conflict. If this is true, we might observe that the basic conflict is never the one on stage but rather the one between the playwright and the audience. The audience's shield of certainty is pelted by the playwright's arrows of doubt. For this reason, it is the tragic destiny of drama to destroy the conditions necessary to its own greatness, to corrode its own foundations. After Sophocles, Euripides. After the conflict between certainty and doubt in the one, the rabid bite of skepticism in the other. Then the history of Greek tragedy comes to a close. After Shakespeare, John Webster. After Ibsen, Alfred Jarry. After O'Neill and Williams, Edward Albee. Drama destroys, or at any rate helps to destroy, the sense of reality on which it feeds.

One way of describing the plight of drama today is to say that its own acids seem mild compared to other acids present in the culture. In 1611, at a time of cultural tension highly productive of drama, John Donne could write, "The new philosophy puts all in doubt." Were one to write such a line today, the reply would be, "*Which* new philosophy puts all *what* in doubt?" The more open and "advanced" society becomes through industrialization and the growth of many political and intellectual opinions, the more the dramatist feels the uselessness of his task in the face of cultural fragmentation.

Ferdinand Brunetière, whom I mentioned a moment ago, was one of the critics who have drawn a very sharp contrast between the drama and the novel. In his essay on "The Law of the Theatre," written in 1894, he put it in the following way:

> The proper aim of the novel, as of the epic, of which it is only a secondary and derived form—what the naturalists call a sub-species or a variety—the aim of the *Odyssey* as of *Gil Blas*, of the *Knights of the Round Table* as of *Madame Bovary*—is to give us a picture of the influence that is exercised upon us by all that is outside of ourselves. The novel is therefore the contrary of the drama.

The opposition between the drama and the novel is a familiar one, and it is also familiar that the novel has come to occupy a place much closer to the concerns of modern man than the theater. "I should always," wrote Laurence Lerner, "suspect of mere nostalgia a critic who denied (even if he regretted) that [the novel] had become for us the central literary form" (*The Truest Poetry* [London, 1960], pp. 193-194).

Mr. Lerner partly means that the novel has become the most popular form of literature, leaving aside for the moment the McLuhanish question of how popular literature itself may be, no matter of what kind. At the same time the novel has become the most relevant form of literature for modern man's self-understanding. Mr. Lerner means that for us the novel has assumed the place once held by the drama.

It is true that today certain types of literature are perhaps even more popular than the novel; and I do not wish to get into the question of the future of the novel itself, whose ills are being proclaimed and diagnosed on every hand. It may be that discursive prose is the most influential type of literature being written and published today. Here I am concerned with literature written to feed our imaginations, and especially to feed them by the telling of stories. In this respect the contrast between the novel and the drama has yet something to teach us.

Unlike drama, the novel has a capacity to adapt itself kaleidoscopically to a multitude of shifting human perspectives. It is, as we know, closer akin to the motion picture than to the stage. In a novel, as in a film, the most important available technique is the close-up, a device invented not by D. W. Griffith but by Homer and resurrected in our time to revolutionize the art of narrative. (Film cutting, as an aesthetic technique, is an outgrowth of the close-up. Not until the close-up became important did film cutting and the mobility of the camera become important or even much used.)

The novel and the motion picture share a penchant for detail. To be more accurate, I should say a penchant for the *casual* detail. When a playwright focuses upon a detail, he lifts it immediately, and sometimes in spite of himself, from the casual to the symbolic: Desdemona's handkerchief, the boots of Miss Julie's father, the electric light bulb in *A Streetcar Named Desire*, and so on. There are very few purely naturalistic plays because the stage has a tendency to turn *things* into symbols. Thus the progenitor of symbolic drama in the modern theater was naturalism itself, a progression we can see very clearly in the career of Gerhard Hauptmann as well as in Strindberg and many others. When the audience, being assembled in the theater, has its attention called to any detail, it asks, even if unconsciously, Why did you point us to that? What does that detail mean? This question does not arise nearly so fast nor so insistently when one reads a novel. The reason is twofold.

First, one reads a novel by himself, wherever and whenever he pleases. Thus he gives it a different sort of concentration from that which he gives a play, when he is a member of a particular audience at a particular place on a particular evening.

Second, the novel lives before one by virtue of the fact that it *flows*. A play does not flow, not even a play of Chekhov. It marches, or it dances. But a novel flows. Fast or slow, languid or turbulent, straight or meandering, it is a stream. Reading it, I move along the stream of consciousness, or the stream of life, and I am never unduly surprised nor automatically arrested by details encountered on the way. Any detail may be picked out by the novelist, examined, turned over, re-marked upon, and then dropped back into the flux, or left standing on the bank. To be sure, there are limits. The novel's unity and its theme do not allow for the appearance of details from life that are *utterly* irrelevant to the purpose in view, but the degree of that relevance may be very much lower in a novel than in a play, because we move on. The casual detail, interesting in its own right, is covered over in the succession of those that follow.

For this reason, the question of symbolism appears to the novelist quite differently from the way it appears to the dramatist. A play-wright discovers that in his first draft of the play, especially if he is just learning his craft, symbols grow up like weeds. This chair has suddenly turned into a throne. That bird the cat killed is proclaiming itself to be the human soul ravaged by time. And oh, how that potted plant in the window is carrying on! It is about to become Persephone. But suppose the playwright *wants* a symbol in his play. He had better watch out. That iguana under the porch will heave and throw the whole play out of balance.

The novelist has a different problem, provided he really is a novelist and not a playwright in disguise. His task is not to pull out unwanted symbols that grow of their own accord but rather to encourage them, lest they become lost in the flux. A symbolic play can be written by accident. A symbolic novel is an achievement.

This difference indicates the primary reason why the novel has become more directly relevant to modern experience than the drama. The basic temper of our age, philosophically speaking, is positivistic. This calls forth counter-tendencies toward ethereal spirituality, a spirit-uality not oriented positively toward the public order nor the order of human work, but toward fantasy and everything which at the moment goes under the name of the "expansion of consciousness." It is the middle ground that is lost, the ground where one is concerned with the actual created world as the bearer of symbolic and analogical meaning, an idea most strongly expressed in modern times by Gerard Manley Hopkins with the term *inscape*. It is on that middle ground that drama really has to stand. In the last analysis, it may be that the novel does also; but the novel has consorted terribly well with the positivist drift in modern thinking because, as Laurence Lerner said, in the book already cited:

> The rise of the novel goes with and is a symptom of the concern for peo-ple as themselves, not for their symbolic significance, their supernatural backing, their patterning into types, but for their uniqueness.
> (*The Truest Poetry*, p. 193)

Thus, although it may be the case that in the long run the difficulties which have overcome the theater will also overcome the novel, the impact upon the novel is delayed.

It is well known that the theater is undergoing a crisis, and perhaps that it has lost any great degree of social importance. When we mention these things, it is important to think not merely of the *symptoms* of the theatrical crisis. Such symptoms are the decline in the size of the theater audience, the scarcity of good new plays, the inconvenience of going to the theater, the tone of grey disappointment that accompanies most of our visits there, the competition from movies and TV, the high cost of tickets—in short, everything that seems to conspire to make theater-going more of an ordeal than a joy. These I regard as symptoms. They are the symptoms of a crisis in our *idea* of theater, our idea of what kind of place and what kind of activity the theater is, and what, if anything, is its function in our lives. If one speaks of the death of theater, as some do, he refers to the fact that the theater has virtually ceased to serve as an aesthetic focus for our experience.

Here I may turn to the quandary of modern theology. It is most visible in the spirit of skepticism and even atheism among the theologians themselves. I am thinking not only of certain famous theological names recently associated with "Christian atheism" but also of something both broader and deeper. We are living now in a generation of theology after Rudolf Bultmann, and Bultmann himself is simply a late and loud voice in liberal Christian theology raising the kind of question for faith, or rather for credence, that has been implicit, if not explicit, in theology ever since the historical criticism of Scripture was first undertaken. It would not be accurate to suggest that historical criticism of Scripture is the principal source of the quandary of modern theology, but it is a very important part of it, since it pushes theology from history toward myth at a time when there is no adequate way to understand myth philosophically. But let us mention other tendencies as well.

The critique of theological language as meaningless, a position held rigorously by logical positivism, less so by the linguistic analysis that developed out of it, has provided a kind of backdrop for all theological discussion in the last forty years. It has served, whether justifiably or not, to put a question mark over the whole of theological discourse. However, it could not, by itself, have modified greatly the situation that has obtained since the Enlightenment. Its force has been due largely to the fact that it has coincided historically with certain strong moral and psychological arguments against the reality of God. Both Freud and Nietzsche attacked God because of his being the moral judge. They attacked the God who says, "Thou shalt not," and who passes judgment upon man's disobedience. They did this because they thought God was a harmless illusion, a way of rationalizing human weakness. For Nietzsche, this God either covered up or enervated man's will to power. For Freud, he delayed or prevented the development of ego-strength. He masqueraded as the super-ego, condemning the urges of the libido and preventing the ego from asserting fully its independence and rationality. Thus, he stood in the way of the Freudian maxim: Where id was, there shall ego be. In short, Freud felt that God enabled one to rationalize his Oedipus complex. Therefore one had to oppose him in order to mature, just as one has to break psychologically with his own father in order to become fully man.

It would be easy to show how this type of psychological and moral rejection of God has appeared in modern drama as well as in philosophy and psychology. One could refer to Georg Buechner, Friedrich Hebbel, Henrik Ibsen, August Strindberg, Eugene O'Neill and many, many others. Modern drama has certainly helped wage the battle against the moral and psychological authority of God, and thus it has helped to set the stage, so to speak, for the contemporary theology of the death of God, particularly in the form this has taken in the writings of William Hamilton, but also to some extent in Thomas Altizer. But it has done more than that. It has set this stage for all of us and has helped prepare in us something that is at least partly sympathetic to the *cri de coeur* that death of God theology represents.

However, we do not get to the heart of the matter merely by suggesting that some of the major modern dramatists have contributed to the climate of opinion in which the present theological quandary comes to light. It is better to see that there are common factors at work on both drama and theology, that the same forces are inimical to them both.

To find what these forces are, we should look not at certain obvious mistakes the modern age has made, but rather at things the modern age has done well, at things we can hardly imagine it as having done very differently or not having done at all. One such factor, surely, is the development of technology, by which I mean not simply a certain form of knowledge and power but a scientific development that issues in a characteristic way of life, particularly urban life. I have in mind the phenomenon that Harvey Cox and others have called *technopolis*.

Urban life characterized by increasing dependence on types of organization made possible by technology has had a deleterious effect upon the theater and also upon the communities of religious faith that create theology. The irony of this with respect to the theater is easy to see. For technological reasons, the theater today is concentrated in large cities. Theater work in all other communities is dependent on what is done in metropolitan centers. In the United States the life of the theater is almost completely determined by its fate in New York City, the recent development of residential theaters in various other places notwithstanding. At the same time, the city destroys the theater. That is why great hopes come to be pinned on theaters outside of New York; but these hopes are futile, because the same tendencies that make theatrical creativity so difficult in New York are present in the other urban centers as well, though their date of development may be a bit slower. In the long run, they will have, in Atlanta as in New York, the same discouraging effect upon histrionic sensibility.

There are many ways to describe why city life has this effect. The economist and the sociologist have much to say to the point; but I am interested in the matter of aesthetic sensibility, and I suggest that technopolis is anti-histrionic because *technology destroys space.* This dictum is not, of course, a literal statement. It carries a psychological and spiritual import. Technology renders all space the same, tending to neutralize the meaning of space. It erodes the meaningfulness of particular places.

To be well adjusted to technopolis, to live the good life in a modern urban setting, one must be on the move. But this movement is not, strictly speaking, a movement to *places.* Instead, it is movement to where certain people happen to live, to where they gather, to certain equipment (people plus equipment equal "the office") or to where certain events are scheduled. The combination of people, equipment, and events may be called a *cluster.* In technopolis one goes to whatever cluster is important at the moment, and the cluster is far more important than the place.

It was because movement is so important in the city that Harvey Cox, in *The Secular City,* hit upon Exodus as the Biblical image pertinent to our time. But the Exodus image does not really fit, because in the Biblical story the Israelites were very conscious of space, of leaving the *place* called Egypt and moving *through* desert *to* promised land. In technopolis, movement as such has no more meaning than space as such, and for the same reason.

It is not surprising, therefore, that the motion picture and television fare better in technopolis than does the theater. The motion picture camera and the television camera, thanks to "cutting," move with a freedom so nearly absolute that change from place to place ceases to be important. This can be put inversely as well: with a camera, change of location and perspective is everything. It is so omnipresent, so much a part of the camera's innate potentiality, that it comes to be taken almost absolutely for granted. The movement that *is* important in film and television is a movement through time—the movement that is aesthetically arranged by cutting from one image to another regardless of space.

The theater, like dance and unlike cinema, is the art of the use of finite space. It requires a space that does not move, that is fixed, limited, that imposes restraints. The aesthetic of theater is in large part built upon the imaginative overcoming of fixed space, just as the aesthetic of painting is largely built upon the imaginative overcoming of a two-dimensional limitation. When the theater is at its height it binds infinite space into a nutshell, as Hamlet said.

> O God, I could be bounded in a nutshell and count myself a king
> of infinite space, were it not that I have bad dreams.
> (II. ii. 260)

Hamlet was speaking, to be sure, of his mind, but the image was theatrical. His was a theatrical understanding of consciousness: an infinite abound concentrated into a finite arena.

If we have a society which, owing to technology, renders space per se of little account, then the art of the theater must suffer. One reason that repertory theater is difficult is that we prefer to patronize *plays* rather than *theater*. The patronage of individual plays, rather than of the theater as such, indicates a loss of histrionic sensibility. We do not go, ever expectant, to *a* theater-place as to a kind of temple. Instead, we shop. The result is that the playwright has no home, and the result of *that* is that the shopping is poor.

As for theology, it becomes necessary for technopolitan man to envision God in spaceless ways, which is well-nigh impossible. A more accurate description of what has happened in modern society than to say that God has died is to say that he has lost his abode. I speak symbolically again, as when I referred to the theater. We have to do, on the one hand, with an aesthetic sensibility and on the other with a theological sensibility. No space nowadays can symbolize the dwelling-place of God, not primarily because we have learned what theology has almost always known—namely, that such language is indeed symbolic or analogical—but because the analogy has ceased to hold, since its human, experiential term has ceased to function. We cannot speak of a dwelling-place of God because space has been de-symbolized in technopolitan society. We should not laugh when the unsophisticated ask, as children frequently do, where God lives. In the sky, in the church, or where? Literally, the question is absurd and draws our smile. Symbolically, the question is asked by a human being who knows himself to be flesh and blood, therefore an occupant of space, whose imagination is inseparable from his feeling for place and three-dimensionality. The question, Where does God live? means, What is the ultimate place where I belong? What is the space of my being?

Once upon a time, I sat in the theater at Epidauros. When I was there, I knew, with an immediate aesthetic perception, that I was in the center of the world, a conviction that could not be dislodged even if at the same time I knew that there might be other centers; and I did not at all want to leave that particular place, although there was no play going on at the moment. It was deserted except for me and a few of my friends. Yet I knew that any actor on that stage, provided he were competent at all, would bring a revelation, for I was in the *theatron,* the place of seeing.

Utterly opposed to the histrionic sensibility and to the idea of theater is the happening, in spite of what a good many of its enthusiasts have said. The happening derives from painting and expresses non-histrionic types of aesthetic response, for it ruthlessly subordinates space to *occurrence.* It is what I call a cluster. Therefore the location of a happening, in the sense of its being a finite space, is not important. In fact, happenings usually avoid the theater. Important instead is the unforeseen, the unpredictable, the occurrence in time, which is the meaning I intend by the word cluster. By contrast, that which is histrionic *fills space.* It fills it with event, to be sure; but it is a filling of space. We do not appreciate this partly because technopolis does not prepare us to and partly because we so rarely see it. However, to cite a recent example, there is no question but that the excellence of the Royal Shakespeare Company's production of Harold Pinter's *The Homecoming* was very largely due to the fact that the company found itself so well able to fill the total space occupied by the setting and the audience. Many spectators observed in *The Homecoming* an articulation of space comparable to the best that can be found in the art of dance. This reminds me to note that the most lively histrionic sensibility to be found in America is that of Martha Graham. She shows us the theatrical root from which have sprung the divergent stems known as drama and dance.

The theater is the marriage of time and space. It is the aesthetic of their fulfillment in purpose.

Still another cause of the loss of the histrionic is to be found in the modern search for meaning, particularly the quest for "authentic existence." There is felt to be an inherent antagonism between authenticity and form. Beginning in the latter part of the eighteenth century, our age has defined authenticity as that which proceeds from man himself and has rebelled against all that originates elsewhere. As if this were not enough, the idea of man himself has been taken to mean the individual. Beyond that, the individual has increasingly been taken to mean the individual in the present moment. Hence, the authentic is often associated with the spontaneous and the immediate. This leads to a revolt against all form that is *given,* a revolt against all received form. Classical form of course was attacked. August Wilhelm von Schlegel called classical form "mechanical" and by that word put it down. He preferred, he said, "organical" form. But the distinction between mechanical and organic form soon breaks down, for the simple reason that any form as such is enduring. Therefore, in the name of authenticity and spontaneity, frequently felt to be the same, the forms of one generation, by whatever adjective they be called, are rejected by the next. With that, we might perhaps be able to live. Indeed, without it we could hardly imagine any continued creativity in cultural history. But it goes deeper than that.

The particular form created a moment ago is rejected now. Not only is the form of a previous generation rejected by this one, but also the form of my creativity a while ago, yesterday or even this morning, which stands there more or less objectively opposed to me, comes to be rejected because it is already outside of me. Existing by virtue of its perduring form, it seems to be over against the *now* of my present authenticity. In certain historical moments this is liberating, but in our culture it has gone on for nearly two centuries and has come to be bad for most of the arts, worst of all for theater.

For some eighty years we have been babbling honorifically about new forms of theater, about experimental theater, about laboratory theater. We seem not to have noticed that it was the word *new* and not the word *forms* that carried our meaning and our intent. It goes almost without notice that the so-called experimentation is done without any controls and is therefore not experiment but sheer innovation. Thus what we are trying desperately to drive out of theater is its ritual quality, its formal rightness. The formal rightness of any play is such that we delight to see it done again and again, perhaps with some variations, but essentially the same. This establishes a kind of ritual character for the theater, and precisely this is today the theater's greatest embarrassment. There is an attempt desperately to drive it out and replace it by that which is casual, unforeseen, impromptu— a notion that consorts well with an aesthetic that is frequently called "disposable art."

It is ironic that we are doing this just at the time when, because of the knowledge available to us through historical research, we have become acutely aware of the ritual quality of all theater. The ritual origin of theater and its latent ritualistic tendencies are common knowledge. But since we do not like ritual and certainly do not trust it, we tend to push that very quality to extremes in order to destroy it, by a strategy of turning form into formal*ism.* This is the tack taken by the so-called *avant garde* theater.

The intensified formalism of Jean Genet results in very exciting theater. Genet is unique in having a very firm ritual instinct and the effect in his particular case is not negative. In Beckett and Ionesco, however, it is; also in Pinter and Albee and by far the majority of the lesser playwrights of the moment. In historical perspective most drama since World War II must be seen as anti-ritual, an attempt to kill form with formalism.

It is the same in religion. Driven out of his space, God has also been driven out of ritual form. Almost the worst thing that a critic can say of a religious practice nowadays is that it is ritual. The symbolic character of ritual is less and less appreciated, although theoretically it has seldom been appreciated more. Existentially it carries no high value. We discern this in an instant when we realize that the word *ritual,* used as an adjective, is almost an antonym of the term *authentic.*

These factors, taken together, show that the notion of vicarious experience is very much in decline. Instead, there is a great longing for, and very much talk about, various types of immediate identification. The motion picture screen and the television screen tend to present us with images and characters with whom we identify immediately, and this is a different thing from vicarious experience.

When the Elizabethans went to the theater, they did not see in Macbeth, Lear, Antony, or Coriolanus mirror images of themselves. Nor did they see characters with whom they might immediately identify. They saw heroic individuals in extraordinary stories, expressing themselves in extraordinary language. The audience brought to the theater a willingness to extend itself, to participate vicariously in an action that would probably never unfold the same way in real life. The diminution of the capacity for vicarious experience began with the rise of the middle class. This class was the most self-preoccupied of all people in the history of the world. The reason was that the only hold it had on reality was money. Whoever owes his position in the world to money will tend to regard himself as a subject of unlimited interest. Money is not inherently interesting. The bourgeois, having only money to point to as his work, being therefore essentially uncreative, points to himself and his family as subjects that are interesting. He comes to see the world as an extension of himself. Uncreative in his work, he is actually afraid of vicarious experience, for he fears losing the only reality he knows, namely, himself. Hence, it is the bourgeoisie, more than the workers, who destroy the public and replace it by mass society. Perhaps the worker has been standardized by the conditions of his employment, but the bourgeois consciously *standardizes himself* in order that he may believe in himself by seeing how similar he is to his neighbor. It is the loss of capacity for vicarious experience—the ability to participate in the experience of another, who is unlike myself and whom I shall have to relate to myself by an act of imaginative correlation—it is this loss which is so terribly important in the loss of the histrionic and which accounts for the phenomenon with which we are all familiar about the drama, namely, the decreasing importance in it of that element which Aristotle called the soul of tragedy, the plot or the *mythos*.

Northrop Frye has called our attention to the fact that periods of high tragedy (what he calls the "high mimetic") are periods in which the form of the aesthetic work is paramount and in which the relation of that form to life will have to be regarded as allegorical. I would prefer the term *analogical* to *allegorical*. Nevertheless, the main point is clear: from the formally mimetic to life, a passage has to be made by some kind of indirect interpretation in which an imaginative stretching is required. One has to see correspondences between things that are dissimilar but that share certain unstated yet fundamental properties. This has gone for most people, and with it has gone the great importance that used to be attached to plot. Not only plot, but also story. And as story and plot decline, so also does the importance of character.

In an article on character and theater in the *Tulane Drama Review*, Summer 1966, the psychiatrist, Donald M. Kaplan, called attention to the problems that actors face when they are called upon to do something on stage other than to portray roles. He quotes from a piece Michael Smith had written in *The Village Voice* describing his attempts to stage a one-act play by Sam Shepherd called *Icarus' Mother*. Smith had said:

> The actors had trouble. When, for example, two men were called upon to make smoke signals, they wanted to know exactly what they were doing and why they were doing it, and it was insufficient to tell them, although true, that all they were doing was making smoke signals, and the reason was Shepherd's and the play's rather than theirs. My first fault was failing to make this clear.

Upon this Donald Kaplan comments:

> If that is all they want their actors to do, they must use children. Called upon to make some signals on stage, children would never ask exactly what they were doing. They would simply make smoke signals, but trained adult actors just can't do this.

The loss of vicarious experience, the loss of plot and story, the loss of character—these proceeding from the loss of the sense of finite space and of ritual form—all this is meant by the loss of the histrionic. And if this poses certain radical questions about the future existence of theater, it also has something to do with the quandary in which modern theology finds itself.

The roots of theology lie in the Biblical witness to the divine activity and in the religious experience of the community of faith created by that activity. Thus both the Biblical and the ecclesiastical understandings of God have largely been shaped by elements that are, if not identical with the histrionic, at any rate parallel to it and consonant with it. Since modern experience is increasingly out of touch with that histrionic quality, the principal concepts of theology are gradually eroded of their cognitive content. I am thinking of such concepts as creation, sin, incarnation, redemption, salvation, perhaps providence. These terms were never oriented primarily toward scientific or even proto-scientific modes of understanding. They are not oriented principally toward the world of nature, though they imply certain things about nature. Their orientation was basically anthropological in the sense that they proceeded from basic apperceptions about being human and carrying on a human life. They rested to a large extent upon histrionic sensibility, man's sense of himself as an occupant of space, an actor in ritual, one capable of going out of himself by imaginative reach and returning to himself by the incorporation of his imaginative adventure. The loss of the histrionic creates a quandary for theology because it tends to render of no credit the content of the theological vocabulary and syntax.

I do not know whether anything can be done about the condition that I have described. It is not my intention to prescribe a remedy but only to describe the situation in a more accurate way than seems previously to have been done.

It has been thought, for instance, that the problems confronting modern theology are due to the philosophical situation. I doubt that this is the case. I rather think that the philosophical situation is itself more or less determined by the loss of the histrionic. It has also been thought that the problems of modern theology had principally to do with a choice of vocabulary and that if a way could be found to translate traditional theological vocabulary into contemporary terms, the problems would be overcome. I had to learn some years ago that this is not the case, because it was frequently felt that to translate theology into drama would contribute to its revived understanding. Confronted with such a request, I became aware that the attempt would only compound the problem, for reasons that should be clear from what I have already said.

Again, it has been thought that the crisis of theology is fundamentally a crisis of faith. That no doubt is true, but it is near to being a tautology. It is not as if there were no religious or even Christian disposition in many persons today. That factor is probably more or less constant in various cultural periods. At any rate, it can only be discussed when we have made the movement from faith to theology; that is to say, when we have begun to articulate faith. It is there, right early, that we begin to encounter the problems of the funding of our language and syntax that I have described.

Modern man is, for better or worse, and whether consciously or unconsciously, attempting to find some mode of self-understanding that is different from the histrionic, to see himself as something other than an actor upon a world stage, to see himself as oriented other than in space, and to see the patterns of his life in something other than ritual form. The question is whether that is possible.

Speaking for myself, I do not yet see that it is. At any rate, I rather expect that it will be to the students and practitioners of psychology that we will have to look for some kind of evaluative judgments about whether there are indeed non-histrionic models for the growth and maturation of human beings. Are there modes other than the dramatic for productively understanding what it is that occurs and should occur in the growth of the child from infancy to old age? If there are, then perhaps we shall be able to enter upon a new cultural period that can be no less exalted in its own way than have certain periods of the past. But it may be that this is not possible and that the loss of the histrionic portends a general loss of culture and of human self-understanding.

At any rate, it is something like this context that I see for the quandary of modern theology, and I do not yet see that it is possible for aesthetic movements in culture to be able to come to the theologian's rescue. I rather expect that we shall have to wait and see whether the loss of the histrionic means the loss of man or whether it simply means his transmutation into a kind of humanity that has not yet been envisioned.

III: RELIGIOUS DIMENSIONS IN MODERN LITERATURE

FRANZ KAFKA: THE ATHEIST'S PROBLEM OF GOD

Gabriel Vahanian

Kafka the lucid could not help it if his morbidity was to become an instrument of frustrated catharsis for our generation; nor could he prevent his logic from enshrining the absurd in the breast of modern man. Neither a totalitarian nor a moralist, he denounced the morality of dogmatism as well as the dogmatism of religion. And when in his work he passes over God in silence, he forces us to realize that God is no longer the missing link we boast of in. justifying ourselves or our loud religiosities.

Not a prophet, nor claiming to be one, it is not Kafka's fault if we find in his work, in the illusory world of his tales and parables, the mirror that reflects the upside-down image of our present condition.

He received no mandate ever from anyone, did not even speak in his own name. Simply seeking to grasp the illusion of a reality—his own—that cannot comprehend itself, he now confronts us with the reality of our own illusion—with no other reality than that of our illusions about God, about man, about the world, justice, and humanity.

Coming from the very heart of man's night, Kafka's voice immediately dispels the deafness into which we have complacently sunk our hearing. But what we hear is not what he said. What we understand is not what he meant. Yet he did say it and he did mean it. But each of us can grasp and understand it only in his own way. We could apply to him his parable of the Sirens: "These are the seductive voices of the night; the Sirens, too, sang that way. It would be doing them an injustice to think that they wanted to seduce; they knew they had claws and sterile wombs, and they lamented this aloud. They could not help it if their laments sounded so beautiful."[1]

And what was it Kafka lamented so loudly and so beautifully? It was the possibility of our being many selves at once or alternately, of being more than oneself and by the same token less than oneself; in other words, it was the impossibility of being oneself, of taking up residence in oneself or, to recall Saint Augustine, of resting in

---

[1] Kafka, *Parables* (New York, 1947), p. 79.

oneself. But I am preaching. Kafka himself was no preacher: he did not embellish and try to improve upon his master's teachings. By the time of Kafka, anyway, no teaching was left that could sustain improvement. Is that not why he did not talk about God—or, for that matter, about man? He merely describes the situation of man, the logic of its incoherence as well as the contradictions of its logic.

What is man? A *flatus vocis,* a name reduced to its anonymous initial, a word that does not become flesh. "I lack nothing," observes Kafka, "except myself." He who so much loved precision, Max Brod tells us in his biography,[2] never cared fully to explain his characters. He believed in a world of exactness, in the indestructible, and yet uncertainty rules over his universe; man is frustrated from attaining the fullness of his being. He is nameless, because God is dead.

Or is it so? For we must remember that Kafka does not preach, either for or against God. He does not say that this is what man is like without God, namely wretched and desperate. Nor does he say that the idea of God is absurd. What, then, is he saying? Perhaps, that it is man's wretchedness itself that is absurd, because it prevents us from knowing our real condition as well as the real world unfailingly, although it exists. As Max Brod writes, "truth is visible everywhere. It shines through the nets of what we call 'reality.' "[3]

Man has been secularized. He has been thoroughly *laïcisé.* In 1914, Kafka enters in his diary this reflection: "What do I have in common with the Jews? I have hardly anything in common with myself, and I should keep quiet in a corner, content that I can breathe." Having nothing in common with himself, man has nothing in common with God, either. Of course, Kafka does not say that, since he never mentions God in his stories. With or without God, man is that being which has nothing in common with itself. Even less does he have anything in common with God. And it is hard to say which comes first, the absence of God or man's absence from himself.

Or are we digressing from Kafka by reading between the lines? Indeed, it might be objected, is not Kafka simply proclaiming the death of God? The answer is twofold. We must admit, to be sure, that Kafka is recording the cultural dimension of that event. As to whether, on the other hand, he also proclaims such an event, we may not answer this question affirmatively before we have realized, as Jean Starobinski points out in his introduction to *La Colonie pénitentiaire,* that this blasphemy—if blasphemy there is—is also a prayer, an invocation.[4] Admittedly, like all logic, the logic of blasphemy, too, imposes itself. It is self-evident and ineluctable, like a trial verdict

---

[2] Max Brod, *Franz Kafka* (Berlin & Frankfurt-am-Main, 1954), pp. 68-69.
[3] *Ibid.,* p. 65.
[4] Jean Starobinski, introduction to *La Colonie pénitentiaire* (Paris, 1945), pp. 29-30.

that has been handed down beforehand. But, unshakable as logic can be, it breaks down before the will to live (cf. Jean Wahl, *Esquisse pour une histoire de l'existentialisme*):

> "No one can say that we are wanting in faith. The mere fact of our living is itself inexhaustible in its proof of faith.
> "You call that a proof of faith? But one simply cannot live.
> "In that very 'simply cannot' lies the insane power of faith; in that denial it embodies itself."[5]

What kind of denial, of negation are we dealing with here? Clearly, we are first of all dealing with the negation into which life incarnates itself. As Camus would say: "I rebel, therefore we are." Kafka's man is a man who says no; more precisely, he ends up saying no simply because he has been saying nothing all along. But he cannot quite live on the logic of this no. Existence does not merely resolve itself into logical consistency. Thus, Kafka, who does not fully give us the key that would help us decipher his characters, hardly finishes his stories even when they are complete. He heralds the world of Picasso's *Guernica* as well as the advent of radical immanentism. He shows, too, that man cannot dwell in a universe of radical immanentism.

Kafka's particular merit is to have succeeded in translating into immanentist terms the values of a transcendental universe now discredited. Like Camus, he realized that the human spirit could conceive of the universe only from two possible angles—namely, that of the sacred (or that of grace) and that of rebellion.[6] These two are for both authors mutually exclusive. But unlike Camus, Kafka would also add that the universe of rebellion is (if one may say so) self-exclusive or self-negating; that is to say, it is one in which man lacks nothing but himself even when, as in *The Judgment*, all that is exhibited is not the irrationality of the Father's sentence, of God's justice, but the self-righteousness of Georg Bendemann and the senility of his father.

Kafka is not so much writing allegorical stories in which one thing consistently stands for another—for example the castle for God's grace—as he is writing about grace in immanentist terms, the only terms now meaningfully available. Perhaps this was a risky shot, an impossible bet. It can hardly be alleged that Kafka was a religious writer in the traditional sense, although he did consider the task of existing to be an act of faith, an invocation, a prayer, the only one that can be uttered when God is dead, that is, when God, ceasing to be a cultural accessory of man's self-understanding, can no longer be taken for granted.

Nor is Kafka writing symbolic novels in the traditional sense. He

---

[5] Kafka, "Reflections," in *The Great Wall of China* (New York, 1946), p. 307.
[6] Albert Camus, "Remarque sur la révolte," in *L'Existence* (Paris, 1945), p. 15.

does not postulate the meaningfulness of a universe bearing out God's design for his creation and for man. To be sure, once God is thus posited as the universal hypothesis, it is easy to find symbols that point to his reality. But this kind of symbolism makes sense only in the context of a transcendental *Weltanschauung*, or, better, in the context of a sacramental universe in which nature points to a supernatural world. But, Kafka's world is one that has lost its sacral dimension. It does not presuppose any reality from which it receives its meaning and to which it points. As the French critic Jean Paulhan has remarked apropos of modern painting, Kafka's world is replete with signs and symbols crying out for that which they signify and that which they symbolize. Unfortunately, the power of the symbol does not come from its own capacity to point to that which is symbolized but lies in its capacity to receive, like a receptacle, and to communicate or mediate that which is symbolized. From the traditional point of view, the power of the symbol lies just in this charismatic instrumentality—in that through it, so to speak, the word becomes flesh.

Clearly, Kafka understood that it was no longer so for modern man. Modern man has the symbol but not the meaning. "We are digging the pit of Babel,"[7] as he put it. Or, "if it had been possible to build the tower of Babel without ascending it, the work would have been permitted."[8] This impotence of the symbol is further stressed in *The Great Wall of China*, where the riddle of existence takes the form of the problem: how to build a round tower on the foundations of a wall that is not circular? And whatever else the following "reflection" means, we can sense that, quite appropriately, it clarifies the analysis that concerns us here: "What is laid upon us is to accomplish the negative; the positive is already given."[9] Man has the words, but not the Word. In contrast with Sartre, Kafka says: "There is a goal, but no way; what we call the way is only wavering."[10]

Not that self-deification is the task of man, as is the case with Sartre; but the Word cannot be extracted from the words of man; it can only take flesh in them in the same way that God "dwells" in the Ark of the Covenant, and that happens through no merit either of the words or of the Ark, for their efficacy is charismatic. Perhaps this explains why Kafka's world looks so much like yours and mine, and is at the same time so fantastically different. We tend to act like positivists, he does not. No wonder, then, that the doorkeeper's words in the fragment "Before the Law," included also in *The Trial*,

---

[7] Kafka, "Fragments," in *Dearest Father* (New York, 1954), p. 349.

[8] "Reflections," *op. cit.*, p. 282.

[9] *Ibid.*, p. 284.

[10] *Ibid.*, p. 283.

seems to address each of us: "No one else could ever be admitted here, since this gate was made only for you. I am now going to shut it."[11] There is no direct access from man to God, especially if—to refer to Sartre's caustic gloss—not only is the gate made only for each of us, but each of us makes his own gate. We cannot achieve authentic existence self-sufficiently. How, then, are we to achieve it?

Kafka sought it through his writing. Literature became his means of grace, his way of salvation. He wrote in his diaries: "I am more and more unable to think, to observe, to determine the truth of things, to remember, to speak, to share an experience; I am turning to stone, this is the truth. . . . If I can't take refuge in some work, I am lost." "But I will write in spite of everything, absolutely; it is my struggle for self-preservation."[12] Writing he considered as a form of prayer. There is no doubt that his greatest satisfaction, however ephemeral, came from it. Like Flaubert, as Max Brod tells us in his biography, Kafka sacrificed everything to his idol. One thing, however, he could not sacrifice to it, and that was what the God of the Old Testament required of man—a contrite heart. In this light alone can we understand Kafka's entry for the 25th of September, 1917, in which he declares that he could not be happy unless he succeeded in introducing the world to the true, the pure, the indestructible.

In The Trial, Joseph K. sees in a dream the artist Titorelli, who is the official painter of the tribunal and has some definite information concerning the outcome of the trial. Joseph K. asks him what the three possibilities are. Finally, the painter acquiesces and, "having performed a mysterious metamorphosis, he conducts Joseph K. towards his deliverance, and disappears. Art is not salvation."[13] "Art," Kafka wrote, "sacrifices and cancels itself."[14] It cannot name the unnamable. It cannot invent that which is symbolized. Nor could man be happy in imitating God.

But in acknowledging the failure of art, Kafka admits something else, too: his novels are not temples sheltering relics of obsolete symbols, purely and simply. Neither are they some kind of invocation to an unknown God. Rather, they are an unknown man's invocation to God. Or else why should Kafka have written? Obviously, he did not think that faith was something into which man could grow by himself, even if, in The Castle, he portrayed the land surveyor K as someone who seeks but one thing, to cease being a stranger, to be admitted into the community, to be accepted.

[11] Kafka, "Before the Law," The Penal Colony, Stories and Short Pieces (New York, 1948), p. 150; The Trial (New York, Mod. Lib.), p. 269.
[12] Quoted by J. H. Miller in The Tragic Vision and the Christian Faith, Nathan Scott, ed. (New York, 1957), p. 292.
[13] Marthe Robert, Kafka (Paris, 1960), p. 66.
[14] Kafka, "Eight Octavo Notebooks," in Dearest Father, p. 154.

In "Pourquoi parler" (*Nouvelle Revue Française*, December, 1962), Brice Parain notes that what Western culture is seeking today is perhaps a new religion, a new faith. "But a religion, or a faith, regardless of how greatly the need is felt, one cannot give to oneself." This would contradict the very definition of faith. Only a Messiah can give it. Meanwhile one can only pray. "But in order to pray, one must already have faith," and in whose name shall one pray? The situation thus seems to be without exit, and just at this point we seem to have rejoined Kafka. Or have we? Indeed, we have come to a gate and it is locked. Trying one key after another might occupy us a whole lifetime, but it will not unlock the gate. No cage ever went looking for a bird.[15] "From a certain point onward there is no longer any turning back. That is the point that must be reached."[16]

What is this point of no return? It is the incommensurability between God and man, yes, between God's justice and man's justice; the point of no return lies in the awareness that life cannot be corseted in the straitjacket of logical consistency. From a human point of view, life is the sum total of its contradictions, as Sartre would say. Quite simply, however, Kafka's problem is that of Abraham and that of Job. The only difference consists in the fact that Kafka apprehends his situation in the context not of a transcendental but of an immanentist universe. That probably is the reason God does not come into the picture.

But we must consider a further aspect of Kafka's statement of the problem. Not only is there no common measure between God's justice and man's; from where modern man stands, he can hope to understand God's justice even less than Job did. Accordingly, faith is all the more necessary if man wants to continue assuming responsibility for his existence: besides, "how could one help but go on living?"

Justice is always that of others. It has no common measure with one's own. Man is hence guilty and innocent alike. "We cannot assert the innocence of anyone," writes Camus in *The Fall*, "whereas we can state with certainty the guilt of all."[17] Quite simply, man is guilty precisely because he claims that he is innocent. In a letter to F. B., which he reproduces in his diaries (October 1, 1917), Kafka writes: "Should I examine myself thoroughly in order to know my ultimate goal, I would realize that I do not truly aspire to be good and conform to the exigencies of a supreme Tribunal. . . . One thing alone matters . . . this human tribunal which, besides, I seek to cheat without committing any fraud. . . ."[18] Kafka knows that this sounds like com-

15 "Reflections," *op. cit.*, p. 281.
16 *Ibid.*, p. 279.
17 Camus, *The Fall* (New York, 1957), p. 110.
18 Marthe Robert, *Kafka*, p. 178.

mitting a fraud in order to establish one's innocence. In fact, no sooner than begun, such an undertaking demonstrates its own futility by forcing man to face the real nature of the dilemma that splits him in the very heart of his being. On the one hand, "God is not needed to create guilt or to punish. . . . God's sole usefulness would be to guarantee innocence."[19] On the other hand, unable to claim innocence as his own victory, man cannot guarantee his existence either. He fails.

But we have not grasped the full meaning of this failure until we have finally consented to consider it as the failure and crisis of atheism, of innocence attempting to authenticate itself. Existence is not possible, man cannot live unless he is innocent, and if, more significantly, his innocence is guaranteed: man thus fails, but in an ultimate sense he can fail only because of God's absence—or, before God only. The crisis of man without God is thus the crisis of man before God. Once secularized, innocence defeats itself, whereas in the strange solidarity of guilt from which no one is excluded, much less by putting on the mask of innocence, "every man testifies to the crime of all the others."[20] Before whom? Oneself? Obviously this would be ludicrous. Before God, then? We might recall, here, Kafka's relationship with his father. He can assert himself only against his father, but he cannot conceive either rest or happiness without his father.[21]

The fundamental difference between Kafka and the atheist consists in that Kafka never cites God in his stories; he does not take God's name in vain or make graven images. Indeed, one might go so far as to say that Kafka's man almost belies Calvin's understanding of man as an idol-maker. *Almost:* to wit, the father's verdict in the *Judgment* is preceded by this remark: "An innocent child, yes, that you were, truly, but still more truly you have been a devilish human being!—And therefore take note: I sentence you now to death by drowning."[22]

Atheism objects that God is what each one conceives somewhat after his own fashion. By contrast, Kafka's insight is incomparably more perspicacious. No doubt, he sees the validity of the atheist's objection. He even makes it his own. But, while seemingly asserting it himself, he also invalidates it in one stroke by showing that it is a *trompe-l'oeil.* His point is well taken: one cannot use the absence of God in order to justify one's innocence anymore than one can use God to justify one's morality or one's religion. God is no exhibit in man's trial, no mere supporting document of man's case for him-

---

[19] Camus, *The Fall,* pp. 110, 111.

[20] *Ibid.,* p. 110.

[21] Cf. Claude Mauriac, *The New Literature* (New York, 1959). *La littérature contemporaire* (Paris, 1958), p. 24.

[22] Kafka, "Judgment," *Selected Stories of Franz Kafka* (New York, 1952, Mod. Lib.), p. 18.

self. One cannot justify one's innocence. Nor can one choose to be innocent, any more. than one can, as Groethuysen says apropos of *The Trial*, "choose one's own crime."[23] One knows too much to believe in one's innocence, much less to be innocent. To be means to be guilty. Indeed, should he be innocent, man could not bear his condition. Only the devilish, or inauthentic, man would dare make such a claim of innocence: at best, he uses it to hide himself, just as, in other climates and under different auspices, he can parade his religiosity in order better to conceal the face of God.

Clearly, on this point, Kafka's understanding of man's predicament, irrefragably though unexpectedly, quite conforms with biblical thought. Here too, one must add, Kafka does not merely reproduce biblical thought. That would scarcely make sense in a universe the frame of reference of which exhibits qualities that are incongruous with the biblical conception. Though Kafka seems to contradict the latter, he actually reiterates the biblical insight into the nature of man in terms of the only available universe of discourse of all those that are possible— his own, and our, immanentist world view. Indeed, both from Kafka's and the biblical points of view, to be means to be guilty. According to Genesis, the history of man begins with his fall. The state of Adamic innocence is not a human quality per se: it belongs to God, as Karl Barth points out, and not to man.[24] It qualifies man as God's creature. Being the seal of God on his creation, as it were, it signifies God's claim on man and on his allegiance. Accordingly, the notion of fallenness presupposes God's claim on man. Sinfulness implies that man should know why he is guilty, but does not. It means, however, that man claims innocence as his own quality, and that he wants to become like God but turns out to be his own idol. This is exactly the conclusion Kafka reaches by coming from the opposite direction. He writes: "The state in which we find ourselves is sinful, quite independently of guilt."[25]

In the last analysis, innocence comes to signify for Kafka the responsibility we must assume: it is our necessity to be—and to be guilty, for the simple reason that man sets up gods where there is no God and becomes an idolater, that is, a man without God: "The choice was put to them whether they would like to be kings or king's couriers," Kafka writes in his parable of the Couriers. "Like children they all wanted to be couriers. So now there are a great many couriers, they post through the world, and, as there are no kings left, shout

---

[23] Bernard Groethuysen, "A propos de Kafka," in Kafka, *Le Procès* (Paris, 1948), p. 7.
[24] Karl Barth, *Kirchliche Dogmatik* (Zollikon-Zürich, 1945), III/I, pp. 351-352; cf. Henri Bouillard, *Karl Barth* (Paris, 1957), II, p. 201, n. 1.
[25] Kafka, "Reflections," *op. cit.*, p. 79.

to each other their meaningless and obsolete messages. They would gladly put an end to their wretched lives, but they dare not because of their oath of service."[26]

Thus innocence is the incapacity of knowing in the name of whom or of what we may assume such responsibility. "It is a mandate. Because of my very nature I can assume nothing other than a mandate I have received from no one." Neither can he, on the other hand, refuse to accept such a mandate, if only because of his "oath of service." "It is in this contradiction and ever in this contradiction that I can live."[27] In the light of Kafka's logic, what else can this mean than that innocence is the illusion by which self-contradiction attempts to put up with itself, or simply the rationalization of meaninglessness? Besides, to whom is the courier without a king to deliver his meaningless message? Therefore, the innocent is like one who would proclaim his innocence, but there is nobody who listens or even hears what he proclaims in the first place. Innocence cannot be proved, especially if existence is the sum total of its contradictions. Ultimately, the innocent looks like one who would confess his sinfulness—but, he thinks, there is only that which denies him. Or is there?

We have now come to the fundamental implication of Kafka's work. Let us state it gradually. By his very nature man is against God. But he cannot be without him. Neither the claiming of innocence nor atheism—which in effect amounts to the same thing—can resolve this contradiction. As Camus put it, the ultimate attempt of the land surveyor is to find God through that which denies him.[28] But Camus, too, immediately misses the point. What denies God is not his inscrutability or his indifference, nor is it his injustice. What attempts to deny God and fails is man's indifference and man's injustice, just as, on another level, it is equally man's *trompe-l'oeil* religiosity and morality, that is to say, his pretension to deity. The God against whom Kafka rebels, the God who for him is dead, in the last analysis, is not the Wholly Other but that which we mistake for God by writing man in capital letters—the universal hypothesis that serves no other purpose than as a prop to justify our pretenses, our contradictions. No more than it was possible to build the tower of Babel without ascending it, can God be reached by simply assembling our contradictions and pretenses as "a tower with its top in the heavens." Climb as high as we may the scaffolding of our innocence, God is not "its top in the heavens."

What this means is that any tower of Babel, since it must be built by ascending it, makes God unnecessary. This applies to our denial

---

[26] *Ibid.*, p. 289; *Parables*, p. 117.
[27] Kafka, *Journal intime* (Paris, 1945), p. 222.
[28] Camus, *Le Mythe de Sisyphe* (Paris, 1942), p. 181.

of God as well as to our religious systems: they are the necessary scaffolding that prevents the building of the tower. God cannot be reached or denied if man must climb the scaffolding of self-justification. God is no *tour de force* by which existence may authenticate itself and thus invalidate God. Accordingly, *mutatis mutandis,* in the context of an immanentist universe the atheist faces the same predicament as does the theist in the context of a transcendental universe.

The difference may be expressed in the following manner. The dilemma of the theist is that he takes God for granted and ends by building a tower of Babel. The dilemma of the atheist, on the other hand, lies in that he eliminates God but cannot avoid him. It is the dilemma, furthermore, of the contemporary world. Being immanentist, modern man's world view, so to speak, seeks to dig the pit of Babel. No more than the tower, does it succeed in eliminating God. In other words, God is no longer necessary, he is inevitable.

Would it be too much, from this vantage point, to say that the atheist is the herald of that God who is no longer necessary—no longer the necessary cog of a universal machine, no longer a missing link? Or, to borrow a biblical phrase, the atheist is the herald of the coming God, that God who precisely is no longer necessary in the immanentist framework of our universe. Exactly this, one could legitimately argue, is the point of the question asked in the New Testament: "When the Son of Man comes will he find faith on earth?" As Kafka himself wrote: "The Messiah will come only when he is no longer necessary; he will come only on the day after his arrival; he will come, not on the last day, but on the very last."[29]

Meanwhile, Kafka remarks, life is such a distraction that it prevents us even from realizing what we are distracted from. To be, therefore, is to be guilty. By the same token, existing is itself an act of faith. To live means to believe. To have faith means to be freed from our pretension to dispense with God as well as from our false conceptions of God (as all our conceptions are): "Believing means liberating the indestructible element in oneself, or more accurately, liberating oneself, or more accurately, being indestructible, or more accurately being."[30] Indeed, "man cannot live without an enduring trust in something indestructible in himself. Yet while doing that he may all his life be unaware of that indestructible thing and of that trust in it. One of the possible ways in which this permanent unawareness may be expressed is to have faith in a personal God."[31] Only thus can what we call the way cease from being mere wavering. Hidden or revealed the goal is there. But the ways of man do not lead to it.

[29] *Parables,* p. 65. Also, "The Eight Octavo Notebooks," *op. cit.,* p. 78.
[30] "The Eight Octavo Notebooks," *op. cit.,* p. 78.
[31] "Reflections," *op. cit.,* pp. 52-53.

Something always obstructs them: it is the bush, the same that was burning and yet was not consumed: "The thornbush is the old obstacle in the road. It must catch fire if you want to go further."[32]

We have, indeed, come a long way from Abraham, the father of faith, who put his own faith into question by his willingness to sacrifice Isaac, the child he and Sara had in their old age. But the radical immanentism that informs existence today gives us only the illusion that Abraham's story is improbable, chiefly because God's absence is the only reality we can experience, because he has become unnecessary. But God is inevitable. And man still wishes to imitate Abraham—if only he could be another Abraham. But supposing he could be, he would have no Isaac to sacrifice. To an age for which God is dead, Kafka seems to be saying: if it were possible to believe in God without sacrificing Isaac God would be dead.

---

[32] "The Eight Octavo Notebooks," *op. cit.*, p. 75.

CHRIST AS TRAGIC HERO:
CONRAD'S LORD JIM

Edwin Moseley

Writing in the last decade of the nineteenth century and for almost twenty-five years thereafter, Joseph Conrad was considerably bothered by the themes and techniques of the literary naturalists. They were expressing themselves on the continent and in America with self-conscious forthrightness about the complete physicality of man. In "Prince Roman" (1911) Conrad was just as explicit in his non-naturalism as Zola, Norris, Sinclair, *et al.* were inclined to be in their opposing theses. He accused "the vulgar refinement of modern thought" of being incapable of "a certain greatness of soul" and "a sincerity of feeling." To Conrad, the new thought omitted what was necessary for understanding "the august simplicity of a sentiment proceeding from the very nature of things and men." The specific sentiment that he had in mind was "patriotism," for which his protagonist, Prince Roman, had an impressive capacity. A decade later belief in sacrifice for a social cause, national or otherwise, was the concept most de-bunked by a young generation brought up intellectually on naturalism or directed to it by their experience in the First World War and the disillusioning days that followed. In the very year of Conrad's death, Hemingway was to depict modern man's futile search for a soul in *The Sun Also Rises,* and four years later he was to make in *A Farewell to Arms* the much quoted statement: "Abstract words such as glory, honor, courage, or hallow were obscene beside the concrete names of villages, the numbers of roads, the names of rivers, the numbers of regiments and the dates."

Two separate worlds of thinking and of writing, each sensitively aware of the other, are reflected in the quotations from Conrad and Hemingway. To Conrad there was an essence beyond the observable, and man had a capacity for reaching and expressing it. Any denial of this capacity was a "vulgar refinement." To the early Hemingway the verbal expression of such a capacity was mere rationalization, "obscene" in its very hypocrisy.

Still, Conrad was hardly naïve about the pretenses of man to himself. At the beginning of the century he had published in *Heart of Darkness* a devastating criticism of European imperialism and colonization, attacking incidentally patterns of behavior which in part led to the first great world conflict of our century. In a ritualistic journey of learning up the Congo, he has Marlow discover that Kurtz, a symbol of European civilization in his amazing intelligence, his artistic expressiveness, and his humanitarian sense, is capable of avarice, lust, tyranny, even murder. In fact, Conrad describes Kurtz's decay and Marlow's journey to recognition of it in terms that are at once as biological and as psychological as those of any Darwin-and-Freud-influenced naturalist. "Going up that river," he writes, "was like traveling back to the earliest beginnings of the world, when vegetation rioted on the earth and the big trees were kings," as if he is designating an atavistic return to some stage of nature even before the animals and man evolved. Or again, on such a journey "one's past came back to one . . . in the shape of an unrestful and noisy dream." In a kind of nightmare he is recalling experiences suppressed and forgotten or facing the id, which has been hidden beneath the "monkey tricks" of honorific manners and occupations. Apparently Conrad could be fashionably scientific about the animal-part of man that even centuries of culture and years of education could not undo.

But the admission of a basic animalism in man and of the ineffectualness of learned controls did not destroy Conrad's faith in human nature. Within the limits of his story, he proves both logically for his own satisfaction and empirically for the satisfaction of his scientifically-minded contemporaries that man has a moral sense as *inborn* as the flesh and its passions. On the way up the Congo to the "heart of darkness," the natives working on the boat have carried with them a supply of "rotten hippo meat," which is soon exhausted by consumption and destruction. The accompanying pilgrims throw part of it overboard, theoretically because they cannot stand its odor but actually, says Marlow, because "you can't breathe dead hippo waking, sleeping, and eating, and at the same time keep your precarious grip on existence." The jungle is ironically having its effect on white men and professed Christians. Having lost their meat, the natives then exist on a minimum of food—so far as Marlow can see, on inadequate particles of half-cooked dough. He wonders "why in the name of all the gnawing devils of hunger they didn't go for us," for after all they were *taught* cannibalism as strongly as the European was *taught* humanitarianism. Marlow, in contemporary psychological terms, looks at them "with a curiosity of their impulses, motives, capacities, weaknesses, when brought to the test of an inexorable physical necessity." He discovers "something restraining," not "superstition, disgust, patience, fear—or some kind of primitive honor," but a kind of "scruple" beyond any "earthly reason." His logical conclusion is that since the natives are drastically hungry and since their learned mores do not forbid eating other human beings, some *innate* restraint, some natural moral sense, must exist in man even in his most primitive state. If the symbolic savagery of Kurtz, the educated European, illustrates the natural animality of man despite his learned manners and morals, the restraint of the cannibals illustrates likewise the natural scruple of man even if he has learned no morals, in the traditional Western sense. The natives' control is decidedly not the Freudian superego, that metaphor of what the parents, teachers, preachers, and policemen tell us is right, that learned shell of social direction. It is more the universal reason glorified in the eighteenth and early nineteenth century as a part of man, who served as a battlefield for the hero reason and the villain passion.

One more point needs pursuing before Conrad proves the *natural* dualism of man. If man can regress in the manifold sense of Kurtz individually, or of Marlow figuratively in his journal toward Kurtz, can man fallen re-exercise his moral capacity? The structure of *Heart of Darkness* takes the reader step by step from "civilization" to the center of the jungle where Marlow struggles to save Kurtz, and thereby himself, as his constant admission of the "fascination of the abomination" suggests, and then step by step from the jungle back to the Western world, all within the vast and subtle structure of Marlow's time-full memory and timeless wisdom. On the way back Kurtz, dissipated, dying, a mere voice, literally and figuratively, looks into the depths of himself and whispers the terrible words of moral evaluation: "The horror, the horror." Conrad emphasizes again man's moral sense in the ability of the human being to observe his catastrophe and evaluate it with self-condemnatory confession. Certainly here is something akin to tragedy, not of the individual but of every man. ". . . then they very nearly buried me," says Marlow in complete identification with the European-trained Kurtz. Kurtz had "no restraint, no faith, and no fear," but struggled "with his soul" and reachieved in his self-evaluation "an affirmation, a moral victory paid for by innumerable defeats, by abominable terrors, by abominable satisfactions." It is this cycle of experience that demands from Marlow humble "loyalty to Kurtz" and in fact loyalty to himself, for it assures that whatever man does or whatever happens to him, as the case may be, he has the ability to cope with it in thoughts and words, to rise above it as it were. The experience of Kurtz is as cathartic for Marlow, and implicitly for the reader, as Aristotle declared that of the tragic hero to be for the members of the Greek audience.

Conrad has dramatically demonstrated a twofold nature of man compatible with the orthodox dualism of Christianity and countless other religious-and-philosophical traditions. There has always been the contention that the emphasis on Christ as both god and man and on man as both the spirit and the body was in part the Greek influence in an Hebraic culture. Plato's famous metaphor pictured man as a celestial chariot driver of a team of two horses, one horse, a milder, fairer one, naturally straining upward and the other horse, a wilder, darker one, ever tugging downward. The duty of the driver, a symbol of man's innate reason and moral sense, was to keep the two horses working together on a straight road through the sky. Of course, it would be fine if both horses should soar upward and land the driver on the top of Mount Olympus with the gods. But the very nature of the wild one made this an impossibility, and the admirable best that the driver could aim at was to keep the disparate horses working some compromise as a functioning team. This twofold concept of man's nature hardly starts with Plato or with any designated culture, for it is as old as the prehistoric wonderings about how night becomes day, how winter becomes spring, how man is born and dies, only to leave a son behind him. Where does man come from, where does he go, and how does he continue the life on this earth? If winter becomes spring, man dead must become man alive in some mysterious and hence worshipful way. Even within the limits of Western culture, the familiar polar words for the dualistic nature of man are manifold: soul and body, spirit and flesh, immortality and mortality, the reason and the passions, and so on to Conrad's "innate strength" and "the jungle" within. Freud's id and superego are not the same kind of opposition. Like the body, the flesh, the passions, the id is tied up with the physical and hence emotional make-up of man. But unlike them, it is in itself a natural complex of both desirable and undesirable elements according to conventional evaluations. The superego, the metaphor for these evaluations, is a *learned* control in contradistinction to the *inborn* goodness or morality that soul, spirit, reason suggest. The orthodox religious concepts involve an acceptance on faith of an immortal spark that tempers the flesh and returns to the Immortal Spark after the flesh is dead. The thinking of the nineteenth century which Conrad was criticizing was monistic in its emphasis on scientific observation and prediction. The nearest the new naturalism came to religious reverence for a God reflected in the godhead was a somewhat timid agnosticism.

In my discussion of Steinbeck later, I emphasize the difficulty of maintaining the early naturalist position in practice. There is no such thing as objectivity in art or in anything else, but the young and self-conscious naturalists such as Zola in France and Frank Norris in America contended that there was. To them, the function of the artist was to describe, not to explain or to judge. At least this is what they said in the manifestoes, being forced by a kind of hydrostatic paradox of controversy into an extreme and stark stand. Literary manifestoes are always a kind of caricature in contrast to the actual practice of those who sign their names to blast at their more traditional contemporaries. Somehow the naturalist felt that if he were going to free himself from current myths about the universe, society, and man, he must first *describe* and be careful not to impose patterns. The patterns of life might be *induced* from described *facts;* they should not be accepted *on faith* and *in spite of*. Another illusion of the early naturalist was that he could develop and utilize a detached style compatible with his theme of detachment. Again, the proclamation that he would free himself of abstractions and subjective pourings-out of self has led to an equation of so-called realistic techniques with naturalistic theses. A self-proclaimed naturalist might start out *describing* his society, but his very choice of words to convey the *awful* plight of man reveals his feeling for man. A familiar pattern was from "Here it is, like it or not" to "Here it is, you can't like it, what shall we *do* to change it?" Or from stating that God is Indifferent Hap instead of Benevolent Reason to wondering, if man *is* in this fix, what each man as a part of Man can do to relieve it even a little. A recognition that man himself is not rational man in control of his world involved experimentation in methods aimed at emphasizing the basically emotional nature of man. Paradoxically, expressing most effectively the emotions of natural man that the naturalist discovered were the very impressionistic methods often contrasted to the prosaic realism that the professed naturalists were so proud of. Conrad, I should say, is bothered by the theoretical naturalism and its self-conscious practice, the new literary scientism in content and in technique. He is bothered, in effect, by what the word *naturalist* continues to suggest to us at the first level of its meaning even if we are aware of its inconsistencies in practice and of its paradoxical development.

The only dualism conceivable for the strict naturalist was an external dualism between what man pretends to do and what man does, as for example in the monopolist who preaches "free enterprise." And since to the behaviorist, man is what he does, even this naïve dualism vanishes. In 1929, *A Farewell to Arms* appeared significantly at the end of a decade of taken-for-granted naturalism. In that very year, Joseph Wood Krutch lamented forcefully that a non-dualistic concept of man made tragedy in either the classical or the Renaissance sense an impossibility for creator or appreciator except as an academic problem. In tragedy, as has been suggested in the example of Kurtz, man is faced with catastrophe that some combination of God, the universe, society, and his own nature brings upon him. But the tragic protagonist proves that he is after all more than an animal: that he has free will, a moral sense, a place, albeit small, in a vast and supernatural order of things and that the creation which includes him is a dualistic creation. Without an implicit dualism, such as that which Conrad worked so meticulously to dramatize, the final catastrophe may be simply oppressive rather than ennobling and man may evolve as merely a pathetic creature, all the more foolish because his ideals are ridiculously high, misleading, or lacking.

Tragedy in one way or another is a religious mode and pathos is not. The very function of Greek tragedy in its original purpose as a part of the Dionysian festival, or its more sophisticated purpose as an artistic cathartic, is consciously spiritual. *Oedipus Rex*, for example, criticizes the belief in *physical* saviors. Young Oedipus, arriving cocksurely at Thebes, saves the city from the inscrutable monster, the Sphinx. To do so, he has answered "man" to the Sphinx's bewildering question of what moves first on four feet, then two, then three, but is weakest when it moves on four. Oedipus then conducts himself as a melodramatic hero, accepting the thanks of the people and the traditional prize of a royal marriage and the throne. But the very point of the play is to remind us that physical saviors are as nothing beside the spiritual saviors who choose to become the scapegoats for all mankind and to do penance before the gods or God, as the case may be, for man's manifold pride. It was impossible for Oedipus as the youthful revitalizer of the impotent city to accept the values of sacrifice, humility, faith that he achieves by the end of the drama. These come only with experience, and as Oedipus' answer to the Sphinx should have told him, experience is an inevitably crippling, hurtful, suffering experience, justifiable because it enables man to transcend the physical limitations of his world and his flesh. To the early Greeks, the story of Oedipus reflected that of Dionysus, whose joyful resurrection after various associations with persecution and death was celebrated each spring in the theater. Tragedy as the celebration of spiritual rebirth had to assume man made in the image of God.

In our climate of cultural relativity it need hardly be pointed out that Dionysus and Christ are alike the suffering gods, the tragic gods, who go through the pain and the exile of winter to become in spring the embodiment of life that is stronger than death. It is as natural for the Western writer of tragedy to make Christ his objective correlative, against which he measures the experience of man, as it was for the Greek playwright to build his tragedy around the stories of Dionysus. Both figures are topical dramatizations of the archetype of the sacrificial hero.

For Conrad, who insisted on the innate nobility, the symbolic god-
liness of man, in the face of a contrary climate of opinion, the conception and the creation of tragedy were practically a moral responsibility. This obligation he fulfilled impressively in *Lord Jim*, the full-
length novel written at the turn of the century, a few years after
Heart of Darkness. Conrad implies his thesis near the beginning of
the novel when the seaman Jim is being examined for his compulsive
desertion of pilgrims on a supposedly sinking ship. Again through
Marlow, Conrad insists that man's actions are somehow related to his
"soul" rather than to his "liver" and that there is considerably more
to man than the "facts" of his observable behavior. Marlow, incidentally, has already been put through the journey of learning to the
"heart of darkness," which taught him so impressively the dualistic
nature of man. If we accept the statements of Jim's emotions on face
value rather than as rationalizations, we must agree with Conrad that
his protagonist has some sort of "soul," for Jim cannot live with himself until he has done penance for his moral failure. In the person
of a minor character such as Brierly, the apparently perfect seaman
who commits suicide when forced to judge himself through Jim,
Conrad emphasizes that the failure of Jim is potentially the failure
of every man and that Jim in his own penance will become the scapegoat for every man.

Conrad gives Jim the opportunity for a dedicated life in an isolated
world when he has the godlike Stein assign him to the managership
of Patusan, the settlement up the river. Jim attempts to rule the people
through the techniques of love and understanding, but predictably
his moral strength is his political weakness. Jim refuses to liquidate
the decadent faction of the Rajah who formerly exploited the people,
or to punish the satanic Brown in whom he recognizes every man's
pathetic situation, or to resist the leader of the people whom he has
served best, although he is wrongly blamed for the death of the
leader's son. Lord Jim, as the people call him, is betrayed and finally
killed as an evil spirit by those to whom he has shown varying degrees
of kindness. He refuses the plea of his mistress-wife to fight or to flee
certain death, and slowly approaches the old chief Doramin, the
grieving father who wants vengeance for the death of his son Dain
Waris. Marlow, as usual, is narrating:

> "He hath taken it upon his own head," a voice said aloud. He heard this
> and turned to the crowd. "Yes. Upon my head." A few people recoiled.
> Jim waited a while before Doramin, and then said gently, "I am come in
> sorrow." He waited again. "I am come ready and unarmed," he repeated.

Marlow's epitaph for Jim expresses a conflict between describing Jim
on the one hand as a psychologically convincing man and on the
other as a veritable god who has briefly visited the earth:

Now he is no more, there are days when the reality of his existence comes to me with an immense, with an overwhelming force; and yet upon my honour there are moments, too, when he passes from my eyes like a disembodied spirit astray amongst the passions of this earth, ready to surrender himself faithfully to the claim of his own world of shades.

Who knows? . . .

Earlier, Conrad has allowed Marlow a conjecture that suggests the spiritual nature of tragic heroes even in the Renaissance, when playwrights were more disposed to a kind of secular dualism—if the phrase is not entirely contradictory. ". . . is not mankind itself," asks Marlow, "pushing on its blind way, driven by a dream of its greatness and its power upon the dark paths of excessive cruelty and excessive devotion. And what is the pursuit of truth, after all?" The excesses which demand punishment sound like a devious route to transcendence, but Conrad and the traditional writers of tragedy point to it as the only way. Holding on almost defiantly to his dualistic concept of the nature of man, Conrad says in effect: the story of Lord Jim has the elements of tragedy if modern thinkers will allow as much. And in his very imagery he implies that there is Christ in any tragic figure regardless of the nature of his excess.

How has Conrad succeeded in conveying to his reader meanings above and beyond but within the literal level of his action? I should like to suggest one way.

The unique metaphor is related to wit: it is a play on ideas through a play on words, the primary way after all that we can demonstrate our conceptual play. The phraseology of *play* immediately suggests the pun, which in its single-word expression of differences tends to be a kind of concentrated metaphor. The ordinary pun is dull in that the likeness related to differences is simply the obvious and coincidental one of the sameness of sound, but the puns which are pivotal to dramatic art involve meaningful likeness as well as ironic difference. The significant artistic pun is related to metaphor, irony, and—to throw us into another complex of ideas—symbolism. One might venture to suggest that effective drama revolves around a central, dominating pun.

Before going on with *Lord Jim,* reconsider Conrad's controlling pun in *Heart of Darkness,* that is, his use of *jungle* and *civilization.* Conventionally, the Westerner associates *civilization* with such externals as dress, furniture, art, manners, mores, laws. The imagery with which he traditionally surrounds his civilization is that of light and whiteness which it is his mission to bring to darkness and blackness. In *Heart of Darkness* the ostensibly civilized is the truly savage: Brussels, the European center of the trading company, is a "whited sepulcher," a place of true darkness and true savagery. As the center of the corrupt trading company, it is the heart of darkness in an important sense of the phrase. The civilized man, climaxed in the over-educated Kurtz, is the chief personification of savagery and darkness, the man who gives in most completely to the jungle around and within him. True civilization lies in the black cannibals, who exercise intuitively their inner strength. One pun, then, is *civilization;* another more complex pun is *jungle.* Both words have extensional and intensional meanings which deny each other.

Lord Jim employs the same pun in a way, but more important imagery than that of *civilization* and *jungle* has to do with *Western* and *Eastern* and, again, *white* and *black.* Traditionally, to Conrad's English reader, *civilization, Western,* and *white* are related in connotation as are *savagery, primitivism; Eastern, Oriental; black, brown, colored. Lord Jim* is divided into two parts. At the beginning Jim is one of a crew on a ship, a separate world as Conrad describes it. As navigator, he is entrusted with steering the pilgrims on their quest for salvation through a visit to Mecca. The pilgrims are colored, Oriental peoples; Jim is a white, Western man. The other members of the crew are also white and Western, forming with Jim a kind of microcosm of the European macrocosm. An inscrutable crisis occurs at sea, and Jim jumps, deserting his charge. Whether he jumps compulsively or deliberately is beside the point. The fact remains that, like the amoral ones who have chosen to desert, Jim is guilty of jumping. Conrad surrounds the jumping from the ship into the boat with *fallen angel* and *descent into hades* imagery. Jim has committed the damnable and is judged by a panel of men, who actually are no less condemnable than the next man, whatever their appearances may be. Jim, who starts life with romantic illusions of becoming a hero, specifically a *savior* of man in shipwrecks at sea, suddenly finds himself in the *same boat with other men,* indeed with the lowest of other men. More simply, one might say that he finds after all that he is a man, hence an inevitable traitor to his ideals and charges, damnable, guilty, low, fallen—if one likes—into the heart of darkness. Conrad suggests, with contempt for the phrase, that Jim the white man has failed to bear his burden of the colored pilgrims and, in serious tone, that Jim a man has failed to fulfill his responsibility to other men and to himself in this our world. The difference between Jim and the other crewmen in the first half of the book is that Jim faces formal judgment by a board of investigation whereas the others escape by amoral indifference, physical illness, and the convenient fantasies of delirium. Even so, the facing of judgment by law is not the essential distinguishing quality of Jim; it is his insistence on judging himself though the trial is over and done with and his identity is for all practical purposes hidden. Conrad starts with Jim's fall, or rather jump, and proceeds to reinforce Jim's insistence on self-flagellation unrelated to the public opinion of men. Then, halfway through the book, he has the godlike Stein isolate Jim from that part of the Eastern world with which Western "civilization" is constantly in touch. Once more Jim is in the position of figurative navigator in a microcosm of a world in which people depend on him as the bearer of their burdens. One almost thinks of the first half of the book as the Old Testament, in which man fails his responsibility and is driven from place to place as if seeking somewhere to hide his guilt. In this half of the book Jim is the archetypal Adam; he is clearly Everyman. Similarly, the second half of the book is a kind of New Testament, in which the protagonist is no longer Man but a god who assumes the shape of man to show him by a life of sacrifice the way to redemption. In this half of the book, as we have previously suggested, Jim develops as the archetypal Christ; he is clearly the sacrificial scapegoat for Everyman.

It is in the dualism of man's nature and the dualism of Christ-as-Man that Conrad employs his *white-and-black* pun. Consider *white* as the color of man's skin, as a synonym for Western as in "Western culture," as similar in connotation with *light* both as a shade and as a metaphor for truth, knowledge, goodness, as in association with *up, heaven, transcendence.* And consider *black* as the color of man's skin, as a synonym for *colored* as in the culture of the colored peoples, as similar in connotation with *dark* as a shade and a metaphor for ignorance, falsehood, depravity, as in association with *down, hell, damnation.* Now proceed to the series of ideas with which Conrad keeps playing. *White* men think themselves better than *black* men, but they are all *men,* neither better nor worse than each other, but all imperfect, *black* with the *white* speck of the soul, or whatever it is, tucked away somewhere in the *blackness* of the flesh and of the world. Under the illusion and pretense of thorough *whiteness* (for example, they rationalize their evil ways with such high-sounding statements as the *black* man is the *white* man's burden), they *must* express their *black* ways by virtue of their very nature, which is both *black* and *white* but more easily the former than the latter. Actually, the *white* speck is brought out only by facing the truth of one's *blackness,* accepting responsibility for it, suffering and sacrificing for it. In this sense, Christ, the *white* one, appeared in the guise of man, the *black* one; he alone was *truly* the *white* man assuming the *black* man's, every man's, burden and dying for it. Jim in the first half of the book is a *white* man in the most naïve sense of the word, existing under the delusion that he is different from, better than other men. In the last half of the book he becomes the true *white* man in his giving of himself as the scapegoat for all men, *white* and *black.* Interestingly, the final devil whom Jim faces is a *white* man named *Brown,* who tempts and tests Lord Jim as Satan taunted Christ. Marlow recalls his final sight of Jim in imagery pertinent to the dominant pun of color: "his smooth tan-and-pink face with a white line on the forehead, and the youthful eyes darkened by excitement to a profound, unfathomable blue."

We can make Conrad's *black-and-white* pun inclusive if we extend its association to *Eastern* and *Occidental, death* and *life.* We need not take the time to do so in any detail, but think of *Occidental* as a direction, a section, a culture, as the place of the setting sun, as literally falling, as death, as darkness, and think of *Oriental* as a direction, a section, a culture, as the place of the rising sun, as literally rising, as birth and rebirth, as the source of light. The ironies, the metaphors, the clusters of imagery, the symbols, the supreme puns are marvelously interwoven by Conrad.

In contrast to the hectic realism of the early naturalists, Conrad's methods were consciously subjective and symbolic. Writers of fiction are inclined within the scope of their stories to talk about their methods either directly as omniscient authors or indirectly through the characters whom they create as central intelligences. In *Heart of Darkness,* for example, Conrad contrasts "the direct simplicity of the yarns of seamen" with the atypical story-telling of Marlow: "to him the meaning of an episode was not inside like a kernel but outside, enveloping the tale which brought it out only as a glow brings out a haze, in the likeness of one of these misty halos that sometimes are made visible by the spectral illumination of moonshine." This is a statement of an interest in mood, in overall effect, in the complex associations of a thing, the kind of less-academic impressionism for which Ryder the painter is known, rather than in the vividness and completeness of detail and the painfully chronological order of the self-consciously naturalistic school. The method is carried even further in *Lord Jim* where the superficiality of fact is the essential emphasis of the theme of dualism. "Facts! They demanded facts from him, as if facts could explain anything!" says Conrad about Jim's failure of his ideals in his apparently clear-cut desertion of the ship full of pilgrims. "The facts those men were so eager to know had been visible, tangible, open to the senses, occupying their place in space and time, requiring for their existence a fourteen-hundred-ton steamer and twenty-seven minutes to the watch," he writes later as if he is parodying the new realism of the literary scientists. But he adds, "they [the facts] made a whole that had features, shades of expression, a complicated aspect that could be remembered by the eye, and something else besides, something invisible, a directing spirit of perdition that dwelt within, like a malevolent soul in a detestable body." The attempt to define the "something else" makes for the weaving of events back and forth, a repetitiveness that grows out of the diligent search for understanding, a wealth of abstract and subjective words such as the naturalist tried to avoid. All in all, these add up to the implicit rejection of objectivity and the approach to a variety of stream-of-consciousness, despite the emphasis of critics on Conrad as a traditional writer. The traditionalism lies in the attitudes, in the orthodox dualism, the consequent concept of tragedy, the availability of Christ as a serious frame of reference, but the style that is most functional for these "non-factual" attitudes is almost a kind of literary impressionism.

The sense of something beyond the observable leads, too, to a conscious employment of symbolism. Answering a gentleman who had both criticized and praised his works, Conrad wrote in 1918:

> Coming now to the subject of your inquiry, I wish at first to put before you a general proposition: that a work of art is very seldom limited to one exclusive meaning and not necessarily tending to a definite conclusion. And this for the reason that the nearer it approaches art, the more it acquires a symbolic character. This statement may surprise you, who may imagine that I am alluding to the Symbolist School of poets and prose writers. Theirs, however, is only a literary proceeding against which I have nothing to say. I am concerned here with something much larger. But no doubt you have meditated on this and kindred questions yourself.
> So I will only call your attention to the fact that the symbolic conception of a work of art has this advantage, that it makes a triple appeal covering the whole field of life. All the great creations of literature have been symbolic, and in that way have gained in complexity, in power, in depth and in beauty.

This brings us back to the imagery throughout *Lord Jim,* which persistently reminds us of Christ as a symbol of man's dualistic nature. ". . . a directing spirit of perdition that dwelt within, like a malevolent soul in a detestable body," may sound more Manichean than Christian. Still, there is certainly something mystical about God willing and Christ insisting upon the crucifixion, that climax of "perdition" that is followed, however, by absolution, also related to a "soul in a detestable body." The Christ-figure is, as we have suggested, a tragic-archetype, and despite the outline of mortal sin, absolution through sacrifice, and resultant immortality, the archetype assumes innumerable dramatic forms.

The form that the Christ-symbol takes is not irrelevant to the climate of opinion of a particular time or to the artist's unique experience, even though tradition or the collective unconscious or human nature or the laws of nature and society may delimit the different Christs with a significant likeness. Almost every important writer in our milieu has at one time or another utilized Christ as a *leit-motif* or as a major symbol. I am not referring to the flood of novels which attempt to recreate a facet of the Scriptures for better or for worse, such as *Ben Hur, Quo Vadis, The Nazarene, The Robe,* but to sincere books which enrich contemporary themes by the employment of the chief objective correlative of our culture. Symbolism may have become synonymous with literary experimentalism to a reading public which theoretically wants only a "good story" without "hidden meanings." Ironically, however, the most repeated cluster of symbols is abstracted from the traditional Christian lore, in which the popular reader of the Western World professes at least a vague belief. The correlative of Christ is the *something* through which the Western writer frequently gets at *everything.*

BIBLIOGRAPHICAL NOTE:
THE HISTORY OF IDEAS

Conrad's "Prince Roman" is included in the Viking *Portable Conrad* (New York, 1947) as is his letter to Barrett H. Clark which I have just quoted. The approaches to Conrad are manifold, but I am more interested in this chapter in approaches to tragedy such as Richard B. Sewall's *The Vision of Tragedy* (New Haven, 1959), Francis Fergusson's *The Idea of a Theater* (Princeton, 1949), and Bernard Knox's *Oedipus at Thebes* (New Haven, 1957). Joseph Wood Krutch's famous essay on "The Tragic Fallacy" was a chapter in *The Modern Temper* (New York, 1929), a book which talks about climate of opinion in an interesting and dramatically clear way that the writers of histories-of-ideas rarely achieve. In *The Modern Temper* Mr. Krutch is of course talking on a level and to an audience different from those of Arthur O. Lovejoy in his *Essays on the History of Ideas* (Baltimore, 1948), but in the end Krutch's kind of sincere and discursive book may be considerably more significant. George Santayana's "Tragic Philosophy," included in M. D. Zabel's edition of *Literary Opinion in America* (New York, 1937), is pertinent to our concern in this chapter both with tragedy and with the ideas implicit in literature. Charles Child Walcutt's *American Literary Naturalism: A Divided Stream* (Minneapolis, 1956) is a readable and valuable discussion of naturalism in idea and in practice.

CAMUS' SISYPHEAN HERO

David Anderson

Among post-war writers in Europe who, while sharing to the full in the 'absurdist' experience of a Sartre, have nevertheless succeeded in giving shape to a human protest which is both individual and corporate, the name of Albert Camus stands high. His famous novel *The Plague* has a quality of moral affirmation which lifts it above the negativities of mere nihilism and imparts to it a tragic grandeur.

The Mediterranean 'climate' of much of the work of Camus, with its delight in sea and sun and its enjoyment of human beauty, has reminded some readers of Ancient Greece. There is also more than a suggestion of Greek drama in his most important writing, and his thought is easier to grasp if we look first at his essay entitled *Le Mythe de Sisyphe*.[1]

The gods condemned Sisyphus to roll a rock to the top of a mountain from which the rock immediately rolled down to the bottom and the laborious toil had to begin again. As Camus says, the gods 'rightly thought that there is no punishment more terrible than work which is useless and without hope'. The moments of greatest interest in the labour of Sisyphus are those in which he walks down the mountain after his rock. What are his thoughts? These are his moments of reflection—this hour which is like a respite is the time in which Sisyphus thinks about his destiny. And because of this power of thought he is stronger than his rock. It is the human capacity for reflection that enables us to recognize our destiny as tragic; yet in the midst of this tragedy there is also joy. The rock is Sisyphus' rock and he has the power to seize his destiny and make it his own. He marches down the mountain with heavy, measured tread towards the torment that has no end. But 'the struggle to the summit is enough of itself to fill a man's heart. It is necessary to imagine that Sisyphus was happy.'

Here, then, we have a curious paradox. The existence of man is absurd —even man himself is absurd—and yet his ability to pass this judgment is a cause of joy for it proves that he is greater than his meaningless

---

[1] A. Camus, *The Myth of Sisyphus*, Hamish Hamilton, London 1955 and Alfred A. Knopf, New York 1955.

destiny. We are reminded here of the famous passage in Pascal's *Pensées* about the 'thinking reed'. 'It is not from space that I must seek my dignity', says Pascal, 'but from the government of my thought. I shall have no more if I possess worlds. By space the universe encompasses and swallows me up like an atom; by thought I comprehend the world.' The judgment of man's consciousness, as Camus points out in *The Rebel*,[2] can be extended even to death, which seems to make indifference the final word. Sacrificial death, so far from being the ultimate absurdity, is the demonstration of freedom and the creation of 'honour'. 'Kaliayev climbs the gallows and visibly designates to all his fellow-men the exact limit where the honour of man begins and ends.'[3]

For Camus, the greatness of man, that which releases him from absurdity, lies in his 'consciousness' and his power of rebellion—a rebellion which Camus calls 'metaphysical'. It is a rebellion, not so much against the terms in which existence is given, as against the submissiveness, the unthinking acceptance, which allows those terms to determine human reality. This Sisyphean theme is the basis of Camus' novel, *The Plague*,[4] which could be said to be an extended working out, in a modern setting, of the old myth.

2

The story tells of an outbreak of bubonic plague in the North African town of Oran. It begins among the rats, but rapidly spreads to the people until a state of emergency has to be declared and the town gates are locked. No one may enter or leave—the inhabitants are forced into a Sisyphean drama, from which there is no escape.

The plague itself is open to a number of possible explanations. There is little doubt that a parallel can be drawn between the situation in Oran and that of German-occupied France from 1940 to 1945, during which period in fact Camus started to write his novel. But as Philip Thody points out, 'it would be limiting to see *La Peste* as the description of a particular historical experience . . . it opens out into a much wider context'.[5] What Camus seems to have in mind is the Sisyphean nature of human existence itself.[6] The human struggle never ends because there

---

[2] A. Camus, *The Rebel*, Hamish Hamilton, London 1953 and Alfred A. Knopf, New York 1954.

[3] *The Rebel*, p. 253. Camus is referring to the Russian terrorist who murdered the Grand Duke Sergei in 1905. This is the subject of his play, *Les Justes*. The point is that the rebel is prepared to *give* his life, whereas the revolutionary will only *risk* it.

[4] A. Camus, *The Plague*, Hamish Hamilton, London 1948, Penguin Books, 1960 and Alfred A. Knopf, New York 1948. The page references are to the Penguin edition.

[5] P. Thody, *Albert Camus 1913-1960*, Hamish Hamilton, London 1961 and The Macmillan Co., New York 1962.

[6] In *Le Mythe de Sisyphe*, Camus mentions the modern working man's repetitive labour and calls Sisyphus 'the proletarian of the gods'. Another person whose work is markedly Sisyphean is, of course, the housewife.

is no power to enter the world from outside, no *deus ex machina*, to call a halt to the conditions in which the only meaningful option is the rebellion against them. The plague, as Camus tells us at the end of the novel, is never finally conquered.

> Rieux remembered . . . that the plague bacillus never dies or disappears for good; that it can lie dormant for years and years in furniture and linen-chests; that it bides its time in bedrooms, cellars, trunks, and bookshelves; and that perhaps the day would come when, for the bane and enlightening of men, it roused up its rats again and sent them forth to die in a happy city (p. 252).

The detailed horror of the plague is movingly realized by Camus. The disease falls upon the town apocalyptically, disclosing by its own monstrous senselessness the far less obvious but no less senseless character of the everyday existence of its citizens. The plague does not destroy meaning: it reveals meaninglessness as already present in the banal routines of work and pleasure. There is a man trying to write a novel who has produced only the first sentence which he constantly revises. There is another man whose spare-time occupation is to stand on the balcony of his house and spit at cats in the street below. These men are living a Sisyphean existence *but they do not recognize it,* and the same is true of the vast majority of the citizens of Oran. Only *consciousness,* says Camus in *Le Mythe de Sisyphe,* can reveal the tragedy and the joy secreted in absurdity, and only the rebellion which follows from this recognition can force meaning into solid, recognizable form. The people of Oran hope foolishly for a remission of the plague or for escape from it: they have failed to realize that the plague is inherent in existence itself, and that the only course open to man is to accept its challenge and fight for his 'honour'.

There are, however, in Oran a small number of Sisyphean heroes—men who are prepared to march down the mountain with heavy, measured tread and prove that they are stronger than the plague which destroys them. These are the men who recognize absurdity and accept its conditions, but who fight it relentlessly without expecting any absolute to vindicate or terminate their struggle. There is the hero and narrator of the story, Dr Rieux, who directs the medical operations and believes that 'honesty consists in doing my job'. There is Tarrou, a man who wants to be 'a saint without God', who organizes 'sanitary squads' to patrol the streets and find victims of the disease. There is Rambert, a journalist, who tries to escape from the plague-stricken town to rejoin the woman he loves; but he decides not to go, because 'it may be shameful to be happy by oneself'. There is Othon, a stiff, unsympathetic magistrate, who, after his little boy dies of the plague, volunteers to help in the isolation camp. The greatness of man is revealed by these men: they prove that 'there are more things in men to admire than to despise'.

What, then, is the substance of this Camusian rebellion? Can it be defined? There is a scene when an old man named Grand is looking at a shop-window decorated for Christmas. He is remembering his wife as a young girl in the early days of their marriage before she left him. Rieux sees Grand but is himself unnoticed.

> And he knew, also, what the old man was thinking as his tears flowed, and he, Rieux, thought it too: that a loveless world is a dead world and always there comes an hour when one is weary of prisons, of one's work, and of devotion to duty, and all one craves for is a loved face, the warmth and wonder of a loving heart. . . . At this moment he suffered with Grand's sorrow, and what filled his breast was the passionate indignation we feel when confronted by the anguish all men share (pp. 213-14).

This passionate indignation is at the heart of the rebellion. It is the sense of outrage one feels at the death in agony of a little boy; it is the struggle to save a friend's life and the smile of comradeship on his lips when, after all, he dies; it is recognition of the harm human beings do to one another, because we are all 'plague-stricken' and we must try to infect as few people as possible. Rebellion is also to go for a swim for friendship's sake, 'because really it's too damn silly living only in and for the plague. Of course a man should fight for the victims, but, if he ceases caring for anything outside that, what's the use of his fighting?'[7] And the record of the plague, the account of it which Rieux has written,

> could be only the record of what had had to be done, and what assuredly would have to be done again in the never-ending fight against terror and its relentless onslaughts, despite their personal afflictions, by all who, while unable to be saints but refusing to bow down to pestilences, strive their utmost to be healers (pp. 251-2).

Conquest of the absurd is found in the work of compassion—the honour of man begins with his willingness to offer himself in sacrificial death. But it also ends there, for there is nothing beyond death to make the sacrifice permanently effective. The pestilence always reasserts itself, the stone always rolls back down the mountain, and we are 'toujours en marche'. The universe does not resonate in tune with the actions of men and there are no absolutes to exempt them from their endless struggle. Indeed, absolutes are themselves principles of death. When men *act* in the name of absolutes they soon forget that there is an intermingling

---

[7] I find myself thinking here of the irony that, on the day after the Russian invasion of Czechoslovakia, Rostropovitch was playing the Dvořák cello concerto with the Russian State Orchestra in the Albert Hall, London. There was some heckling from the audience, but not much. The dominating feeling seemed to be that the music and the players were expressing a universal humanity which was itself the most radical criticism of tyranny. This was something outside the plague which validated the human struggle and reminded us that there are still more things in men to admire than to despise.

of evil with good in every human action, they forget their own inescapable contingency, they forget 'la mesure'. They begin to regard *themselves* as absolutes, so that they murder in order to prevent murder, they commit acts of injustice in order to establish justice.

Equally, when men *submit* to absolutes the result is death. The priest in *The Plague* tells his congregation that 'plague is the flail of God and the world his threshing-floor'; man's part must therefore be to accept it as the divine judgment, to refuse the rebellion which questions the divine verdict, to submit to the sentence of God. The priest dies with his face to the wall having refused medical help. He dies in the terrible solitude of obedience to God. Perhaps it was not even the plague that killed him; perhaps he died simply because he gave in. Submission to the will of God means repudiation of human values—values which man, not God, creates; values which must constantly be recreated, for they 'are never given once for all and the fight to uphold them must go on unceasingly'. 'To leave all justice to God', says Camus in *The Rebel*, 'is to sanctify injustice', and that is why 'it is better to die on one's feet than live on one's knees'.

In the work of Camus, then, we see the human rebellion hurling itself against a meaningless universe and claiming for itself the power to justify happiness. The rebellion is not an individual act of Promethean defiance, but a work of human compassion, and it neither seeks nor requires any absolute to vindicate it. In the words of Colin Smith, 'Rebellion has its own meaning as the final action of which man is capable when everything else dissolves into irrationality and death.' The meaning is in the rebellion itself: it is not in the *results* of rebellion, which may be nothing but failure and which in any case can never create permanent values. All we know is that the irrational and deathly conditions which demand rebellion will never be other than they are, and that rebellion itself will always be the only way open to man to establish his 'honour'. This means that the fight must go on unceasingly: the honour of man is lost when he submits to the false absolutes of bourgeois morality or political or religious dogmas. It is also lost when he forgets his own profound implication in the deathly conditions against which he fights: for man is himself 'plague-stricken' and cannot help doing harm even when he would do good. He is bound to be a 'murderer'; the best he can do is to try to be an 'innocent murderer', one who at least does not do harm deliberately. This requires vigilance and clarity. Our involvement in tragic guilt is inescapable: even Christ, says Clamence in *The Fall*,[8] shared in it when the Innocents were slaughtered because of him, and perhaps Clamence is right when he says that the

---

[8] A. Camus, *The Fall*, Hamish Hamilton, London 1957, Penguin Books 1963 and Alfred A. Knopf, New York 1957.

cry of Rachel weeping for her children rang for ever in his ears. So the
rebellion is not much to set against the plague and the labour of
Sisyphus; not much, but enough. It *must* be enough: 'it is necessary to
imagine that Sisyphus was happy'.

3

The obvious difference between Camus and Sartre is that the former
gives an important place to human relatedness and avoids the latter's
loveless individualism. For both writers there can be only one kind of
meaning, and that is the meaning created by man himself; but for Camus
this meaning is found not so much in individual as in corporate action,
and the metaphysical rebellion which he demands issues in a sense of
human solidarity. This is the exit from absurdity: 'In absurdist experience suffering is individual. But from the moment that a movement of
rebellion begins, suffering is seen as a collective experience—as the
experience of everyone.'[9] Rebellion is 'the clue which lures the individual
from his solitude . . . I *rebel*—therefore we *exist*'. In *The Plague*, this
thesis is demonstrated most clearly by Othon, a magistrate. He has
always been a cold, aloof man, regulating his life by principles rather
than compassion. He suffers the terrible death of his little boy almost
in silence: this is the experience of absurdity by which all principles
are shattered and in which we are alone; but when Othon is sent to
the isolation camp—it is a rule that all who have been in contact with a
plague-victim must go into isolation for some weeks—he performs various menial tasks and soon becomes a useful member of the camp. He
has now entered the ranks of the rebels, which means that he has begun
to recognize the corporate nature of suffering and is exposed to human
need. When he is discharged from the camp, he asks Rieux if he can go
back to work there—and Rieux notices that there is 'a sudden gentleness
in those hard, inexpressive eyes'. It is thus the rebellion that draws man
out of his individual solitude and impels him towards others. 'The individual is not, in himself, an embodiment of the values he wishes to
defend. It needs at least all humanity to comprise them.' Therefore the
fact of rebellion implies the existence of a human nature: 'why rebel if
there is nothing worth preserving in oneself?' Camus asks. Man does
not begin, as he does in Sartre, at the absolute zero of individual responsibility where he must project himself out of the undefined mass of
being; man for Camus is one who has in him the power to rebel against
the absurdity of his existence, and Camus seems to imply that this

---

[9] *The Rebel*, p. 28. Raymond Williams argues that this move from individual to collective experience may be merely 'rhetorical' here, but is convincingly 'actual' in *The
Plague*. See *Modern Tragedy*, pp. 181-2.

power is man's defining characteristic which makes it possible to speak of a 'human nature'. I shall argue later that Camus does not succeed in showing why this 'metaphysical' rebellion should express itself in terms of compassion and sacrifice rather than in terms of self-interest. For the moment, however, we notice Camus' insistence that the power to rebel can all too easily be lost when men simply accept the senselessness of their existence in a universe which offers them nothing but disorder and outrage. To abdicate from the rebellion against such a universe is to lose one's manhood—to become inhuman.

We must remember, however, that the rebellion contains no absolute to make human action unambiguous or to create conditions from which absurdity is banished. The values we seek are found in the act of rebellion itself: once they are erected into an ideology, once they take the form of an End which is thought to be independent of human action and capable of automatic realization—then they cease to be human values and become instead the cause of inhuman tyranny or of indifference towards the concrete needs of suffering humanity. It is on these grounds that Camus rejects Christianity, with which, at first sight, his understanding has so much in common. He points out that 'there is an act of metaphysical rebellion at the beginning of Christianity',—by which, presumably, he means the cross of Christ. We have already noticed the view of Camus that a man's offering of himself in sacrificial death is the only way by which he can establish his 'honour'; it is a 'metaphysical' victory because in fact the absurdity of death *is* the final word and the joy which can be wrested out of this tragic destiny does not alter its inevitability or make it any the less absurd. But Camus parts company with the Christian scheme when it asserts the resurrection of Christ and announces the kingdom of Heaven. These dogmas, he says, render the cross 'futile'. This conclusion will not surprise us if we have followed the Camusian repudiation of 'absolutes'. To put it into traditional terms, Camus cannot subscribe to any 'objective' theory of the atonement: the cross is meaningful because it typifies the human rebellion against the senselessness of existence, but we make a serious mistake if we think that it has created new conditions in which meaning has somehow become 'given' and permanent. This is precisely the mistake which the Church *has* made. If there is resurrection, if a supernatural order has now imposed its solutions upon absurdity, then Christ's death is no longer the desperate throw of man against futility; it is surrender, not rebellion, and it is therefore 'inhuman' in the sense that it ends by denying the need for rebellion and proclaims acceptance as the way of salvation. So man loses one of his essential dimensions, and turns into an ideology the values which have no existence except in unceasing, ever-renewed struggle.

Camus distinguishes sharply between 'the only two possible worlds that can exist for the human mind': they are 'the world of grace' and 'the rebel world'.[10] The former is Christian, the latter is not. Either we deny all power to justify ourselves and wait submissively for supernatural blessings; or we decide that meaning can come only from our own efforts, and act accordingly. The priest, Paneloux, in *The Plague*, believes in the world of grace even though the fact of human suffering refutes its existence: the doctor, Rieux, fights against the plague without belief—simply because that is where 'honesty' leads. The result is that Paneloux passes more and more deeply into solitude while Rieux finds in himself an increasing identification with others. And this is the criterion by which rebellion is to be judged—whether or not it succeeds in creating human solidarity. It is true that rebellion can be lost or distorted 'through lassitude or folly', and then it becomes 'an accomplice to murder'; absurdity is fundamentally the denial of love, and the rebel must maintain perpetual vigilance lest he 'fasten infection' on others and thus become an instrument of the very absurdity against which he fights. But the Christian has lost this fight before he even begins. His beliefs lead him along one of two courses: either he seeks to impose his 'absolutes' upon others and thus becomes a tyrant, forgetting that he is himself not an absolute but a pestiferous human being; or he submits tamely to absurdity and tries to assure himself that suffering will have its compensation in eternal life, thus despairing of present human transcendence and passing by the healing task in which men find unity.

4

One sometimes feels with Camus, as one does with Sartre, that the writer's theory fails to give an adequate account of his own artistic creation. Is it really possible for man to fight for ever in a hopeless war? Has not Camus turned absurdity itself into an absolute? Is it necessary to assert categorically that there is no meaning except what man creates? or that belief in 'resurrection' makes the human rebellion futile? Does not Camus fail to answer the crucial question—why should man be a rebel at all if there is nothing outside himself by which his actions may be supported? If the existence of all objective moral values is denied, it is hard to see how we can fail to arrive at a totally nihilistic conclusion. As it is, in Camus one suspects the presence of a categorical imperative in rebellion itself: we rebel, not to assert values and not to claim solidarity with other men—for it is only when we have *begun* to rebel that these products reveal themselves; we rebel simply because we must. But why must we? Is it really possible to accept Rieux's explanation that he is simply 'doing his job'? What is it that prompts a man

---

[10] *The Rebel,* p. 27.

to stay with the victims of the plague—why should he seek to be a true healer, at the cost, it may be, of his own life, against the strong instinct of self-preservation? Even Rambert, the self-centred journalist, whose only thought is to escape from the plague-stricken town in order that he may rejoin the woman he loves—even Rambert finally recognizes an imperative in the claims of the victims and decides to stay. Decisions like this are really as absurd and inexplicable as the plague itself. But Rieux, after an initial moment of surprise, accepts Rambert's decision in a matter-of-fact way which, one feels, is something less than adequate to its extraordinariness. One would have expected him to take less for granted this evidence of self-denying values in man. But we know that Camus has decided that he must avoid any hint of imperatives which might imply some kind of *religious* interpretation of human awareness. Only absurdity can safely be absolutized because only a very few religious fanatics, like Paneloux, can persuade themselves that the Absurd is God. The rest is relative and impermanent; and it can never win.

But there is much of the work of Camus to which the appropriate response is one of gratitude. *The Plague* is one of those rare novels which release the tragic protest and deepen our awareness of what is 'genuinely human'. We recognize ourselves in it, and yet we did not know that we could be as admirable as this. Given the conditions of the plague, we might all hope to act like a Rieux or a Tarrou or an Othon.

Camus is surely right in thinking that to understand oneself as 'genuinely human' is to understand oneself as a rebel. It is important, however, to remove political overtones from the word 'rebel'. While it is true that the human rebellion may and often will find political forms of expression, the 'metaphysical' rebellion of which Camus speaks refers to something which pre-exists specific forms of rebellion and stands for a characteristic of our existential awareness as such. The word is not used to mean an attempt to overthrow some constituted authority: it points rather to the vision, the questioning, the *protest* which man finds in himself. The starting-point of rebellion is the recognition that the world provides no objective correlate which is coincident with man's interior vision, and it lays upon him the necessity of acting in the light of that vision while refusing to be an instrument of the forces which threaten it. For Camus, the human struggle lies in the attempt to create order and meaning under the overarching absurdity of the universe. Principally, this is the work of alleviating suffering and of refusing to be a carrier of the plague-germ; it is the willingness to give one's life for others and to decline escape-routes; and it must never become an attempt to impose some absolutist programme upon other people.

In the sense in which Camus uses the term, we would all be proud to be called 'rebels', though we might have to admit that it is a hard vocation and that we seldom live up to it. Most of us are so busy trying to adjust ourselves to the changes and complexities of modern life that we seem to have little energy for rebellion; a letter to *The Times* is hardly at the level of heroism which Camus requires, and we can nearly always find reasons for thinking that conformity is the highest virtue in most areas of work and service. It could be argued that, for many of us, absurdity comes not through apocalyptic events but through the very systems by which we try to control and ease our existence. We shall have occasion to think about this when we look at the novels of Kafka. For the moment, however, let us see whether we can agree with Camus that rebellion *is* an essential dimension in our self-understanding and that the sickness of our age lies in our failure to maintain the interior vision out of which it springs.

It could be that our rebellion is a consequence of our *fallen* nature and that we would make a serious mistake if we held it to be characteristic of true humanity. We notice that there is no instance in the Old Testament where the verb 'rebel' and its cognates is used in anything other than a bad sense. Most of the uses of the word refer to rebellion against God. For the OT writers, rebellion is precisely that which introduces disorder and misery into human affairs: it is the 'stiff-necked' and 'gainsaying' attitude which refuses the God who stretches out his hands to his people. Clearly, rebellion against God is not a virtue, and out of this general conviction the view could develop that *any* rebellion of man against the conditions of his life must be understood as defiance of the God who is alone responsible for those conditions and who 'unites in himself absolute power with absolute justice, goodness, and wisdom'.[11] Thus Jephthah's daughter submissively accepts her fate as the divine will, and Job's protests are silenced by the inscrutable majesty of the Creator.

This view is very close to that of the priest in *The Plague*, but Camus is wrong in thinking that it is Christian. Even in the OT there is plenty of evidence for belief in the share of man in the creation of meanings and in the improvement of the conditions of his life. Of course man falls into disaster and ridicule when he thinks he knows better than God: how can he pit himself against the Lord of the whole earth without presumption? But the God he serves is not an inscrutable tyrant. He declares his purpose through his servants the prophets and invites the partnership of man in his actions. It is true that events may often seem to be contrary to the divine purpose and the conditions of life may sometimes appear intractable, but the faith of the OT is the faith that

---

[11] I am referring to an article in *The Listener* (September 2, 1955) by D. Daiches Raphael entitled *Tragedy and Religion*. He argues that tragedy depends upon the human rebellion and is therefore incompatible with 'the religion of the Bible'.

God is present in bad times as well as good, and that the frustration of his purposes is due not to his own failure but to that of his human agents. Of course there are limits to human understanding beyond which God *is* inscrutable and his ways past tracing out; if this were not so, God would be nothing more than an idol—a projection of human fantasies and ambitions claiming authoritative status. But the prophets of Israel will have none of this. The divine word is not an echo of human ambitions: it is a word of judgment as well as promise; it summons men to depart from iniquity and to ally themselves with the divine compassion.

There are thus two kinds of rebellion open to man: the false, self-destroying kind which is rebellion *against* God; and the true, liberating and life-giving kind which is rebellion *with* God. To obey God is to become a rebel against sin and evil, against all that separates man from the source of life and virtue, against all the destructive forces inside and outside man which masquerade as God. To obey God is also to align oneself with meanings and values which have their source in God but which man himself is called to actualize in human history—in politics, economics, social organization, as well as in the individual himself. The fact that these meanings and values always transcend the power of man to grasp or achieve is the reason why the human rebellion always has a Sisyphean character and never attains finality; at the same time, it also forces upon man the realization that he is not God. Only a transcendent God can give the lie to the absolutist claims of man; only a transcendent God is our safeguard against attributing divine authority to human programmes. Camus is right when he points to the terrible consequences which follow when man introduces 'absolutes' into his affairs and claims to be acting in their name.[12] But this is precisely the primal sin of man in the biblical doctrine: 'ye shall be as gods' are the words which lead to the Fall; it is man at the height of his aspiration who forgets the limits of rebellion and plunges into disorder and misery. But without the transcendent God to remind him of his imperfect insights and the hidden 'cellarage' of his self-regard, there is no reason why he should ever do otherwise or understand the cause of his collapse.

The transcendence of God is therefore both the source of the human rebellion and its limitation. It is the source because man finds himself grasped by a power other than himself and in touch with values which are independent of his own projects: it is the limitation because the very values which summon him to rebellion also reveal the ambiguity of his motives and the inadequacy of his achievement. Man is neither the passive recipient of imposed meanings nor the inventor of all the

---

12 Compare Simone Weil: 'We must always be prepared to change sides with Justice—that fugitive from the winning camp.'

meaning there is.[13] In the secular order he is an 'applied scientist' whose
job is to actualize in human life at every level the truths which have
their origin in God, but without supposing that either his knowledge of
those truths or its application is final.

5

It is clear that Jesus was himself a 'rebel', and if proof were needed that
rebellion is characteristic of what is genuinely human, then surely it is
here. Of course, to call Jesus a rebel is to apply to him a word which
neither the NT nor the Church uses of him: apart from its almost inescapable political resonances, the word perhaps implies a certain imma-
turity as of a young man asserting his independence. But we have seen
that the Camusian meaning is very different. To be a rebel is to live
by an interior vision, a categorical imperative, which refuses to bow
down to pestilences and demands that men shall be healers. In this
sense, Jesus was the greatest of all rebels. The point need not be
laboured: the works of healing and feeding, the refusal to coerce, the
willingness to die—all are evident in the gospels. It is not surprising
that there is much in *The Plague* to remind us of Christ; indeed, one
feels that Camus was somewhat haunted by the gospel Figure even
though he had to repudiate Christian theology.

In the preface to the American edition of his earlier novel, *The Outsider,* Camus remarked that its hero, Meursault, was 'the only kind of
Christ we deserve'.[14] This was no doubt a deliberately provocative
statement—Camus admits that he speaks with a certain irony—but the
hint is certainly worth following up. At first sight it is not easy to see
Meursault as a Christ-figure even in an ironical sense. He is characterized by 'a complete indifference to anything except immediate physical sensations, together with an absolute refusal to lie about his own
emotions' (Thody). What Camus has in mind in his half-identification
of Meursault with Christ is perhaps his silence before his judges, his
refusal to plead for acquittal in a way which would endorse the false
bourgeois morality in the light of which the trial is conducted. Meursault is accused of shooting an Arab, which indeed he had done in a
moment of half-consciousness when he was blinded by the sun, but it
is not so much because of the deed that he is condemned to death as
because of the complete indifference he displays during his trial. He is
a man who is intensely in love with life, especially in the physical
sensations produced by light and colour and movement, but he stands

[13] Here I dissent from Harvey Cox, *The Secular City,* SCM Press, 1965, p. 72.
[14] A. Camus, *The Outsider,* Hamish Hamilton, London 1946 and Penguin Books,
1961. American title, *The Stranger,* Alfred A. Knopf, New York 1946.

outside all the normal structures of social relatedness and the moral values by which they are sustained. Meursault had not wept at his mother's funeral; he had refused promotion at work; he had had no feelings of romantic love for Marie, his girlfriend; he showed no remorse over his killing of the Arab. He is condemned because he is callous, indifferent, and contemptuous. The trial simply fails to touch his central being.

Meursault understands himself and his life in terms which are entirely foreign to the conventional outlook of his judges. He cannot defend himself without expressing a sorrow he does not feel, and to express such sorrow would be to play the bourgeois game of pretending that life has meaning and that the authorities know what it is. But Meursault is the 'absurd man' of *Le Mythe de Sisyphe* who knows that there are no meanings and who sees through the pretence and hypocrisy of official morality. It is in the light of this detached interior conviction that Meursault faces his judges and finally prepares to climb the scaffold. He is prepared to die for the sake of the truth. He resembles Christ in his silent rejection of the official *mores* at his trial and in the condemnation which rejection brings upon himself. He is, in short, a 'metaphysical' rebel who chooses 'the benign indifference of the universe' just as Sisyphus 'chooses' his rock and Rieux 'chooses' the plague—because that is where honesty leads. The destiny of the outsider is to be condemned and by his condemnation to reveal the corruption of consciousness in the human system by which he is judged. Meursault and the other Camusian heroes 'choose' an absurdity by which all human systems are revealed as lies. Christ chooses the cross, with similar effect. But there is one great difference. The choice of Meursault leaves us with absurdity as the final word, whereas the choice of Christ reaches out to a meaning beyond absurdity by which the tragic worth of our mundane existence is affirmed.

For Meursault is a Christ *manqué*, the only Christ we deserve. Camus cannot accept the belief that Christ has defeated absurdity and has decisively altered the conditions in which the human struggle takes place. It may indeed seem impossible to combine the human rebellion with obedience to a divine will and to claim that the work of Christ has a finality which is denied to ours. Yet we have to assert about Jesus two seemingly contradictory truths: that he thought and acted in terms of an absolute and referred his own will to that of the heavenly Father; and that his life was characterized, as ours is, by responsibility, by doubt, inner conflict, and the final absurdity of death. 'Him who knew no sin,' said St Paul, 'God made to be sin on our behalf,'[15] pointing us to the solution of the difficult problem of how the truth of God can be

---

[15] II Cor. 5.21 (RV).

actualized within the Sisyphean existence of man without the imposition of an absolute which would bring the human rebellion to an end.

6

The answer, I believe, is to be found by considering the nature of the divine absolute which Jesus embodied and actualized. That absolute is love, and in understanding this we are at once removing from our thought any notion of coercion or violence or arbitrariness. For love is characterized, not by any exercise of arbitrary power, nor by the imposition of rules or formulas, but by the very opposite of all this—by self-giving, by identification, by acceptance of responsibility for human suffering. As Berdyaev has said, God has not even the power of a gendarme: his power towards men is of a different order from that of coercive authority. It follows that love is present only where there *is* self-giving and participation with others, and this means that not even God can create conditions in which love works like a computer carrying out a programmed operation. The human rebellion is not made superfluous by Christ: on the contrary, it is underwritten and reinforced. Christ has shown that we do not fight in darkness and isolation, but as it were in company with God himself. The resurrection does not make our rebellion 'futile' as Camus says: to say that it does is to regard it as an act of arbitrary power by a god from the machine. But Christians do not think of the resurrection as an eleventh-hour retrieval of disaster: it is understood as the culmination of the love of Christ, the proof that his way is the authentic way and that reality endorses it. From Christ we learn that rebellion *is* the only way open to man to establish his 'honour', and at the same time we discover that the Sisyphean cycle has been broken. The war is not hopeless. The honour of man begins on a cross but it does not end there, for the values actualized by Christ within the human context have been taken into the divine context and stamped with an eternal guarantee. The interior vision of man is matched and transcended by the actuality of Christ; the absolute is not absurdity but love, and the strange work of love overcomes absurdity.

> For the creation was subjected to vanity . . . in hope that the creation itself also shall be delivered from the bondage of corruption into the liberty of the glory of the children of God.

I think we must say that Camus is mistaken when he places in opposition to each other the world of grace and the rebel world. To live by grace is to live as a 'rebel' and to find one's power of rebellion increased. This may seem a startling statement to those who see in the Church nothing but submission and inaction, but I agree with Harvey Cox in his belief that it is one of the great biblical correctives to the distortions of 'tradition'. Catholic and Protestant alike have too often understood 'grace' or 'justification' in essentially *static* terms having little to do with the ongoing challenge of the secular conditions of man's existence. This is not to deny the Church's historic role in the relief of need and suffering, but generally speaking this role has been performed without much radical questioning by the Church of the political, social, and economic orders themselves.[16] But twentieth-century man has become convinced that there is a human duty to contrive changes in these orders for the betterment of human life,[17] and this discovery has brought under question the Church's 'metaphysical' understanding of salvation as a 'state of grace' defined by its detachment from and therefore its essential *acquiescence in* the secular orders of existence. This is, of course, part of the Camusian case against Christianity—that it leads men to abdicate from the human duty of rebellion in favour of meanings and values which are prefabricated and other-worldly, with the corollary that life on earth is something to be endured rather than improved and enjoyed. There is, no doubt, such a thing as Christian fortitude when circumstances cannot be altered, but Camus is undoubtedly right in thinking that fortitude must not be allowed to become a total substitute for rebellion. To borrow van Buren's metaphor, when there is a fire at sea the important thing is not to try to understand oneself as a man on board a burning ship but to put the fire out.[18] Modern man has come to the conclusion that if God is to be found at all he is to be found in the secular meanings and challenges which confront him in the actualities of his existence. The theological case for this view has been argued by a good number of contemporary theologians, among them Harvey Cox whose stimulating book *The Secular City*[19] shows how much modern biblical scholarship has contributed to this more pragmatic type of religious awareness. The Christian Faith is seen not so much as the guarantee of eternal salvation but rather as the charter for human action by which man is liberated for secular programmes and invited to collaborate with God and his fellow-men in the better ordering of life.

---

[16] Commenting on the attitude of the early Christians to the Roman civilization around them, F. R. Barry says, 'The existing structures of human life—rich and poor, masters and slaves—were just there, whether so ordained by God's creation or, as Christian theology was to suggest later, permitted as consequences of the Fall. They made no attempt to alter or reform them'. *Christian Ethics and Secular Society*, p. 114, Hodder & Stoughton, 1966. The whole chapter on 'The Christian Society' may be consulted.

[17] This, of course, goes back at least as far as nineteenth-century Comtism.

[18] P. van Buren, *The Secular Meaning of the Gospel*, SCM Press, London 1963, Penguin Books, 1968 and The Macmillan Co., New York 1963.

[19] Harvey E. Cox, *The Secular City*, SCM Press, London 1965, Penguin Books, 1968 and The Macmillan Co., New York 1965. The page references are to the original edition.

There is no difficulty in showing that this understanding has biblical support; but it is not the whole story.

7

The trouble with 'correctives' is that they usually correct too much and end up as substitutes. Biblical understanding does not require us to choose between grace and rebellion; nor does it require us to abandon belief in metaphysical values which pre-exist human programmes and give them direction and impetus. To live by grace in the NT sense is to be seized by a power which forces men out of their self-centered prisons into the world of sin and suffering and need where Christ himself operated—a power which, at least in some measure, reproduces the victorious rebellion of Christ. Let us concede that the Church has not always exhibited this power, that it has too often been concerned only with the perpetuation of its own existence, and has, as Berdyaev says, attempted to live by law rather than by the creative energy of the Spirit.[20] Against this betrayal of its origins the emphasis today on secular action is a recovery by the Church of New Testament truth. But it is not true that we discover the meanings and values by which we ought to live only as we take up the secular challenge: if this were so, there would be no sufficient reason for taking up the challenge at all. As Tillich points out,[21] dynamics without form drives man in all directions without any definite aim and content, and the drive is likely to be, not towards the secular challenge, but towards the preoccupations of self-interest. On the other hand, to take some kind of form *out* of the dynamics in which it occurs and then impose it on dynamics to which it does not belong is to act in terms of an absolute which, as Camus has warned us, is destructive and deathly. But the NT does not offer us either of these alternatives: it offers us Jesus Christ and the creative life of the Spirit— and if we may continue with Tillich's terminology, Jesus is the *form* and the Spirit is the *dynamics* of the Christian life. But to refer to Christ as 'form' is, we believe, to make an assertion not only about the human context but also about the *divine* context, and this means that there is a permanence, a transcendence about Christ which places him 'beyond, behind, and above the passing flux of things' (Whitehead) and makes him a source of meanings and values relevant to but not limited by our partial, finite perspectives. To speak of the Holy Spirit as 'dynamics' is to assert the working out, the incarnation of those meanings and values in the contemporary human context. In other words, there is both a

---

[20] *Spirit and Reality*. Berdyaev's argument that the Church has denied the creativeness of the Spirit by its emphasis upon 'obedience' is very relevant here.

[21] P. Tillich, *Systematic Theology, Vol. II*, James Nisbet, Welwyn, Garden City 1957, p. 74 and University of Chicago Press, 1951.

givenness and a potentiality in Christian faith, both the permanent achievement of Christ and the potential actualization of that achievement by man in the structures of his historical existence. As Reinhold Niebuhr says,[22] the view that all things have their source in God must always be balanced by the view that all things have their fulfilment in God: without the latter, the former becomes a mere pantheistic acceptance of life as it is—which Camus and others rightly condemn. We have already seen that fulfilment has nothing to do with the laying down of dogmatic pre-emptions or of submission to a pre-ordained divine programme. Nevertheless, we do not act blindly in meeting the secular challenge, nor is our task merely the pragmatic one of trying something to see if it works only to end up with Sisyphus at the bottom of the mountain because absurdity always has the last word. We act in a world in which Christ has already acted, and we seek to align ourselves with him in the belief that his way—the way of love—is the way things ultimately are and that in him our work will not be in vain. The fact that our achievement falls far short of his reminds us that we are still 'pestiferous' men and ought to keep us from the presumptuousness of claiming absolute authority for our programmes or finality for our insights.

In conclusion, it is interesting and indeed devastating to notice the way in which the word 'theology' is being used today in political contexts. To refer to a political doctrine as 'theology' is to imply blind belief in and wholesale application of views which are now irrelevant to the political realities of the time. Nothing could reveal more clearly the secular opinion of what Theology itself is, and it is right that modern theologians should repudiate it by their emphasis upon the disclosure of theological truth within the concrete realities of our mundane existence. But as I have tried to argue, the truth that is in Jesus belongs to the divine as well as to the human context and necessarily transcends and questions our secular structures. There is an inescapable sense in which Theology *is* a setting out of timeless, 'metaphysical' truth: that truth is, I believe, the content, the style, the substance of the divine rebellion, initiated and endorsed by God, actualized in the world by Christ, and made permanently available to all who align themselves with the way of Christ through the Holy Spirit 'for the bane and enlightening of men'. To be a Christian is to have one's own tragic protest taken up into the Protest of Christ and to find that in him it meets a reality beyond our dreaming.

Those who believe that they believe in God, but without any passion in

22 R. Niebuhr, *An Interpretation of Christian Ethics*, Harper & Row, New York 1935 and Living Age Books, 1956, p. 137.

their heart, without anguish of mind, without uncertainty, without doubt, without an element of despair even in their consolation, believe only in the God-Idea, not in God himself.[23]

---

[23] Unamuno, *The Tragic Sense of Life*, Macmillan, London 1921 and Collins Fontana Books, 1962, p. 193.

D. H. LAWRENCE: THE QUARREL WITH CHRISTIANITY

Graham Hough

. . . Lawrence's practical recommendations for the reform of society vary between the politics of cloud-cuckoo-land and the politics of the sergeants' mess. But the defect is largely a defect of executive power, and his most incondite or ill-considered practical precepts turn out to be linked with ideas of fundamental importance. The history of his political ideas is really an eccentric and not very significant branch of his ideas about religion—especially the great historical and institutional religion of his own culture, Christianity. And to trace Lawrence's relation to Christianity genetically, from the first tentative agnosticism of his letter to his sister to *The Man Who Died* and the *Last Poems,* would be to trace the whole course of his work again from another and more specialised point of view. Let us here attempt something more summary, a synoptic view, neglecting chronology, a composite photograph made up of many shots, not all wholly compatible with each other, but still capable of fusion into a comprehensible whole. We might start at any one of a number of points—so let us start at the one we have in any case reached—his anti-democratic political doctrine.

After innumerable attempts at defining the basis of his objection to democracy, scattered through his work from *Women in Love* onwards, Lawrence gets it out most clearly at the eleventh hour in *Apocalypse:*

> The mass of men have only the tiniest touch of individuality, if any. The mass of men live and move, think and feel collectively, and have practically no individual emotions, feelings or thoughts at all. They are fragments of the collective or social consciousness. It has always been so, and it always will be so.[1]

---

[1] *Apocalypse,* Viking Press, p. 215. Page references are not helpful for most of Lawrence's works, as there are a number of editions in wide circulation. The following plan has been adopted. The provenance of quotations from the novels, tales and poems is indicated as clearly as possible in the text; for the novels, chapter references are given, in Roman figures, immediately after the quotations. Other references are given in footnotes.

Which has not prevented him saying earlier that the end of all education and social life is the development of the individual. So it is—but
only so far as the individual exists. And in most men the individual
exists very little, the rest of them being realised in their share of the
collectivity.

Most men are largely citizens, members of the community, collective
men. And "as a citizen, as a collective being, man has his fulfilment in
the gratification of his power sense". A man may wish to be a unit of
pure altruistic love, but since he is inescapably a member of the political
community, he is also inescapably a unit of worldly power. A man must
be both a unit of love and a unit of power; he must satisfy himself both
in the love-mode and the power-mode. This theme, appearing in almost
the last words Lawrence wrote, goes back to a far earlier period of his
career. It is expressed in almost similar terms in the last chapter of
Aaron's Rod.

> I told you there were two urges—two great life-urges, didn't I? There
> may be more. But it comes on me so strongly, now, that there are two:
> love and power. And we've been trying to work ourselves, at least as in-
> dividuals, from the love-urge exclusively, hating the power-urge and
> repressing it. And now I find we've got to accept the very thing we've
> hated.
> We've exhausted our love-urge, for the moment. And yet we try to
> force it to continue working. So we get inevitably anarchy and murder.
> It's no good. We've got to accept the power motive, accept it in deep
> responsibility.[2]

And this is as good a point as any to enter Lawrence's long quarrel
with Christianity. For Christianity as Lawrence always sees it is the
attempt to live from the love-motive alone—to make love, *caritas*, pure
altruism the only motive in life. "The essence of Christianity is a love
of mankind." Of course this takes no account whatever of historic and
doctrinal Christianity in all its developed complexity; still worse, from
the Christian point of view, it takes no account of the *source* of that love,
which should be the motive of all faith and all action. Still, in a thousand
places in his fiction and expository writing Lawrence makes the identification between Christianity and the doctrine of pure, universal, altruistic love. It is against this doctrine of Kangaroo's that Somers revolts,
exalts his own dark god and preserves his integrity. It is against this
doctrine that Don Ramón revolts and triumphs over in the person of
Doña Carlota. It is against this doctrine that the Ursula of *The Rainbow*
revolts when she shakes the little sister who has slapped her face, and
feels the better for it—"unchristian but clean." On every level from the
prophetic to the trivial Lawrence sees Christianity as the love-ideal and
rejects it.

---

[2] *Aaron's Rod*, Chap. XXI.

Two thousand years ago Western man embarked on the attempt to live from the love-motive alone. Sometimes Lawrence puts it a few hundred years earlier, with Platonism and the rise of the higher religions. He refers to this momentous step in the history of humanity in at least two different ways. Sometimes he sees it as a great rejection, a failure of courage, a refusal of the responsibility of life, sometimes as a necessary development, living and valid for its time and for centuries to come, but now at an end. Perhaps the second judgment represents his steadiest and most central belief.

> I know the greatness of Christianity: it is a past greatness. I know that, but for those early Christians, we should never have emerged from the chaos and hopeless disaster of the Dark Ages. If I had lived in the year 400, pray God, I should have been a true and passionate Christian. The adventurer.
> But now I live in 1924, and the Christian venture is done. The adventure is gone out of Christianity. We must start on a new venture towards God.[3]

In either case, the love-mode is exhausted. Christianity is kept going by a barren effort of will, it has no longer any connection with the deep sources of life; and the consequences of this continuing will-driven automatism of love is to be seen everywhere in the modern world.

The psychological and personal consequences have been touched on sufficiently often already. The withered and fluttering figure of Doña Carlota is supposed to represent the etiolation of spiritual love; and the unsleeping will behind it has strained her relation to Don Ramón beyond the breaking point. When Kangaroo proposes to love Somers, Somers reflects: "He doesn't love *me*, he just turns a great general emotion on me, like a tap. . . . Damn his love, he wants to *force* me."[4] Hermione wants to love Birkin spiritually, and when Birkin, to preserve his integrity, has to reject her, she tries to knock his brains out. Farther back still, the unhappy Paul of *Sons and Lovers* is in the toils of a 'spiritual' love which should have been a happy physical relation, but can never become so because of Miriam's fixed spiritual will; and his situation is complicated because there is another woman, his mother, who also wants to possess his soul. The common element in all these admittedly complex and varying situations is a love which is cut off from the natural carnal roots of love, and continues to exist as a function of the will. It is sterile in itself and becomes life-exhausting to whoever exercises it. Since it is something imposed on the object of love, not a reciprocal relation, it becomes inevitably a kind of spiritual bullying, and must inevitably be rejected by anyone who wishes to preserve his individual being. And all this in Lawrence's eyes is an inevitable consequence in

---

[3] "Books," *Phoenix*, Viking Press, p. 734.
[4] *Kangaroo,* Chap. XI.

personal relations of the Christian love-doctrine, the Christian discipline of the heart.

There is an analogous development in public life. The universal sentiment of love for mankind is similarly cut off from the natural roots of human comradeship, the warm, carnal physical community; known, for instance, by men working together in a common manual task or playing together in a ritual dance. These are communities of power, and have behind them the inexhaustible vitality of a common physical life. The love of mankind offers only a community of sentiment, and can be maintained only as a fixed direction of the will. So, like private spiritual love, it becomes a kind of bullying. *Sois mon frère ou je te tue.* Hence the devastating wars by which Christendom has been riven. Further, this kind of love is not a true communal feeling at all, it is a product of the individual will, of the ego, of all that is most personal and least deeply rooted in man. It demands that each man shall be an individual power-house of universal love. This has two consequences. The first, only clearly apparent late in the Christian cycle, but its inevitable and logical development, is democracy. Each individual must love all others, equally and impartially—the Whitmanesque universal brotherhood. The mysteries of power and lordship are denied—for they would be a break in the uniformity of universal love. So that universal love becomes a forcing of the same ideal sentiment on all alike; or looked at in reverse, a claim by each individual alike for the same universal consideration. And this claim is false, for all men do not possess individuality in the same measure. And this brings us to the second consequence of the demand for universal love—it involves the demand that all men shall be fully individuals, and that each shall be a separate individual source of universal spiritual love. It is a demand for the impossible, and it falsifies the whole relation of man to man.

> In democracy, bullying inevitably takes the place of power. Bullying is the negative form of power. The modern Christian state is a soul-destroying force, for it is made up of fragments which have no organic whole, only a collective whole. In a hierarchy each part is organic and vital, as my finger is an organic and vital part of me. But a democracy is bound in the end to be obscene, for it is composed of myriads of disunited fragments, each fragment assuming to itself a false wholeness, a false individuality. Modern democracy is made up of millions of fractional parts all asserting their own wholeness.[5]

Christianity, in fact, is designed for a world of free, pure, bodiless individuals, not for a world of men—men, who exist largely in their undifferentiated physical community, most of whom are capable of very little individual spiritual development. "Christianity, then, is the ideal,

---

[5] *Apocalypse*, p. 217.

but it is impossible."[6] Lawrence agrees with Dostoevsky's Grand Inquisitor, as he makes plain in an introduction that he wrote to that dialogue. Christ loved man, but loved him in the wrong way. The following words of the Inquisitor might almost have been written by Lawrence himself: "By showing him so much respect, thou didst, as it were, cease to feel for him—thou who hast loved him more than thyself. Respecting him less, thou wouldst have asked less of him. That would have been more like love, for his burden would have been lighter." Or, as Lawrence paraphrases it: "To be able to live at all, mankind must be loved more tolerantly and more contemptuously than Jesus loved it, loved for all that, more truly, since it is loved for itself, for what it is, not for what it ought to be, free and limitless."[7]

But man is not free and limitless. He needs earthly bread, the satisfaction of his physical appetites, and he needs to acknowledge that satisfaction as a divine gift. And he needs authority, someone to bow down to, the acknowledgment of power—not the spiritual power of an unseen god, but embodied power in the flesh. To restore health to the community of men it is first necessary to accept the power-motive again, to acknowledge the legitimacy of both individual authority and collective power. The mass of undeveloped mankind will find their vicarious fulfilment in this acknowledgment. Lawrence worries constantly over this problem of power from *Aaron's Rod* to *The Plumed Serpent*, and never successfully. His negative analyses of the corruptions of 'white' love and democratic humanitarianism are piercing and profound; yet the dark god of power who is to be not destructive but life-giving is never successfully evoked. The attempts to embody him in fiction produce fascist leaders or posturing mountebanks. It might be said that this is exactly what such attempts produce in life—these are the only practical embodiments of the dark god. History since Lawrence's death might well seem to confirm the accusation. I think Lawrence could still reply that this is not so; it is precisely because the reality of power is shirked by the general "democratic" presuppositions that, like all realities that have been denied and suppressed, it reasserts itself in violent and terrible explosions. If the reality had always been admitted to its rightful place, the explosions would not have been necessary.

He would in part be right. The most committed liberal democrat would be free to admit that the calamities of the last thirty years are in part a result of the decadence of his own ideals, a decadence evident in the general loss of all sense both of the proper mode of exercising authority and the proper mode of submitting to it. This decay is not yet arrested, and Lawrence is one of its sharpest analysts. He was asking a real question, though he never found an answer.

[6] *Phoenix*, p. 284.
[7] *Phoenix*, p. 285.

It may be that Lawrence had himself too many relics of Christianity in his heart ever to be able to cope with the problem of earthly power, or even thoroughly to accept the necessity he asserted. Certainly he knew too little of how it works and how it is obtained. What could a man who had never had an ordinary job, never had a place in a community of men, never exercised or submitted to authority, know of political reality? His characters become steadily less convincing the nearer they come to exercising political power. The only way Lawrence can realise power and convey the sense of it, unhampered by ignorance or an inner resistance, is when it is displayed in nature. Lou Carrington submits to the "wild spirit" she finds in the mountains of Taos, but it is hard to see her submitting to any human embodiment of it. Lawrence becomes aware of this failure himself, for after *The Plumed Serpent* we hear less of the power-mode. He is still equally concerned with the failure of 'Christian' love, but he is now inclined to find the alternative in "a new tenderness", a fleshly tenderness. *Lady Chatterley* is supposed to be the illustration of this tenderness, and the story which explores its relation to Christianity is *The Man Who Died*.

As Lawrence's attention shifts from power to sensual tenderness as the alternative to Christian love, the opposition becomes less intense; and it becomes easier for him to represent his doctrine as a completion of Christianity rather than a contradiction. Spiritual love and sensual love are, after all, both forms of love: and the Christian depreciation of sexuality[8] is an accident rather than the essence of its doctrine. *The Man Who Died,* therefore, comes nearer to being a reconciliation with Christianity than anything else Lawrence wrote. In other places sensual love is seen as the negation of 'white' love, *agape,* Christian love. Here we come near to seeing it as a transcendence, reached by death and re-birth. And this means that it represents, not the climax of his art, which it certainly is not, but a climactic point in the development of his thought.

This story of the rejected prophet, almost killed, left for dead, returning painfully to life, and finding it, not in the resumption of his mission but in the knowledge of a woman—this story of the resurrection is certainly Lawrence's most audacious enterprise. Many readers have found in it the final evidence of the arrogance, the ignorant presumption of which Lawrence has often been accused. To take a story so tremendous, so profoundly interwoven with the life of our civilisation, and "to try to improve on it", as I have heard it said, may well seem to suggest some-

---

[8] I take it for granted that Christianity does depreciate sexuality, or at most make reluctant concessions to it; and that Lawrence was right in believing this, wherever else he was wrong; and that the Chestertonian (and post-Chestertonian) trick of representing Christianity as a robustly Rabelaisian sort of faith is a vulgar propagandist perversion.

thing of the kind. I think the charge can be dismissed if we are careful enough to see what Lawrence was trying to do. Although the prophet is unnamed, the identification with Jesus is not disguised. The Crucifixion, the Entombment, St. Mary Magdalen, the journey to Emmaus are all explicitly referred to. Yet what is the Jesus to whom the story refers? The "historical Jesus", the Lamb of God who takes away the sins of the world, the Christ who shall come again with glory to judge the living and the dead? Surely none of these. Lawrence had believed since he was twenty that Jesus was "as human as we are"; but he is not trying to provide a demythologised historical version of his end, more acceptable to positivists than a supernatural resurrection. George Moore attempts something of the kind in *The Brook Kerith;* but not Lawrence. And the cosmic and eschatological bearings of the Gospel story concern him even less. There is no suggestion anywhere in his tale that the death and resurrection of Jesus is a mystery of redemption or that it affects the destiny of mankind. Lawrence is concerned with two aspects of the Christian myth, and two only: one, the value of Christian love; the other, the personal destiny of Jesus the teacher. What he has done is not to vulgarise or reduce the splendours and mysteries of traditional Christology; he simply leaves them on one side. He has taken Jesus as what he believed him to be, a human teacher; he sees what he believes to be the consequences of his teaching, and tries according to his own lights to push beyond it. Certainly an audacious attempt, possibly a misguided one, but to anyone who cares to read what Lawrence wrote, not to rest on a conceptual summary, it will not, I think, appear as an attempt made without due reverence.

The story was originally called *The Escaped Cock* and ended at Part I, with the prophet setting out alone to walk through the world, vividly aware of life in the flesh, but as yet without any active participation in it. The central symbol of this part of the story is the cock itself, tied by the leg by the vulgar peasant, released by the prophet. The first act of his re-born existence is to let it fly free; and its newfound freedom is a symbol of his own sensuous faculties, imprisoned during the years of his mission and almost extinguished during his passion and death. For it has been a real death. With great discretion Lawrence avoids the question of a miraculous resurrection. What does it matter? One who has suffered, as the prophet has done, the extremity of physical and spiritual torment has in effect died; and if his vital powers should, miraculously or unmiraculously, return, it is a real re-birth. In the concentration-camp world that we have produced after twenty centuries of Christian civilisation there are many people who know this. At first the prophet walks in the world like one who is still not of it.

He felt the cool silkiness of the young wheat under his feet that had been dead, and the roughishness of its separate life was apparent to him. At the edges of rocks, he saw the silky, silvery-haired buds of the scarlet anemone bending downwards. And they too were in another world. In his own world he was alone, utterly alone.

He can feel no kinship with the tender life of the young spring; and this may serve to remind us how different Lawrence's nature religion is from the Wordsworthianism of the nineteenth century. Lawrence is more aware of the tormenting complexity of human experience, of the indirectness, even the contrariety of the relation between man and external nature. Man cannot learn of man by passively receiving impulses from a vernal wood, but only by adventures in the world of men. The prophet awakens to the new life of the body only when he realises that the peasant woman desires him. He does not desire her; he has died and does not desire anything; anyway, he knows that she is hard, short-sighted and greedy. But the knowledge of her desire awakens in him a new realisation.

> Risen from the dead, he had realised at last that the body, too, has its little life; and beyond that, the greater life. He was virgin, in recoil from the little, greedy life of the body. But now he knew that virginity is a form of greed; and that the body rises again to give and to take, to take and to give, ungreedily.

So he does not reject her harshly—"he spoke a quiet pleasant word to her and turned away".

But he has another and sterner rejection to make, the rejection of his own former mission, and of Madeleine, the woman who had believed in him. They meet, and she wishes him to come back to her and the disciples. But he only replies that the day of his interference with others is done, the teacher and the saviour are dead in him. In a sense he accepts this death: betrayal and death are the natural end of such a mission. "I wanted to be greater than the limits of my own hands and feet, so I brought betrayal on myself." This is what happens to the man who would embrace multitudes when he has never truly embraced even one. On his second meeting with Madeleine he again rejects her entreaties, saying that he must ascend to the Father. She does not understand, and he does not explain; but the reader will remember that in Lawrence's mythology the Father was also the Flesh.

Madeleine, who wants to devote everything to him, is also under the spell of a hard necessity. In her life as a carnal sinner she had taken more than she gave. Now she wants to give without taking, and that is denied her. The prophet prefers the society of the peasants, for their earthy inert companionship "would put no compulsion on him". He dreads the love of which he had once been the preacher, the love that compels.

The central symbol of the second part of the story is the priestess. She is a priestess of Isis in search of the dead Osiris, and like the prophet she is virgin. She had known many men in her youth, Caesar and Antony among them, but had remained always cool and untouched; and an old philosopher had told her that women such as she must reject the splendid and the assertive and wait for the re-born man.

The lovely description of her temple and its setting is a delicate Mediterranean landscape, nature at its most humane, friendly and responsive. At the moment when the stranger lands on her shores—the stranger who is the prophet on his travels—she is idly watching two slaves, a boy and a girl. The boy beats the girl, and in a moment of half-frightened excitement copulates with her, scared and shamefaced. The priestess turns away indifferently. These are the loves of slaves; whatever fulfilment she is to find has no more in common with these vulgar couplings than with the loves of Caesars. When the stranger-prophet asks for shelter he is given it, indifferently and impersonally. A slave suspects that he is an escaped malefactor, and the priestess goes to look at him as he sleeps.

> She had no interest in men, particularly in the servile class. Yet she looked at the sleeping face. It was worn, hollow, and rather ugly. But, a true priestess, she saw the other kind of beauty in it, the sheer stillness of the deeper life.
> . . . There was a beauty of much suffering, and the strange calm candour of finer life in the whole delicate ugliness of the face. For the first time, she was touched on the quick at the sight of a man, as if the tip of a fine flame of living had touched her. It was the first time.

Both the prophet and the priestess are separate, cut off from the common life around them. She is surrounded only by slaves, and she found slaves repellent. "They were so embedded in their lesser life, and their appetites and their small consciousness were a little disgusting." And as for the prophet—"He had come back to life, but not the same life that he had left, the life of the little people and the little day. Re-born, he was in the other life, the greater day of the human consciousness." Both are aristocrats of the spirit and both are incomplete— she because she is the living representative of Isis in search of Osiris; and he because he has died and come back to the world and still dreads its contact. She realises that she has not yet found her Osiris, and he realises that there is the whole vista of a new life before him that he has not yet been able to touch.

And when she becomes Isis to his Osiris (for there are no surprises in this story), we are to see it not only as the satisfaction of a long-denied bodily hunger (it is that, too), but as the consummation for each of them of a solitary life of spiritual exploration—a spiritual journey that can never be complete until it has reached carnal fruition that will alter its whole meaning. She who has played out her life as a drama of search has now found. "And she said to herself, 'He is Osiris. I wish to know no more'." And he who has died, returned to the world, but not yet felt himself to be living again, knows that he is risen from the dead when he feels desire for the woman and the power to satisfy it. When the life of the little world, in the shape of the slaves and the Roman soldiers, breaks in upon these Christian-Osirian mysteries, the prophet takes a boat and slips away, healed, whole, risen in the body, content to take what may come on another day.

Æsthetically, no doubt, the story was more satisfying in its first form, when it ended with the prophet's rejection of his old mission and his yet unfulfilled knowledge that a new life awaits him. The temptation to be explicit about what cannot properly be explained is always the *ignis fatuus* for which Lawrence is content to lose his way. The attempt to *present* the experience of one who has stepped inside the gates of death and come out again seems foredoomed to failure. As it turns out, the failure is of a different kind from that which might have been expected. It is a breakdown of continuity, not a breakdown of expression. The idyll of the stranger and the priestess is beautifully done; the balance between fabulous remoteness and concrete sensuous realisation is delicately held; and Lawrence convinces us as he rarely does that the conjunction he describes is that of two rare beings, each with an exquisitely specialized individual life, yet satisfying each other completely by meeting on a ground which is beyond the personal life of either. And over it all is shed like sunshine the warm tolerant beauty of the ancient Mediterranean world—a beauty which may be partly the product of Arcadian fantasy, but still forms a real and living part of European experience.

All this is true. But it is also true that it is hard to accept the stranger of the second part of the book as identical with the prophet of the first. In the first part the broad, unspecific outlines of fable are filled out with what we know of the Gospel narrative, which is still very close to us. The invented myth is given density and immediacy by its dependence on the great public myth. In the second part the invented myth stands alone, and like all products of the pure personal imagination, it is thinner than what history or the mythopoeic faculty of a whole culture supplies. The stranger in the second part is not so much a different person as a person out of a different story; the change is a change in the mode of conception. For the tale has two kinds of significance, unequally distributed—the one more prominent in the first part, the other in the later addition.

It can be interpreted synchronically or diachronically, to borrow terms from the linguists. Synchronically, it is simply what Lawrence first called it—a story of the Resurrection, deriving much of its strength from its background in the Gospel narrative, passing over into a more rootless fantasy as this recedes into the distance. Its theme is the necessity of rejecting the Christian love-ideal for a man who has really risen in the flesh. And right or wrong, we recognise this as an integral part of the Laurentian thesis. The second part of the story is a more arbitrary invention, and as such abides our question. Should the fulfilment of the flesh, the obvious natural destiny of mortal creatures, be discovered so late and after such long wandering? Should it, for the sake of Lawrence's thesis, be a healer for creatures who have been so long estranged from the roots of life? Could it be so, for beings who have been so long specialised in other directions, one of whom has suffered to death? It would be absurd to press these questions too hard, but they do at least begin to obtrude themselves. They can be answered by seeing the tale in the second way, diachronically; not as the story of a particular man at a particular time, but as an allegory of the course of Christian civilisation. The death of the prophet is also a symbol of the death of the Christian dispensation. Christian civilisation is dying after two thousand years. But the story of man is a continuity, and no culture ever really dies: it comes to life again, to a new life, which it is at first incapable of realising and is unable to face. The passion and death of the prophet are the death-agonies of Christian culture ("Ours is a tragic age," as Lawrence said at the beginning of *Lady Chatterley*), and the second part of the story is a foreshadowing of the new dispensation that is to come. But it is a new dispensation reached only by death and re-birth. The fleshly tenderness that is to replace Christian love in the new order can never be the pristine, unembarrassed pagan delectation. The one thing a post-Christian can never be is a pagan, C. S. Lewis has remarked; and Lawrence is showing his sense of this. Christianity may be brought into touch again with the old nature-mysteries of death and re-birth, as it is in this tale; but they will be changed in the process. The fleshly healing is painfully, almost fearfully accepted by the priestess and the prophet, after years of deprivation and a season of anguish; and so it must be in the history of Western man. It will not be among *hommes moyens sensuels* that the new apprehension of life is born. Theirs is the "little day", as it always has been, under any dispensation. But to encompass this in the greater day will be the task precisely of those who have most completely submitted to the old spiritual disciplines. True, the mission of Christianity has to be rejected, but it has been lived through before it has been rejected, and nothing can ever be the same again. If a new order is to come into being, it will in all its splendor and joy be the inheritor of the Christian abnegation and suffering.

I believe that this, or something like it, is what Lawrence is saying in *The Man Who Died*, and that this is the most developed state of his relation to Christianity. The hostility had, after all, never been unmitigated. "Give me the mystery and let the world live for me"—Kate's cry in *The Plumed Serpent* was Lawrence's own. And Christianity, at any rate Catholic Christianity, was at least a guardian of the mystery in the midst of the desert of mechanised civilisation. As Lawrence sees it, Catholicism had even preserved some of the old earthy pagan consciousness, and through the cycle of the liturgical year had kept in touch with the rhythm of the seasons, the essential rhythm of man's life on earth. As the inheritor of the sense of vital mystery which was the essence of religion, the Catholic Church seemed at times to him a vehicle of hope. It was a sympathy of sentiment only, not at all of dogma, intermittently awakened in Lawrence by his love for the Mediterranean world. Far stronger was the perpetual intellectual and moral preoccupation with Christian civilisation and Christian ethics; a preoccupation so intense that he is able to orientate himself only by taking bearings on the Christian position he had abandoned.

For of course he had abandoned it; and the Christians (there are some) who would use Lawrence's stream to turn their own mills have need of caution. He often looks at Christianity with sympathy, but to do so he always has to turn it upside down. A choice had to be made, and Lawrence, in fact, made it in early life. However he may use Christian language, he uses it to a different end. For Christianity the life of the flesh receives its sanction and purpose from a life of the spirit which is eternal and transcendent. For Lawrence the life of the spirit has its justification in enriching and glorifying the life of the flesh of which it is in any case an epiphenomenon. It is at once an older and a newer religion that he is celebrating with what were almost his last words.

> For man, the vast marvel is to be alive. For man, as for flower, beast and bird, the supreme triumph is to be most vividly, most perfectly alive. Whatever the unborn and the dead may know, they cannot know the beauty, the marvel of being alive in the flesh. The dead may look after the afterwards. But the magnificent here and now of life in the flesh is ours, and ours alone, and ours only for a time. We ought to dance with rapture that we should be alive and in the flesh, and part of the living, incarnate cosmos. I am part of the sun as my eye is part of me. That I am part of the earth my feet know perfectly, and my blood is part of the sea. My soul knows that I am part of the human race, my soul is an organic part of the great human soul, as my spirit is part of my nation. In my own very self I am part of my family. There is nothing of me that is alone and absolute except my mind, and we shall find that the mind has no existence by itself, it is only the glitter of the sun on the surface of the waters.[9]

This is an old religion because it is the pantheistic animism that we suppose to have prevailed over the world "before we pieced our

---

[9] *Apocalypse*, p. 223.

thoughts into philosophy"; it is new because for the modern world it is not something that can be accepted as a matter of course; if it is found at all, it is attended with all the excitement of rediscovery. For Lawrence it was a real rediscovery, not bookish or archaeological; achieved through living experience, not through grubbing in *The Golden Bough* or tracing Tibetan mandalas.

Practically there is only one choice open to the modern Western man who feels the necessity for a religious apprehension of the world. It is the choice between some kind of supernaturalist theism[10] and some kind of naturalist pantheism. Lawrence chose the second. Those who choose (or are chosen by) theism are likely to end up as Christians. Pure theism is not a faith with much staying power, and the attractive force of the only great historic theism of our culture is so great, and the shocks of living so numerous, that Christianity of one kind or another is likely to receive into its fold all theists except a few insulated academic philosophers. Even Lawrence felt the attraction, though he resisted it and took the other course. He took the other course; and this means that to theists, *a fortiori* to Christians, what he has to say about human destiny can never be more than peripheral. Why should they exercise themselves overmuch about a thinker who has rejected what to them is self-evident?

For Lawrence's polemics do nothing, and can do nothing, against real Christianity. Of course real Christianity is *not* what Lawrence says it is; its essence is *not* love for mankind, meaning by this as Lawrence does a merely natural sentiment, generated within the human ego. Christianity knows as well as Lawrence did that such a love is impossible. But then the essence of Christianity is what Lawrence has rejected in advance—the faith that there is another kind of love, outside the natural order altogether, offered to humanity as grace, mediated by the Incarnation, by which all things become possible, even the subsistence of charity in the human heart. Between those who believe in the reality of the supernatural and those who do not no argument is possible; there is no common ground. Lawrence never attempts to assail the supernatural foundations of Christianity, he tacitly assumes that they are unreal and concentrates his fire on the human and ethical consequences of its doctrines. The Christian may reject his criticism altogether, though I think he would find this difficult; or he may reply that what Lawrence is attacking is only a human perversion of Christian love; and this may well be true. Even admitting this argument, it is also true that the perversion is common and widespread, and that Lawrence's polemics have a real and not insignificant object. But there is, I think, a further point.

10 "Theism: Belief in a personal God, capable of making Himself known by supernatural revelation."—*Universal English Dictionary*, ed. H. C. Wyld.

Real Christianity is an increasingly rare phenomenon in the more or less educated Western world from which Lawrence drew most of his observations; pseudo-Christianity is a much more massive and widespread affair. By pseudo-Christianity I mean an acceptance of the verbal habits, emotional predispositions and some of the ideals of conduct of real Christianity, without any profound and fundamental belief in their supernatural foundation. This is Lawrence's actual target, though he failed to distinguish its nature; and it is not impossible that real Christianity might even be helped by his searching analysis of the imitation.

Romantic love I believe to be equally immune to his attacks. Romantic love is a psychic fact; it is something that occurs, and its peculiarity is that when it occurs it is absolute and compelling. It may be an artificial channel, but it is by now so deeply worn that any waters which find their way into it flow with a force that no verbal argument can alter or modify. Lawrence can only be effective, as he is, against its vulgar or sentimental accretions. There is no need to use the historical and pragmatic argument that we *ought* not to give up the train of feeling that has been the refiner of the European heart for eight hundred years. Lawrence may be an emotional barbarian for rejecting the whole code of courtesy and chivalry, and we have the right to reject him in consequence. But it hardly matters; this particular citadel is impregnable if sparsely garrisoned. He can blow up Poe, but not the *Vita Nuova*. All he can do, and this in part he has probably done, is to create a moral climate in which it is difficult for the sentiments of the *Vita Nuova*, and all their progeny, to occur again.

In his campaign against democracy the situation is rather different. Nothing that Lawrence says is of any great moment to democracy as a convenient piece of political machinery, a reasonably handy and equitable way of getting government by consent. But against democratic egalitarianism as the ideal of human relationship he has dealt heavy blows. What is more, he has replaced it by another, and as I think more permanent, ideal, with as much respect for the human person and without the falsity and illusion—an ideal which is capable of ennobling authority, not merely of dethroning it. Men are radically unequal, if you compare them; and there are times when both intellectual honesty and personal honour demand that we should admit it. But the ideal is to stand at a point where you do not attempt to compare men at all, for each is unique. This does not so much confute egalitarianism as render it irrelevant.

Having identified the object of Lawrence's criticism, we can now recognise its immense corrosive power. Its peculiarly devastating influence is not a matter of rhetoric; it does not depend nearly as much as has been supposed on the evocative or prophetic force of his language, and it can only lose by the frequent cloudiness and ill-temper. The real weight of his criticism does not lie here at all; it is something more intellectual, in the very substance of his thought. It lies in his power to show the rotting and corrupting effect of unliving and unrooted ideals. It is not merely that they are unreal, but that their unreality is poisonous. Lawrence shows this, and does not merely talk about it. Many writers show up false patterns of life—it is the staple, for example, of an exceedingly unrevolutionary ironist like Thackeray. But there is always the tacit allowance—we are constantly tempted to make it—that a false ideal can be pragmatically useful or serve instead of a better. Lawrence's criticism is more fundamental and more penetrating largely because he destroys this comfortable compromise.

But the world has not lacked for negative and cathartic critics, especially in this century; and it is not in the end with them that one is tempted to rank Lawrence. He is indeed a destroyer of shams and falsities, but it is also necessary to discover what it is that makes him so much more than this. Those who find the best of Lawrence in the travel books and the descriptive writing would balance the destructive force with what they find there, and make the positive side of Lawrence a sort of simple natural religion. But those who do so are making Lawrence's message into a more inviting and digestible matter than it really is. The intimate and joyful contemplation of the natural scene is the consolation rather than the business of his life. Where Lawrence's powers are working most vigorously, it is the Dionysiac fervour of his destruction that is most striking; and it can be so intense that it becomes a positive value in itself. The triumphant welcome Lawrence can give to the forces which are to extinguish all ordinary personal and social values is akin, or at least analogous to, the mystic's joy in the extinction of his personality. The ecstasy with which Nietzsche in *The Birth of Tragedy* welcomes the merging of all separate entities in the Dionysian flood is the only literary parallel to Lawrence's vision, if we are really to see it as it is, not merely to extract from it those parts that are most agreeable to us.

Lawrence had read Nietzsche in youth, and through his wife he was always subject to Germanic influences. It is probable that his doctrine would not have been what it is if the Nietzschean influence had not been felt. But I am not suggesting a direct influence here, and the moment the comparison is made a vital difference is to be observed. Nietzsche sees the Apollo-Dionysus dichotomy (much like the dichotomy that runs through Lawrence's thought) as tragic. He first becomes aware of it when he is explaining the origin of tragedy—both tragedy as a literary form and the tragic sense of life. And he accepts and welcomes the necessity of tragedy. In Lawrence there is none of this acceptance. His fiction never even approaches the tragic mode; and the violence, the cruelty, the extreme situations in his stories, are never seen in a tragic light. That is why the cruelty in Lawrence's fiction so often seems naked and unresolved—there is almost a deliberate refusal of the tragic vision. "Tragedy ought to be a great big kick at misery," he wrote. Maybe so, but only when the extremes of misery and suffering have been faced, contemplated and accepted. The suffering experienced or caused by Lawrence's characters is never faced with that degree of fullness and realisation. The suffering of Miriam, of Clifford Chatterley, the full horror of the mutually destructive relation between Ursula and Gerald Crich—it is hardly too much to say that they are avoided; perhaps rightly for Lawrence's purpose; but that implies a limitation of his purpose. The full human implications of the situations in which his characters find themselves are never completely realised. And his vision of the destiny of man, for all the conflict and destruction by the way, reaches its consummation not in the tragic but in the idyllic mode—in the vision of some quasi-pastoral perfection in the past or the future, with the really terrifying conflicts all vanished away.

This I believe points to the most serious limitation of Lawrence's thought. To be alive in the flesh is magnificent, and Lawrence has expressed his sense of it magnificently. But if it is the only supreme value, man is irrevocably immersed in the transitory and the contingent, irremediably at the mercy of physical accident and physical change. And however much Lawrence may hate fixity and achieve a poetic and metaphysical exaltation by glorifying the flux, man is also a being who has a passion for the absolute, the changeless, the unconditioned. This predicament is a tragic one, perhaps the root of all tragedy. Yet Lawrence fails or refuses to see it in a tragic light.

> Man is in love, and loves what vanishes,
> What more is there to say?

Yeats' stoic question, for all its laconic brevity, contains the essence of this tragedy as nothing in Lawrence does.

To inquire why the tragic sense is absent in Lawrence leads in the end to the discovery that he is not wholly free from the sentimental idealisation that he wishes to destroy. The forms of life that Lawrence condemns are all actual enough; we recognise at once their counterparts in the contemporary world. Those which he exalts all lack reality. He projects them into some imaginary future, as much a fantasy as Morris's News from Nowhere, where men wear red trousers on their proud limbs and hierarchically dance in celebration of the life-force. Or he retrieves them from the past—some lost Indian culture, or the Etruscan civilisation whose great advantage for his purpose is that we know almost nothing about it. The construction of such myths is probably as old as civilisation itself, and Lawrence has as much right to his imaginative indulgence as anyone. But it is imaginative indulgence rather than the rigour of the whole truth.

Yet Lawrence does, after all, claim to be doing something more, and I for one wish to claim it for him. If what he does is to subject current ideals to a corrosive criticism, bring the edifice crashing down, and then sidestep from the resultant catastrophe into a fantasy world, his achievement would be less than we feel it to be. There must be something else. It has been admitted that he does not feel with the force of full commitment the tragic bearing of his doctrine. Why does the impression of personal integrity remain so strong? It can only be because Lawrence personally manages to transcend tragedy—if the paradox may be allowed—as the saints transcend it. I am not trying to predicate sanctity of Lawrence, and it is an analogy, not an identity, that is suggested. But the selfless, obliterating joy of identification with the energies of life wipes out all individual loss, limitation and incompleteness for Lawrence as the saints' all-obliterating love of another God does for them. This self-annihilating joy becomes more intense as Lawrence approaches the end of his life. We can see its effects in *Apocalypse* and *Last Poems*. As he becomes less alive in the flesh, all the ecstasy that comes, as he tells us, from being alive in the flesh becomes more real and more acute.

Then at the last we begin to wonder whether words are not slipping beneath us, and whether Lawrence has not been betrayed by his own terminology. This ecstasy that we can only experience while we are in the body becomes by a strange paradox more intense as the life of the body ebbs away. At the end of his days, at the last extremity of sickness and physical misery, when his life, in his own words, is only the leavings of a life, Lawrence finds:

> *still among it all, snatches of lovely oblivion, snatches of renewal,*
> *odd, wintry flowers upon the withered stem, yet new, strange flowers,*
> *such as my life has not brought forth before, new blossoms of me.*[11]

Is it possible that these moments have their source in the flesh that is now almost worn away? We are driven to believe that Lawrence has unwittingly brought the serpent into his own earthly paradise—the soul with all its maladies, but also with its central spark of unconditioned, inexhaustible life. At the end of "The Ship of Death", when everything has disappeared down the flood of darkness, "still out of eternity, a thread of light separates itself on the blackness"; and by its light it is possible to see that the soul is still there;

> *and the little ship wings home, faltering and lapsing*
> *on the pink flood,*
> *and the frail soul steps out.*

---

[11] "Shadows," *Last Poems*.

And then, having followed Lawrence so far, it would perhaps be possible to go back to the beginning, to tread the same path again, tracing the same pattern, but giving a different value to the symbols— and to find that the flesh had never been the flesh in any common acceptance of the term, and that the frail soul had been there all the time.

It is the genial corollary of Lawrence's impetuous and metaphorical way of thinking, even of his capriciousness, his uncertainty of tone and temper, that new growing points are to be found in his writing where we least expect them. When he seems to have carried one train of speculation to the point of exhaustion, a new, small shoot of life unexpectedly appears. This happens throughout his work, which seen as a whole presents a picture of energies flowing and ebbing, but continually pushing out in new directions. Not least at the end of his life, when the man who had exalted the natural forces of the body as the source of supreme good surveys the prospect of these forces burnt to ashes, and finds even in the ashes a new living flame. Here, as in other ways, he has earned the right to make the phoenix his symbol.

WILLIAM BUTLER YEATS:
THE RELIGION OF A POET

Austin Warren

Yeats needed religion less as a man than as a poet, and his need was epistemological and metaphysical: he needed to believe that poetry is a form of knowledge and power, not of amusement. One might say of the early Yeats that he thought of poetry as incantation and meant the word as more than metaphor; of the later Yeats, one would have to say that his metaphors were meant as more than illustrative analogies. Of symbolism, the juncture between religion and poetry, he could never have admitted its "mereness": symbols are vehicles as well as intimations. If mathematical and chemical formulas are recipes for the control of matter, images and liturgy have power over minds; they reach farther and deeper than do abstractions. Men become what they contemplate.

The last decades of the nineteenth century did not lack the sense, now become more ominous, of being at the "end of our time." Men were asking, practically—not as ritual prelude to catechetical instruction—whether life was worth living. They were doubting the gain of improved instrumentalities. Unable to hold their old faith, they were unable to relinquish it and were tormented by their indecision. "Seigneur, prenez pitié du chrétien qui doute, de l'incrédule qui voudrait croire." Des Esseintes's melodramatic cry, muted, can be heard in the suave, sad pages of *Marius*. Frederick Myers writes, in 1900, of "the deep disquiet of our time. . . . On the one hand, health, intelligence, morality,—all such boons as the steady progress of planetary evolution can win for man,—are being achieved in increasing measure. On the other hand, this very sanity, this very prosperity, do but bring out in stronger relief the underlying *Weltschmerz*, the decline of any real belief in the dignity, the meaning, the endlessness of life."

Young Yeats read Darwin and Huxley and accepted them as "established authority." But upon consideration he saw that their beliefs contravened his imagination; and he could not accept as doctrines their assumptions and methods. While others lauded "progress," he turned to that kind of traditionary primitivism which supposes central insights into human nature to occur more easily at the beginning of a culture than at the end of a civilization. Like A.E. he was not a university man; he had indeed a prejudice against meek readers in libraries; and—by reaction as well as chance, doubtless—he sought out first the unprofessional books professing to teach wisdom of life. In search of a philosophy "at once logical and boundless" he read Baron Reichenbach on Odic Force, Boehme, Swedenborg. An "authoritative religion," he decided, could be assembled from the affirmations of the poets—especially Spenser, Blake, and Shelley.

His emancipated father took no stock in religion; and it was this parental unbelief which forced the son to examine the arguments and evidences with care. "I weighed this matter perpetually with great anxiety, for I did not think I could live without religion." Much later, writing of his occult studies, he protests that he has not taken them up "wilfully nor through love of strangeness nor love of excitement . . . but because unaccountable things had happened even in my childhood and because of an ungovernable craving."

The grandparents were Anglicans of the Evangelical persuasion; and they took the child to church, where he found pleasure in the hymns, the sermon, and the poetry of Ecclesiastes and the Apocalypse—predictable tastes. In later life he occasionally visited Anglican churches; but, as an Irish boy in a London school, under a clerical headmaster "as temperate in his religious life as in all else," he had been repelled by the ease with which English religion passed into respectability. Nor could the moderations and negations of the altarless Church of Ireland be expected to attract the devotion of a young man in search of symbolism and audacity. And "Protestant Ireland seemed to think of nothing but getting on in the world."

Despite his close friendships with Dowson and Lionel Johnson and his subsequent association with Baron von Hügel, Yeats never seriously considered becoming a Catholic. Though impressed by the neo-Catholic movement among the young French intellectuals (Claudel, Péguy, Psichari), he was also puzzled: such concern for the church as he had known in the nineties was the concern of Barbey d'Aurevilly and Huysmans—Catholics with a taste for magic, sadism, or Satanism. To be sure, Celtic Ireland is also Catholic. But in *Ireland's Literary Renaissance* (1916), Ernest Boyd, who can cite only Katherine Tynan as a Catholic writer, remarks the Irish impossibility of *grands convertis* like Huysmans or Verlaine. The "Protestantism of the Irish Catholic is such as to deprive the Church of precisely those elements which are favourable to literary and intellectual development, and have rallied so many artists to her support." If the Church of Ireland is very Protestant, so, and in another sense, is the Catholic church in Ireland. And so, to find a faith really suited to the Irish genius, the 'Dublin mystics' (as Boyd calls Eglinton and A.E.) adopted the ancient Irish pantheon, the *Tuatha De Danann*, and the *sidhe*. With his friends, Yeats turned from St. Patrick (whether Catholic or Anglican) to Oisin and Niamh and Aengus. He began to chart the Sacred Mountains of Ireland on his map, to wander about raths and fairy hills, to question old peasants; he longed to be carried away by the fairies; he found beneath the Catholic stratum more primitive deposits of faith. A countrywoman told him that she disbelieved in ghosts and hell—the latter, an invention of priests for their own profit; "but there are fairies," she hastened to supplement, "and little leprechauns, and waterhorses and fallen angels": Whatever else one doubts, one never doubts the fairies, for—as another peasant said to the same inquirer, "They stand to reason."

Thus encouraged, Yeats rejected Christian authority. There must, he maintains, be a "tradition of belief older than that of any European Church, and founded upon the experience of the world before the modern bias." He writes to a French friend: "I have not found my tradition in the Catholic Church, which was not the church of my childhood, but where the tradition is, as I believe, more universal and more ancient." And to this position he persuaded Lady Gregory. "I have longed to turn Catholic that I might be nearer to the people," she testified; "but you have taught me that paganism brings me nearer still."

Of course Yeats pointed out to Lady Gregory that neither she nor her peasants were pure pagans; and in earlier days he did not oppose such a properly contaminated Christianity as a peasant might practice or an esoteric Christian speculatively construct. Both *The Celtic Twilight* (1893) and *The Secret Rose* (1896) use thematically the interplays—the rivalries and interpenetrations—of the Christian and the pagan. In "The Crucifixion of the Outcast," the White Friars put to death a pagan gleeman because his mythic songs, so different from those of their own pious poets, arouse "forgotten longing in their hearts." But when, in another story, Puritan troopers break down the door of the abbey and shoot the White Friars at the altar, and the abbot, crucifix high over his head, condemns the profaners to dwell among the ungovernable shadows, it is the Gaelic deities who lead them to destruction. One and the same "happy theologian" has visions of Christ and of the people of fairy.

Yeats himself early became a pagan. Reading *Walden*, he was inspired to conquer bodily desire and become a hermit: living "as Thoreau lived, seeking wisdom"; it was this desire for the ascetic's solitude which he commemorated in the early popular lyric, "The Lake Isle of Innisfree." Recurrent for him, throughout his life, is the image of Milton's hermetic scholar.

> Or let my lamp at midnight hour
> Be seen in some high lonely tower,
> Where I may oft outwatch the Bear
> With Thrice-Great Hermes, or unsphere
> The spirit of Plato. . . .

But such desire for solitude and lonely contemplation is less characteristic of his confessedly gregarious spirit than a series of entries into esoteric cults, communion of adepts.

In 1885, when he was twenty, he met with A. P. Sinnett's *Esoteric Buddhism,* a chief scripture of the Theosophical movement; he interested his friend, Charles Johnson, who founded the Hermetic Society, soon renamed the Dublin Lodge of the Theosophical Society. In London, shortly after, Yeats nightly frequented the establishment of Theosophy's discoverer and founder, Mme Helena Blavatsky. The Society for Psychical Research had just finished its scrutiny of the Theosophical revelations; it had pronounced them fraudulent, and the movement had dwindled. But Yeats felt an instinctive admiration, not subsequently renounced, for this "sort of old Irish peasant woman with an air of humour and audacious power," this "great passionate nature, a sort of female Dr. Johnson, impressive . . . to every man or woman who had themselves any richness." One night a week she answered questions on her system, was calm and philosophic; on other evenings she was busy, shrewd, racily humorous—played patience, reckoning her score on the green baize table top while cranks "from half Europe and from all America" talked into her imperturbable ears.

Esoteric Buddhism, Yeats's introduction to Theosophy, purports to publish the secret teaching of spiritual adepts living in the remotest Himalayas. As a movement, Theosophy offers itself as an interpretation of the inner meaning of world religion, Christian as well as Buddhist; it attaches much historical importance to Alexandrian Neo-Platonism, both pagan and Christian, as its ancestor; it has developed, historically, from the spiritualist movement; it is sympathetic in its attitude toward astrology, alchemy, and such. Like pure Buddhism, Theosophy has no God, and consequently no atonement and no prayer. It teaches the Hindu and Buddhist doctrine of karma: that our rewards or punishments in future incarnations proceed, as by natural law, from our characters in the last. Like Buddhism, it exhorts to the destruction of desire and anticipates the eventual release from the wheel of existence and entrance into nirvana.

At the British Museum, Yeats encountered S. L. MacGregor Mathers, Bergson's brother-in-law. Mathers, who had assisted Mme Blavatsky in her *Secret Doctrine* and translated *The Kabbalah Unveiled,* founded, at London, the Iris-Urania Temple of the Hermetic Students of the Golden Dawn, an order which professed to derive its rituals from old Rosicrucian manuscripts. Yeats was initiated into the order in its first year, 1887; and Mathers had a long, deep, and acknowledged influence over him. In "All Souls Night" of 1920, Yeats remembers his adept:

> *I call up MacGregor from the grave. . . .*
> *He had much industry at setting out,*

Much boisterous courage, before loneliness
Had driven him crazed;
For meditations upon unknown thought
Make human intercourse grow less and less. . . .

It was presumably Mathers who introduced Yeats to the "Christian Cabbala"a name loosely given to writings of the sixteenth and seventeenth centuries, notably those of Pico della Mirandola, Reuchlin, Cornelius Agrippa, Henry More, and *The Kabbala Denudata* of Rosenroth.[1] Yeats frequently cites Agrippa's *De occulta philosophia,* a work which has much to say of magic and magical images and astrology and the World Soul. According to Agrippa, all terrestrial things owe their power to their celestial patterns; and by a proper knowledge of their correspondences we may use the earthly images to induce the occult powers. Each sign of the zodiac, each face of each sign, each planet, has its image; and these images imprinted in seals and rings, made at proper times and of proper materials, can effect these powers; so, too, can images not celestial which are made at the astrologically proper times: thus, to procure love one devises figures embracing one another; to bring about disaster, one breaks an image.

Under Mathers' instruction, Yeats learned how to paint cabalistic symbols on cards and how to use them for evoking states of reverie in himself and sometimes trance states in others. Yeats tells some extraordinary stories of these experiments; but at the end of "Hodos chameliontos," he passes a judgment of rejection, not denying power to the symbols chosen but perceiving that irresponsible play with them brings danger. The images that really matter to men of genius and culture are the images which are not chosen but given; and the unity of a culture comes from a given image—the figure of Apollo or of Christ.

In Paris at the end of the century, Yeats scrutinized the chief occultists. With the followers of the eighteenth-century mystic, Saint-Martin, he tested the vision-producing potency of hashish. He met a young Arabic scholar possessing a ring of alchemical gold. He visited the "mysterious house" of Marquis Stanislas de Guaita, founder (in 1889) of the Ordre Kabbalistique de la Rose-Croix and author of *La Clef de la magie noire* and *Le Serpent de la Genèse;* admired the Marquis as "the one eloquent learned scholar who has written of magic in our generation." He met also the great Sar Péladan, founder (in 1890) of yet another, a professedly Catholic, order of the Rosy Cross. Péladan, described by Max Nordau in his once famous *Degeneration,* claimed to be the descendant of the old Magi, the inheritor of the arcane wisdom of Zoroaster, Pythagoras, and Orpheus; and his order purported to revive and unite with

---

[1] Cf. J. L. Blau, *The Christian Interpretation of the Cabala in the Renaissance* (New York, 1944). For Mathers' Order and its contexts, cf. A. E. Waite, *Brotherhood of the Rosy Cross* (London, 1924); and Alvin B. Kuhn, *Theosophy. . .* (New York, 1930).

the Rosicrucians the Knights Templars and the order of the Holy Grail. The Rosicrucians, professing to reconcile Christianity with Cabalism, provided Yeats with his obsessive symbol of the rose—especially the "Rose upon the Rood of Time" (1893); and in his essay of 1895, "The Body of the Father Christian Rosencrux," he symbolizes an old myth of the order, according to which two hundred and fifty years after the founder's death, his disciples found in a sealed temple his imperishable body.

In "Hodos chameliontos," Yeats confesses that he had himself ambitions of becoming founder of a "mystical order" which should buy or hire a castle in Lough Kay, a castle affording at one end "a stone platform where meditative persons might pace to and fro." This castle on the rock would provide a place "where its members could retire for a while for contemplation, and establish mysteries like those of Eleusis and Samothrace." For ten years (1888-98?) he sought "to find philosophy and create ritual for the Order." Perhaps, as for Boehme, Swedenborg, and Blake, so again the gates of revelation would open; and he was prepared that the new scripture should, like that of the great mystics whom he had read, use Christian symbols as well as pagan. "Is it true that our air is disturbed, as Mallarmé said, by 'the trembling of the veil of the temple, or that our whole age is seeking to bring forth a sacred book?' Some of us thought that book near towards the end of last century, but the tide sank again."

Acquaintance with Theosophists, Cabalists, and Rosicrucians lay behind Yeats's endeavor to write a novel, the hero of which should "see all the modern visionary sects pass before his bewildered eyes, as Flaubert's St. Anthony saw the Christian sects." This abandoned manuscript of 1896, which must have owed much to Pater as well as to Flaubert, may well be represented by the three tales, "Rosa Alchemica," "The Magi," and "The Tables of the Law," published in 1897 and introducing the figures of Michael Robartes and Owen Aherne, the adepts who reappear in "The Phases of the Moon" and elsewhere. Told in the elaborate, thick harmonies of the *Imaginary Portraits,* these stories summon up adepts in risk of losing their sanity as they have already lost their taste for human intercourse, even for intercourse with other students—men like Pater's Van Storck, like Huysmans's Des Esseintes, like Villiers' Axel. The narrator is a reformed adept, now a Catholic, who, though conscious of the malign in esoteric cults, has but half suppressed his desire for the dangerous, for that "indefinite world" which invites the soul to waver, wander, and perish. While professing renunciation, the vain soul still hovers over her former state, proud to have sinned. The other tales offer the same image of the divided soul. In the second, Owen Aherne has grown wise to his own damnation. It has been revealed to him that only through sin and separation from God can he come to God; but he cannot sin, he cannot pray. "I have seen the Whole," he says, "and how can I come again to belief that a part is the whole?" In the third tale, concerned with the return of the Magi and the beginning of a new cycle, a Second Coming, the teller speaks of dreading the illusions which accompany any age of revelation; and he concludes: "I no longer live an elaborate and haughty life, but seek to lose myself among the prayers and the sorrows of the multitude. I pray best in poor chapels, where the frieze coats brush past me as I kneel, and when I pray against demons. . . ." Despite their perioded style, these pieces have their power and horror—a horror drawn not from blasphemy or diabolism but from the fear of madness.

All the cults to which Yeats attached himself vary a single pattern—that of an arcane wisdom traditionally clothed in myth but now, to some group of initiates, "unveiled"; all of them—even theosophy, the most elaborate of the systems—are inclusive of magic, alchemy, astrology, and spiritualism. These concerns of Yeats are all defined and defended by Mme Blavatsky, who devoted the first volume of her *Isis Unveiled* to magic, past and present; who asserted that "astrology is to exact astronomy what psychology is to exact physiology"; and who pointed out that, under the emblems of sulphur, mercury, and salt, alchemy may concern itself with human and cosmic mysteries.

Yeats played with alchemy and its symbolisms. He imagined himself as writing a little work, in the style of Sir Thomas Browne, which should interpret the alchemic quest as the "transmutation of life into art." He learned to cast horoscopes; in the Preface to his early novel, *John Sherman,* he writes: "I am something of an astrologer, and can see" in these pages a young man "born when the Water-Carrier Aquarius was on the horizon, at pains to overcome Saturn in Saturn's hour, just as I can see in much that follows his struggle with the still all-too-unconquered Moon, and at last, as I think, the summons of the prouder Sun." Technical terms of the 'science' are not infrequent in *A Vision;* more significant, however, is the general analogy between the "Twenty-eight Incarnations" and the structure of a popular manual like Evangeline Adams' *Astrology* (1927). Both offer sequences of characterological types, illustrated from the biography of genius; both offer shrewd, suggestive analyses of types and individuals. But, unlike Miss Adams, Yeats is not offering a literal equation of celestial influences and terrestrial products; he professes that the fitting of the lunar series into the solar year is purely arbitrary and that the whole series is a "parable." In a fashion for which astrologers offer no authority, he orders his types so that they constitute a gradual progression from the most objective to the most subjective and back again; and he combines a psychology with a history by making the same diagram serve at once for a vertical view of two thousand years (the Great Wheel, comprising twenty-eight successive incarnations) and a horizontal view of all types contemporarily occurrent.

His degree of faith in the predictive power of horoscopes is difficult to estimate; but it is not difficult to conjecture the imaginative and philosophical value which the 'science' held for him: it lay in the honorific connection astrology establishes between man and nature and in its imprecise determinism of the individual and the state.

One must be at least equally cautious in estimating Yeats's attitude toward spiritualism, apparently the latest to develop of his occult interests. He was critical of alleged communications with the dead and the interpretation of the 'messages.' He did not forget the warnings of Swedenborg (whose *Heaven and Hell* he read in his youth) that the spirits who can reach men through mediums are either earthbound or devils counterfeiting the virtuous dead. In his discourse prefatory to "The Words upon the Window-Pane," he argues that every manifestation of a spirit is "first of all a secondary personality or dramatisation created by, in, or through the medium." He even suggests, though he but half accepts his suggestion, the theory that the communicators of *A Vision* were not spirits of the dead but the "personalities of a dream" shared by his wife and him; the test of truth for him lies certainly not in the mode of its delivery but in its coherence and illumination. For the credulous "millions who have substituted the séance-room for the church" he had only pity and contempt.

Whatever the precise nature of his interest in spiritualism it had little to do with curiosity concerning man's post-mortem existence and much to do with possible unseen worlds surrounding man now. In his *Human Personality* (1903), a book admired by William James and A.E. and surely known to Yeats, Myers discovers the cure for man's "spiritual solitude" in the law of telepathy, defined as the transference of ideas and images from living brain to living brain and as communion between incarnate and discarnate spirits. From the painful sense of the self's isolation, Yeats turned to the doctrine that beneath our conscious selves there is a communal psyche, an *Anima mundi*. The sharing of the same dream by two living persons and the invasion of the living man's dream by the dead man's memories are beliefs interconnected in Yeats's faith: they are parts of the same release from the uniqueness of the self.

How far Yeats believed in these mysterious worlds and powers is a question to which his critics have long addressed themselves. The answer has often been skeptical. Before the publication of *A Vision*, Yeats was customarily, in contrast to A.E., viewed as one who toyed with mysticism, used it for literary effect. And certainly *The Celtic Twilight* (1893) is full of hints that Yeats is being romantic and misty and that the real Yeats is the shrewd observer who says of "A Visionary" (clearly A.E.) that there is in him "the vast and vague extravagance that lies at the bottom of the Celtic heart." But there are intimations of another attitude, hints of a Pyrrhonism which finds dreams as credible as facts, of a fideism which is not disturbed by the current and changing 'truths' of science. "Everything exists, everything is true" is one fashion of putting this; another is to ask, rhetorically, "When all is said and done, how do we not know but that our own unreason may be better than another's truth?"

Autobiographically considering his earlier self, Yeats suggests the Pascalian antithesis between the reasons of the head and the reasons of the heart: "My critical mind—was it friend or enemy?—mocked, and yet I was delighted." And of his youthful talks with peasants: "I did not believe with my intellect that you could be carried away body and soul, but I believed with my emotions, and the belief of the country people made that easy." But when he conversed with educated people he grew timid: "I was always ready to deny or turn into a joke what was for all that my secret fanaticism. When I had read Darwin and Huxley and believed as they did, I wanted, because an established authority was upon my side, to argue with everybody." Even in *A Vision* Yeats leaves room for the reader to think that he is being offered prose commentary on the symbolism of the poems.

Yet, if the earlier Yeats is whimsical or otherwise evasive on the subject of the occult, the later Yeats has cut himself off from such ambiguity. With whatever hesitations, cautions, and reserves, he ranges himself on the side of the supernaturalists. Responsibility of belief markedly increases from *The Celtic Twilight* to *A Vision.* In the Preface to the 1902 edition of the former, he announced, "I shall publish in a little while a big book about the commonwealth of faery, and shall try to make it systematic and learned enough to buy pardon for this handful of dreams." This announcement, which his critics took as further whimsy, indicates rather that Yeats was unsatisfied to leave his convictions in the twilight of poetic prose, that intellectual integrity required him to produce some philosophical defense of his convictions. The essays called "Magic" (1901) and "Per amica silentia lunae" (1917) represent preliminary efforts at such defense; but it is *A Vision* which, incorporating and developing the earlier ideas of the *Anima mundi,* of the self and its antithetic mask, especially fulfils the intention of 1902. "Learned" and "systematic" are relative terms, of course; but they can stand as descriptive of the intention toward which Yeats moved.

Until comparatively late, he had restricted his reading to the 'poets and the mystics,' avoided the philosophers, even the philosophers of mysticism—as though the purity of his intuitive belief might be violated by acquaintance with rival positions and criteria. But now, after making the initial notes for *A Vision,* he reads Plotinus, medieval philosophy, Berkeley, Hegel, Wundt, McTaggart, willing not only to see his own 'philosophy' in terms of its historical parallels and oppositions but to make it as coherent as possible; and he reads biography and especially history with the intent of grounding his myth in the world of secular fact. This movement from the Rosicrucians to Plotinus and Berkeley is strikingly paralleled by the increasing comprehensiveness of Yeats's mythic Ireland. Whereas in the *Twilight* and the *Rose* he almost limits himself to the lore of peasants and the "pride of the adept," to a pre-Christian, or, failing that, a pre-Reformation, Ireland, the later Yeats is able to find heroes in the persons of the Anglo-Irish Augustans—Swift, Burke, Goldsmith, and Berkeley—and to find Irish philosophy in their writings.

> *And haughtier-headed Burke that proved the State a tree,*
> *That this unconquerable labyrinth of the birds, century after century,*
> *Cast but dead leaves to mathematical equality;*
> *And God-appointed Berkeley that proved all things a dream,*
> *That this pragmatical, preposterous pig of a world,*
>   *its farrow that so solid seem*
> *Must vanish on the instant if the mind but change its theme. . . .*

Yeats's early traffic with ghosts, sorcerers, and fairies was, probably, instigated by a desire to loosen the bonds of logic. In his essay on "Demonology" Emerson speaks of the great interest which dreams, animal magnetism, and omens have for "some minds. They run into this twilight and say, 'There's more here than is dreamed of in your philosophy.'" Young Yeats was surely one of these 'minds'; he desired to say: Life is not all rule, order, reason, system, common sense; nature and the human mind have their 'night-side' of the subconscious, of dusk and half-lights. Religion he saw as the search for the irrational, the irruptive, the unpredictable. But, without exaggerating the antithesis, one may represent the later Yeats as finding its own logic and order in the supernatural.

In all these respects, Yeats may be judged to have matured. In his early traffic with Rosicrucians and Cabalists, he is disarmingly easy to satirize as the adolescent enamored of ritual wardrobes, passwords, and the "pride of the adept"; the self-awareness of the later Yeats is, in the earlier, sometimes theatrical, posed. Yet the maturity is anticipated in certain persistencies—belief in the imagination, balance of sensibility and sense, moral courage. Like his contemporary, Irving Babbitt, Yeats could stand removed from the current intellectual orthodoxy without losing either his sharp sense of dissent or his own faith. He was not afraid to seem adolescent until he could achieve maturity on something like his own terms and win, by steadfast adherence, some respect for his outmoded causes. After 1900 we hear little more of arcane societies; Yeats turns from planning an occult ecclesiasticism to the organization of an Irish Theatre. The occult pursuits consolidate into a general defense of a more variously comprehensive universe than a positivist science will admit.

A central property of Yeats's religion which remains unchanged from youth to age is its lack of a consequent ethics. His old companion in theosophy, A.E., was fond of quoting the injunction, "For every step that you take in the pursuit of the hidden knowledge, take three steps in the perfecting of your own character." But Yeats, so far as one can see, never postulated an ascetical discipline preliminary to a religious experience. He had his moral code, and he had his ritual; but, as in primitive religions, the two were unrelated. Catholic Christianity is mystical, sacramental, ethical, and seeks, at whatever tension, to realize this character. With liberal Protestantism, the numinous disappears as *Aberglaube*, and religion becomes morality. In Yeats, religion returns to its pre-Christian and indeed pre-monotheistic character, becoming the search for knowledge of the unseen and for gnostic power.

Temperamentally, Yeats seems to have been an optimistic monist. If his magic seems generally 'white,' if he had no appetite for diabolism or blasphemy, he was correspondingly free from any sense of sin or need of redemption. In the broad sense, he remained, in *A Vision*, theosophic, by implication entertaining the belief in karma, reincarnation, and the eventual delivery from rebirth into the peace of nirvana; but it does not appear that his 'heart' ever accepted the Orient's pessimistic view of existence or the ethical release of the Four Noble Truths. Such a statement, however, needs modification; if the earlier Yeats identifies vision with reverie and virtue with abstention from Philistine ambitions, the later Yeats, with his doctrine of the will and its achievement of its True Mask, holds a more strenuous conception. And the later Yeats finds in the grasp of a "Vision of Evil" a chief differentiation between great poets like Villon, Dante (and himself), and such, for his last judgment, superficial poets as Emerson, Whitman, and A.E. Though his is a vision not of man's sin but of necessary pain, an unflinching view of world history which moves characteristically not by smooth progressions but by revolutions, reversals, and brutalities, it is an advance in Yeats's apprehension that he insists upon this realism.

T. S. ELIOT: FROM ASH WEDNESDAY TO MURDER IN THE CATHEDRAL

R. P. Blackmur

If you want a text to head and animate a discussion of Mr. Eliot's work from *Ash Wednesday* to *Murder in the Cathedral*, there is none better—for exactness, for ambiguity, and for a capacity to irritate those unlikely otherwise to respond—than the following sentence drawn from *After Strange Gods,* which summarizes Mr. Eliot's answer to the charge of incoherence between his verse and his critical prose. "I should say that in one's prose reflexions one may be legitimately occupied with ideals, whereas in the writing of verse one can only deal with actuality." Here Mr. Eliot shows his characteristic talent for making statements of position which mislead some, drive others to labored exegesis, but end by seeming self-evident and a piece with the body of his work. In this instance what is misleading is not in the words but in the common and not always tacit assumption that poetry aims to transcend or idealize the actual; which may be so of some poetry, of official poetry for example, but cannot well be so without vitiating it, of poetry like Mr. Eliot's which has a dramatic or moral cast. Conflict of character, mixture of motive, and the declaration of human purpose and being, cannot be presented (however much they may be argued) except in terms of good and evil, which makes the most actual realm we know.

It is the criterion of the actual, of the important orders among it, and the means of approach that differ; and if we call the differences verbal, intending to belittle them, it is because we wish to escape the pressure of imaginative labor inherent in any genuine picture of the actual—as if the actual were free and ascertainable to all comers at the turn of a tap, instead of being, as it is, a remaining mystery even when long ardor has won knowledge of it. The actual, for poetry, or for Mr. Eliot's poetry, resides perhaps among "the deeper, unnamed feelings which form the substratum of our being, to which we rarely penetrate"; a notion, and Mr. Eliot's phrasing of it, to which this essay will return. Now, you might say that for the realm of the actual so conceived the psychoanalysts have a means of approach but no criterion, and the Nazis have a criterion which for their purpose makes means of approach

superfluous. Mr. Eliot has a criterion and a means which
tangled but which cannot be separated. But it is not a
many can adopt today. As it happens, the three major ad
of the actual—the Church of the great Christmas, philos
cludes Plato, Montaigne, and Spinoza, and, third, that nan
of the supernatural in daily life which includes folk ma
Christian religion; as it happens all three are in our day
models of escape or their animating influence is ignored. This is because
of the tireless human genius for evasion and the inexhaustible human
appetite for facts of the kinds that have use but cannot declare meaning:
the statistical facts of science; it has nothing to do with the adequacy
of the criteria themselves. Which indicates only that a man must achieve
his own criterion individually and that it may appear disguised.

Mr. Eliot's criterion is the Christianity of the Church of England;
and he is in the process of achieving it for himself. He provides us with
an example of a powerful poetic imagination feeding on a corpus of
insight either foreign or stultifying to the imaginative habit of most of
us, and sustained by an active and inclusive discipline beyond our
conscious needs. He is as far from us as Mr. Yeats, our one indubitable
major poet, is with his fairies and lunar phases; and as close, in his best
work, as Mr. Yeats in his, in an immitigable grasp of reality. It is a
question which is the outsider. Mr. Yeats finds Christianity as unsatis-
fying for himself, finally, as any Huxley;[1] and Mr. Eliot has emphasized,
with reference to Mr. Yeats, that you cannot take heaven by magic, has
argued in several places recently that you cannot substitute a private
for an institutional religion or philosophy. Both men write verse with
the authority and the application of an orthodoxy. It may be that both
are outsiders, if we conceive, as it may be fruitful to do, that the prevailing essences of English and American civilization are heterodox—when
the mere sight of any orthodoxy, of any whole view, may be entertained
as dramatic and profoundly tragic. Some such notion was perhaps tacitly
present in Mr. Eliot's mind when he wrote the following sentence: "At
the moment when one writes, one is what one is, and the damage of a
lifetime, and of having been born into an unsettled society, cannot be
repaired at the moment of composition." At least it is in terms derived
from such a notion that the spectator can see the tragedy in the lives
of such writers as D. H. Lawrence and Hart Crane—perhaps no less in

---

[1] I hope to consider in another place the extraordinary strength in representing reality which Mr. Yeats derives from his own resort to the supernatural; a strength so
great that it corrects every *material* extravagance of his doctrine. Here I merely quote
three lines addressed to a modern Catholic.

Homer is my example and his unchristened heart.
The lion and the honeycomb, what has Scripture said?
So get you gone, Von Hügel, though with blessings on your head.

life of Dante—though the writers themselves may have seen only the pursuit of a task.[2]

Here two interesting and fundamental problems are raised—that of the truth of an orthodoxy and that of the tragedy of an orthodox mind in a heterodox world; one is for theology and the other for imaginative representation; but neither can be here our concern. Our own problem is no less interesting and I think no less fundamental; the problem of the moral and technical validity of Mr. Eliot's Christianity as it labors to seize the actual for representation in his poetry. Validity is not truth in an ascertainable sense, but amounts to truth in a patent sense. We are faced in Mr. Eliot's recent verse with a new and rising strength patently connected with his Christianity; and the Christian discipline is dominant and elemental in the two plays, *The Rock* and *Murder in the Cathedral*. It might formerly have been thought odd to call attention to a writer's religion as still earlier his religious conformity would have been the final test of his value. Now a man's religion is the last thing we can take for granted about him, which is as it should be; and when a writer shows the animating presence of religion in his work, and to the advantage of his work, the nature of that presence and its linkage deserve at least once our earnest examination. Interest will be clearly seen if the statement can be accepted that there has hardly been a poet of similar magnitude in English whose work, not devotional in character, shows the operative, dramatic presence of Christianity. Many poets have relied, like Wordsworth, upon a religion to which they did not adhere, and many have used such a religion provisionally as a foil from the rack; but there are only rarely examples of poets or poems where deliberate affirmative use is made of religion for dramatic purposes. It is true, after the middle age, in the ages of Faith muddled with reason, the Church would not have tolerated such a use at lay hands. There is Milton unarguably; but I should like to submit that Milton's religious dramatizations are theological in an age of theology and that what I am anxious to discriminate in Mr. Eliot is in the dramatization of the turbulent feelings and the voids beneath the theology. Then there is Blake, whose religion was not Christian and often not religion at all but whose religious convictions permeated his prophetic books; but Blake's religion was self-manufactured as well as self-achieved, with the consequence that it as frequently clogged as freed his insight. Here we are concerned with the operative advantage of an objective religion on the material of dramatic poetry.

That is, the great interest, here as in any domain of criticism, is in the

---

[2] It is notable that from another point of view Henry James saw the artist as an interesting theme for fiction only in his guise as a failure; his success was wholly in his work. See the Prefaces to *The Tragic Muse, The Author of Beltraffio,* and *The Lesson of the Master.*

facts that can be stated about the relation between Mr.
and his religion. No fact requires so much emphasis as
just as Mr. Yeats's poetry is not magic, Mr. Eliot's poetry
Religion and magic are backgrounds, and the actual (whic
the experience of magic and religion) is so to speak the
each; the poet is in the area between, and in the light of th
upon the other. But there is no way in which, say, the mys
of the Mass can enter directly into the material of poetry; nor on the
other hand can poetry alone satisfy the legitimate aspirations of religion.
For all I know the Church may hold differently; these propositions are
meant to apply from the point of view of poetry alone, which we may
think of here as looking for light upon its subject matter. The Church,
which is religion embodied, articulated, and groomed, concentrates and
spurs the sensibility, directing it with an engine for the judgment of good
and evil upon the real world; but it does not alter, it only shapes and
guides the apprehension and feeling of the real world. The facts of
religion enlighten the facts of the actual, from which they are believed
to spring.[3]

The act of enlightening or of being enlightened cannot, except for
the great mystic, amount to identification of the object with the light in
which it was seen; and in poetry it is only the devotional order which
would desire such identification. Mr. Eliot's poetry is not devotional,
unless we accept the notion that the love of God is best exercised in the
knowledge of his works; a notion which would include Shakespeare as
above all a devotional poet since he mirrored more of the actual man
than any poet we know. But that is not what we mean by devotional
poetry and it is ruining the heart of a word to sustain the pretense that
we do. We mean as a rule poetry that constructs, or as we say expresses,
a personal emotion about God, and I think it requires something approaching a saint to be very often successful in such constructions; and
a saint, as Mr. Eliot observes, would limit himself if he undertook much
devotional poetry. Otherwise, whatever the sincerity, private devotions
are likely to go by rote and intention rather than rise to a represented
state; there enters too much the question of what ought to be felt to
the denigration (and I should say to God's eye) of what is actually
felt—and it is this characteristic predicament of the devout which
cripples the development of poets like Hopkins and Crashaw so that we
value them most in other, hindered qualities than the devout. It is perhaps indicative in this context of devotional poetry considered as poetry
to remember how few from twenty Christian centuries are the great

[3] The facts of science may similarly enlighten, providing there is a medium of poetic
imagination; this although Mr. Eliot finds, correctly, the falsely poetic astronomy of
our day quite vitiated. It was, says Mr. Eliot, the eternal *silence* of the immense spaces
that terrified Pascal.

ers. It would seem that an earnest repetition of the General Con-
ssion is a more devout if less emotional act than the composition of
a poem.

Mr. Eliot's poetry is not devotional in any sense of which we have
been speaking, but, for the outsider—and we are all outsiders when we
speak of poetry—it is the more religious for that. It is religious in the
sense that Mr. Eliot believes the poetry of Villon and Baudelaire to be
religious—only an educated Villon and a healthy Baudelaire: it is pene-
trated and animated and its significance is determined by Christian
feeling, and especially by the Christian distinction of Good and Evil.
This feeling and this distinction have in his prose reflections led him
to certain extravagances—I remember as superlative a paper contributed
to a Unitarian monthly attacking the liberal element, which ended magnificently: "They are right. They are damned."—but in his verse, where
he has limited himself, if sometimes obscurely, to the actual, there is no
resulting extravagance, but the liberation of increased scope and that
strength of charitable understanding which is apparently most often
possible through Christian judgment.[4]

That is, the Church is in Mr. Eliot's poetry his view of life; it recognizes and points the issues and shapes their poetic course; it is the
rationale of his drama and the witness of its fate; it is, in short, a way
of handling poetic material to its best advantage. It may be much more—
as there is always life itself beyond the poetry that declares it; here
nothing but the poetry is in question. If we consider the series of poems
united in *Ash Wednesday* apart from the influence of that view of life
we shall be left in as much of a muddle as if we consider them apart
from the influence which Mr. Eliot's merely poetic habits exert upon
their Christianity. We should have, in the one case, an emotional elegy
without much point but human weakness; and in the other, if we recognized the Christianity and nothing else, we should have only a collection
of ritual trappings and reminiscences.

I do not know if there have been efforts to appreciate the Christian
tags alone; but I know that so intelligent a critic as Mr. Edmund Wilson
(in *Axel's Castle*) missed the Christian *significance* in the poem and
saw only a revelation of human weakness and an escapist's despair.
Mr. Wilson had a non-literary axe to grind. Mr. I. A. Richards, who had,
as Mr. Eliot would say, more nearly the benefits of a Christian education, saw, even if he did not share, the Christian light, although that is
not what he calls it. Mr. Richards saw what the poem was about; that
it was not a revelation of human weakness and an attempt at escape
but a summoning of human strength and an effort to extinguish both

---

[4] The least charity is moral indifference, and Mr. Eliot's attacks upon it (in *After Strange Gods*) are just, whether you share his Christianity or not; but his principles are not the only ones to secure the end in view.

hope and despair in the face of death. The poem is neither the devotion of a weary soul nor an emotional elegy; it is, like almost all of Mr. Eliot's poetry, a dramatized projection of experience. As it happens the experience has a religious bias; which means that it calls on specific Christian beliefs to make the projection actual.

That the poem relies on other devices of the poetic imagination is obvious, and that these in their turn make the Christian beliefs actual for the poem—as Shakespeare's devices made Othello's jealousy actual— should be equally obvious. Here I want to emphasize that the abnegation in the first section of the poem is Christian abnegation (it is introduced, after all, by the governing title *Ash Wednesday,* which begins the forty days of fast and penance before the resurrection, and which also commemorates the temptation and triumph in the wilderness); and Christian abnegation is an act of strength not weakness, whereby you give up what you can of the evil of the flesh for the good of the soul. The conception is certainly not limited to Christianity; as an ethical myth it is common to most philosophies and religions; but its most dramatic because most specifically familiar form is certainly that rehearsed by the Christian Church. That Mr. Eliot should make serious use of it, aside from his private religion, is natural; and it ought to have helped rather than hindered the understanding of the fundamental human feelings his poem dramatized. Mr. Wilson should have recognized its presence, and had he done so could not have mistaken the intent of the poem, however much for other reasons he might have judged it inadequate, for many persons, to its theme.

Similarly—if there is need for a further example—in the quoted words of Arnaut Daniel in the fourth section, we should, to gain anything like their full significance, not only be aware of their literary origin in the *Purgatorio,* not only feel the weight of Dante at our backs, but also should feel the force of the Christian teaching which made the words poignant for Dante—and so for Mr. Eliot. This or its equivalent. Knowing such matters for poetry is not so hard as it seems when the process is described; perhaps in this case, if the mind strikes instinctively at all the right attitude, the context of the poem will force the right meaning into the reader's mind once the literal meaning is understood. *Sovegna vos:* Be mindful of me, remember my pain. Arnaut wishes Dante to remember him in the willfully accepted, refining fires of purgatory. It is characteristic of the meaning and integral to the association from which it springs that the words appear in Dante's Provençal. Had Mr. Eliot translated them they would have lost their identity and their air of specific origin; their being a quotation, and the reader knowing them so, commits them to a certain life and excludes other lives; nor could they have brought with them, in bare English, the very Christian context we wish to emphasize.

A different, but associated, effect is secured by the fact that the line which, with variations, opens the first and the last of these poems, appears in Mr. Eliot's English rather than in Guido Cavalcanti's Italian: at least I assume the line would own its source. Cavalcanti's line reads: *"Perch'io non spero di tornar già mai"*; Mr. Eliot's first version reads: "Because I do not hope to turn again," and his second: "Although I do not hope to turn again." The difference between "Because" and "Although" is deliberate and for the attentive reader will add much to the meaning. Mr. I. A. Richards has commented on the distinction in *On Imagination.* But the point I wish to make here is not about the general influence of either form of the line; the unwary reader can determine that for himself. My point is smaller, at least initially, and consists in stating two or three facts, and the first fact is very small indeed. *"Perche"* may be rendered either "because" or "although," depending on the context, here supplied by Mr. Eliot. The second fact is a little larger; although Mr. Eliot may greatly admire the Ballata from which the line was taken, it was not its import in that poem which concerned him in his own, so that to have quoted it in the original would either have given a wrong impression of import or have prefaced a serious work with a meretricious literary ornament. The Italian line (with its overtones about turning and renunciation of many orders) gave him material to remodel for his own purposes in his own poem—with yet a sediment, perhaps, of objective source to act as a mooring. As it happens, which is why the line is discussed here at all, it is indissolubly associated in both its forms with the "great" lines in the poem: the prayer—

> *Teach us to care and not to care*
> *Teach us to sit still.*

This is a Christian prayer (not, as I gather Mr. Wilson would have it, at all mystical) and represents in an ultimate form for poetry one of the great aspects of the Church—its humility. That it also represents, in another interpretation, a great aspect of Confucianism is immaterial; as it is immaterial that by still another interpretation it represents the heart of Roman stoicism. Mr. Eliot came to it through the Church, or his poem did, and he brought Guido's line with him;[5] and the line as used has a dominant Christian flavor which cannot be expunged. There is thus a transformation of tone in this quotation quite different but to be associated with the quotation of Arnaut's phrase. As materials in the poem, one exerted Christian feeling in its own right, and the other was made to carry Christian feeling by the context—and feeling of the deep and nameless order which is the reality of Mr. Eliot's poetry.

---

[5] It is amusing but not inconsistent to reflect that Mr. Eliot has noted that Guido was a heretic.

The reader may rightly wonder if he is expected to get at Mr. Eliot's reality so indirectly and through the coils of such close-wound ellipsis; and especially will he wonder if he had read Mr. Eliot's assertion that he would like an audience that could neither read nor write, and this because, as he says, "it is the half-educated and ill-educated, rather than the uneducated, who stand" in the poet's way. Well, the uneducated hardly exist with relation to Mr. Eliot's poetry; and very few of his audience can be said to be rightly educated for it—certainly not this writer; most of us come to his poetry very ill-educated indeed. If modern readers did not as a class have to make up for the defects of their education in the lost cause of Christianity—if we did not find Christianity fascinating because strange, and dramatic because full of a *hubris* we could no more emulate than that of Oedipus—there would be neither occasion nor point for this particular essay. We have a special work of imaginative recovery to do before we can use Mr. Eliot's poetry to the full. However a later day may see it in perspective, to us Mr. Eliot must be of our time less because he seems to spring from it than because he imposes upon us a deep reminder of a part of our heritage which we have lost except for the stereotypes of spiritual manners. These stereotypes form our natural nexus with the impetus or drive of his poetry; and it is as we see them filled out, refreshed, re-embodied, that his poems become actual for us. Mr. Eliot is perhaps not himself in a position to sympathize with this operation of imaginative recovery; at any rate he rejected the to us plausible statement of Mr. Richards that *The Waste Land* was poetry devoid of beliefs. Mr. Eliot would prefer the advantage of a literal to that of an imaginative faith, immersion to empathy; and he has very much doubted, in his moral judgment of Thomas Hardy, whether what he says could "convey very much to anyone for whom the doctrine of Original Sin is not a very real and tremendous thing." The answer to that is that we do need to know that the doctrine of Original Sin is a reality for Mr. Eliot, and how much so, in order to determine both what light it sheds on Hardy and how to combine it with other insights into Hardy; but we do not need to share Mr. Eliot's conviction of literal application. Indeed, many of us would feel that we had impoverished our belief by making it too easy if we did share the conviction. Here is the crux of the whole situation between Mr. Eliot and those outside the Faith. The literal believer takes his myths, which he does not call myths, as supernatural archetypes of reality; the imaginative believer, who is not a "believer" at all, takes his myths for the meaning there is in their changing application. The practical consequences may be similar, since experience and interest are limited for data to the natural world, but the labor of understanding and the value assigned will be different for each. Thus Mr. Eliot and Mr. Richards are both correct—although neither would accept my way of saying so. *The Waste Land* is full of beliefs (especially, for this essay, a belief in the myth of Gethsemane) and is not limited by them but freed once they are understood to be imaginative. Only Mr. Eliot is correct for himself alone, while Mr. Richards is correct for others as well. Our labor is to recapture the imaginative burden and to avoid the literal like death.

If Mr. Eliot could not accept this notion in the abstract, he employs something very like it in his practical view of poetry, and by doing so he suggests an admirable solution for the reader's difficulties with his own poems and especially the difficulty with their Christian elements. This is the notion of different levels of significance and response. "In a play of Shakespeare," says Mr. Eliot, "you get several levels of significance. For the simplest auditors there is the plot, for the more thoughtful the character and the conflict of character, for the more literary the words and phrasing, for the more musically sensitive the rhythm, and for auditors of greater sensitiveness and understanding a meaning which reveals itself gradually. And I do not believe that the classification of audience is so clear-cut as this; but rather that the sensitiveness of every auditor is acted upon by all these elements at once, though in different degrees of consciousness. At none of these levels is the auditor bothered by the presence of what he does not understand, or by the presence of that in which he is not interested."

I propose to apply a little later the burden of these sentences where they properly belong: to the two plays, *The Rock* and *Murder in the Cathedral.* Meanwhile let us twist the reference slightly and apply it to our present problem: the reader's relation to the Christian element among other elements in such poems as *Ash Wednesday,* merely substituting within the quotation the word readers for audience or auditors. Clearly there are different levels of significance at which the poem can be read; there are the levels responded to by Mr. Richards and Mr. Wilson; and there is the simplest level where there is "only" the poem to consider. But if the formula is applicable with any justice it is because Mr. Eliot's contention is correct that "The sensitiveness of every reader is acted upon by all these elements at once," and because, further, "at none of these levels is the reader bothered by the presence of what he does not understand, or the presence of that in which he is not interested." In that case we must admit that most readers do not count for more than the simplest form of excitement and vicarious mewing; which is the truth—and it is upon that class that the existence of poetry relies. Then there is a class a little higher in the scale, the class that propagates poetry without understanding it in any conscious sense; this is the class Mr. Wilson describes, the class of young poets who, after *The Waste Land* began to sink in, "took to inhabiting exclusively barren beaches, cactus-grown deserts, and dusty attics overrun with rats." Possibly these classes are unconsciously affected by all or almost all the possible levels of significance, including those of which the author was unaware; which makes occasion both for pride and prospective humiliation in the poet. I think the notion has something Christian in it; something that smells of grace; and has very little to do with any conception of popular poetry addressed to an audience that can neither read nor write. However that may be, there remains the class that preserves and supports poetry, a class the members of which unfortunately cannot stop short on the level of their unconscious appreciation but necessarily go on, risking any sort of error and ultimate mistake, until they are satisfied as to what a poem means. This may not be the class for which Mr. Eliot or any poet writes; but it includes that very small sub-class of readers of "greater sensitiveness and understanding" for whom the meaning of a poem reveals itself gradually. It is the class for and by both the good and bad members of which honest literary criticism is written.

And it is this class which, confronted by a sensibility so powerful and so foreign as Mr. Eliot's, is determined to get at the means as well as the meaning. It is in that sense that Mr. Eliot's poetry may be a spiritual exercise of great scope. This class, then, apprehending the dominant presence of Christian doctrine and feeling in Mr. Eliot's work, must reach something like the following conclusions as representing provisional truths. The Church is the vehicle through which human purpose is to be seen and its teachings prod and vitalize the poetic sensibility engaged with the actual and with the substrata of the actual. Furthermore, and directly for poetry, the Church presents a gift of moral and philosophical form of a pre-logical character; and it is a great advantage for a poet to find his material fitting into a form whose reason is in mystery rather than logic, and no less reason for that. It is perhaps this insight into the nature of the Church's authority that brought Mr. Eliot to his most magnificent statement about poetry. "The essential advantage for a poet is not to have a beautiful world with which to deal: it is to be able to see beneath both beauty and ugliness; to see the boredom, and the horror, and the glory."

But since this class of reader is not itself Christian—any more than poetry is itself Christian—it will be to our advantage and to that of poetry to remind ourselves emphatically of what Mr. Eliot has himself several times insisted, that the presence of Christianity does not make a poem good. It is the poetry that must be good. Good Christianity will be a very watery thing adulterated with bad poetry, and good poetry can overcome a good deal of defection in a Christian poet's Christianity —as it does in Dante's hate. In admitting and enforcing the advantage of the Church, we commit ourselves, and before measuring our appreciation, to define the limits, both moral and operative, contained in our admission. There are some orders of charity in moral judgment which the doctrines of the Church cannot encompass; there are some experiences, that is, that the Church cannot faithfully mirror because it has no clues or has not the right clues to the reality involved. Thus we find Mr. Eliot refusing to understand Shelley and *Lady Chatterley's Lover;* and we find him also complaining of Irving Babbitt, whom he admired, that he made too much use of the Eastern Philosophies. I doubt, too, if the Church would be the right docent for an inspection of the drama of personality unfolded by Freudian psychology; it would see a different drama. . . . And we have, too, to decide provisionally what the Church, as a supernatural reference, makes up for, and what—whether we miss it or not—it fails to make up for; which is not at all easy to do. Perhaps we may say that the doctrines of the Church (we are not concerned, in poetry, with ritual worship) idealize a pretty complete set of human aspirations, and do this by appealing to a supernatural order. That is a great deal; but for poetry the Church does more. As these ideals are applied for judgment and light, all human action, struggle, and conflict, and all human feelings, too, gain a special significance. For us, as outsiders, the significance becomes greater if we remember that it is a special, a predicted significance, and that other ideals would give a different significance or none at all. Taken as a whole, the Church, by insisting on being right, became one of the great heresies of the human mind.

Our final obligation with respect to the Church is our smallest but most specific: to deal with it as an element of metric, only to be understood in composition with the other elements. We shall have emphasized and exaggerated in order to accomplish a reduction. But as the Church is not itself logical neither are the other elements in the composition. We have collections of elements, of qualities, which appear side by side, engaged, or entangled, or separate, of which the product is a whole varying with each combination. And a mind, too, such as we wish to think of as whole, is subject to the "damage of a lifetime," and we must think of the pressure and stress of that damage, omnipresent, agonizing, even though we cannot and would not wish to say what at the moment it is: unless we say vaguely that it is the personality.

To put together indications of the qualities of a mind and of its suffusing personality is a labor for which there are models but no principles; there is no logical structure; and the more plausible the picture made the more likely it is to be untrustworthy. Mr. Eliot's mind, let us say, is a mind of contrasts which sharpen rather than soften the longer they are weighed. It is the last mind which, in this century, one would have expected to enter the Church in a lay capacity. The worldliness of its prose weapons, its security of posture, its wit, its ability for penetrating doubt and destructive definition, its eye for startling fact and talent for nailing it down in flight, hardly go with what we think of today as English or American religious feeling. We are accustomed to emotionalism and fanaticism in religious thought and looseness in religious feeling; the very qualities which are the natural targets of Mr. Eliot's weapons. Possibly it may be that we are unfamiliar with good contemporary Christian writers; they could hardly infect the popular press. Possibly, or even probably, it was these very qualities which, after the demolition of the pretense of value in post-war society, drove him into the Church as the one institution unaffected by the pretense or its demolition. Perhaps the teaching of Irving Babbitt, less by its preliminary richness than by its final inadequacy, was an important influence: we see in Mr. Eliot at least one of the virtues which Babbitt inculcated—Mr. Eliot is never expansive, either in verse or in prose, and expansiveness was a bugaboo to Babbitt.

However that may be, within the Church or not, Mr. Eliot's mind has preserved its worldly qualities. His prose reflections remain elegant, hard (and in a sense easy—as in manners), controlled, urbane (without the dissimulation associated with ecclesiastical urbanity), and foolproof. One would say that the mind was self-assured and might pontificate; but there is a redeeming quality of reserve about the assurance of his rare dogmatic extravagances, a reserve which may be taken as the accompaniment of scrupulous emotion and humility. This is—except the reserve—the shell which a mind must needs wear in order to get along without being victimized, and in order to deal, without escape, with things as they are on the surface. It is the part of a mind which is educable from outside, without regard to its inner bias.

Beneath the shell is a body of feeling and a group of convictions. Mr. Eliot is one of the few persons to whom convictions may be ascribed without also the ascription of fanaticism. Prejudice, which he has, is only a by-product of conviction and need be raised as an issue only when the conviction goes wrong; and intolerance, which he condones, is in the intellectual field only the expected consequence of conviction. With a little skill one learns to allow for prejudice and intolerance in Mr. Eliot's mind as we do for any convicted mind. His convictions are those which stem from the Church, from the history of Christian peoples, and from the classical cultures: including the convictions which represent Sophocles, Dante, and Shakespeare, as well as those which represent Original Sin, the Resurrection, and the sin of Spiritual Pride. However complexly arrived at, and with whatever, as the outsider must think them, tactful evasions in application, his convictions are directly and nobly held. If they enhance narrowness and put some human problems on too simple a plane they yet unflaggingly enforce depth. The mind reaches down until it touches bottom. Its weakness is that it does not always take in what it passes.

But a mind furnished only with convictions would be like a room furnished only with light; the brighter the more barren. Mr. Eliot's convictions light a sensibility stocked with feelings and observations and able to go on feeling and observing, where the feelings are more important than the observations. It is this body of feelings, and not any intermediately necessary intellectualizations of them, which are his ultimate concern; and ours, when we can bear on them. We may note here the frequency in his work of physiological images to symbolize the ways of knowing and the quality of things known; the roots and tentacles and all the anatomical details. Concerned with the material of life actually lived, his convictions only confirm a form for the material, make it available, release contact with it; as I suppose, in the other direction, convictions only confirm a form for the feeling of faith. And for these operations all learning is only a waiting, a reminiscence, and a key. It is the presence of this material, living and seen, if underneath, that makes Mr. Eliot master of the big words which, when directly charged, are our only names for its manifestations as emotion. Both in his poetry when he needs to and in his prose when he cares to, Mr. Eliot is free to use all those large emotional words with absolute precision of contact which your ordinary writer has to avoid as mere omnibuses of dead emotion.

It is natural then, in connection with these remarks, that in his prose writing, whether early or late, whether in essays or controversy, appreciation or judgment, Mr. Eliot is master of the compressed insight, the sudden illumination, the felt comparison, the seminal suggestion, and a stable point of view; and it is equally in course that we should find him master of persuasive and decimating rhetoric rather than of sustained argument and exhaustive analysis. He sees and his words persuade us of the fact that he has seen and of the living aspect of what he saw; but his words hardly touch, directly, the objective validity of what he saw. This explains the scope of his influence. There is no question that he has seen what he asserts; in the field of literature his eye for facts is extraordinarily keen, though like a sharpshooter's it hits only what it is looking for. There is no question, either, if you share his point of view even provisionally, that his weapons of attack penetrate if they do not dispatch their victims. That there is more to be seen, his scruples make him admit. But as for the objects of his attack, not his scruples but his methods leave some of them alive. You cannot kill an idea unless you have first embraced it, and Mr. Eliot is chary of embraces. This explains, too, why some of his followers have turned against him and why others are content to parrot him. He has an air of authority in his prose, an air of having said or implied to the point of proof everything that could be said; when as a matter of fact he has merely said what he felt and demonstrated his own conviction. Conviction in the end is opinion and personality, which however greatly valuable cannot satisfy those who wrongly expect more. Those who parrot Mr. Eliot think they share his conviction but do not understand or possess his personality. Those who have, dissatisfied, turned against him have merely for the most part expected too much. The rest of us, if we regard his prose argument as we do his poetry—as a personal edifice—will be content with what he is.

To argue that the poetry is written by the same mind and intellectually in much the same way as the prose is to show, in this order, all we need to know. It explains what he leaves out and gives a right emphasis to what he puts in; and if we add, once again, that his mind runs almost instinctively to dramatic projections, we understand what kind of organization his work has—and it has one, deeply innervated. And I do not mean to beg the question when I say, as Mr. Eliot said of Shakespeare, that he is himself the unity of his work; that is the only kind of unity, the only circulating energy which we call organization, that we are ever likely to find in the mass of a man's work. We need to remember only that this unity, this effect of organization, will appear differently in works of criticism and works of poetry, and that it will be more manifest, though less arguable, in the poetry than in the criticism. The poetry is the concrete—as concrete as the poet can make it—presentation of experience as emotion. If it is successful it is self-evident; it is subject neither to denial nor modification but only to the greater labor of recognition. To say again what we have been saying all along, that is why we can assent to matters in poetry the intellectual formulation of which would leave us cold or in opposition. Poetry can use all ideas; argument only the logically consistent. Mr. Eliot put it very well for readers of his own verse when he wrote for readers of Dante that you may distinguish understanding from belief. "I will not deny," he says, "that it may be in practice easier for a Catholic to grasp the meaning, in many places, than for the ordinary agnostic; but that is not because the Catholic believes, but because he has been instructed. It is a matter of knowledge and ignorance, not of belief or scepticism." And a little later he puts the advantage for readers of poetry "of a coherent traditional system of dogma and morals like the Catholic: it stands apart, for understanding and assent even without belief, from the single individual who propounds it." That is why in our own context we can understand Mr. Eliot and cannot understand Mr. Pound. The unity that is Mr. Eliot has an objective intellectual version in his Christianity. The unity of Mr. Pound—if there is one—is in a confusion of incoherent, if often too explicitly declared, beliefs.

Christianity, then, is the emphatic form his sensibility fills; it is an artificial question which comes first. It is what happens to the sensibility that counts; the life lived and the death seen. That is the substantial preoccupation of the poet and the reader's gain. The emotion leans for expression on anything it can. Mr. Eliot's sensibility is typical of the poet's, as that of many poets is not. There is no wastage, little thinning out, and the least possible resort to dead form, form without motion. It is a sensibility that cannot deal with the merely surface report—what we used to call naturalism—and be content, but must deal with centers, surds, insights, illuminations, witnessed in chosen, obsessive images. These, as presented, seize enough of the life lived, the death seen, to give the emotion of the actuality of the rest. These we use as poetry; some will keep and some will wear out, as they continue or fail to strike reality as we can bear to know it.[6]

For opposite reasons, this essay can present texts for study neither of the apposite Christian form nor of the private sensibility that fills it; it merely emphasizes—with as much repetition as the reader is likely to put up with—that knowledge is better than ignorance for the one, and that the other exists to implement the first. There is the Church for inspection and there are the poems to read. There remains the common labor of literary criticism: the collection of facts about literary works, and comment on the management, the craft or technique, of those works; and this labor, in so far as it leaves the reader in the works themselves, is the only one in itself worth doing. All that has been said so far is conditional and preliminary and also a postscript to reading. The modern reader is not fitted to appreciate either a mind or its works conceived in relation to Christianity as a living discipline; and the effort to appreciate as dead manners what is live blood is as vain as it is likely to prove repulsive. If I have shown to what degree the reader must perform an imaginative resurrection, I have so far done enough.

For Mr. Eliot does spill blood for ink and his discipline does live. It is a commonplace assertion that Mr. Eliot has shaped both his Christianity and his technique to forward the expressive needs of his mind. Here let us keep to the technique; it involves the other; and say that he has deliberately shaped and annealed and alloyed and purified it: the object being a medium of language to enhold the terms of feeling and the sign of the substance felt so as to arouse, sustain, and transform interest at different levels of response; and that he has done so, besides, under the severest of disciplines, adherence to the standard of the good writing that has interested him. I do not say that he has succeeded altogether. Such a technique is the greatest *practical* ambition possible

---

[6] It is perhaps relevant to quote here part of Mr. Eliot's comment on Arnold's "Poetry is at bottom a criticism of life," in the essay on Arnold in *The Use of Poetry*. "At bottom: that is a great way down; the bottom is the bottom. At the bottom of the abyss is what few ever see, and what those cannot bear to look at for long; and it is not a 'criticism of life.' If we mean life as a whole—not that Arnold ever saw life as a whole —from top to bottom, can anything that we can say of it ultimately, of that awful mystery, be called criticism?" Here Mr. Eliot, as he commonly does at important junctures, which are never arguable, resorts to the emotional version of the actual concerned. The "abyss" is one of his obsessive images.

to secure; it takes long to come by and is slow to direct, since if it is to be adequate it must include the craft of presenting everything that is valuable. Very young poets confuse technique either with tricks, dodges, and devices, which are only a part of it, or with doodads.

> Ambition comes when early force is spent
> And when we find no longer all things possible.

Perhaps I twist a little Mr. Eliot's implications, but it seems to me that the great temptations to which a poet's technique are exposed are the early temptation of the adventitious—the nearest weapon and the nearest subject—, and the temptation of repetition, which comes later, and of which it is the sin that the result is bound to be meretricious. These are fundamentals for all techniques and there are modifications for each; the whole technique of any one poem can never be the whole technique of any other poem, since, such is the limitation of human experience, a new poem is more likely to represent a growth of technique than a *growth* (I do not say change) of subject matter.

Nor will such a technique, for all readers or perhaps for any, ever be completely achieved except in the sum of the greatest poets. There are too many expectations, just enough in their sincerity, that can neither be gratified nor eradicated. There are those, for an extreme example, who expect an art of happiness. But the fact is that the rest of us, whose expectations are less gross, can hardly ever at a given time get over expecting a technique to show us what is not there; nor can we invariably "let" ourselves see what is there.

Confronted by *The Rock* and *Murder in the Cathedral*, it is at once clear, first, that it is Mr. Eliot's technique rather than his subject matter that has grown, and, second, that this technique, new or old, radically limits the number and kind of our expectations. The scope of his poetry, its final magnitude, is a different matter, and the impurity or bloom of the contemporaneous must be rubbed away before it can be determined. What I mean here is that we get neither the kind nor variety of emotional satisfaction from either of his plays that we get from Noel Coward or Congreve or Shakespeare. We are not titivated or stroked; we do not see society brushed with the pure light of its manners; there is no broad display of human passion and purpose; we get the drama of the Church struggling against society toward God, which is something new (for those who like newness) in English drama; we get the way of the Church against the way of the World. And we get the awful harm as well as the good done men and women in the course of the struggle. It is this harm and this good, this sense of irreparable damage and intransigent glory, as it is in contact with this struggle, that makes the drama actual. It is not spiritual drama; it is not like Dante the drama of damnation, penance, and beatitude; it is the drama of human emotions actualized in the light of spiritual drama. The spirit is there, and intellect, and theology; but all these through actualized emotions of the experience of good and evil, of fraud and ambition, self-deceit and nobility, and the communal humility of the poor—which is a humility beneath Christian humility. This is what we get most in *Murder in the Cathedral,* and what we crucially fail to get in *The Rock.*

It is the substance of this (the same utter view of life) that we get in another way in "Mr. Eliot's Sunday Morning Service" and "The Hippopotamus"—these the tough anticlerical way; and in still other ways it is the same substance in "Prufrock," "Gerontion," and *The Waste Land.* The substance is permanent; the flux representative. If we take all the poems together with this substance in mind one charge that has been made against them should disappear—that they resent the present and fly into some paradise of the past. On the contrary, they measure the present by living standards which most people relegate to the past. The distinction is sharp; it is between poetry that would have been a shell of mere disillusion and poetry that is alive, and beyond disillusion. As Mr. Eliot himself remarked, *The Waste Land* only showed certain people their own illusion of disillusionment. It is this fundamental identity of substance which marks the unity of his work; that a variety of subjects and diverse approaches conspire to complete, to develop, a single judgment.

The changes—and no one would confuse or wrongly date two of Mr. Eliot's poems—are in the changes and growth of technique. The deliberate principle of growth has been in the direction of appealing to more levels of response, of reaching, finally, the widest possible audience, by attempting to secure in the poetry a base level of significance to which any mind might be expected to respond, without loss or injury to any other level of significance. It is in the light of this re-interpretation that Mr. Eliot's desire for an illiterate audience should be considered. That it is obvious does not make it any less telling, or any less inspiring to work toward, or—remembering the tacit dogma of difficulty held by so many poets—any less refreshing for the prospective reader. That this direction is not a guess on my own part and that he meant his notion of levels of significance in Shakespeare to apply to his own poetry, Mr. Eliot provides a candid text to show. It is at the very end of *The Use of Poetry.* With the great model of Shakespeare, the modern poet would like to write plays. "He would like to be something of a popular entertainer, and be able to think his own thoughts behind a tragic or a comic mask. He would like to convey the pleasures of poetry, not only to a larger audience, but to larger groups of people collectively; and the theatre is the best place to do it. . . . Furthermore, the theatre, by the technical exactions which it makes and limitations which it imposes upon the author, by the obligation to keep for a definite length of time the sustained interest of a large and unprepared and not wholly perceptive group of people, by its problems which have constantly to be solved, has enough to keep the poet's *conscious* mind fully occupied."

The best of Mr. Eliot's paragraph I have omitted: sentences that give the emotion of being a poet. What I have quoted is that part of his prose reflections concerned with the ideal behind the two plays. It is extraordinary how much of what we want to know these three sentences can be made to explain. The only emphasis needed is this: that the obligation to keep an audience interested is only indirectly connected with the real interest of the plays. It is primarily a technical obligation; it points to and prepares for the real interest by seeming to be connected with it; and the great liability or technical danger is that the two interests may be confused without being identified, as the great gain is when the two interests are, in crisis, actually identified.

I do not think that in his two plays Mr. Eliot has realized either the radical limitations of his substance or the insuperable limitations of the theater. The two do not always cooperate and they sometimes overlap. Perhaps it is better so; the comparative failure which says most, like *Hamlet,* is better than the relative success, like *The Coward,* that says least. The elements of failure must be nevertheless pointed out both when they spread rot and when they are surpassed. *The Rock* gives us an example of failure by confusion of interest which is nearly fatal, and *Murder in the Cathedral* gives us an example of success by fusion of interests.

Contrary to custom in English drama, it is the objective, the witnessing, the only indirectly participating, passages in these plays that are the finest poetry and that do the most work. These are the Choruses: in *The Rock* the chorus that represents the voice of the Church, and in *Murder in the Cathedral* the chorus of the women of Canterbury. In *The Rock* there are also choruses of the unemployed, of workmen, and some songs used as ritual chorus. In *Murder in the Cathedral* there is a kind of grand chorus of Priests, Tempters, and Chorus proper, which is used once, in the crisis of the first part. Whereas the traditional uses of the chorus are to comment on and to integrate action, here they are the integrity of the action itself, its actuality. Their relation to the "ordinary" version of the action, the rest of the play, is different in the two plays; and the quality of the work they do is different. It is these differences, in the light of the notion of levels of significance and response and in connection with the effort to maintain interest of both orders, that I wish to lay down the bare bones of. They carry the flesh.

The Rock is a pageant play, superficially about the difficulties, the necessity, and the justification of building a church in modern London. The pageant is a loose form and condones the introduction of a great variety of material; and so we are shown, upon the recurring focal scene of a church foundation actually in progress, a variety of episodes in the history of London churches. The theme and much of the incident were no doubt set; it is not a promising theme in which to expand a substance as concentrated as Mr. Eliot's, it is too generous and like the form chosen too loose, and too inherently facile of execution. Where almost anything will do passably there is nothing that will do well. The resulting text is not as drama very promising either. It is the sort of thing that, as a whole, depends on lushness of production and the personality of per-formance. At Sadler's Wells it may have been magnificent, but not be-cause of Mr. Eliot's poetry; and as it is now, a reader's text, what was important and the very life of the performance—the incident, the fun, the church-supper social comment, and the good-humored satire—reduce the effect of the poetry because it points away from the poetry instead of toward it. Bad verse cannot point to good poetry, and there is here the first bad verse Mr. Eliot has allowed himself to print, as well as his first bad jokes. The whole play has an air of following the counsel of the Chorus to the worshipers.

> Be not too curious of Good and Evil;
> Seek not to count the future waves of Time;
> But be ye satisfied that you have light
> Enough to take your step and find your foothold.

It is all satisfied and nearly all spelt in capital letters. Whether the expected nature of the audience was responsible, the form chosen, or whether Mr. Eliot was mistaken about both, the fact is that the level of interest appealed to by the whole play is too low to make passage to the higher levels natural. The general level lacks emotional proba-bility and therefore lacks actuality. It is dead-level writing. The reader satisfied with the dead level can hardly be expected to perceive, even unconsciously, the higher levels; and the reader interested in the higher levels cannot but find his interest vitiated by finding it constantly let down. Take the episode of the Crusades. The conversation between the man and his betrothed is one thing, a flat appeal to stereotyped emotion; the taking of the Cross, with its sonorous Latin dressing, is another, an appeal by the direct use of ritual, on another plane, to the stereotype of the conversation; neither is actualized. The actuality is in the Chorus; but the Chorus is not the same thing in a different form, it is another thing altogether. There is a gap between, which is not crossed, and the relations between the three are disproportional. We hear a distinct voice from another world, which is the real world, and which is the real poem; the actuality of which the other voices are only the substitute and the sham. And the Chorus, in this instance, perhaps loses some of its effect because it comes first, prefacing what it does not perform, and because its phrasing depends on the statements it makes rather than makes the statements.

> *Not avarice, lechery, treachery,*
> *Envy, sloth, gluttony, jealousy, pride:*
> *It was not these that made the Crusades,*
> *But these that unmade them.*
>
>   ✿   ✿   ✿   ✿   ✿
>
> *Our age is an age of moderate virtue*
> *And of moderate vice*
> *When men will not lay down the Cross*
> *Because they will never assume it.*

Mr. Eliot has not here levied enough upon that other actuality, the actuality bred in the fitting of words together; which is not the same thing as fitting notions together. These strictures apply throughout the episodes of the play and to most of the Choruses to the episodes. It is only rarely, in some of the songs and parts of the general choruses, that we get lines like these, when the poetry escapes the Oppressor.

> *Our gaze is submarine, our eyes look upward*
> *And see the light that fractures through unquiet water.*
> *We see the light but see not whence it comes.*

The Oppressor was the misconceived need of expressing the Church at the level of general interest, instead of intensifying the actuality envisaged by the Church in terms of a represented interest.

This last is what Mr. Eliot has done in his second play, *Murder in the Cathedral,* and I think that the play could not have been better constructed with a view to representing in a self-contained form the mutually interrelated play of different levels of significance, from the lowest to the highest. I do not expect to have exhausted anything but its general interest for a long time to come and I do expect its actual significance—its revelation of essential human strength and weakness—to grow the whole time. Yet it deals with an emotion I can hardly expect to share, which very few can ever expect to share, except as a last possibility, and which is certainly not an emotion of general interest at all; it deals with the special emotion of Christian martyrdom. Martyrdom is as far removed from common experience as the state of beatitude to which it leads; and it is much further removed, too, from ordinary interests than is the episodic material of *The Rock.* The view of life is as seriously held in either play, and the emotion is in itself as valid in one as in the other; they are in fact substantially the same. The whole difference between the failure of the first and the success of the second play depends on the lowest level of poetic intensity employed. If anything, the lowest level of significance (that is, the broadest, appealing to more, and more varied minds) is lower in the second play than the first; and this fact is in itself an element of formal strength and a verification of Mr. Eliot's ideal theory. It almost seems as if in *The Rock* Mr. Eliot had confused conventional significance with basic significance, but in his second play had clarified the confusion.

Applying Mr. Eliot's sentences about levels of significance, we can say that there is for everyone the expectation (we can hardly call it a plot) and ominous atmosphere of murder and death; for others there are the strong rhythms, the pounding alliterations, and the emphatic rhymes; for others the conflict, not of character, but of forces characterized in individual types; for others the tragedy or triumph of faith at the hands of the world; and for others the gradually unfolding meaning in the profound and ambiguous revelation of the expense of martyrdom in good *and* evil as seen in certain speeches of Thomas and in the choruses of the old women of Canterbury. It is the *expense* of martyrdom as a supreme form of human greatness, its expense for the martyr himself and for those less great but bound with it, its expense of good and evil and suffering, rather than its mere glory or its mere tragedy, that seems to me a major part of the play's meaning. Greatness of any kind forces to a crisis the fundamental life and the fundamental death in life both for the great themselves and for those who are affected by it. Martyrdom is the Christian form of personal greatness, and as with other forms of greatness, no human judgment or representation of it can fail of a terrible humility and a terrifying ambiguity. It is the limit of actuality in what Mr. Eliot calls the abyss.

I do not expect to prove that the emotional substance of which these remarks are a re-formulation may be found in *Murder in the Cathedral*. There is no proof of the actual but the experience. But if the reader will first realize that the predicament of Thomas Becket is the predicament of human greatness, and that its example affects him, the reader, by reading over the dialogue between Thomas and the Fourth Tempter and Thomas' final speech in Part One, he will at least have put himself in the frame of mind to perceive the higher levels of significance, and the identification of all levels in the six long choruses and the play as a whole. It may be impertinent to point out as a clue or indication, that the Fourth Tempter's last speech repeats, as addressed to Thomas, Thomas' speech on his first appearance in the play, where the words are applied to the Chorus:

> *They know and do not know, what it is to act or suffer.*
> *They know and do not know, that acting is suffering,*
> *And suffering action. Neither does the actor suffer*
> *Nor the patient act. But both are fixed*
> *In an eternal action, an eternal patience*
> *To which all must consent that it may be willed*
> *And which all must suffer that they may will it,*
> *That the pattern may subsist, that the wheel may turn and still*
> *Be forever still.*

And it may be superfluous to note that in the last of Thomas' speech at the end of Part One, he addresses you, the reader, you, the audience. Impertinent or superfluous the emphasis will not be amiss.

The Choruses, which flow from the expression of the common necessities of the poor up to, and in the same language, the expression of Christian dogma, may be said to exist by themselves, but their instance is the greatness of Thomas, as the death in them is Thomas' death. Thomas exists by himself, too, and his particular struggle, but both are made actual in relation to the Choruses. They are separate but related; they combine and produce a new thing not in the elements themselves. But the Choruses themselves have interrelated parts which work together by fate because they were rightly chosen and not because, in any ordinary sense, they have natural affinity for each other. The kinds of parts and their proportional bulk are not fixed but vary with the purpose of the particular Chorus; but the predominant elements are the concrete immanence of death and death in life, and the rudimentary, the simple, the inescapable conditions of living, and there is besides the concrete emotion of the hell on earth which is the absence or the losing of God. It is the death and the coming of it, of the Archbishop which measures and instigates all the Chorus has to say; but neither that death, nor its coming, nor its Christian greatness create its words; rather what it says is the actual experience from which the Christian greatness springs. That is why the chorus is composed of poor women, ordinary women, with ordinary lives and fates and desires, women with a fundamental turbulence of resentment at the expense of greatness.

> *What is woven on the loom of fate*
> *What is woven in the councils of princes*
> *Is woven also in our veins, our brains,*
> *Is woven like a pattern of living worms*
> *In the guts of the women of Canterbury.*

It is against this, the common denominator of all experience, that the extraordinary experience of Thomas is seen, and by it made real.

It is shameful to quote for illustration when half the virtue is lost without the context, but I nevertheless quote two passages, one for concreteness of sensual image and as an example of internal rhyme, and the other to show how actual an emotion the expectation of death can be, and how dramatic.

> *I have eaten*
> *Smooth creatures still living, with the strong salt taste of living things under the*
> *sea; I have tasted*
> *The living lobster, the crab, the oyster, the whelk and the prawn; and they live*
> *and spawn in my bowels, and my bowels dissolve in the light of dawn.*

Chorus, Priests and Tempters alternately

c. Is it the owl that calls, or a signal between the trees?
p. Is the window-bar made fast, is the door under lock and bolt?
t. Is it rain that taps at the window, is it wind that pokes at the door?
c. Does the torch flame in the hall, the candle in the room?
p. Does the watchman walk by the wall?
t. Does the mastiff prowl by the gate?
c. Death has a hundred hands and walks by a thousand ways.
p. He may come in the sight of all, he may pass unseen unheard.
t. Come whispering through the ear, or a sudden shock on the skull.
c. A man may walk with a lamp at night, and yet be drowned in a ditch.
p. A man may climb the stair in the day, and slip on a broken step.
t. A man may sit at meat, and feel the cold in his groin.

These are the easy things that come first; but without them, the other meaning that comes gradually would not come at all; they are its basis, in poetry as in life. "The world," says Mr. Eliot, "is trying the experiment of attempting to form a civilised but non-Christian mentality." He believes the experiment will fail; and I think we may be sure it will fail unless it includes in itself the insight, in Christian terms or not, of which Mr. Eliot gives an actual representation. Meanwhile he redeems the time.

MR. W. H. AUDEN: TOWARDS A
NEW CHRISTIAN SYNTHESIS

Amos Wilder

Here is where W. H. Auden, who is a very Protestant kind of Anglo-Catholic, takes on a representative significance.[1] Eliot has also in his own way negotiated his Odyssey through the various perils, temptations, and disasters of our world. But in Auden we see modern men exposed to the risks and costs of our situation on all fronts. He takes a swarm of spears into his breast. He is initiated into our intellectual as well as our social dilemmas. And he has fought through all our issues and wrestled with our distempers without adventitious aids or extrinsic authoritarian props. His work is peculiarly representative and instructive because all these dilemmas are taken up and canvassed in his poems directly. In Eliot much lies below the surface or is taken for granted. In him, at least in the later work, we have the outcome; in Auden, the debate. Auden offers us the forum of the modern consciousness. This makes his work difficult, especially in view of its philosophical content. Both poets are moreover highly allusive. In Auden's case a rich topical allusiveness is added to the symbolical allusiveness of any modern poet. One needs to be alert to all sorts of modern curiosity and science as well as to general literature to follow him. But this is what qualifies him as an interpreter. His poetry knows how to make room for the outlook of Montaigne as well as Pascal, for Nietzsche as well as Kierkegaard, for Marx and Freud as well as for Dante. Auden represents the new Christian synthesis in the making. He starts with the disarray and the sense of meaninglessness of the time but he gives it a Christian construction.

> *We are afraid*
> *Of pain but more afraid of silence; for no nightmare*

---

[1] In the following discussion we have in mind especially the more recent of Auden's works: *The Double Man* (New York: Random House, 1941); *For The Time Being*, including "A Christmas Oratorio" (New York: Random House, 1944); *The Age of Anxiety* (New York: Random House, 1947). *The Collected Poetry of W. H. Auden* (New York: Random House, 1945), includes the first two works named and much of his earlier writing.

> *Of hostile objects could be as terrible as this Void.*
> *This is the Abomination. This is the Wrath of God.*[2]

Auden's earlier work carried no confessional labels upon it but was dense with social ethical concerns and the responsibilities of the individual as was the case with so many of the writers of the thirties. A dozen or more years given to exposure of the disorder of western life precede his arrival in this country well before the Second World War. His volume, *Another Time,* published in 1940,[3] evidences the lucidity of his analysis of the times and the extraordinary versatility of his indictments and warnings. He points out in poem XXIV that the democracies had long been inviting the Furies, luring the "crooked wing," the Terrible Presences. "We conjured them here like a lying map." For individual vices add up to public disaster. By intimate anarchies, by self-deceptions, and glossed-over violence, by personal indiscipline—"a father's rage" or "a mother's distorting mirror"—we ourselves have smoothed the way for wholesale convulsions. Not only does the tiger make easy entrance and find himself quite at home in the familiar surroundings of a heartless state, but also

> *. . . the ape*
> *Is really at home in the parish*
> *Of grimacing and licking.*

The course of events was to bring a rude disclosure of the character of the Almighty. In "Spain, 1937" God berates men for thinking that he was altogether such a one as themselves:

> *To you I'm the*
> *Yes-man, the bar-companion, the easily-duped.*

But events reveal his implacable aspects, and when sobered nations plead to him in panic, there is no deliverance:

> *History to the defeated*
> *May say Alas but cannot help or pardon.*

In this volume Auden rebuked democratic idealists who assigned all the fault to the fascists, and who oversimplified by announcing that the devil had broken parole and that they must go to war to chain him up again. He castigated factories "where lives are made for a temporary use, like collars or chairs." He wrote hauntingly of the refugees. He satirized Christians who escaped the real guilt by routines of cultic expiation. Recurrent in this as in his later volumes

---

[2] *For the Time Being,* p. 67.
[3] New York: Random House.

is the insight that social tyrannies in either totalitarian states or in democracies flourish on the maladies and sins of the individual. These tyrannies live on "lucrative patterns of frustration"; the masses tolerate and nourish their masters as a compensation for their own obscure hurts and cravings. When Auden pursues the basic problem of salvation to any length he turns to the insights and language of psychology. The splendid tribute, "In Memory of Sigmund Freud," found in this volume shows that, at least at this time, the cure was to be sought in self-knowledge, in sunlight admitted to the deep places, in honesty, in self-pardon. Thence would come wholeness and reconciliation and man's "dark, disordered city" would be sweetened. In Freud the writer found one who

> *went his way,*
> *Down among the Lost People like Dante, down*
> *To the stinking fosse where the injured*
> *Lead the ugly life of the rejected.*

In his work published since that volume, beginning with *The Double Man*, 1941, Auden continues the use of Freudian tools in his analyses of society but a new range of reference and allusion comes into the poetry and prose drawn frequently from writings of a theological character including Pascal, Kierkegaard, Tillich and the Christian classics. In his most recent work, notably in the "Christmas Oratorio," it is evident that he has adopted not only an explicit Christian frame of reference but a Catholic formulation of it. In the "Oratorio" the formulation in terms of the Word, the Child, the Miracle, is not necessarily Catholic in a dogmatic sense, and may be thought of as a borrowing for the occasion, appropriate to the particular Christian saga used. Moreover, the combination of the Christian themes with all manner of psychological and philosophical elements indicates that the dogmatic elements are not taken over in any stereotyped form.

The idea of original sin which, at least in the sense of moral derangement and incapacity, marks the work of all the more notable modern writers except D. H. Lawrence and the Marxists, is presented in terms that are more Protestant than Catholic. The influence upon this writer of contemporary neo-Protestant theologians is generally recognized and the repeated use of Kierkegaard's categories radically modifies the Catholic vehicle employed. The most Catholic statement this writer has so far made is the paper contributed to the Yale Divinity School series of Beecher Lectures in the spring of 1950. As we have said above (Ch. I) he here drew a systematic line between the layman and the priest of so sharp a character as to presuppose a completely Catholic view of the church, grace and the sacraments.

On the other hand, in a paper submitted in connection with the Princeton Bicentennial conferences in 1948 he distinguished three contemporary solutions of the modern predicament of belief: (1) Greek humanism: identification with "immortal contemplative mind"; (2) primitive religion: modern versions of sacrifice and magic; (3) Christian humanism: acceptance of the revelation of the truth by God to man, with the consequent conversion of man's Flesh (body and mind) by the Spirit. Notable in the argument was the demonstration of the failure of secular humanism and the invocation here of Kierkegaard, Nietzsche and Freud. The first of these made it clear once and for all that the objective thinker, the scientific humanist, forgets that he is in an existential situation: he leaves out three-quarters of the problem. Nietzsche and Freud showed further that every humanist, scientific or contemplative, is a "haunted thinker," and, moreover, that his supposed objective "truth" is only strategy and mask, i.e., rationalization.

Auden's view of the relations of poetry and religion rewards study. This writer unquestionably uses his poetic gift for didactic purposes and betrays that "interfering spirit of righteousness" which was assigned to the Puritans long ago. In his practice Auden offers us a Christian witness directed both to our social and our spiritual need. In his theory, however, he warns against confusing the poet and the prophet.[4] The temptation of poetry in our period has been to occupy the religious vacuum consequent upon modern disbelief. The poet must be more modest, says Auden. Jacques Maritain in his own way has pointed out the same danger. The older patterns of poetry have of late been enriched by the free use of symbol drawn from the unconscious. The poets have learned much as to resources for communication from the deeper life of the soul: "the contemplation of the depths" as Maritain calls it. Upon such contemplation there ensues a "release of images." The breakdown of traditions in our time invites the poet to such exploration and to the surrealist or apocalyptic expression that is appropriate. Maritain holds that this is all to the good if the modern poet avoids the danger here of confusing such prerational experience and such oracular deliverances with grace itself or genuine religious authority.

Auden agrees here. The poet must not ascribe to himself the role of seer or prophet. If he does so he degrades himself into a magician. That is, he is manipulating, exploiting certain phenomena of the psyche or of esthetic experience for ulterior purposes. Auden speaks

---

[4] "Criticism in a Mass Society," in *The Intent of the Critic*, ed. by Donald A. Stauffer (Princeton: Princeton University Press, 1941), pp. 127-147. Also, "Squares and Oblongs," in *Poets at Work*, Essays by Rudolf Arnheim, etc., Introduction by Charles D. Abbott (New York: Harcourt, Brace, 1948), pp. 163-181.

of him as a purveyor of "spurious emotions," and sees him really as motivated by an impious impulse to "make free with necessity." He becomes a false "healer." No, the poet must be more modest. He must look on his work as a higher kind of play, a kind of artifice, a "game of knowledge," "a bringing to consciousness (by naming them) of emotions and their hidden relationships." Auden's diatribe here is directed not only against prophets of a pagan mysticism or vitalism but also against the sway of sentimentalism in traditional poetry.

It is a Protestant instinct in him, intensified by the dialectical rigor borrowed from Kierkegaard, which breeds this caution against all the intoxications and disorders of contemporary art. But Auden overstates himself. He arraigns that whole tradition from the Greeks to the present which assigns a quasi-religious authority to the poet. He rejects Aristotle's conception of *katharsis* in connection with the function of the drama. He accuses Milton of assigning too important a function to the poet. He is especially scornful of Shelley and ridicules the latter's claim that the poets are the "unacknowledged legislators of the world." He appears to be animated by such a fear of false prophets in an age of Pied Pipers that he would abase the poets completely, or at least confine them to a kind of "intellectual play," or an intellectual-imaginative artifice.

His plea for modesty among the poets is most pungently expressed in his paper, "Squares and Oblongs," in *Poets at Work:*

> The Prophet says to men: "Thus saith the Lord." The poet says firstly to God: "Lord, do I mean what you say?" And secondly to men: "Do you mean what I mean?" Agit Prop [i.e., the agitator propagandist] says to men: "You mean what I say and to hell with the Lord who, even if he exists, is rotten with liberalism, anyway."[5]

Thus Auden would dissociate the poet from all propaganda, even for the best causes.

But he vastly oversimplifies the matter. Even if a deliberate didacticism is to be excluded, yet values, presuppositions, and norms transpire in every poet and it is a matter of importance even esthetically what these are. Auden recognizes as much in other statements. Furthermore his own work shows it. He is himself the teacher, the didactic writer, sometimes in the bad sense where his plastic imagination fails, often in a persuasive and admirable way. Thus he teaches original sin and yet freedom and responsibility; he urges lucidity and honesty; he preaches social democracy; he insists on the unity of truth against all contemporary relativism; while art is

---

[5] P. 177.

not life he holds that we must recognize the interdependence of ethics, politics, science, and esthetics. He holds that *The Waste Land* (by T. S. Eliot) shows us that to be without belief is to be lost.

In his "A Christmas Oratorio" Auden celebrates the incarnation in a way that often reminds us of T. S. Eliot.

> *We who must die demand a miracle.*
> *How could the Eternal do a temporal act,*
> *The Infinite become a finite fact?*
> *Nothing can save us that is possible:*
> *We who must die demand a miracle.*[6]

What is distinctive is the orchestration of the different facets of the incarnation in terms of the familiar images of secularism and of the present social and psychological situation. From a theological point of view the "Meditation of Simeon" is specially interesting. The poet is careful to exclude all docetism, a danger to which the Catholic emphasis on the incarnation is always exposed. Here the Flesh is united to the Word "without magical transformation" (p. 117), and so "by Him is the perpetual recurrence of Art assured." That is, our human life remains human and our Christian art remains human. There is no false cleavage between the Flesh and the Spirit, though the former is saved by the latter. Again, writes Auden, the Word is united to the Flesh "without loss of perfection" (pp. 117, 118). This not only safeguards the finality and ultimacy of the redemption and solves the problem of the One and the Many, but so "Science is assured," "because in Him abstraction finds a passionate 'For-the-Sake-Of.'" The point here is that truth is really *given*, so that science and philosophy can know that they are not wandering in the dark. Thus also they receive a vital motivation to their tasks.

Auden then succeeds both in registering what is, in effect, a Protestant protest against false culture and false prophets, and in presenting a positive faith and morality in Anglo-Catholic terms. What makes both highly significant, however, is that in him the Christian tradition is wedded intimately to the empirical circumstances, the spiritual and intellectual climate of today. In him we see the initiation of the religious spirit into the full gamut of the modern experience: modern science, modern psychology, modern sociology, the modern sensibility and alienation. Here he enables us all better to understand ourselves—more effectively in breadth and in depth than in height, indeed. This empiricism and realism with the consequent relevance of his solutions we may put down to his long detachment from any binding Catholic pattern of life and symbolism.

---

[6] *For the Time Being*, p. 68.

Auden exemplifies only one of the ways in which Protestantism has artistic expression. He is the secularist who has returned to the faith and who possesses and exploits the full panoply of the modern man in his Christian utterance. But there are also poets and artists of Protestant connection whose faith is vital in their work but who have not had his wide initiation. They can speak to those within the fold but not to those without. They have not sojourned in the wilderness and their immunities have narrowed their significance. Yet like many gifted Catholic poets their songs may be all the more unsullied, not to say intelligible, in view of this handicap! Finally there are the poets without ostensible religious preoccupation who nevertheless derive from Protestantism. Many of the most significant talents of our time are to be counted here. They are the ones of whom we have spoken earlier in whom Protestantism acts as a leaven rather than a tradition. They are children of the church who have been caught up in the dilemma of the age, who are struggling at first hand with its major heresies, and whose faith is "for the time being" uncrystallized. But they carry with them, unrecognized and under disguises, the faith of their background, and in their isolated and pioneering situations contribute to the new Christian synthesis. A relevant and powerful version of Christianity for the time to come will emerge as much from the explorations of such prodigals as from the stay-at-homes of the tradition, as the case of Auden himself shows. But our special gratitude will go to those who today in the new accents of today show themselves victorious over the ills that paralyze so many, who render harmless the toxins and miasmic vapors all about us, and who so fulfill the promise of the gospel: "*They shall speak with new tongues;* they shall take up serpents; and if they drink any deadly thing, it shall not hurt them; they shall lay hands on the sick, and they shall recover."

WILLIAM FAULKNER: VISION OF GOOD AND EVIL

Cleanth Brooks

Professor Randall Stewart, in his very stimulating little book *American Literature and Christian Doctrine,* asserts that "Faulkner embodies and dramatizes the basic Christian concepts so effectively that he can with justice be regarded as one of the most profoundly Christian writers in our time. There is everywhere in his writings the basic premise of Original Sin: everywhere the conflict between the flesh and the spirit. One finds also the necessity of discipline, of trial by fire in the furnace of affliction, of sacrifice and the sacrificial death, of redemption through sacrifice. Man in Faulkner is a heroic, tragic figure." This is a view with which I am in basic sympathy. I agree heartily with Professor Stewart on the matter of Faulkner's concern with what he calls "original sin," and with Faulkner's emphasis upon discipline, sacrifice, and redemption. But to call Faulkner "one of the most profoundly Christian writers in our time" seems somewhat incautious. Perhaps it would be safer to say that Faulkner is a profoundly religious writer; that his characters come out of a Christian environment, and represent, whatever their shortcomings and whatever their theological heresies, Christian concerns; and that they are finally to be understood only by reference to Christian premises.

Probably the best place to start is with the term "original sin." The point of reference might very well be T. E. Hulme, one of the profoundly seminal influences on our time, though a critic and philosopher whom Faulkner probably never read. In "Humanism and the Religious Attitude" Hulme argued for a return to orthodox doctrine. His concern with religion, however, had nothing to do with recapturing what he called "the sentiment of Fra Angelico." Rather, "What is important," he asserted, "is what nobody seems to realize—the dogmas like that of Original Sin, which are the closest expression of the categories of the religious attitude. That man is in no sense perfect, but a wretched creature, who can apprehend perfection. It is not, then, that I put up with the dogma for the sake of the sentiment, but that I may possibly swallow the sentiment for the sake of the dogma."

Hulme's position as stated here would seem to smack of scholastic Calvinism rather than of the tradition of Catholic Christianity. His emphasis at least suggests that nature is radically evil and not merely gone wrong somehow—corrupted by a fall. But if Hulme's passage is so tinged, that very fact may make it the more relevant to Faulkner, who shows, in some aspects, the influence of Southern Puritanism.

Be that as it may, Hulme's is not a didactic theory of literature, which stresses some direct preachment to be made. On the contrary, his "classicism" derives from a clear distinction between religious doctrine and poetic structure. It is romantic poetry which blurs that distinction, competing with religion by trying to drag in the infinite. With romanticism we enter the area of "spilt religion," and romantic "damp and fogginess." For Hulme, the classic attitude involves a recognition of man's limitations—his finitude. Since the classical view of man recognizes his limitations and does not presume upon them, the classical attitude, Hulme argues, is a religious attitude. For Hulme is quite convinced that man, though capable of recognizing goodness, is not naturally good. It is only by discipline that he can achieve something of value.

The whole point is an important one, for Faulkner's positive beliefs are often identified with some kind of romantic primitivism. Thus his concern with idiots and children and uneducated rural people, both white and Negro, is sometimes interpreted to mean that man is made evil only by his environment with its corrupting restrictions and inhibitions, and that if man could only realize his deeper impulses, he would be good.[1]

Allied to this misconception is another, namely that Faulkner's characters have no power of choice, being merely the creatures of their drives and needs, and that they are determined by their environment and are helplessly adrift upon the tides of circumstance. It is true that many of his characters are obsessed creatures or badly warped by traumatic experiences, or that they are presented by Faulkner as acting under some kind of compulsion. But his characters are not mere products of an environment. They have the power of choice, they make decisions, and they win their goodness through effort and discipline.

If Faulkner does not believe that man is naturally good and needs only to realize his natural impulses, and if he does believe that man has free will and must act responsibly and discipline himself, then

---

[1] Faulkner, a few years ago, in defining his notion of Christianity, called it a "code of behavior by means of which (man) makes himself a better human being than his nature wants to be, if he follows his nature only" (*Paris Review*, Spring 1956, p. 42).

these beliefs are indeed worth stressing, for they are calculated to separate him sharply from writers of a more naturalistic and secularistic temper. But I grant that to attribute to Faulkner a belief in original sin or in man's need for discipline would not necessarily prove him a Christian. The concept of grace, for example, is either lacking or at least not clearly evident in Faulkner's work.

Let us begin, then, by examining Faulkner's criticism of secularism and rationalism. A very important theme in his earlier work is the discovery of evil, which is part of man's initiation into the nature of reality. That brilliant and horrifying early novel *Sanctuary* is, it seems to me, to be understood primarily in terms of such an initiation. Horace Benbow is the sentimental idealist, the man of academic temper, who finds out that the world is not a place of moral tidiness or even of justice. He discovers with increasing horror that evil is rooted in the very nature of things. As an intellectual, he likes to ponder meanings and events, he has a great capacity for belief in ideas, and a great confidence in the efficacy of reason. What he comes to discover is the horrifying presence of evil, its insidiousness, and its penetration of every kind of rational or civilized order. There is in this story, to be sure, the unnatural rape of the seventeen-year-old girl by the gangster Popeye, and the story of Popeye's wanton murder of Tommy, but Horace Benbow might conceivably accept both of these things as the kinds of cruel accidents to which human life is subject. What crumples him up is the moral corruption of the girl, which follows on her rape: she actually accepts her life in the brothel and testifies at the trial in favor of the man who had abducted her. What Horace also discovers is that the forces of law and order are also corruptible. His opponent in the trial, the district attorney, plays fast and loose with the evidence and actually ensures that the innocent man will not only be convicted but burned to death by a mob. And what perhaps Horace himself does not discover (but it is made plainly evident to the reader) is that Horace's betrayal at the trial is finally a bosom betrayal: Horace's own sister gives the district attorney the tip-off that will allow him to defeat her brother and make a mockery of justice. Indeed, Horace's sister, the calm and serene Narcissa, is, next to Popeye, the most terrifying person in the novel. She simply does not want her brother associated with people like the accused man, Lee Goodwin, the bootlegger, and his common-law wife. She exclaims to her brother, "I don't see that it makes any difference who [committed the murder]. The question is, are you going to stay mixed up with it?" And she sees to it with quiet and efficient ruthlessness that the trial ends at the first possible date, even though this costs an innocent man's life.

Sanctuary is clearly Faulkner's bitterest novel. It is a novel in which the initiation which every male must undergo is experienced in its most shattering and disillusioning form. Horace not only discovers the existence of evil: he experiences it, not as an abstract idea but as an integral portion of reality. After he has had his interview with Temple Drake in the brothel, he thinks: "Perhaps it is upon the instant that we realize, admit, that there is a logical pattern to evil, that we die," and he thinks of the expression he had once seen in the eyes of a dead child and in the eyes of the other dead: "the cooling indignation, the shocked despair fading, leaving two empty globes in which the motionless work lurked profoundly in miniature."

One of the most important connections has already been touched upon in what I have said earlier. Horace Benbow's initiation into the nature of reality and the nature of evil is intimately associated with his discovery of the true nature of woman. His discovery is quite typical of Faulkner's male characters. In the Faulknerian notion of things, men have to lose their innocence, confront the hard choice, and through a process of initiation discover reality. The women are already in possession of this knowledge, naturally and instinctively. That is why in moments of bitterness Faulkner's male characters—Mr. Compson in *The Sound and the Fury*, for example—assert that women are not innocent. Mr. Compson tells his son Quentin: "Women are like that[;] they don't acquire knowledge of people[. Men] are for that[. Women] are just born with a practical fertility of suspicion. . . . they have an affinity for evil[—]for supplying whatever the evil lacks in itself [—]drawing it about them instinctively as you do bed clothing in slumber. . . ." Again, "Women only use other people's codes of honour."

I suppose that we need not take these Schopenhauerian profundities of the bourbon-soaked Mr. Compson too seriously. It might on the whole be more accurate to say that Faulkner's women lack the callow idealism of the men, have fewer illusions about human nature, and are less trammeled by legalistic distinctions and niceties of any code of conduct.

Faulkner's view of women, then, is radically old-fashioned—even medieval. Woman is the source and sustainer of virtue and also a prime source of evil. She can be either, because she is, as man is not, always a little beyond good and evil. With her powerful natural drives and her instinct for the concrete and personal, she does not need to agonize over her decisions. There is no code for her to master—no initiation for her to undergo. For this reason she has access to a wisdom which is veiled from man; and man's codes, good or bad, are always, in their formal abstraction, a little absurd in her eyes. Women are close to nature; the feminine principle is closely related to the instinctive and natural: woman typically manifests pathos rather than ethos.

A little later I shall have something more to say about Faulkner's characters in confrontation with nature. At this point, however, I want to go back and refer to another aspect of *Sanctuary*. The worst villains in Faulkner are cut off from nature. They have in some profound way denied their nature, like Flem Snopes in *The Hamlet*, who has no natural vices, only the unnatural vice of a pure lust for power and money. In *Sanctuary* Popeye is depicted as a sort of *ludus naturae*. Everybody has noticed the way in which he is described, as if he were a kind of automaton, with eyes like "two knobs of soft black rubber." As Horace watches him across the spring, Popeye's "face had a queer, bloodless color, as though seen by electric light; against the sunny silence, in his slanted straw hat and his slightly akimbo arms, he had that vicious depthless quality of stamped tin." Faulkner's two figures of speech are brilliantly used here. They serve to rob Popeye of substance and to turn him into a sinister black silhouette against the spring landscape. The phrase "as though seen by electric light" justifies the description of his queer, bloodless color, but it does more than this. Juxtaposed as it is to the phrase "against the sunny silence," it stresses the sense of the contrived, the artificial, as though Popeye constituted a kind of monstrous affront to the natural scene. These suggestions of a shadowy lack of substance are confirmed at the end of the sentence with the closing phrase: "depthless quality of stamped tin." Faulkner relentlessly forces this notion of the unnatural: Popeye deliberately spits into the spring, he cringes in terror from the low swooping owl, he is afraid of the dark.

Popeye has no natural vices either. He cannot drink. Since he is impotent, he is forced to use unnatural means in his rape of Temple. As a consequence, some readers take Popeye to be a kind of allegorical figure, a representation of the inhumanly mechanistic forces of our society. We may say that Popeye is quite literally a monster, remembering that the Latin *monstrum* signifies something that lies outside the ordinary course of nature.

Though Popeye represents an extreme case, in this matter he is typical of all of Faulkner's villains. For example, Thomas Sutpen, in *Absalom, Absalom!*, is a man of great courage and heroic stature, who challenges the role of a tragic protagonist. Yet he has about him this same rigid and mechanical quality. Sutpen, as an acquaintance observes, believes "that the ingredients of morality were like the ingredients of pie or cake and once you had measured them and balanced them and mixed them and put them into the oven it was all finished and nothing but pie or cake could come out."

Sutpen has a great plan in mind, his "design," he calls it—which involves his building a great plantation house and setting up a dynasty. As he tells General Compson, "I had a design. To accomplish it I should require money, a house, and a plantation, slaves, a family—incidentally, of course, a wife." But when he finds later that his wife has a trace of Negro blood, he puts her aside, and he does it with an air of honest grievance. He says, "[Her parents] deliberately withheld from me the one fact which I have reason to know they were aware would have caused me to decline the entire matter, otherwise they would not have withheld it from me—a fact which I did not learn until after my son was born. And even then I did not act hastily. I could have reminded them of these wasted years, these years which would now leave me behind with my schedule. . . ." (The last term is significant: Sutpen, modern man that he is, works in accordance with a timetable.) He tells General Compson that when he put aside his wife and child, "his conscience had bothered him somewhat at first but that he had argued calmly and logically with his conscience until it was settled." General Compson is aghast at this revelation of moral myopia. He calls it "innocence," and by the term he means a blindness to the nature of reality. And since the writer is Faulkner, the blindness involves a blindness to the nature of woman. For Sutpen has actually believed that by providing a more than just property settlement he could reconcile his wife to his abandoning her. General Compson had thrown up his hands and exclaimed: "Good God, man . . . what kind of conscience [did you have] to trade with which would have warranted you in the belief that you could have bought immunity from her for no other coin but justice?—"

Evil for Faulkner, then, involves a violation of nature and runs counter to the natural appetites and affections. And yet, as we have seen, the converse is not true; Faulkner does not consider the natural and instinctive and impulsive as automatically and necessarily good. Here I think rests the best warrant for maintaining that Faulkner holds an orthodox view of man and reality. For his men, at least, cannot be content merely with being natural. They cannot live merely by their instincts and natural appetites. They must confront the fact of evil. They are constrained to moral choices. They have to undergo a test of their courage, in making and abiding by the choice. They achieve goodness by discipline and effort. This proposition is perhaps most fully and brilliantly illustrated in Faulkner's story, "The Bear." Isaac McCaslin, when he comes of age, decides to repudiate his inheritance. He refuses to accept his father's plantation and chooses to earn his living as a carpenter and to live in a rented room. There are two powerful motives that shape this decision: the sacramental view of nature which he has been taught by the old hunter, Sam

Fathers, and the discovery of his grandfather's guilt in his treatment of one of his slaves: the grandfather had incestuously begotten a child upon his own half-Negro daughter.

"The Bear" is thus a story of penance and expiation, as also of a difficult moral decision made and maintained, but since it is so well known and has received so much commentary, I want to illustrate Faulkner's characteristic drama of moral choice from a less familiar story, "An Odor of Verbena," which is the concluding section of Faulkner's too little appreciated but brilliant novel *The Unvanquished*. As this episode opens, word has come to Bayard Sartoris, a young man of twenty-four off at law school, that his father has been assassinated by a political enemy. Ringo, the young Negro man of his own age and his boyhood companion, has ridden to the little town where Bayard is at law school to bring the news. Bayard knows what is expected of him—the date is 1874, the tradition of the code of honor still lingers, the devastating Civil War and the Reconstruction have contorted the land with violence, and Bayard knows that the community expects him to call his father's assassin to account. Even the quiet and gentle Judge Wilkins with whom he is studying law expects him to do so, and though he speaks to the boy with pity ("Bayard, my son, my dear son"), he offers him not only his horse but his pistol as well. Certainly also Bayard's father's Civil War troop expect him to avenge his father. Bayard's young stepmother, eight years older than he, expects it. Speaking in a "silvery ecstatic voice" like the priestess of a rite wrought up to a point of hysteria, she offers Bayard the pistols when he returns to the family home. Even Ringo expects it.

Some years before, when Bayard and Ringo were sixteen, at the very end of the Civil War, when the region had become a no-man's land terrorized by bushwhackers, Bayard's grandmother had been killed by a ruffian named Grumby, and Bayard and Ringo had followed him for weeks until finally they had run him down and killed him. Bayard had loved his grandmother and was resolved that her murderer should be punished. But there was no law and order in this troubled time to which he could appeal; the two sixteen-year-old boys had to undertake the punishment themselves.

Now as the two young men ride back to Jefferson, Ringo says to Bayard, "We could bushwhack him. . . . Like we done Grumby that day. But I reckon that wouldn't suit that white skin you walks around in." Bayard in fact has resolved that he will not kill again.

The motive for this decision is complex. For one thing, he realizes that his father had become a proud and abstracted and ruthless man. Bayard had loved his father but is well aware that his father had pressed his opponent, Redmond, far too hard. George Wyatt, the countryman who had served under his father, earlier had in fact come to Bayard to ask him to restrain his father: "'Right or wrong,' he said, 'us boys and most of the other folks in this county know John's right. But he ought to let Redmond alone. I know what's wrong: he's had to kill too many folks, and that's bad for a man. We all know Colonel's brave as a lion, but Redmond ain't no coward either and they ain't any use in making a brave man that made one mistake eat crow all the time. Can't you talk to him?'"

Another powerful motive is evidently the psychic wound that Bayard has suffered in the killing of Grumby. He has executed vengeance once, and in that instance there were extenuating circumstances to justify his taking the law into his own hands. But this case is different, and as he says to himself before he begins his journey home, "If there [is] anything at all in the Book, anything of hope and peace for [God's] blind and bewildered spawn," the command "*Thou Shalt not kill*" must be it." Finally, and not least, there is the example of his own father. Even his father had decided that there had been too much killing. Two months before, he had told Bayard: "Now I shall do a little moral house cleaning. I am tired of killing men, no matter what the necessity or the end." Thus Bayard, in resolving not to avenge his father, may be said to be following his father's own resolve.

But Bayard, as a member of a tightly knit community, does not want to be branded as a coward; he respects his community's opinion, and he feels compelled to live up to what the community expects of him. And so he resolves, though the reader does not learn of it until late in the story, to face Redmond, but to face him unarmed.

There is one person who understands his dilemma and can support him in his decision. It is his Aunt Jenny, who tells him when he arrives home that night: "'Yes. All right. Don't let it be Drusilla, poor hysterical young woman. And don't let it be [your father], Bayard, because he's dead now. And don't let it be George Wyatt and those others who will be waiting for you tomorrow morning. I know you are not afraid.' 'But what good will that do?' I said. 'What good will that do?' . . . 'I must live with myself, you see.' 'Then it's not just Drusilla? Not just him? Not just George Wyatt and Jefferson?' 'No,' I said."

It is indeed not just Drusilla and George Wyatt and the other outsiders that are forcing Bayard to take his proposed course of action. As he tells his aunt, it is not enough that *she* knows that he is not afraid. He must prove it to himself. "I must live with myself," he says. This is the situation of many a Faulkner character. He must live with himself. He must prove to himself that he possesses the requisite courage.

Bayard is fortunate. The man that he goes to meet is also brave, also decent. He has decided that, having killed the father, he will not kill the young son. Thus, when Bayard walks up the stairs past the small faded sign "*B. J. Redmond. Atty at Law*" and opens the door, he sees Redmond sitting "behind the desk, not much taller than Father, but thicker as a man gets that spends most of his time sitting and listening to people, freshly shaven and with fresh linen; a lawyer yet it was not a lawyer's face—a face much thinner than the body would indicate, strained (and yes, tragic; I know that now) and exhausted beneath the neat recent steady strokes of the razor, holding a pistol flat on the desk before him, loose beneath his hand and aimed at nothing." Redmond fires twice but Bayard can see that the gun was not aimed at him and that the misses are deliberate. Then Redmond gets up from his desk, blunders down the stairs and walks on out past George Wyatt and the six other members of Colonel Sartoris' old troop. He "walked through the middle of them with his hat on and his head up (they told me how someone shouted at him: 'Have you killed that boy too?') saying no word, staring straight ahead and with his back to them, on to the station where the south-bound train was just in and got on it with no baggage, nothing, and went away from Jefferson and from Mississippi and never came back."

George Wyatt rushes up to Bayard, mistakenly thinking that he had taken Redmond's pistol away from him and then missed him, missed him twice. "Then he answered himself . . . 'No; wait. You walked in here without even a pocket knife and let him miss you twice. My God in heaven.'" But he adds, " 'You ain't done anything to be ashamed of. I wouldn't have done it that way, myself. I'd a shot at him once, anyway. But that's your way or you wouldn't have done it.' " And even Drusilla, the wrought-up priestess of violence, before she leaves the house forever to go back to her kinsfolk in Alabama, leaves on Bayard's pillow a sprig of verbena because it is the odor of courage, "that odor which she said you could smell alone above the smell of horses," as a token that she too has accepted his act as brave and honorable.

One further observation: as I have already remarked, it is the men who have to be initiated into the meaning of reality, who have to observe a code of conduct, who have to prove themselves worthy. Aunt Jenny, as a woman, is outside the code. Indeed she sees the code as absurd and quixotic, though she knows that Bayard as a man will have to observe it. And what shall we say of Drusilla, who is a woman, and yet is the very high priestess of the code? Drusilla is the masculinized woman, who as a type occurs more than once in Faulkner. Drusilla's story is that she has lost her fiancé early in the war and finally in her boredom and despair has actually ridden with the Confederate cavalry. She is brave and Faulkner gives her her due, but he is not celebrating her as a kind of Confederate Joan of Arc. Her action exacts its penalty and she ends a warped and twisted woman, truly a victim of the war.

I realize that I am risking oversimplification in pressing some of these issues so hard—for example, the contrast between man and woman, in their relation to nature and to their characteristic roles as active and passive. One may be disposed to doubt that even a traditional writer writing about a traditional society would stylize these relationships as much as I have suggested Faulkner has. Yet I am very anxious to sketch in, even at the risk of overbold strokes, the general nature of Faulkner's conception of good and evil, and so I mean to stand by this summary: Faulkner sees the role of man as active; man makes choices and lives up to the choices. Faulkner sees the role of woman as characteristically fostering and sustaining. She undergirds society, upholding the family and community mores, sending her men out into battle, including the ethical battle. This generalization I believe, is, if oversimplified, basically true. And I should like to relate it to Faulkner's "Calvinistic" Protestantism. Insofar as his Calvinism represents a violent repression and constriction of natural impulse, a denial of nature itself, Faulkner tends to regard it as a terrible and evil thing. And the natural foil to characters who have so hardened their hearts in accordance with their notion of a harsh and vindictive God is the feminine principle as exemplified by a person like Lena Grove, the heroine of *Light in August*. Lena has a childlike confidence in herself and in mankind. She is a creature of warm natural sympathies and a deep instinctive commitment to her natural function.

But Faulkner has still another relation to Calvinistic Protestantism. Insofar as the tradition insists that man must be brought up to the urgency of decision, must be set tests of courage and endurance, must have his sinews strung tight for some moral leap or his back braced so as to stand firm against the push of circumstance, Faulkner evidently derives from this tradition. From it may be derived the very necessity that compels his male characters to undergo an initiation. The required initiation may be analogous to the crisis of conversion and the character's successful entrance into knowledge of himself, analogous to the sinner's experiencing salvation.

On the conscious level, Faulkner is obviously a Protestant anticleric, fascinated, but also infuriated, by some of the more violently repressive features of the religion that dominates his country. This matter is easily illustrated. One of his masterpieces, *Light in August*, provides a stinging criticism of the harsher aspects of Protestantism.

Indeed a basic theme in *Light in August* is man's strained attempt to hold himself up in a rigid aloofness above the relaxed female world. The struggle to do so is, as Faulkner portrays it in this novel, at once monstrous, comic, and heroic, as the various characters take up their special postures.

In a character like old Doc Hines, there is a definite distortion and perversion. His fury at "bitchery and abomination" is the fury of a crazed man. In her conversation with Bunch and Hightower, Mrs. Hines states quite precisely what has happened to her husband: he began "then to take God's name in vain and in pride to justify and excuse the devil that was in him." His attribution of his furies to God is quite literally a taking of God's name in vain, blasphemy. The tendency to call one's own hates the vengeance of a just God is a sin to which Protestantism has always been prone. But not merely Southern Protestantism and, of course, not merely Protestantism as such.

Calvin Burden represents another instance of the militant Protestant, but this man's heartiness and boisterous energy have something of the quality of comedy. He is the son of a Unitarian minister; but when he runs away to the West, he becomes a Roman Catholic and lives for a year in a monastery. Then, on his marriage, he repudiates the Catholic Church, choosing for the scene of his formal repudiation "a saloon, insisting that every one present listen to him and state their objections." Then, though he cannot read the English Bible—he had learned from the priests in California to read Spanish—he begins to instruct his child in the true religion, interspersing his readings to the child in Spanish with "extemporised dissertations composed half of the bleak and bloodless logic which he remembered from his father on interminable New England Sundays and half of immediate hellfire and tangible brimstone." Perhaps he differs from the bulk of doctrinaire hellfire and brimstone Protestants in not being a "proselyter" or a "missionary." But everything else marks him as truly of the breed: his intensity, his stern authoritarianism, and his violence. He has killed a man in an argument over slavery and he threatens to "frail the tar" out of his children if they do not learn to hate what he hates—hell and slaveholders.

The case of the Rev. Gail Hightower is one of the most interesting of all. He is the only one of these Protestants who has had formal theological training. Because of that fact one might expect him to be the most doctrinaire. He is not. He seems at the beginning of the book the most tolerant and pitying of all the characters, the one who recoils in horror at man's capacity for evil and man's propensity to crucify his fellows: he is a man whose only defense against violence is nonresistance. One may be inclined to say that Hightower had rebelled against his Calvinist training and repudiated the jealous and repressive God. Certainly, there is truth in this notion. Hightower is a disillusioned man and a man who has learned something from his sufferings. But there is a sense in which he has never broken out of the mold: he still stresses a God of justice rather than of mercy, for his sincerest belief is that he has somehow "bought immunity." He exclaims: "I have paid. I have paid"—in confidence that God is an honest merchant who has receipted his bill and will honor his title to the precious merchandise he has purchased at such cost.

Lastly there is the case of Joe Christmas, the violent rebel against hellfire Protestantism. His detachment from any kind of human community is shocking. Here is a man who has no family ties, no continuity with the past, no place in any community whatsoever. He is a man who has literally tried to kick the earth out from under his feet. Yet his very alienation and his insistence upon his own individual integrity are touched with the tragically heroic. As a child he is conscious that he is being hounded by old Doc Hines; he resists stubbornly the discipline imposed by his foster father McEachern, whom he finally brains with a chair; and when his paramour, Joanna Burden, threatens him with hell and insists that he kneel with her and pray for forgiveness, he decapitates her. Yet there is a most important sense in which Joe Christmas is the sternest and most doctrinaire Calvinist in the book.

He imbibes more from the training of his foster father than he realizes. For all that he strains in fierce resistance against him, he "could depend" on "the hard, just, ruthless man." It is the "soft kindness" of the woman, his foster mother, that he abominates. If one mark of the Calvinists in this novel is their fear and distrust of women and their hatred of the female principle, then Joe Christmas is eminently qualified to take a place among them. He even has affinities with his old childhood ogre, Doc Hines, and Hines' fury at the bitchery of women and the abomination of Negro blood. Joe, hearing the "fecundmellow" voices of Negro women, feels that he and "all other manshaped life about him" had been returned to the "lightless hot wet primogenitive Female" and runs from the scene in a kind of panic.

Christmas too wants not mercy but justice, is afraid of the claims of love and its obligations, and yearns only for a vindication of his identity and integrity—a vindication made the more difficult by his not really knowing precisely what he would vindicate. When he puts aside the temptation to marry Joanna and win ease and security, he does it by saying: "If I give in now, I will deny all the thirty years that I have lived to make me what I chose to be." Finally, Joe is something of a fatalist, and his fatalism is a kind of perversion of Calvinist determinism. On his way to murder Joanna, "he believed with calm paradox that he was the volitionless servant of the fatality in which he believed that he did not believe." But so "fated" is his act of murder that he keeps saying to himself "I had to do it"—using the past tense, as if the act had already been performed.

Lena (along with Eula of *The Hamlet*) has sometimes been called an earth goddess. The description does have a certain aptness when applied to Eula, especially in some of the more rhapsodic passages of *The Hamlet*. But it is a little highfalutin for Lena. It is more accurate to say that Lena is one of Faulkner's several embodiments of the female principle—indeed one of the purest and least complicated of his embodiments. Her rapport with nature is close. She is never baffled as to what course of action to take. She is never torn by doubts and indecisions. There is no painful introspection. This serene composure has frequently been put down to sheer mindlessness, and Lena, to be sure, is a very simple young woman. But Faulkner himself undoubtedly attributes most of Lena's quiet force to her female nature. In this novel the principal male characters suffer alienation. They are separated from the community, are in rebellion against it—and against nature. But Lena moves serenely into the community, and it gathers itself about her with protective gestures. Its response to her, of course, is rooted in a deep and sound instinct: Lena embodies the principle upon which any human community is founded. She is the carrier of life and she has to be protected and nurtured if there is to be any human community at all.

I have said that *Light in August* depicts man's strained attempt to hold himself up in rigid aloofness above the relaxed female world. In terms of the plot, Lena is the direct means by which Byron Bunch and the indirect means by which Hightower are redeemed from their pallid half lives and brought back into the community. This coming back into the community is an essential part of the redemption. Unless the controlling purposes of the individuals are related to those that other men share, and in which the individual can participate, he is indeed isolated, and is forced to fall back upon his personal values, with all the risk of fanaticism and distortion to which such isolation is liable.

The community is at once the field for man's action and the norm by which his action is judged and regulated. It sometimes seems that the sense of an organic community has all but disappeared from modern fiction, and the disappearance accounts for the terrifying self-consciousness and subjectivity of a great deal of modern writing. That Faulkner has some sense of an organic community still behind him is among his most important resources as a writer.

In *Light in August* Faulkner uses Lena to confirm an ideal of integrity and wholeness in the light of which the alienated characters are judged; and this is essentially the function of Dilsey, the Negro servant in *The Sound and the Fury*, regarded by many people as Faulkner's masterpiece. Dilsey's role, to be sure, is more positive than Lena's. She has affinities not with the pagan goddess but with the Christian saint. She is not the young woman and young mother that Lena is. She is an older woman and an older mother, and she is the sustaining force—the only possible sustaining force of a broken and corrupted family.

Yet Dilsey's primary role is generally similar to Lena's: she affirms the ideal of wholeness in a family which shows in every other member splintering and disintegration. *The Sound and the Fury* can be regarded as a study in the fragmentation of modern man. There is Benjy, the idiot brother who represents the life of the instincts and the unreflective emotions; there is Quentin, the intellectual and artistic brother, who is conscious of his own weakness and failure and yet so hagridden by impossible ideals that he finally turns away from life altogether and commits suicide; and there is Jason, the brother who represents an aggressive and destructive rationalism that dissolves all family and community loyalties and attachments. There has been a somewhat strained attempt to portray the brothers in Freudian terms: Benjy as the *id,* Quentin as the tortured *ego,* and Jason as the tyrannical and cruel *super-ego.* Faulkner's own way of regarding the three brothers (as implied in the appendix he supplied for the Modern Library edition) is interesting. Benjy is an idiot, of course; Quentin, in his obsession, is obviously half-mad; and Jason is perfectly sane, the first "sane" Compson for generations. Faulkner's mocking choice of the term "sane" to characterize Jason's coldly monstrous self-serving (all of Faulkner's villains, let me repeat, are characterized by this devouring and destructive rationalism) is highly significant. It is as if Faulkner argued that mere sanity were not enough—indeed that pure sanity was inhuman. The good man has to transcend his mere intellect with some overflow of generosity and love.

But we ought not to confine ourselves to the three brothers, for Dilsey is being contrasted not merely with them but with the whole of the family. There is Mr. Compson, who has been defeated by life and has sunk into whisky and fatalism. There is Mrs. Compson, the mother, whom Faulkner calls a "cold, weak" person. She is the whining, self-centered hypochondriac who has poisoned the whole family relationship. She is evidently a primary cause of her husband's cynicism; she has spoiled and corrupted her favorite son, Jason; and she has withheld her love from the other children. Quentin, on the day of his suicide, can say to himself bitterly, "If I only had a mother."

Mrs. Compson is all that Dilsey is not. It is the mother role that she has abandoned that Dilsey is compelled to assume. There is lastly the daughter of the family, Candace, who in her own way also represents the dissolution of the family. Candace has become a wanton. Sex is her particular escape from an unsatisfactory home, and she is subject to her own kind of specialization, the semiprofessionalism of a sexual adventuress.

In contrast with this splintered family, Dilsey maintains a wholeness. Indeed, Dilsey's wholeness constitutes her holiness. (It is well to remember that *whole* and *holy* are related and come from the same root.) In Dilsey the life of the instincts, including the sex drive, the life of the emotions, and the life of ideal values and of rationality are related meaningfully to one another. To say this is to say, of course, that Dilsey is a profoundly religious person. Her life with its round of daily tasks and responsibilities is related to the larger life of eternity and eternal values. Dilsey does not have to strain to make meaningful some particular desire or dream or need. Her world is a solid and meaningful world. It is filled with pain, toil, and difficulty, but it is not wrenched by agonizing doubts and perplexities.

I said a moment ago that Dilsey was sometimes compared to the saint and in what I am going to say I do not mean to deprive her of her properly deserved halo. But we must not allow the term to sentimentalize her. If she treats with compassion the idiot Benjy, saying "You's de Lawd's chile, anyway," she is quite capable of dealing summarily with her own child, Luster, when he needs a rebuke: "Lemme tell you somethin, nigger boy, you got jes es much Compson devilment in you es any of em. Is you right sho you never broke dat window?" Dilsey's earthiness and her human exasperations are very much in evidence in this novel. Because they are, Dilsey's "saintliness" is altogether credible and convincing.

One may say in general of Faulkner's Negroes that they remain close to a concrete world of values—less perverted by abstraction—more honest in recognizing what is essential and elemental than are most of the white people. Faulkner certainly does not assume any inherent virtue in the Negro race. But he does find among his Negro characters less false pride, less false idealism, more seasoned discipline in the elemental human relationships. The Negro virtues which Faulkner praises in "The Bear" are endurance, patience, honesty, courage, and the love of children—white or black. Dilsey, then, is not a primitive figure who through some mystique of race or healthiness of natural impulses is good. Dilsey is unsophisticated and warmhearted, but she is no noble savage. Her role is in its general dimensions comparable to that of her white sisters such as the matriarchs Aunt Jenny and Mrs. Rosa Millard, fostering and sustaining forces.

If she goes beyond them in exemplifying the feminine principle at its best, still hers is no mere goodness by and of nature, if one means by this a goodness that justifies a faith in man as man. Dilsey does not believe in man; she believes in God.

To try for a summary of a very difficult and complicated topic: Evil for Faulkner involves the violation of the natural and the denial of the human. As Isaac's older kinsman says in "The Bear," "Courage and honor and pride, and pity and love of justice and of liberty. They all touch the heart, and what the heart holds to becomes truth, as far as we know truth." A meanness of spirit and coldness of calculation which would deny the virtues that touch the heart is by that very fact proven false. Yet Faulkner is no disciple of Jean-Jacques Rousseau. He has no illusions that man is naturally good or that he can safely trust to his instincts and emotions. Man is capable of evil, and this means that goodness has to be achieved by struggle and discipline and effort. Like T. S. Eliot, Faulkner has small faith in social arrangements so perfectly organized that nobody has to take the trouble to be good. Finally Faulkner's noblest characters are willing to face the fact that most men can learn the deepest truths about themselves and about reality only through suffering. Hurt and pain and loss are not mere accidents to which the human being is subject; nor are they mere punishments incurred by human error; they can be the means to the deeper knowledge and to the more abundant life.

A RITUAL OF TRANSFIGURATION:
THE OLD MAN AND THE SEA

Arvin R. Wells

The Old Man and the Sea develops a familiar Hemingway theme—
the theme of the undefeated. Like other Hemingway treatments of
the same theme, this one presents the story of a moral triumph which
has as its absolutely necessary condition an apparently smashing
defeat. The literary lineage of the old fisherman himself goes back
to several Hemingway "code heroes," and, as Philip Young observed,

> Particularly he is related to men like . . . Manuel Garcia, "The Unde-
> feated" bullfighters, who lose[s], in one way, but win[s] in another. Like
> Manuel, Santiago is a fighter whose best days are behind him and, worse,
> is wholly down on his luck. But he still dares, and sticks to the rules, and
> will not quit when he is licked. He is undefeated, he endures, and his loss,
> therefore, in the manner of it, is itself a victory.[1]

This, in effect, is what it means to be a Hemingway "code hero,"
but the manner of Santiago's loss and of Hemingway's presentation
of it is such that it sets the old fisherman apart from all predecessors.
He is the apotheosis of the code hero; his experience is not only a
confirmation of personal dignity and courage but what is perhaps
best called a ritual of transfiguration.

The sense of ritual accompanies the whole action from the opening
dialogues between Santiago and Manolin, in which ritualized questions and responses serve to sustain an innocent illusion of uncom-
promised respect and dignity, to the final disposal of the remains of
the great fish. This sense of ritual action is fostered by the simplicity
of the style, by verbal repetition, by the deliberateness with which
even small acts are performed, and by the old fisherman's own sense
of mystery, and it is re-enforced by what might be called reminiscences
of Christianity, present in the story sometimes as symbol, sometimes
as direct allusion and sometimes merely as a matter of tone. The
transfiguration that is at the heart of the story, however, is no Christian

---

[1] Philip Young, *Ernest Hemingway* (Rinehart & Co.: New York, 1952), p. 96.

"A *Ritual of Transfiguration*: The Old Man and the Sea." *From* The University
Review, *XXX (Autumn 1963). Copyright © 1963 by the University of Missouri
at Kansas City. Reprinted by permission of* The University Review *and the
author.*

mystery; it is "in the manner of it" fundamentally and essentially pagan.

This is not to say that there isn't something of the Christian saint about Santiago. He has achieved the most difficult and saintly of all Christian virtues, humility, a humility so absolute that it involves "no loss of true pride."[2] There is even in him a suggestion of Saint Francis, in his response to animal life and especially to birds—the "small delicate black terns" and the small warbler that comes to rest on his fishing line. Moreover, at various moments in the story Santiago affirms the major Christian virtues: Faith—" 'He hasn't much faith!' 'No . . . But we have' " (10-11). Hope—"It is silly not to hope, he thought. Besides, I believe it is a sin" (104-05). And charity—the old fisherman's generous, unsentimental love of men and animals. But as the old fisherman moves away from the shore and out into the sea, it becomes apparent that, if in any sense he is or is to become a saint, his sainthood is of a non-Christian order.

His "charity" arises, not from the feeling that all are God's creatures, but from a sense that he and all natural creatures participate in the same pattern of necessity and are subject to the same judgment: "Take a good rest, small bird,' he said. 'Then go in and take your chance like any man or bird or fish' " (55). His relation to the sea and to the life of the sea is intensely personal and pagan. The sea is "la mar"; it is feminine, not quite personified, but capable, in a moment of fantasy, of taking a lover beneath a blanket of yellow seaweed. It gives forth life and reabsorbs it: the old man is fascinated by the sight of a dead fish growing smaller and smaller as it sinks.

Moreover, for him the realm of nature and the realm of morality are coexistent; the creatures of the sea express for him all that he knows about life—the falseness of the Portuguese man-of-war, the playfulness of the dolphin, the nobility and endurance of the marlin. If there is a god in Santiago's life (he says he is not religious), it is the sea, and the sea, as traditionally, is life itself, which Santiago both loves and mistrusts but to which he can commit himself because he knows "many tricks" and because he can endure. Though he does not make of them grounds for superiority, he has, nonetheless, his intelligence and his will.

Similarly, Santiago's faith and hope rest, not upon any belief in a just and benevolent God, but upon his belief in man's ability to endure suffering. This basis of hope is implicit even in the early pages of the story. When we first see Santiago, he appears immensely old, he has been 84 days without catching a fish, and he carries a

---

[2] Ernest Hemingway, *The Old Man and the Sea*, The Scribner Library (New York, 1952), p. 14. All future references to *The Old Man and the Sea* are to page numbers in this edition, cited parenthetically in the text.

sail which, furled, "looked like the flag of permanent defeat" (9). Yet, "his hope and his confidence had never gone" (13); he only needs luck, and in the past he has been lucky. Significantly, the signs of that luck are visible in the old man's hands: "His hands had the deep-creased scars from handling heavy fish on the cords. But none of these scars were fresh. They were as old as erosions in a fishless desert" (10). Clearly, in Santiago's world, luck and pain are closely related. Luck is something that comes and goes, and a man may hope for it from day to day, but it is meaningless unless he can endure pain.

In the first few pages of the story the word "faith" appears twice—once, when the old fisherman affirms that he has faith, and then again later, in a very different context. During a conversation about baseball, Santiago says to Manolin, "Have faith in the Yankees my son. Think of the great DiMaggio" (17). A bit later this attitude is further elaborated in talk between the boy and the fisherman.

> "In the American league it is the Yankees as I said," the old man said happily.
> "They lost today," the boy told him.
> "That means nothing. The great DiMaggio is himself again."
> "They have other men on the team."
> "Naturally. But he makes the difference." (21)

One can have faith in the Yankees, because DiMaggio makes the difference. In just what way he makes the difference becomes clear only later.

During the long ordeal of his struggle with the great fish and then against the sharks, the old man thinks repeatedly of DiMaggio, wondering whether or not DiMaggio would approve of the way in which he has fished and endured. Behind this is no merely childlike idolization of a baseball player. The DiMaggio of these reveries is first of all a man with a mysterious and painful ailment, a bone spur; he is, in other words, a man who performs well against the handicap of pain. And it is this that makes the difference. One can afford to place his faith where he finds the power to endure suffering, and this power Santiago finds in himself and in other men. In the end, for him, pain becomes literally the means of distinguishing reality from unreality—"He had only to look at his hands and feel his back against the stern to know that this had truly happened and was not a dream" (98); and it is all but synonymous with life itself—"He put his two hands together and felt the palms . . . and he could bring the pain of life by simply opening and closing them" (116). The power to endure suffering, then, which is in man, gives the power of mastery over life and thus a basis for hope and faith.

In a sense, *The Old Man and the Sea* is a study in pain, in the endurance of pain and in the value of that endurance. The old fisherman fishes as much for a chance to prove himself as he does for a living, and, though he fails to bring the giant marlin to market, he wins the supreme chance to prove himself in the terms he best understands. Starting in simple physical pain, he transcends, through his agony, his own heroic ideal, personified in DiMaggio, and ends in the attitude of the crucified Christ: "He slept face down on the newspapers with his arms out straight and the palms of his hands up" (122). All this he endures without compromising his code either as man or fisherman; he succeeds in showing "what a man can do and what a man endures" (66).

Hemingway's story, however, does not place a final emphasis upon endurance as a value in itself. Within the pattern of the story, endurance like pain is a necessary condition, not so much of victory but of being "undefeated." The fundamental qualities of the old man's character—his humility, his simple and pagan reverence for the conditions and processes of life, and his capacity for suffering—serve to transform his struggle into something which he himself vaguely feels to be a mystery, and his defeat into a triumph as much as the divinity of Christ transforms the terror and sorrow of the Crucifixion into the promise of life.

Before the old fisherman is himself identified by obvious allusion with the crucified Christ, he is identified with Cain and with the crucifiers of Christ. Once he has hooked the great fish, all of his generalized sense of humble brotherhood with other creatures of the sea concentrates upon this one magnificent marlin. Repeatedly, he addresses the fish as "brother"; the taut line that connects them becomes an expression of an equally strong bond of suffering and, on the fisherman's part, of love. Yet, at the same time, he is relentlessly determined to capture and kill the marlin, as Cain killed his brother and as the Roman soldiers killed Christ. That the great fish is somehow to be associated with Christ is not left to conjecture based on traditional symbolism. " 'Christ,' " Santiago exclaims in wonder. " 'I did not know he was so big.' 'I'll kill him though . . . In all his greatness and his glory' " (66). Significantly this is the only place in the story where the expletive, Christ, is used, and the echo in the second sentence is unmistakable—"for thine is the kingdom and the power and the glory forever." When Santiago does slay the fish, he drives the harpoon into his side below the chest fin, "that rose high in the air to the altitude of the man's chest" (94), and pierces the heart. Then the fish rises into the air and hangs there a moment, and there is "some great strangeness" (98) in it.

The old fisherman is not unaware of the paradox of his situation.

He thinks, "It is good that we do not have to try to kill the sun or the moon or the stars. It is enough to live on the sea and kill our true brothers" (75). He thinks on occasion that perhaps he should not have been a fisherman; yet the question is scarcely admissible. He was born to be a fisherman; he is a fisherman of necessity, and he must kill the giant fish out of a necessity that is deeper than hunger.

Santiago is, of course, incapable of articulating just what this necessity is, but the pattern of the story makes it clear enough. All the qualities which Santiago sees in the great fish—beauty, nobility, courage, calmness and endurance—are the qualities which he values most; they are the qualities which *redeem* life from meaninglessness and futility (this is perhaps the fundamental link in the story between the fish and Christ); and they are the qualities that Santiago wishes to confirm in himself. Paradoxically the only means he has of confirming them in himself is by exercising them in opposition to the fish. He must, symbolically, slay the lord of life in order to achieve a spiritual identity with him.

Thus the central event of the story is one in which the redemption of life and the destruction of life, affirmation and guilt, are locked in a single action. While he actually is battling the great fish, there is some thought of injustice but none of guilt in the old man's mind. There is only the bond of love and suffering and the sense of mystery, the sense of some deep necessity that the old man cannot quite bring into consciousness. But after the first shark, the Mako shark, has mutilated the fish, thoughts of sin come to tease the old man's mind. "Perhaps it was a sin to kill the fish. I suppose it was even though I did it to keep me alive and feed many people. But then everything is a sin . . . everything kills everything else" (105-6).

The old man, who has said he is not religious, cannot quite believe in sin in the orthodox Christian understanding of the word; yet, he cannot evade the sense of sin in connection with his killing of the fish. He has chosen "to go there to find him beyond all people" (50). He may argue, "I did it to keep me alive and feed many people" (105), but he knows, as he confesses, that the boy Manolin keeps him alive, and he has said earlier that no one is worthy to eat of the great fish. Here again in the idea of worthiness with its suggestion of communion, the Christian allusion is clear, but in the context of the story worthiness is something acquired in action, by being great in the same way the fish is great.

The old man cannot resolve the question of guilt for himself; he can only oppose to it his conviction of necessity: "You were born to be a fisherman as the fish was born to be a fish" (105). And in the fight against the sharks, the feeling of sin is lost and replaced by something more congenial to the spirit of the old man, something like the idea of *hybris*.

> And what beat you? he thought.
> "Nothing," he said aloud. "I went out too far." (120)

While the question of sin and guilt persists, however, the old man tries to deal with it honestly, and having counseled himself against rationalization, he leans forward, almost unconsciously tears a piece of the flesh from the giant marlin, and eats of the fish of which no one is worthy to eat.

It is only after this act, which the reader has been prepared to recognize as a kind of communion, that we meet the first of the allusions that serve to refer the old man's experience to the Passion of Christ. As he sees the first of the shovel-nose sharks approaching, the old man utters a cry: "'Ay,' he said aloud." And the reader is told, "There is no translation for this word and perhaps it is just a noise such as a man might make, involuntarily, feeling the nail go through his hands and into the wood" (107).

Before this, all symbols associated with and all allusions made to Christ's Passion have been applied to the giant fish. Now begins a process of transfer from the fish to the man. As he leaves the skiff, the old man falls and lies for a moment with the mast across his shoulders; he must sit down five times before he reaches his shack on the hill, and when he reaches the shack, he lies down in the attitude of the crucified Christ.

The point of this accumulation of allusions is not simply, as Philip Young has suggested, that life crucifies even the strong and noble in the end and that the important thing is how one takes it when it comes. The transfer of Christian symbols and allusions from the great fish to the fisherman is, in fact, only part, perhaps only the most obvious part, of a fairly complex process through which identity is established between them.

Santiago fights and kills the great marlin "out of pride," out of the desire to show that he is like the great fish. What he seeks is identity. He affirms continually his own feeling of brotherhood, but, in another sense, brotherhood can be affirmed only in a struggle that must end in the death of the fish. In a moment of semi-delirium just before he kills the fish, the old man's sense of identity with him becomes so intense that he thinks, "Never have I seen a greater, or more beautiful, or a calmer or more noble thing than you, brother. Come on and kill me. I do not care who kills who" (92).

After the fish is dead the old man has a strong desire to touch him, to confirm the reality of the fish and, thereby, the reality of what he has proven of himself. The delusion of confused identities persists as the old man, seeing the giant carcass of the fish alongside, wonders, "Is he bringing me in or am I bringing him in?" (99). When the fish is hit and mutilated by the first shark, the old fisherman feels "as though he himself were hit" (103). Later, when, without pride, almost unconsciously the old man eats of the fish, the fish becomes a part of his life. Almost immediately the *galanos* approach, and we encounter the first of the allusions that refer the old man's experience to the Passion of Christ. The pattern is extremely tight and neat: just as the great marlin in his noble but futile struggle to preserve his life becomes identified symbolically with the crucified Christ, so the old man in his noble but futile struggle to preserve the fish from the sharks becomes identified with the same figure.

Seen as a part of this general pattern, the fact of crucifixion no longer suggests either, on the one hand, a vague evocation of Christianity or, on the other, merely the supreme experience of "the pain of life" and the supreme test of endurance. It is the final seal of the old man's triumph. Through the tragic image of Christ in his agony, the identity of the fisherman with the fish, that is, with the essentially pagan virtues which the fish represents, is finally affirmed. The justification for this non-Christian use of Christian symbolism stems not only from the fact that the giant marlin expresses in action all those qualities that, for the old man, redeem life, but from the fact that the Crucifixion is a consummate metaphor for the medium of suffering, endurance, and apparent defeat through which the old man achieves his at least momentary transfiguration.

When the old man reaches shore he has only the skeleton of the marlin. The experience has been stripped of its practical and material aspects, and even the great skeleton is at last only so much more garbage waiting to go out with the tide. At most it serves to give the other fishermen a clue as to what the struggle must have been; to the outsiders, the man and woman tourists who look down from the terrace, it is all but meaningless. They perceive some strange beauty in the thing itself, but they cannot distinguish even the elementary terms of the experience.

> "I didn't know sharks had such handsome, beautifully formed tails."
> "I didn't either," her male companion said. (127)

Having lost his fish to the least worthy of opponents, the shovel-nose sharks that are just moving appetites, even the old man is unclear about what he has accomplished, and the boy, Manolin, whose admiration and pity counterpoint the old man's humility, must order the experience for him.

"They beat me, Manolin," he said. "They truly beat me."
"*He* didn't beat you. Not the fish."
"No. Truly. It was afterwards." (124)

Finally the old fisherman seems almost indifferent to the great struggle; he is beyond it; it is complete in itself, and the others may take
from it what they can: the head of the marlin to Pedrico, the spear
to Manolin, the uncomprehending glimpse of the skeleton to the two
tourists. But the gap between what the experience has actually been
and what the others can gather from the remains is strongly suggested
by the total lack of connection between their concern with the skeleton and the dream of the lions which fills the old man's sleep at the
close of the story.

In a sense, the old man's final reward for having endured is the
freedom which he finally has to dream, uninterrupted, of the lions
that he had once seen playing like cats upon the shores of Africa and
that somehow now are "the main thing that is left" (66). The dream
has come before during the story, but always before the old man was
called back to a reality of further action and further suffering. Now,
that reality is held at a distance. For the old man there is a childlike
happiness and reassurance in seeing the great beasts at play. What
the lions represent beyond this is broadly suggested by the details of
the dream in their relation to the general pattern of action and symbol.

The lions, traditionally, are the noblest of the great beasts in comparison with which man, according to the old fisherman, "is not much."
They are the kings of the jungle, primal nature, which they dominate
by their courage, their strength, their fierceness and their supposed
pride. They are both like and unlike the great marlin: like him in
that they have the qualities that redeem life and are in this way the
lords of life; unlike him in that their beauty and nobility are compounded with fierceness and therefore inspire not only awe but fear.
In the dream, however, the lions come out from the jungle and down
onto the beach to play on the sand; they have put aside their majesty
and have grown domestic and familiar. It is as if they gave themselves
up to the old man, to his love, without the necessity of further trial
or guilt or suffering.

As the lions come out of the jungle and fill the old man's sleep,
their cat-like playfulness, free of threat or challenge, suggests a harmony between the old man and the heroic qualities which the lions
possess and the giant marlin possessed and which the old man has
fought to realize in himself. Most simply, perhaps, they suggest an
achieved intimacy between the old man and the proud and often
fierce heart of nature that for him is the repository of values.

RELIGIOUS ASPECTS IN THE
NOVELS OF GRAHAM GREENE

A. A. DeVitis

Anyone approaching the work of Graham Greene is immediately confronted by a number of literary, scholarly, and, perhaps, theological problems; for Greene's career since the publication in 1929 of his first novel, *The Man Within,* has led him into many aspects of creative and imaginative literature. As well as his serious novels, he has written thrillers (which he calls "entertainments"), plays, motion picture scripts, essays, and several dozen short stories; more recently he has edited books for The Bodley Head Press. He has, besides, written countless reviews of novels and motion pictures for the *Spectator* and the *Times* but these enterprises date to his early career in the field of letters. In this category can be placed those pieces that appear from time to time in various magazines and journals from remote areas of the globe—from Indo-China, Cuba, and Haiti, places that frequently serve as locales for both his novels and his entertainments. Still, Greene is best known for his spy stories, such as *The Ministry of Fear* and *The Third Man,* and for his serious "novels," books that deal with "religious" problems.

According to many of his critics, Greene is a divided novelist who frequently doesn't know exactly where to place his emphasis—on action and suspense, as in the entertainments; or on characterization and philosophical speculation, as in the novels. To many of his readers, his religious, philosophical, and literary preoccupations range from Manicheism to latter-day Existentialism. Others see him simply as a writer whose Roman Catholicism is a device that allows him to comment on and perhaps even to play fast and loose with his one true love, the Church itself.

Perhaps there is a great deal of truth in this last assertion: the majority of his novels deal with people who happen to be Roman Catholics, people caught up in emotional dilemmas that give rise to theological speculations of the most beguiling kind. Frequently the solutions Greene implies for these very human problems do not seem consistent with the teachings of his church; and to that church he must stand as something of an enigma. But when one considers the general movement of Ecumenism, Greene's search for some sort of tolerance and understanding within the confines of his faith does not seem so very far from the new feeling that the Catholic Church has been promulgating. The fact is that since his first novel Greene's career has involved him in an ever-widening circle of interests and beliefs that have taken him farther and farther from dogmatic Roman Catholicism toward a wider-ranging humanism; and it is this tendency towards humanism which places him strictly within the tradition of English letters, and marks at the same time his place as the most compelling and the best of modern novelists.

1

In 1938 appeared *Brighton Rock,* a novel that read much like a detective story, but one that upon reflection hardly seemed a detective story at all. In addition to the obvious paraphernalia of the thriller—the chase, the melodramatic contrivances, the sensational murders—that Greene had made use of in *The Ministry of Fear* and *This Gun for Hire,* Greene presented an obvious allegory. The protagonist, an antihero named Pinkie Brown, was handled with a sophistication rare since Conrad, and the antagonist, a blowsy blonde named Ida Arnold, proved a bewildering as well as bewildered pursuer of the seventeen-year-old racketeer. That there must have been some confusion in Greene's mind about the kind of book he had written is apparent from his first calling *Brighton Rock* an "entertainment," and only later a "novel."

What is apparent now is that *Brighton Rock* was actually an attempt on Greene's part to explain the nature of right and wrong and good and evil in the world of ordinary men and women—good-hearted, generous, fine-feeling people like Ida Arnold. Still and all, people like Ida Arnold found themselves confused and bewildered when entering a world of good and evil, a world in which the values taught and insisted on were those of the Roman Catholic Church. Consequently, one of the most beguiling aspects of the novel is the subtle yet relentless way in which Greene managed to shift his reader's interest away from right and wrong—morally easy Ida—to good and evil—the Roman Catholic girl Rose and the boy Pinkie. As the focus shifted, the reader's affection for Ida diminished, and her undeniable humanity, at first so captivating, became tedious and then even unreal. The allegorical importunities of the theme began to dominate the narrative as the reader understood that Ida was merely a catalyst, the agent that precipitated a reaction that must have occurred in any event.

Within the allegory, Ida's concepts, right and wrong, are secondary to considerations of good and evil. Yet *Brighton Rock* is also a detective story, and within that pattern Ida Arnold exemplifies human nature and human justice—she is like a stick of Brighton rock candy: wherever one bites into it, it spells "Brighton." Ida is, however, an alien in the spiritual drama; she likens herself to a traveler in a foreign country who has neither phrase nor guidebook to help her find her way. She is "a stickler where right's concerned," a competent pursuer of human justice, an avenging spirit, but an alien in a spiritual dilemma. She represents humanity; she is the vitality of most people, and the highest praise she can pay to any activity is that for her it is "fun." The reader sees her at first as friendly, good-natured, morally easy; but as the action progresses her "humanity" seems somehow to diminish as the reality of good and evil, a consideration Ida is not competent to understand, becomes infinitely more meaningful.

In turning to the girl Rose, the reader soon appreciates Greene's frightening comment made on Ida's world of right and wrong, this world of the everyday; for Rose is returned to the worst horror of all, a life without hope. On the recording that Pinkie had made for her she learns what her emotions have kept her incapable of appreciating—that Pinkie despised her and that her chief attraction to him had been her goodness, which he was determined to destroy. At the end of the novel Rose knows that she is pregnant with Pinkie's child; the reader is left to draw the conclusion that her marriage to Pinkie has been the union of heaven and hell. These, briefly noted, are the allegorical importunities of the theme; but the fact that the novel is also a detective story, and a brilliant one at that, should not be overlooked. *Brighton Rock* in 1938 begins for Greene a pattern of interest culminating with *The End of the Affair* in 1951. In the novels written between these dates Greene defines and clarifies his "religious" preoccupations without ever becoming a dogmatist or a religious teacher.

In an essay on the religious aspect of the writing of Henry James, included in *The Lost Childhood*, Greene writes, "The novelist depends preponderantly on his personal experience, the philosopher on correlating the experience of others, and the novelist's philosophy will always be a little lopsided." To this statement might be added a comment from *In Search of a Character* (1961): "I would claim not to be a writer of Catholic novels, but a novelist who in four or five books took characters with Catholic ideas for his material. Nonetheless for years . . . I found myself haunted by people who wanted help with spiritual problems that I was incapable of giving." It would seem then that the sensible approach to a study of the artistry of Graham Greene is to take him at his own word. He is not a "Catholic writer," considering the classification in its narrowest sense; he is not a novelist like G. K. Chesterton or Helen White, who writes remark-ably astute novels for Catholic girls. He is, as he says himself, a novelist who uses as his characters people who happen to be Roman Catholics. The sensible way to approach Greene's craft is to read what he writes about his use of Roman Catholicism as background for characters and plots in *Why Do I Write?*:

> If I may be personal, I belong to a group, the Catholic Church, which would present me with grave problems as a writer were I not saved by my disloyalty. If my conscience were as acute as M. Mauriac's showed it-self to be in his essay *God and Mammon*, I could not write a line. There are leaders of the Church who regard literature as a means to an end, edification. I am not arguing that literature is amoral, but that it presents a different moral, and the personal morality of an individual is seldom identical with the morality of the group to which he belongs. You remem-ber the black and white squares of Bishop Blougram's chess board. As a novelist, I must be allowed to write from the point of view of the black square as well as of the white: doubt and even denial must be given their chance of self-expression, or how is one freer than the Leningrad group?

The Power and the Glory (1940) grew out of a trip Greene took through the Mexican provinces of Tabasco and Chiapas in the late thirties. Here again Roman Catholicism is used as background, and again it is allegory that lends the events of the narrative an excite-ment above and beyond the simple adventure of flight and pursuit. The whisky priest in the Mexican novel is a reluctant recipient of grace, and to many readers this fact immediately transforms the novel into a Catholic document of such mysterious overtones that only the initiate can understand and appreciate it.

Greene's whisky priest is opposed by the lieutenant of the new order, the socialist state; neither protagonist nor antagonist is named, in keeping with the main theme of the novel, which is quite simply the portrayal of the meaning and value of the code handed down by Christianity since its inspiration by and in the New Testament. Yet in the final pages of the novel the priest becomes not so much a champion of Roman Catholicism or Christianity as a champion of the individual: in his dramatic debate with the lieutenant toward the end of the narrative he points out in his simple manner the real dignity of his humanity, something the lieutenant has been only re-luctantly aware of.

The immediate frame of reference in *The Power and the Glory* is specifically the protagonist's Roman Catholicism, yet the ultimate ref-erent is the humanistic ideal. The whisky priest is one who admin-isters the sacraments of his church while in the state of mortal sin; he evades the police of the new state as he evades God, all the while sustaining his courage with drink. The theme of flight and pursuit is thus doubly pointed. In his characterization of the priest Greene consciously works within the anatomy of sainthood, a theme which was to preoccupy him in various ways until the publication of *The End of the Affair*.

In the Mexican novel Greene takes the weak priest who must drink to preserve his courage and through him portrays the thesis that the evil man discovers in himself is an index to his love of God. As a young man the unnamed priest had been good in the narrow and conventional sense. Concerned with sodalities and baptisms, he had been guilty of only venial sins; but he had felt love for no one except himself. Since the outlawing of Roman Catholicism in his province he has fallen to drink—and in a lonely hour fathered a child. It is his acquaintance with evil that allows him to learn about the resources of his religion. Closed in tight in a prison cell, aware with a precocious intensity of the foulness and stench of human misery, he recognizes the reality of evil and, conversely, feels the presence of God: "This place was very like the world; overcrowded with lust and crime and unhappy love; it stank to heaven; but he realized that after all it was possible to find peace there, when you knew for certain that the time was short."

In *Brighton Rock* Greene had sketched the theme of power in the relationship between Pinkie and his adopted father, Kite. In *The Power and the Glory* Greene develops his thesis in terms of the ironical similarities set up between the unnamed priest and lieutenant. It is through this representative of the new order that Greene portrays the vitality and strange beauty of power, subtly relating the cult of power to an ultimate consideration of evil. The battle of individual choice for good or evil is fought in the soul of the priest, who comes to represent individual protest against the degrading urges of power politics. In *The Lawless Roads* of 1939 Greene wrote: "Perhaps the only body in the world to-day which consistently—and sometimes successfully—opposes the totalitarian state is the Catholic Church."

The Power and the Glory, despite the fact that it apologizes in a very real way for the author's faith, nevertheless transcends its narrowly Roman Catholic theme. George Woodcock's observation in *The Writer and Politics* is in this respect cogent:

> [W]hile the police lieutenant remains the representative of a collective idea, the servant of the State, the presence of the Church becomes steadily more distant and shadowy, and the priest seems to stand out more solidly as an individual, without tangible connections or allegiances, fighting a guerilla war for an idea which he considers right. Instead of being the representative of Catholicism, he becomes more and more the type of human person fighting against the unifying urges of a power society, and triumphing even in defeat and destruction, because in this battle there are no fronts and the messages are passed on by examples to other individuals

who continue as rebellious elements in the total St
ground which is never eliminated, because it has
and no headquarters, except in the heart of each m
for freedom.

As the whisky priest confronts the lieutenant a
evil of the organized violence he espouses, the Catl
more and more into the background; and as this l
becomes more and more Everyman, seeking the wa
his own salvation and indicating at the same time
nature of his convictions. In the character of the priest, Greene
creates an important figure in contemporary mythology.

The Heart of the Matter, written in 1948, is the next major novel
to develop and exploit religious considerations. Again there are allegorical importunities, but they are neither as obvious nor as insistent
as they were in *Brighton Rock* and *The Power and the Glory*. In *The*
Heart of the Matter the theme of pity, sketched in both the preceding
novels, is given full expression by means of the central character,
Major Scobie. Once again, this time in the careful characterization of
the protagonist, the reader finds Greene working with myth: like
the whisky priest Scobie escapes the immediate confines of the novel's
situation and plot and becomes a character capable of exciting the
curiosity, the imagination, and the humanity of the reader. The idea
of Scobie remains with the reader long after he has forgotten about
the intrigues of the melodramatic action.

Greene had successfully worked within the anatomy of pity in *The*
Ministry of Fear, the entertainment that immediately preceded *The*
Heart of the Matter; but the theme had not been distinctly related
to a religious context. In both *The Ministry of Fear* and *The Heart*
of the Matter pity is shown to be a force that dominates the personality and the actions of the protagonist, making him subject to the
suffering of the world, the victim of the unhappy and the discon-
tented. This pity is diagnosed as a sort of egotism, insisting as it does
that the individual assume responsibility for his fellow man without
consulting the referents of religion or philosophy. Hence pity is shown
to be an excess, and Greene comments indirectly on the value of a
religious or philosophical orientation that accounts for suffering. The
aspect of pride can be neither overly insisted upon nor ignored:
Scobie's responsibility and concern for unhappiness characterize him
in such a way that he deludes himself, and perhaps the undiscrimi-
nating reader, into thinking that he is essentially humble. And this is
the paradox upon which the characterization is built; Greene challenges the reader to discover the error of Scobie's thought, while at
the same time he makes Scobie so human and so understanding that
his error appears to be noble, as Prometheus's stealing of fire from

appears noble to mankind. What Greene achieves, then, is
ation of a man whose character flaw reaches tragic proportions.
he beguiling problem of whether or not Major Scobie is saved
ccording to the teachings of his Church has aroused much speculation. Scobie's struggle with himself and with his Roman Catholic
God forms the basis of the conflict: it is Scobie's pity that forces him
to suicide. But to abstract from the character's actions Greene's
philosophy or personal belief is absurd, for the novel has been constructed with an artistic consideration in mind, not a philosophical
or a religious one. Both Arthur Rowe and Henry Scobie are moved
by suffering, misery, and ugliness. Unlike Rowe, whose preoccupation
with pity is put down to a childhood loss of innocence, Scobie is
possessed of a love of God that orients his actions and determines
his suicide. The individual struggle is made the first consideration
of the novel; as the character develops, the Roman Catholic Church
fades more and more into the background, becoming a portion of the
Necessity that propels Scobie on his quest for identity and recognition.

As the action of the novel progresses, Scobie's pity and his sense
of responsibility are described as images of his love of God. But
Scobie's personal God is one of infinite mercy and forgiveness. As
Scobie, a police officer in West Africa, goes off to investigate the
suicide of a young district commander, he feels in his heart that his
God will not exact damnation from one so young, so unformed. Father
Clay, the district priest, attempts to reason with Scobie, but is interrupted: " 'Even the Church can't teach me that God doesn't pity
the young . . .' " Scobie prefers the God who died for sinners over
the God of justice and retribution; he chooses the God who allowed
Himself to be crucified to prevent unhappiness over the God of
justice. Scobie, then, trusts his own instincts concerning mercy and
forgiveness above the written law. This is pride, but a pride compounded of a keen awareness and appreciation of unhappiness. For,
paradoxically, it is his pride that makes Scobie humble; his intolerance of suffering is the index of his emotion. Indeed, the opposites
seem irreconcilable, for Scobie accepts personally the responsibility
for sin. But so had Christ. Scobie mistakenly sees himself in relation to
Christ, who died to save mankind from the blight of the first sin.

Scobie is aware of this precarious logic, recognizing the possibility
that the sense of pity he cherishes is an excess; but he knows equally
well that he cannot avoid the call of misery and unhappiness. He
reasons that with death, responsibility ends. " 'There's nothing more
we can do about it,' " he says. " 'We can rest in peace.' "

Scobie's humility is evidenced by his willingness to accept the
teachings of the Catholic Church for himself even though both his
pride and his pity refuse to allow him to accept these same harsh

strictures for others. He knows that if he kills himself to keep from hurting both his wife and his mistress (again he is mistaken, for his experience has shown him that no one person can arrange the happiness of another), he damns himself for all eternity. He does not so much fear hellfire as he does the permanent sense of loss of God that the Church teaches as a condition of hell. To be deprived of the God he loves is the worst torment of all for Scobie, yet he chooses this over giving more hurt to Louise and Helen. Sentimentally he sees himself as Christ committing suicide for mankind.

The Heart of the Matter takes its epigraph from Péguy: "The sinner is at the very heart of Christianity. No one is as competent as the sinner in matters of Christianity. No one, unless it is the saint." In *The Heart of the Matter* Scobie's competence in matters of his religion is shown all too clearly. His love, consistent with his pity, becomes indicative of a universal love. In the process of learning the substance of his religion he realizes the immensity of human love; he places himself alongside God and insists on dealing personally with matters of happiness. Both his pride and his humility, seen as opposite sides of the same coin, conspire against him. Paradoxically, since he refuses to trust the God he loves, he becomes at once Christ and Judas. He dies for man, but in doing so he betrays God.

Ultimately Scobie is a hero of tragic proportions. He knows his antagonist, recognizes his strength. What Scobie cannot accept is an orthodox conception of a God who seems indifferent to the agony of those He has created. He cannot conceive of a God who has not the same sense of pity as himself, and cannot trust a God who allows misery and unhappiness. Scobie is at once a scapegoat and a traitor, and his pity, mistaken though it may be in its applications, becomes his tragic flaw. Whether or not he is damned is unimportant in the consideration of his heroism or the novel's artistry. But Greene invites speculation and comment: the reader's concern for Scobie is, paradoxically, the most telling aspect of Greene's artistry; for Scobie's humanity is what most readers retain from the pages of the novel.

In *The End of the Affair* (1951) Greene creates a situation in which God becomes the lover of the heroine, Sarah Miles. At the expense of incident and action, the aspects of his art which had stood him in best stead in the earlier pieces, he develops the theme that human love, even abandonment to passion, is an index to divine love.

Greene's narrative is set in the midst of contemporary events. Yet his minimizing the allegorical dimension and restricting the action of the novel to a bomb-torn city somehow detracts from the veracity of the presentation: the real world does not here appear as compelling as the symbolically conceived world of Brighton, Mexico, or West Africa.

Sarah Miles becomes a saint and Greene goes so far as to ascribe miracles to her. What the reader would have accepted in the earlier novels as compelling truth becomes in *The End of the Affair* embarrassing insistence on the author's part that his theme is significant and his method artistic. *The End of the Affair* is not completely successful because it is Catholic in the narrowest meaning of the term. *Brighton Rock* and *The Power and the Glory* had been Catholic in a broad sense and, ultimately, had escaped the limitations of Roman Catholicism because of the warm humanism upon which they insisted. However, Evelyn Waugh, who had severely criticized Greene's "theology" in *The Heart of the Matter*, applauded Greene's ability in using the religious theme in *The End of the Affair*, perhaps because he found the theological implications more acceptable within the framework of a Roman Catholic belief closely akin to his own orthodox views. "Mr. Greene is to be congratulated," wrote Waugh in the *Commonweal*, "on a fresh achievement. He shows that in middle life his mind is suppler and his interests wider than in youth. . . . He has triumphantly passed his climacteric where so many talents fail."

The action of *The End of the Affair* is limited chiefly to the ultimately unsuccessful love affair between Sarah Miles and Maurice Bendrix, an author who had not yet made the mistake of becoming popular. In *The Power and the Glory*, Greene had made use of "Bystanders," characters the whisky priest had encountered on his progress to martyrdom. The purpose of introducing these Bystanders into the action had been simply to indicate the force of Catholic action; in other words, to indicate that all the priest represents would continue in one way or another. In *The End of the Affair* Bystanders are made use of again; but here they emerge as important aspects of the plot, for it is their function to authenticate the various "miracles" attributed to Sarah after her death. They also add their perspectives to the story of Sarah, exemplifying various aspects of her character: yet they do not, somehow, succeed.

Paradoxically, *The End of the Affair*, although Greene's least successful novel among those discussed here, is his most artistically conceived and most "modern" novel, if one will except *The Comedians*, published in 1966. The melodramatic and allegorical contrivances, although the theme of flight and pursuit is still the chief pattern of the action, are replaced by the devices of "modern" fiction: the skeptical narrator, stream-of-consciousness technique, flashback, diary, interior reverie, spiritual debate, the found or discovered letter—all are used with discrimination and insight. Indeed, *The End of the*

Affair is the most Jamesian of Greene's novels and also the one that most confirms in his work the influences of François Mauriac and Ford Madox Ford.

The function of Bendrix, Sarah's lover and the chief narrator of the novel, is to maintain a secular perspective on the events of the affair and to comment on the religious—here it might be more applicable to say Catholic—aspects of the theme. Like Charles Ryder in Evelyn Waugh's *Brideshead Revisited*, Bendrix is skeptical about what he calls the religious "hanky-panky" of the action, yet is the one left to make a final assessment of the meaning of the love affair. His last physical action is to begin writing the story of his and Sarah's relationship, and the implication is that perhaps he, too, will learn to accept the reality of a divine force.

Bendrix's account of the affair dwells on its carnal side, its passionate side. Having established this point of view, Greene allows Sarah's diary to fall into her jealous lover's hands; in this way Bendrix becomes aware of the spiritual struggle which is the basis of the novel. A third point of view is achieved by Parkis, an inept detective hired by Bendrix to spy on Sarah; a fourth by Sarah's husband Henry; and a fifth by Richard Smythe, a "rationalist" to whom Sarah goes in her need to deny the God who insists on her sanctity. But it is Bendrix who correlates and assesses these points of view. Here the reader finds himself in the same novelistic milieu that Ford Madox Ford so brilliantly describes in *The Good Soldier*, except that Bendrix's jealousy makes him infinitely more human than Dowell could ever be.

Sarah Miles's reluctant decision to prefer God over Bendrix is occasioned by her promise to give up Bendrix if God will allow him to live: she thinks he has been killed by a bomb that falls on the house where they have been making love. At first she tries to forget the promise, but she cannot. She suffers, as had Major Scobie before her, but her suffering teaches her to believe staunchly in the God who restored Bendrix. Her faith becomes her trust; and Greene insists that this trust is as firm as that which gave strength to the greatest saints. Sarah writes to Bendrix:

> "I believe there's a God—I believe the whole bag of tricks; there's nothing I don't believe; they could subdivide the Trinity into a dozen parts and I'd believe. They could dig up records that Christ had been invented by Pilate to get himself promoted and I'd believe just the same. I've caught belief like a disease. I've fallen into belief like I fell in love."

The End of the Affair is technically Greene's masterpiece. The diary and the journal, the flashback, and the reverie all allow him not only to characterize his actors but also to present the various levels of Sarah and Bendrix's spiritual dilemmas. If *Brighton Rock* and *The*

Power and the Glory owe something to Eliot's *The Waste Land,* then *The End of the Affair* owes as much to *Ash Wednesday,* for penance and acceptance condition the atmosphere of the novel. If Major Scobie fails in matters of trust, it is in these same matters of trust that Sarah Miles triumphs.

2

Allegory and all the excitement occasioned by the contrivances of melodrama had given Greene ample latitude to develop his themes in *Brighton Rock* and *The Power and the Glory,* and, to some extent, in *The Heart of the Matter.* The need to explain, clarify, and define had been a partial stimulus for his writing these books. But in *The End of the Affair* Greene discovered little need to allegorize, and melodrama was kept to a minimum. The four novels indeed describe a single pattern, a movement, from definition and qualification of a religious conviction to a thumping avowal of the reality of goodness in the real world. But one cannot forget that goodness had been present in the world of *Brighton Rock:* one need only compare Rose to Sarah Miles to understand what tremendous strides Greene made between 1938 and 1951 in both characterization and novelistic technique.

Between the publication of *The End of the Affair* in 1951 and the appearance of *The Comedians* in 1966, Greene wrote two major novels, *The Quiet American* in 1955, and *A Burnt-Out Case* in 1961. Set in Indo-China, *The Quiet American* exploits in terms of Conradian doubles the implications of political innocence and philosophical experience. The English journalist Fowler is paralleled by Alden Pyle, a naive American intent on establishing contact with a mysterious power cult headed by an equally mysterious General Thé. While paying lip service to the tenets of contemporary Existential thought, *The Quiet American* is in reality a further illustration of the themes that interested Greene in *The Ministry of Fear* and *The Heart of the Matter:* the fascination of power and its destructive potential.

Pyle's political innocence is paralleled by Fowler's knowledge of the politics centering on the war-ravaged zone surrounding Vietnam and its neighboring countries. At the novel's end Fowler is forced to betray Pyle in order to keep the "innocent" American from contributing to the deaths of innocent people. Criticized by many American reviewers for its anti-American feeling, *The Quiet American* nevertheless makes a cogent point in a startling manner: what Greene intends, first, is to demonstrate satirically his belief that money cannot buy peace and security in a world coerced by power addicts; and, second, to insist that in a world on the brink of destruction, a man

must choose to remain human, even if his choice in
equanimity dearly bought and paid for.

At the end of the novel Fowler says of the man
to the Communists, " 'Am I the only one who really
Although on the surface *The Quiet American* se
the Existentialist formula of engagement and to giv
angoisse necessary to a full appreciation of human
novel actually takes a sidewise glance at the theme
of Major Scobie's sentimentality and high-sounding purpose, Fowler's
reasons for betraying Pyle appear simply as egotism: the aspect of
pity is perhaps replaced by that of compassion, much more difficult
to appreciate. Fowler says, "I know myself and the depth of my
selfishness. I cannot be at ease (and to be at ease is my chief wish)
if someone is in pain. . . . Sometimes this is mistaken by the innocent for unselfishness, when all I am doing is sacrificing a small
good . . . for the sake of a far greater good, a peace of mind, when
I need think only of myself.' " Despite this assertion Fowler wishes
after Pyle's death that there were someone to whom he could say
he was sorry.

In the introduction to *A Burnt-Out Case,* Greene says that the
task of writing the novel proved so difficult that he felt the effort
involved in writing still another to be beyond him. Indeed, there
is something enervated about *A Burnt-Out Case,* even though the
craftsmanship of the novel is superb. The Conradian elements emerge
clearly and forcibly, even humorously at times, but on the whole
the novel remains unconvincing and the hero's plight unmoving. However, the ambience of *The Comedians,* published in 1966, must have
renewed Greene's interest in the art of the novel, and his effort was re-
warded; it is one of the very best of his books and as exciting and
compelling as any of those written between 1929 and 1951.

The Comedians is a black comedy, full of broad farcical touches
paralleled by frightening melodramatic innuendoes. Perhaps the most
significant aspect of the novel is that it gives evidence of a shifting
attitude on Greene's part toward his Maker as well as toward his
fellow man. *The Comedians* also elaborates more fully on the theme
of innocence, best exploited previously in *The Quiet American.* There,
Alden Pyle, thematically Fowler's alter ego, is the committed man;
once investigated, however, the nature of his commitment is found
wanting. Through Pyle Greene attempts to indicate that innocence
uninformed by experience is dangerous in a world menaced by
power cults. In *The Quiet American* Fowler is forced to sacrifice
Pyle to the cause of what he hopes to be higher humanity, although he
is by no means certain of his personal motivations. What Fowler
does know, and know for certain, is that he cannot resist the appeal

bodies mangled by the explosion of Pyle's plastic bombs. In *Burnt-Out Case* the architect Querry makes his voyage into the heart of Africa to rediscover the springs of innocence. Led by Deo Gratias, a mutilated leper, to the very borders of innocence, Pendalé, Querry comes near to rediscovering the goodness he lost years before.

The hero, or rather antihero (for such he is), of *The Comedians* is a man simply named Brown. (There are also characters within the plot called Smith and Jones: the point, perhaps, is to lend an Everyman aspect to the narrative.) With Brown, Greene attempts to define further the nature of innocence and that experience which is its opposite. In Greene's world, power is one of the many disguises of evil, and in *The Comedians* the fear engendered by power becomes the device by which the question of innocence is forced into prominence. The fact of the matter is that Greene in his last three novels has moved away from the highly stylized and symbolical representations—representations first employed in *Brighton Rock* and set aside after *The End of the Affair*—and has entered a new dimension, the outlines of which can only now be perceived.

Greene entitles his latest book *The Comedians*, and in the course of the novel's activity attempts to define what he means by the word "comedians," which, in turn, requires his establishing a definition of comedy. "'Neither of us would ever die for love,'" says Brown to his mistress, Martha. "'We would grieve and separate and find another. We belong to the world of comedy and not of tragedy.'" If *The Comedians* is a comedy, it is certainly not one in the accepted meaning of the term, nor in the Dantean sense; rather, it is Greene's version of contemporary black humor: there is no movement from despair to happiness—there is movement only from horror to despair.

The comedians are the pretenders, those who play a part, those neither good enough nor grand enough for tragedy—perhaps because Greene's world no longer allows for tragic action. Martha's husband, the ambassador of a small, unnamed South American country, says, "'Come on, cheer up . . . let us all be comedians together . . . it's an honorable profession. If we could be good ones the world might gain at least a sense of style.'" But it is difficult to recognize the comedians, for frequently those who appear to be best qualified to play a part reach a point at which the part overwhelms them—the reality and the drama coalesce, or, to borrow Yeats's phrase, the dancer becomes indistinguishable from the dance. Occasionally one who assumes a role becomes the character he portrays, yet ironically the face he presents to the world continues to reveal eccentricity and grotesqueness. The comedians are nevertheless the worthwhile. They form a small troupe of initiates in a power-coerced and fear-ridden world. Still, it would be wrong to call tragedians those who manage to transcend the limitations of the role they play, for Greene's world, having once accommodated tragic action, no longer does so: at the novel's end the Haitian patriots are found symbolically housed in an abandoned insane asylum in Santo Domingo.

This question of innocence is at once the crux of and the key to the novels and the entertainments (*Our Man in Havana* appeared in 1958) published since Greene left off working with the anatomy of sainthood in *The End of the Affair*. In Sarah Miles, the strongest of his women characters, Greene carries the theme he had first presented in *Brighton Rock* to a final and disquieting conclusion—the impossibility of recognizing sainthood in a world hostile to saints, a world seemingly dedicated to the destruction of goodness. The recently published story, "Beneath the Garden," included in the collection significantly entitled *A Sense of Reality* (1963), is a further illustration of Greene's renewed interest in the anatomy of innocence, for that story is an expressionistic, occasionally absurd, and frequently humorous attempt to rediscover the point at which innocence was lost, to be replaced by the cynicism of experience.

The setting of *The Comedians* is contemporary Haiti under the dictatorship of Dr. Duvalier, "Papa Doc." Greene writes:

> Poor Haiti itself and the character of Doctor Duvalier's rule are not invented, the latter not even blackened for dramatic effect. Impossible to deepen the night. The Tontons Macoute are full of men more evil than Concasseur; the interrupted funeral is drawn from fact; many a Joseph limps the streets of Port-au-Prince after his spell of torture, and, though I have never met the young Philipot, I have met guerrillas as courageous and as ill-trained in that former lunatic asylum near Santo Domingo. Only in Santo Domingo have things changed since I began this book—for the worse.

Like a Kafka enigma, Papa Doc remains mysteriously within his palace, his laws enforced by the Tontons Macoute, bogey-men, whose insignia are slouched hats and sunglasses, behind which they hide their uncertainties. The Voodoo element comes into play in the course of the novel's action, and an equation is drawn between Papa Doc and Baron Samedi, the prince of the dead of Voodoo belief. The Tontons approximate a mysterious fraternity of terror infinitely more menacing than that of the cultists. The chief representative of the power cult in the novel is Captain Concasseur, who is responsible for the mutilation and emasculation of Joseph, Brown's servant in the hotel Trianon.

Brown, Smith, and Jones arrive in Port-au-Prince on a Dutch vessel ominously called the *Medea*, Brown to return to his luxury hotel which he has been unsuccessfully trying to sell in the United States; Smith, a former presidential candidate who ran against Truman on

a vegetarian ticket in 1948, together with his wife, to set up a vegetarian center; and Jones, an inept adventurer who calls himself "Major,"
to engage in a military maneuver of dubious nature.

Brown has been conducting a love affair with Martha Pineda, the
wife of a South American diplomat. She is the mother of a five-year-
old child, Angel, whose claims keep her from abandoning her family
for Brown, whom she says she loves. The affair, bittersweet and
reminiscent of many love triangles in Greene's fiction, is resumed the
night Brown returns to Haiti. Brown admits several times that what
he seeks in a love affair is not so much happiness as defeat; and
ironically there is a sort of success at the novel's end—Brown and
Martha both realize once they are safely over the border in Santo
Domingo that their love affair belongs peculiarly to Port-au-Prince,
that it was but the reflection of the horror and terror of the times.

Brown has been brought up a Catholic, but he is unlike the Catholics Greene has previously portrayed. The passionate pity of both
Scobie and Fowler has given way to a tragicomic compassion, which
is also the chief mood of the novel; Brown is much more tolerant
of success than any of Greene's other heroes, but he is infinitely less
loving. His Catholicism is not the leper's bell that it is to both the
whisky priest and Sarah Miles; it is instead a cloak of indifference,
a means whereby the stupidities and the atrocities of the world can
be warded off, and perhaps explained. Brown's Catholicism becomes
for him a standard of measurement, in Haiti a valid one, for Catholicism liberally sprinkled with Voodooism is the religion of the majority.

Through the Smiths, or perhaps because of the Smiths, Greene
expresses a certain amount of anti-American sentiment reminiscent
of *The Quiet American*. Dr. Magiot remarks at one point:

> We are an evil scum floating a few miles from Florida, and no American
> will help us with arms or money or counsel. We learned a few years back
> what their counsel meant. There was a resistance group here who were
> in touch with a sympathizer in the American embassy: they were prom-
> ised all kinds of moral support, but the information went straight back
> to the C.I.A. by a very direct route to Papa Doc. You can imagine what
> happened to the group. The state department didn't want any disturbance
> in the Caribbean.

Although he bears much in common with Alden Pyle of *The Quiet
American*, the good vegetarian Mr. Smith is by no means the same
sort of deluded innocent. He is capable of appreciating the oppor-
tunism and graft-seeking of the corrupt Tontons Macoute; and he
even has the courage to admit that his vision of setting up an American Vegetarian Center in either Port-au-Prince or the new city, Du-
valierville, is impractical. Despite their being vehicles for caustic

satire, Mr. and Mrs. Smith emerge as the two strongest characters in the novel; they are saved by their humanity, by their certainty that there is goodness in the world. Ultimately, it is their dedication to their cause, their sincere and straightforward desire to better the human predicament—by reducing acidity in the human body—that makes them acceptable.

It is also through the Smiths that the theme of commitment enters the novel, again satirically. As in *The Quiet American*, Existentialism is used as a philosophical determinant, but in this novel it is not so much obscured by religious considerations. Furthermore, the jargon of Existentialism is kept to a minimum and the theme emerges more cogently, demonstrated as it is in the action of the comedians who make up the drama.

"Major" Jones, who at first appears to be the biggest fraud of all, one of the "tarts," as he puts it, is a committed man by the novel's end; but his commitment is comically handled. He passes himself off as an organizer of military affairs, but he fools only those who wish to be fooled. He dreams, he invents, and he deludes, at times even himself. But there is something about the man that endears him to others. Tin Tin, the girl at Mère Catherine's bordello, likes him because he makes her laugh; and Brown's mistress Martha, in whose embassy Jones takes shelter when his bogus papers are discovered by Captain Concasseur, likes him too, and for the same reason—he makes her laugh. Brown, we are told, has never learned the trick of laughter.

Together with Dr. Magiot, a committed Communist, Brown arranges for Jones to escape the Tontons and to join the partisans, who under Philipot, a one-time Baudelairean poet, are attempting to unseat Papa Doc in bumbling and ineffectual ways. However, Brown's decision to help the partisans is motivated not by a feeling for the rightness of their cause, or by the danger and the excitement, or by his awareness of the childlike innocence of their exploit, but by the unreasoning jealousy that he feels toward Jones. Again, the reader is reminded of Fowler. Jones is a comedian within the broadest meaning of the term; but unlike Brown who cannot—perhaps because of early Roman Catholic training—he can follow the gleam, and there comes a point where the dream and reality coalesce. In his last glimpse of Jones, the reader sees him limping along, unable to keep up with the partisans because of his flat feet. He remains behind, a comical version of Hemingway's Robert Jordan, to fire upon the Tontons in order to make it possible for those he has grown to love to survive, if only temporarily.

Of all the major comedians, Brown alone remains uncommitted. He is a con man grown old, whose most successful venture had been peddling bad pictures to the nouveaux riches. His mother's post-card had brought him to the Trianon, and one of her first questions had been, "'What part are you playing now?'" After her death, Brown had discovered among her papers a note she had written to her young lover: "'Marcel, I know I'm an old woman and as you say a bit of an actress. But please go on pretending. As long as we pretend we escape. Pretend that I love you like a mistress. Pretend that I would die for you and that you would die for me.'" Brown's love affair with Martha, however, is something more than just pretending; it is a desperate attempt to capture stability in a fear-menaced world, and it is compounded as much of the desire to inflict pain as it is of a desire to dominate. For several years Brown has prospered, achieving a false sense of security; but the coming of Papa Doc and the Tontons has destroyed not only his business but his sense of belonging as well. He finds himself involved with innocence, with the Smiths and with Jones, who, thematically, serve to set off and to illustrate his failure.

The problem of Brown's Roman Catholicism is an important one in understanding both the characterization of Brown himself and the theme of the novel; it is indeed the chief challenge of the book. The Voodoo black mass in which Brown's servant Joseph partici-pates makes a sensational counterpoint to the religious importunities of the novel; the figure of Baron Samedi is associated with Papa Doc, the personification of evil. But the black mass does not necessarily sug-gest a breakdown of religion. At the novel's end, it is contrasted with the mass the priest reads over the body of Joseph in the insane asylum in Santo Domingo where the partisans are cared for. Brown's failure, then, does not illustrate a religious breakdown; it is a failure of character.

Brown's failure is his inability to accept reality, and it can best be explained in Existential terms. He can detect innocence, appreci-ate goodness, admire courage, and—even if for the wrong motives—help the cause of right. But he is so good a comedian that he cannot transcend the limitations imposed by the role. All the religious im-plications seem like so much rationalization on Brown's part, and he fools neither himself nor the reader. Brown can appreciate com-mitment: to retain his self-esteem, to support his ego, he is forced into comedy. Although his sympathies are with Dr. Magiot, Philipot, and the partisan cause, Brown makes no real commitment to any-thing, not to love, not to religion, not to God, not to innocence. It is only right that at the novel's end Brown becomes a partner in the undertaking business. In his black suit and black hat he appears a comic Baron Samedi. He belongs to the world of the dead and not to that of the living, and symbolically and literally he serves the dead.

Since the appearance of *The Man Within* critics have accused Greene of being pessimistic. The truth of the matter is that he is not a cheerful writer, but *The Comedians,* tragicomic though it is, and full of comic touches and humor of a macabre and grotesque nature, is the gloomiest of his novels to date. At least Major Scobie loves God, in his own mistaken way; at least the whisky priest finds honor, albeit unwillingly; and Sarah Miles achieves a sort of gratuitous sainthood. Querry in *A Burnt-Out Case* finds the hint of an explanation; he glimpses Pendelé. But there is only a pathetic part left for Brown to play in *The Comedians.* There is not even the saving factor of remorse as in *The Quiet American;* for Fowler wishes at the end of that novel that there were someone to whom he could say he is sorry for his participation in Pyle's death. Fowler at least is spurred to action after witnessing the carnage caused by Pyle's plastic explosives. He does what he does because he loves. But there is no real love in Brown, only ego. Jones and Smith may indeed illustrate contrasting aspects of the theme of innocence, but within the pattern of the novel they serve merely as foils to set off the failure of the individual.

IGNAZIO SILONE AND THE PSEUDONYMS OF GOD

Robert McAfee Brown

I could easily spin out my existence writing and rewriting the same story in the hope that I might end up understanding it and making it clear to others; just as in the Middle Ages there were monks whose entire lives were devoted to painting the face of Christ over and over again.

—preface to the revised version of Fontamara

1

A first reading of Silone might give the impression that he is "dated." He is clearly writing about the struggle of Italian peasants against fascism in the 1930's, and about the lure of communism during that period as a possible alternative to the status quo. It could be argued that his works are no more than an interesting series of canvases depicting what life was like in a period and geographical setting now remote from us.

But to whatever degree Silone's main works were hammered out on the anvil of concern for the downtrodden and oppressed, and to whatever extent they rose out of particular challenges presented by fascism and communism, their author has rightly seen that the story of the human spirit, threatened but not overcome during that period, is the story of the human spirit threatened but not overcome during every period.

Although the novels as originally written could stand on their own even today, Silone has employed the unusual device of re-writing a number of them, excising the materials that tie them too closely to the period of their origin, in order that the perennial concerns with which they deal may stand out in bolder relief. This he has done so far with *Fontamara* (1934, 1960), *Bread and Wine* (1937, 1962), *The School for Dictators* (1938, 1963), and *The Seed Beneath the Snow* (1942, 1965).

"Ignazio Silone and the Pseudonyms of God." Reprinted from The Shapeless God: Essays on Modern Fiction, Harry J. Mooney, Jr. and Thomas F. Staley, editors, by permission of the University of Pittsburgh Press. © 1968 by the University of Pittsburgh Press.

Whether the device is successful or even wise, the revised novels do force certain ongoing questions upon the reader, the events of the 1930's assume a disturbing relevance in the light of the events of the 1960's, and each one becomes a parable of contemporary human concerns. The parallels between the Italian "liberation" of Ethiopia and the American "liberation" of Vietnam are disturbing; the indictment of the indifference of the Italian church in the 1930's becomes an indictment of the indifference of the American church in the 1960's; and the disillusionment of the revolutionary in Silone's novels may foreshadow some of the problems with which the New Left must shortly come to grips.

The story Silone tells is, as he says, "the same story"—a story that needs retelling for each generation and in terms understandable to each generation. It is a story that is often told without explicit reference to the three-letter word g-o-d, but it is a story that is always grappling with what that word has meant for men, and with what the reality to which it is dimly pointing still means for men. Silone, deeply steeped in a Christian faith he has formally or at least institutionally rejected, finds it impossible to deal with that which has spoken most deeply to the human spirit without employing the imagery of Christian faith and Christian history. It is hard for one of sensitive conscience to affirm God's presence in the kind of world Silone depicts, so gross are the inequities between men, so brutal is the destruction of human values by nature using impersonal power and men using power impersonally. And yet, if God is absent, His absence is a kind of creative one, and is indeed almost a brooding presence, the presence of a God virtually at the mercy of His world; a God who, if He has visited His tortured planet, has gone into hiding; a God who, when He wishes to assert Himself, must employ pseudonyms—false names—in order to communicate a healing word. That Silone has faith in a God not dead but hidden, a God found (when He is found) in the most unlikely places, is surely a central fact in that "same story" which Silone continues "writing and re-writing."

2

Dangerous though it is to use the events of an author's life as a means of understanding his works, the device is particularly helpful in the case of Silone, since his own pilgrimage is so close to that of many of the characters in his novels.

The terrible injustices of life around him were borne in upon Silone at an early age, as he recounts in an episode the reader might imagine to have come from one of his novels:

> I was a child just five years old when, one Sunday, while crossing the little square of my native village with my mother leading me by the hand, I witnessed the cruel, stupid spectacle of one of the local gentry setting his great dog at a poor woman, a seamstress, who was just coming out of church. The wretched woman was flung to the ground, badly mauled, and her dress was torn to ribbons. Indignation in the village was general, but silent. I have never understood how the poor woman ever got the unhappy idea of taking proceedings against the squire; but the only result was to add a mockery of justice to the harm already done. Although, I must repeat, everybody pitied her and many people helped her secretly, the unfortunate woman could not find a single witness prepared to give evidence before the magistrate, nor a lawyer to conduct the prosecution. On the other hand, the squire's supposedly Left-Wing lawyer turned up punctually, and so did a number of bribed witnesses, who perjured themselves by giving a grotesque version of what had happened, and accusing the woman of having provoked the dog. The magistrate—a most worthy, honest person in private life—acquitted the squire and condemned the poor woman to pay the costs.[1]

It became clear to Silone that attempts to combat such gross miscarriages of justice were not going to be effected through ordinary political means, since the whole system was rigged against the peasants. He describes the decision of the large landowner, "the Prince," to run for public office:

> The Prince was deigning to solicit "his" families for their vote so that he could become their deputy in parliament. The agents of the estate, who were working for the Prince, talked in impeccably liberal phrases: "Naturally," said they, "naturally, no one will be forced to vote for the Prince, that's understood; in the same way that no one, naturally, can force the Prince to allow people who don't vote for him to work on his land. This is the period of real liberty for everybody; you're free, and so is the Prince."[2]

The church played no role in the struggle, except to condone by its silence the activities of the landlords against the peasants. Its priests were indifferent to the peasants' fight for justice, and anxious to support the status quo. Silone recalls seeing a puppet show in which the devil marionette asked the village children where the child in the show was hiding. The children instinctively lied to save the child from the devil.

> Our parish priest, a most worthy, cultured and pious person, was not altogether pleased. We had told a lie, he warned us with a worried look. We had told it for good ends, of course, but still it remained a lie. One must never tell lies. "Not even to the devil?" we asked in surprise. "A lie is always a sin," the priest replied. "Even to the magistrate?" asked one of the boys. The priest rebuked him severely. "I'm here to teach you Christian

---

[1] Richard Crossman, ed., *The God That Failed* (New York, 1949), p. 83.
[2] *Ibid.*, p. 86.

doctrine and not to talk nonsense. *What happens outside the church is no concern of mine."*[3]

Faced by injustice and dismayed by the impotence he felt at the possibility of bringing about change through ordinary political means or through the church, Silone joined the Communist party. He was a member for many years. But disillusionment with the party came too, in terms described later in this essay by Uliva, the disillusioned revolutionary of *Bread and Wine*. For Silone, and for Uliva, communism was indeed (in the title of the symposium from which the above excerpts are taken) "the god that failed." An act of faith had been made, an allegiance had been manifested, a commitment had been offered, and the god to whom the faith, the allegiance, and the commitment were made turned out to be a false god, an idol, a human creation rather than a deity worth dying for.

Silone finally left the party. He did not become a cynic, however, and after his departure he could still give voice to a positive credo that had been won at the cost of many scars:

> My faith in Socialism (to which I think I can say my entire life bears testimony) has remained more alive than ever in me. In its essence, it has gone back to what it was when I first revolted against the old social order; a refusal to admit the existence of destiny, an extension of the ethical impulse from the restricted individual and family sphere to the whole domain of human activity, a need for effective brotherhood, an affirmation of the superiority of the human person over all the economic and social mechanisms which oppress him. As the years have gone by, there has been added to this an intuition of man's dignity and a feeling of reverence for that which in man is always trying to outdistance itself, and lies at the root of his eternal disquiet.[4]

3

Where is God in the tangle in which Silone's political concerns have involved him? Where, in the novels written out of this experience, can one look for the divine reality? How does God relate to Silone's "intuition of man's dignity," to his "feeling of reverence for that which in man is always trying to outdistance itself," and to man's "eternal disquiet?" It will not do to try to make an orthodox Christian out of Silone, but as we shall see, he draws heavily on orthodox and Biblical imagery in dealing with the brooding presence of the divine. A description of five interrelated themes may help us to see how the "shapeless god" takes shape in Silone's writings.

1. One might initially expect God would be found within the in-

---

[3] *Ibid.*, p. 85. Italics added. Silone later told the priest that if the devil marionette ever asked where the priest was, he would cheerfully give him the priest's address.

[4] *Ibid.*, pp. 113-114.

stitution that exists to give Him honor and praise, and that the church might be the abode of His human dwelling. But the church, if it once gave witness to a Master who came not to be served but to serve, seemingly does so no more. So there is in Silone's fiction *a strong critique of the church.* Don Benedetto, a priest in *Bread and Wine* who has been removed from his post because of his advanced ideas, suggests to a colleague that the church should condemn Mussolini's war against Ethiopia. Don Angelo, a conservative priest, recounts the conversation to Don Paolo:

> I replied, "But can you imagine what would happen if the Church were openly to condemn the present war? What persecutions it would undergo? What material and moral damage would be done?" You have no idea what Don Benedetto dared to answer me. "My dear Don Angelo," he answered, "can you imagine John the Baptist offering a concordat to Herod to escape decapitation? Can you imagine Jesus offering a concordat to Pontius Pilate to avoid being crucified?"
>
> "That doesn't seem to me to be an anti-Christian answer," said Don Paolo.
>
> "But the Church is not a society in the abstract," said Don Angelo, raising his voice. "It is what it is. It's almost two thousand years old. It's not like a little girl who can permit herself all kinds of headstrong caprices. It's like an old, a very old lady, full of dignity, prestige, traditions, and rights tied to duties. Of course there was Jesus Who was crucified and Who founded her; but after Him there were the apostles and generations upon generations of saints and popes. The Church is no longer a clandestine sect in the catacombs. It has millions and millions of souls in its following who need her protection."[5]

But it is not only the far-off war against Ethiopia that the church will not condemn. There is another war nearer at hand, the war against injustice and poverty, with which the church refuses to involve itself. The story of this futile war is told poignantly in *Fontamara,* Silone's earliest novel. The peasants are tricked out of their water rights. The workers are tricked out of their pay by hidden taxes that become visible too late. When a movement of protest is finally launched, the town is pillaged, the women are raped, and finally the whole of Fontamara is destroyed. The book ends with the despairing cry:

> What can we do?
> After so much suffering, so many tears, and so many wounds, so much hate, injustice, and desperation—
> WHAT CAN WE DO?[6]

What they can do is what the narrators of *Fontamara* did—they can join the revolutionary forces.

---

[5] Ignazio Silone, *Bread and Wine* (New York, 1962), p. 267.
[6] Ignazio Silone, *Fontamara* (New York, 1961), p. 224.

What they cannot do is look to the church for help. The indictment of the church for its silence is epitomized by the dream of Zompa early in the book. The Pope and the Crucifix have a little talk. The Crucifix suggests all sorts of things the Pope could do for the people: the land could be given to the people, for example. The Pope counters that the Prince wouldn't have it, and the Prince is a good Christian. Christ then suggests that the peasants could be exonerated from their taxes; the Pope replies that the government officials couldn't think of that, and they are good Christians too. In response to the suggestion that the peasants be sent a good crop, the Pope replies that if there is a good crop, prices will go down and the merchants will be ruined; and the merchants are likewise good Christians. Finally Christ and the Pope visit the villages, with Christ carrying a knapsack from which the Pope can take anything that will do the peasants some good:

> The two Heavenly Travelers saw the same thing in every village, and what else could they see? The peasants were lamenting, swearing, fighting, not knowing what to wear nor what to eat. So the Pope felt his heart breaking, and he took from the sack a cloud of lice of a new species and sent them to the houses of the poor, saying, "Take them, O beloved children, and scratch. Thus in your moments of temporal hate there will be something to take your thoughts away from sin."[7]

In *Bread and Wine* another priest, Don Piccirelli, writes a paper on "The Scourge of Our Times." Don Benedetto asks him hopefully, "Have you written about war or unemployment?"

> "Those are political questions," answered Don Piccirelli stiffly. "In the diocesan bulletin we deal only with religious questions. From a purely spiritual point of view, the scourge of our times, in my opinion, is an immodest way of dressing."[8]

So much for the church's contribution to the social ills of men. It is no wonder that Rocco, in *A Handful of Blackberries*, gets up one day in the middle of mass and leaves the church, never to return. He suddenly realizes that those present are neither hot nor cold, and that God will spew them out of his mouth. Rocco chooses the poor as his comrades and makes his way into the Communist party, so that he can work for the social justice he has found the church ignoring. If God is a God who cares for those whom He has created, it is clear that the institution perpetuating His name has desecrated that name beyond redemption.

2. Where, then, is God found? Perhaps the God who appears to

---

[7] *Ibid.*, p. 35.
[8] *Bread and Wine*, p. 23.

have been deserted by his church may be working in hidden fashion elsewhere. This possibility brings us to the heart of Silone's theme, his conviction that *God carries on His work through pseudonyms.*

Don Benedetto, the elderly priest in *Bread and Wine,* makes the point most directly: "In times of conspiratorial and secret struggle, the Lord is obliged to hide Himself and assume pseudonyms. Besides, and you know it, He does not attach very much importance to His name. . . . Might not the ideal of social justice that animates the masses today be one of the pseudonyms the Lord is using to free Himself from the control of the churches and the banks?"[9]

Lest this seem too new an idea, too unorthodox in its implications, Don Benedetto makes clear in a conversation with his former student Spina, now a revolutionary, that it has a long history:

> This would not be the first time that the Eternal Father felt obligated to hide Himself and take a pseudonym. As you know, He has never taken the first name and the last name men have fastened on Him very seriously; quite to the contrary, He has warned men not to name Him in vain as His first commandment. And then, the Scriptures are full of clandestine life. Have you ever considered the real meaning of the flight into Egypt? And later, when he was an adult, was not Jesus forced several times to hide Himself and flee from the Judaeans?[10]

Don Benedetto also recalls the story of Elijah's encounter with God (1 Kings 19:9-13). God was not present in the wind or the earthquake or the fire—the accustomed signs of divine theophany in those times. He was present, unexpectedly, in a sound of soft stillness. So too today, he may not be present in the open and public ways men expect him, but may be found in quiet, hidden, unexpected deeds, in the pseudonymous activity of humble men. Reflecting on the Elijah story, Don Benedetto continues, describing certain actions in which he knows Spina to have been involved:

> I, too, in the dregs of my afflictions, have asked myself: where is God and why has He abandoned us? Certainly the loudspeakers and bells announcing the new slaughter were not God. Nor were the cannon shots and the bombing of the Ethiopian villages, of which we read every day in the newspapers. But if one poor man gets up in the middle of the night and writes on the walls of the village with a piece of charcoal or varnish, "Down with the War," the presence of God is undoubtedly behind that man. How can one not recognize the divine light in his scorn of danger and in his love for the so-called enemies? Thus, if some simple workmen

---

[9] *Bread and Wine* (earlier edition: New York, 1946), pp. 247-248.
[10] *Bread and Wine,* p. 274. The latter theme is developed in Silone's stage version of *Bread and Wine,* entitled *And He Did Hide Himself,* the Biblical reference being John 12:36: "These things spake Jesus and departed, and did hide himself from them."

are condemned for these reasons by a special tribunal, there's no need to hesitate to know where God stands.[11]

The unexpectedness of the divine activity, the fact that God may choose to work through pseudonyms is, as Don Benedetto acknowledges, a familiar theme in Jewish and Christian history. The prophet Isaiah warned that in an ensuing battle between Israel and the Assyrians, the power of the Lord would be revealed, but he made clear that the revelation would come not through the chosen people of Israel but through the pagans of Assyria. Assyria would be the "rod of God's anger," even though the king of Assyria had no idea he was being so used, and would have scoffed at the very notion.[12] Paul Tillich often talks in similar fashion of "the latent church," the unexpected instrument through which the divine may manifest itself, and which may be quite different from the institutional church.[13] Pascal similarly puts great store by Isaiah's discussion of the hidden God: "Truly, thou art a God who hidest thyself."[14] God can raise up children of Abraham from the very stones around him. Since the churches do not serve Him, it may be that the revolutionary forces can, and Don Benedetto later says of Spina, "Socialism is his way of serving God."[15]

At different periods of history, God may employ different pseudonyms. During the particular period about which Silone is writing, when the grossest denial of God is the inequity between rich and poor, it can be expected that the manifestations of God's presence will be found not among the rich, not among the landlords, not among the heads of state, but among the peasants. It is therefore highly consistent that the Christ figures in Silone's novels are drawn from among the peasants (Berardo and Murica) or those who identify with the peasants (Spina). The theme is present in *Fontamara*. Berardo, one of the peasants who participates in the abortive uprising against the landlords, is taken to jail, where he gets to know "the Solitary Stranger," the man seeking to organize the peasants. Realizing how important it is for the Solitary Stranger to be at liberty, Berardo confesses to the crimes of which the Solitary Stranger has been charged, in order that the latter may be released. Berardo feels his own life can have a meaning if he dies not for himself but for someone else, and for a cause greater than himself. After Berardo's confession the authorities beat him up, and "finally they led him

---

[11] *Ibid.*, pp. 275-276.
[12] Cf. Isaiah 10:5-19.
[13] Cf. most recently in *Systematic Theology*, III (Chicago: University of Chicago Press, 1963), esp. pp. 152-154.
[14] Blaise Pascal, *Pensées*, Nos. 194, 242. The Scriptural reference is to Isaiah 45:15.
[15] *Bread and Wine*, p. 305.

back to the cell, holding him by the arms and legs, like Christ when he was taken off the Cross."[16]

Berardo lays down his life for his friends, and his action finally galvanizes the peasants into action; they form a newspaper to give voice to their opposition to the landowners. They are crushed, as we have seen earlier, for victory is not yet something that is promised by God to men—a theme to which we shall presently return.

3. Silone, after his espousal of the revolutionary cause, does not become uncritical in that espousal. God may indeed choose to work pseudonymously through the forces of revolution, and socialism may indeed be a way of serving God, but Silone sees clearly that *the revolutionary forces, like the church, may also become corrupted.* When they do, they deny the God they unknowingly have served. The disillusionment of the revolutionary in several of Silone's novels mirrors the disillusionment that emerged from his own years as a communist. In *Bread and Wine*, Uliva, the disillusioned revolutionary, shocks Spina by the forcefulness of his attack upon that in which he once believed. Speaking about what will happen after the revolution, he says,

> Yes, I don't deny that there'll be technical and economic changes. Just as we now have the state railways and the state quinine, salt, matches and tobacco, so then we'll have state bread, state peas and potatoes. Will that be technical progress? Let's admit that it would be. But this technical progress will be an opening wedge for a compulsory official doctrine, for a totalitarian orthodoxy which will use all means, from movies to terrorism, to stamp out any heresy and tyrannize individual thought. The present black inquisition will be followed by a red inquisition. There'll be red censorship instead of the present one, and red deportations will take the place of the ones we have now—and the most favored victims will be dissident revolutionaries. In the same way, just as the present bureaucracy identifies itself with the fatherland and exterminates every opponent, denouncing him as a hireling of the foreigners, your future bureaucracy will identify itself with labor and Socialism and will persecute anyone who continues to think with his own head, as a prized agent of the big landowners and the industrialists. . . .
>
> For a long time I've been bothered about this: why have all revolutions, every single one of them, begun as movements of liberation and ended as tyrannies? Why hasn't even one revolution escaped from this?[17]

Shortly after this outburst Uliva demonstrates the existential reality of his disillusionment by blowing himself and his wife—along with a considerable portion of their apartment house—to bits.

The same theme is stressed in *A Handful of Blackberries.* Rocco, who walked out of church one day and joined the Communist party, makes the discovery that "the Party of today is not what it used to

---

[16] *Fontamara*, p. 211.
[17] *Bread and Wine*, pp. 210-211.

be. It was a party of the persecuted, now it is a party of persecutors."[18] So Rocco has to leave the party as well, and there remains for him only a life of lonely protest against all forms of corruption, a life spent as part of a remnant able to do little but wait for a day of deliverance that has not yet come.

What has gone wrong? Why has the revolutionary cause fallen victim to the malady it was trying to correct? For what reason does it become increasingly difficult for Silone to identify God's pseudonyms with the forces of revolution?

Perhaps the clearest answer is that in his concern for revolution on behalf of man, man himself becomes dehumanized, and must find his way back from impersonal ideology to a recovery of humanity. The progression of attitudes in Spina, whom we first meet as a revolutionary-in-hiding in *Bread and Wine*, is most instructive. At first he is simply one who organizes groups for resistance, rebellion, and, possibly, death. But as the book progresses, his enforced hiding results in his beginning to enter into human relationships, to recover a feeling for *persons*, and to discover that these are more important than impersonal ideologies. He learns that one can find more human solidarity in shared humanity than in shared political convictions. Spina, disguised as Don Paolo, finds a young peasant named Infante, follows him home and starts giving him a political lecture. Infante gives him food. Spina's landlady finally locates him in Infante's hut and urges him to return to the inn for dinner:

> "I'm not hungry," said Don Paolo. "Go back to the inn, because I still have some things to discuss with my friend here."
> "Discuss?" said Matalena. "But don't you realize that he's a deaf-mute and understands nothing but some signs?"
> There was the deaf-mute, seated on the threshold of his hut, next to the priest. Don Paolo looked him in the face and saw how his eyes slowly realized the misunderstanding he had caused.
> The priest said to the woman, "That's all right. Go back to the inn anyway. I'm not hungry."
> The two men stayed there on the threshold of the hut, and he who had the gift of speech was silent. Every once in a while they smiled at one another. . . . After a while Don Paolo got up, shook hands with the deaf-mute and said good night.[19]

This seemingly trivial episode has deep significance for Spina. His concerns shift more and more from politics to human love. In the sequel to *Bread and Wine*, *The Seed Beneath the Snow*, Spina finally moves out of his own house and into the stall with the deaf-mute Infante. A remarkable bond is established between them, as Spina recalls in a conversation later:

18 Ignazio Silone, *A Handful of Blackberries* (New York, 1953), p. 145.
19 *Bread and Wine*, p. 148.

"Brotherhood was the first new word which Infante learned from me. He could already say *bread*, which he pronounced *brod;* and I explained to him with gestures that, in a certain sense, two people who ate the same bread became *brod-ers*, brothers, or companions. So from *brod* for *bread* came brother. The next day, Infante gave some evidence of his intelligence and of his agreement with my way of feeling when he showed me some mice running over the straw in search of bread crumbs. He murmured in my ear, *"Brod-ers."* From then on, he began to offer a piece of bread to the donkey every day, so that he could be a brother too, as he certainly deserved to be. I would like to talk a lot about my time in the stall, Nonna, and whenever I do, I'm trying to explain to you something of the state of my soul. Because I came out of there, if not completely transformed, at least stripped naked. It seems to me that up to that time I was not really myself; that I had been playing a part like an actor in the theatre, preparing a role properly, and declaiming the required formulas. All our life seems a theatrical fiction to me now.[20]

For Spina, what goes on in the stable turns out to be far more important than would have seemed possible to the earlier revolutionary; it establishes a human relationship across seemingly impossible barriers. This kind of relationship becomes more important to Spina than anything else, and finally, at the end of the book, when Infante has killed his father, Spina takes responsibility for the deed, confesses to the crime he did not commit, and lays down his life for his friend.

In *The Secret of Luca*, Andrea Cipriani, a politician, returns to his native village to run for public office. He arrives just at the time that Luca, a simple peasant, is released from jail. Luca has spent a lifetime in jail for a crime he did not commit, and which the people of the village know he did not commit. They are frightened by his return even though he seems to have no vengeance in his heart against those who could have demonstrated his innocence in court and failed to do so. Cipriani determines that he must discover the "secret" of Luca. What would motivate a man to let his life be destroyed in this way? Cipriani's attention is deflected more and more from his politicking as he discovers in Luca a fierce and stubborn integrity that was willing to endure forty years of imprisonment to protect the honor of another individual.

There is a dimension of human understanding that politics does not reveal. This does not mean that politics becomes unimportant, but only that politics needs, visionary as it may sound, to be infused by love. Without this ingredient, the most dedicated revolutionary will fall into the trap Uliva so convincingly sketches. The need is one

---

[20] Ignazio Silone, *The Seed Beneath the Snow* (New York, 1965), pp. 194-195. The same point can be made linguistically from the Latin. *Cum-panis* means, "with bread," and it is the word from which "companion" is derived. Companions are those who share bread together.

that Rocco, both disillusioned churchman and disillusioned revolutionary, comes to sense. Rocco revises Descartes' *Cogito ergo sum* (I think, therefore I am) to *Amo ergo sum* (I love, therefore I am). This, it will be noted, is very different from the formula of another famous revolutionary, Albert Camus, who declared, "I rebel, therefore we are." Perhaps the fullest statement of the principle would even go beyond Rocco, and emerge as *Amo ergo sumus* (I love, therefore we are), since love must leap the boundary from the self to other selves.

Silone thus captures the disillusionment into which the revolutionary can be led and he recognizes the ingredient that must enter into the ethos of the revolutionary if he is to avoid being transmuted into a replica of that which he wishes to overcome. The ingredient is love.

4. Once again, however, Silone does not fall victim of simplistic thinking. He offers no assurance that love will "win" or pay off. The one who loves does so at tremendous risk. And here again the theme of the pseudonyms of God comes to the forefront. For just as human love offers no assurance of success, neither does divine love. In his preface to *And He Did Hide Himself,* a stage version of *Bread and Wine,* Silone makes the point clearly: "In the sacred history of man on earth, it is still, alas, Good Friday. Men who 'hunger and thirst after righteousness' are still derided, persecuted, put to death. The spirit of man is still forced to save itself in hiding."[21]

"In the sacred history of man on earth, it is still, alas, Good Friday." God has come to man, but man has not been willing to receive Him. Man has, in fact, rejected Him. God is present, not as triumphant presence, but as brooding presence, as suffering presence, a suffering into which those who "hunger and thirst after righteousness" can expect to be initiated. In his play, Silone introduces Brother Giocchino, a wandering friar, who has been expelled from his order for giving voice to the dangerous notion that Christ has not risen, that God is still in hiding, that it is still Good Friday. Brother Giocchino says to Uliva: "You have lost heart because you think [God] is here on earth no longer. But I say to you that He is still here on earth; in hiding, certainly, and in agony, but on this earth still. As long as He is not dead, we mustn't despair. And perhaps it is for us to see that he is not allowed to die."[22]

The theme is not incidental to Silone, and he introduces it again in a later novel, *The Seed Beneath the Snow.* Don Marcantonio comments to a carpenter, Master Eutimio: "You forget that Jesus isn't

21 Ignazio Silone, *And He Did Hide Himself* (London, 1946), p. 6.
22 *Ibid.,* pp. 62-63.

on the cross any more. . . . The Church itself teaches that. There are people around here who believe that He's still on the cross, dying right now at this moment," said Master Eutimio seriously. "There are people who are convinced that He never died, and never ascended to heaven. That He's still dying, on this earth. And that would explain a lot."[23] The very symbolism of the book's title reinforces the point. The seed has indeed been planted, but it is still "the seed beneath the snow," the seed that has not yet come to flower. Furthermore, the action of the book takes place during Lent. Both facts suggest a theme of anticipation but not of fulfillment. The theme is reminiscent, as are so many of Silone's themes, of Pascal, who exclaims in the Pensées, "Jesus will be in agony even to the end of the world."[24]

That Christ has come to earth and has been crucified is, of course, part of the central Christian story. It is not the whole of that story, which includes the claim that Christ's death was not the end of the story, and that only in the light of His resurrection from the dead can one really bear the full burden of the message of the cross. There is, however, a Christian sentimentalism that leaps too quickly over Good Friday to Easter Sunday, that seeks victory without defeat and triumph without tragedy. It does not therefore understand the meaning of servanthood and suffering servanthood. In the face of such one-sided claims, Silone's counterclaim, that it is still Good Friday and that Easter has not come, is an important one. No victory worth having is ever cheaply won. Silone, however, refuses to let the unabated optimism of an Easter without Good Friday be transformed into the utter pessimism of a Good Friday without an Easter. For while he says that Easter has not come, he does not say that it cannot come. One can continue to hope, as Brother Giocchino does, and as all men must, but one must not allow his hope to be falsely and prematurely transformed into a nonexistent reality. There is a sober realism here that is clearly appropriated from the gospels, even though Silone himself is unable to make the full affirmation that the gospels make. While man must wait, he nevertheless waits with a certain hope, having seen in anticipation that which one day will be realized fully.

5. The above themes converge in a way that summarizes Silone's concern with God's pseudonyms. If God cannot be seen clearly and distinctly, if He is hidden by pseudonyms and it is still Good Friday, some hints of Him are nevertheless given to men. If he cannot be fully contained in human form or human events, there are at least certain events that help to reveal Him. *Earthly events can image*

---

[23] *The Seed Beneath the Snow*, p. 243.
[24] *Pensées*, No. 552, "The Mystery of Jesus."

divine events. That which we experience in utterly human terms can contain portents of the hidden God.

We have already seen that the death of Berardo was more than the death of a peasant. It was a contemporary reenactment of the death of Christ, a way of dramatizing the truth, "Greater love hath no man than this, that a man lay down his life for his friend."

In *And He Did Hide Himself,* Silone spells out in similar terms the implications of the death of another peasant, Luigi Murica. Murica had been found with a sheet of paper on which was written, "Truth and brotherhood shall triumph over lies and hatred," and "Living Labour shall triumph over money." Three women describe what followed:

> THIRD WOMAN   Then they crowded round him, and put a chamber pot on his head for a crown, and in mockery they said to him: "This is the reign of Truth."
> FIRST WOMAN   The wretches knew not what they did.
> SECOND WOMAN   Then they put a broom in his right hand for a sceptre, and bowing to him they jeered: "This is the reign of brotherhood."
> FIRST WOMAN   The wretches knew not what they did.
> THIRD WOMAN   Then they took a red carpet from the floor and wrapped it round him in mimicry of royal purple.
> FIRST WOMAN   The wretches knew not what they did.
> SECOND WOMAN   Then they blindfolded him and lashed him to a pillar in the barracks yard.
> FIRST WOMAN   The wretches knew not what they did.[25]

The conversation continues, paralleling the passion story.

Back in the village from which Murica had come, friends gather in his parents' home. They sit around the table. The elder Murica gives them food and drink, and the parallel to the holy eucharist, now being enacted in a simple peasant hut, is apparent.

> "It was he," he said, "who helped to sow, to weed, to thresh, to mill grain from which this bread was made. Take it and eat it; this is his bread."
> Some others arrived. The father gave them something to drink and said, "It was he who helped me to prune, to spray, to weed and to harvest the grapes which went into this wine. Drink; this is his wine."[26]

A little later in the meal, Spina comments, "The bread is made from many ears of grain. Therefore it signifies unity. The wine is made from many grapes, and therefore it, too, signifies unity. A unity of similar things, equal and united. Therefore it means truth and brotherhood, too; these are things which go well together." And an old man

---

25 *And He Did Hide Himself,* pp. 102-103.
26 *Bread and Wine,* p. 322.

replies, "The bread and wine of communion. The grain and the grape which has been trampled upon. The body and the blood."[27]

The double meaning of this episode (from which the book's title is taken) is apparent. Bread and wine are necessities of life, imperative for sheer physical survival, and they thus stand for food and drink. But bread and wine stand for more than food and drink. Bread, as we have already seen, stands for companionship, for companions (cum-panis) are those who share their bread; and the bread and wine together, as Spina testifies, stand for unity, and thus for truth and brotherhood.

Silone, however, goes far beyond even such levels of meaning as these, for his account of the meal in the home of Luigi Murica's parents is shot through with allusions to the holy meal of Jesus and his disciples. The point surely is that it is not only the meal consumed at the altar in the church that is a holy meal, but that any meal, even in the rudest peasant's hut, can be a showing forth of the divine through the very vehicles of the earthy. Murica's body has been broken, and Murica's blood has been shed, on behalf of the victims. of injustice, in the name of truth and brotherhood. And since he threshed the grain and trod the grapes, the bread and the wine are indeed "his" bread and "his" wine. But he who lays down his life for his friends witnesses not only to the integrity of his own deed, but witnesses also to the ongoing presence of the hidden God who has adopted the pseudonym of a suffering humanity.

In those moments when men suffer for their fellow men, therefore, they give shape to the "shapeless god" and make clear that God, too, participates in suffering on their behalf. Silone makes apparent that the material can be the vehicle of the spiritual, and his very doing so destroys the propriety of such a way of speaking, for he is saying really that the material and the spiritual are indivisible, and that he who comprehends the one likewise comprehends the other. If it is unlikely that God should be present in a peasant's hut when eating and drinking are taking place, it is just as unlikely that He should be present in a Palestinian peasant's hut as the son of a village carpenter. He may be unexpected in either place, but His presence having been discerned in one place lends credence to His presence in other places as well. Every table can be holy, every meal a eucharist, every deed of love a revelation.

Silone's world is a world still unfinished. It has been confronted by the presence of God, and being unable to bear that presence has tried to destroy it. It has not succeeded in destroying that presence,

---

[27] *Ibid.*, p. 323. The theme is present from earliest times in the second-century document, the *Didache,* and is incorporated in most subsequent liturgies.

although it has succeeded in forcing the divine into hiding, into the adoption of pseudonyms. But the divine continues to call upon men to discover Him in most unlikely places—in the man who writes in chalk "Down with the war," in the peasant who confesses to the crimes of another, in the revolutionary who teaches a deaf-mute the meaning of companionship—and thereby to assist Him in the work of bringing His own creation to completion. He is a strange, a hidden, a shapeless, a pseudonymous God, this God of Silone. But if men miss His presence in the world, it is not because He is not there, but simply because they have been looking for Him in the wrong places.

LORD OF THE FLIES:
THE POWER OF BEELZEBUB

Paul Elmen

The book which succeeded Salinger's *Catcher in the Rye* as the book most often discussed in Student Unions, English literature classrooms, and literary seminars, was *The Lord of the Flies*. Why the book should have sold so modestly when it appeared in 1955, and why it became a *succès d'estime* a decade later, is a problem in literary double-take which I leave to literary historians and owners of bookshops. Whatever the answer, *Lord of the Flies* fascinated the critical intelligence of the middle sixties.

Its theme was the death of innocence. Possibly the secret of the book's appeal was the obscure congruence between its thesis and the social history of our land. It has often been observed that we Americans moved through a similar crisis in our national history, having passed through the bland insouciance of our pioneer days to the reluctant maturity that we now enjoy as a world power. Our national novels have often portrayed this ripening of the ingenue: *Huckleberry Finn, The Great Gatsby, Catcher in the Rye*. In each case the hero loses his Adamic innocence and takes an awkward role in the world of grown-ups. The *Spannung* between the fragile structures of society and the primordial vitalities which explode beneath them is part of the American saga, exemplified in Western stories as well as in our political life; and it is the theme also of *Lord of the Flies*.

Golding's novel is about a company of English schoolboys, refugees from an atomic war, who have been deposited for safe-keeping on an uninhabited island of the South Seas. Attempting to carry on in the traditions of home before the holocaust, they organize into a makeshift community in order to find food and shelter and to tend the signal fire which will lead to their rescue. But dissension springs up among the boys. Worse still, an unspeakable threat appears on the mountain. By degrees the boys degenerate from the carefree lads of the opening chapter, frolicking like choirboys on a picnic, to the savage killers of the final chapter, who stalk their prey like animals.

Ralph is the boys' choice as leader. He is a tall, good-looking twelve-year-old who struggles to keep a minimal order, but who cannot understand or deal with the wild, subterranean forces that threaten his command. He is helped by Piggy, a fat, asthmatic proto-intellectual who uses his thick glasses to start the signal fire; and by Simon, a frail, Christlike figure who despite his shyness is the only boy brave enough to climb the mountain and confront the nameless terror thought to be there.

Leading the disruptive forces is Jack Merridew, a coarse redhead whose chagrin at not being chosen leader causes him to neglect the signal fire and to turn his food hunters into a terroristic band. As the novel opens he approaches with some marching choirboys from "the darkness of the forest." At first Jack cannot see Ralph, whose back is to the sun. Significantly his first command to the choirboys is that they remove their robes, which are marked with the sign of the cross. His confederate is Roger, a sadist, who later becomes the murderer of Piggy.

The novel clearly is about the fortunes of a few individuals who are at the same time representative people: singular little boys, who are also exemplars of the conservatives, the intellectuals, the criminals. Golding is clearly concerned with a universal theme, but his setting—an island like Tahiti—is strikingly vivid and comes alive for us like a successful Kodachrome, and his action—the refuge from an atomic blast—has also a singular quality, never having happened elsewhere. Always there is a contrapuntal motion between the odd and the familiar. As in *King Lear*, the underlying theme is the descent into animality. Chapter One, "The Sound of the Shell," introduces the conch that the boys use to call assemblies and to recognize speakers in the forum, thus serving in the novelist's shorthand for decorum, sanity, and free speech in a free society; the last chapter is "The Cry of Hunters," and between these chapters the democratic society has become a wolf pack. The agent for this deterioration is "the Thing," a nameless Beast or malignancy that seems to live on the mountain and turns what might have been a paradise à la Gaugin into an island hell. He is Beelzebub, whom the Pharisees called "prince of the devils," by etymology "Lord of the Flies," the Miltonic deity who presides over offal and carrion.

Golding has taken a steady look at the mystery of evil: the ancestral bias toward death and destruction that lurks just below the surface of polite behavior, biding its time, until a flaw appears in the conventions of society and the obscene deity appears. His archetypal topic—the loss of innocence—has been documented as well by Henry James, Conrad, Faulkner, Malraux, Camus, Graham Greene, and is certainly part of the distinctive anxiety of our time. The special kind of evil—the terrifying loss of humanity suffered by survivors of an atomic blast—is also the theme of Aldous Huxley's *Ape and Essence* (1948) and Walter M. Miller's *A Canticle for Leibowitz* (1959).

But *Lord of the Flies* is descended directly from the archetype of all such adventures, Daniel De Foe's *Robinson Crusoe* (1719). De Foe drew the rough outline that many lesser hands have filled in: there is a disaster that spares a few survivors, there is a lucky landing on an island that turns out to be a place of safety but also a place of mysterious danger, there is a struggle before the eventual rescue. Crusoe is the quintessential Englishman, who believes in God but who does not waste time brooding about Beelzebub and Gabriel. He busies himself instead by turning his primitive acre into a copy of a Sussex farm. Not only is his English common sense on his side, but God is there too. More ready than Golding to ascend a pulpit, De Foe tells the story, as he explains in his preface, "to justify the Wisdom of Providence in all the Variety of our Circumstance."

More immediately, *Lord of the Flies* is descended from an adventure story read by English boys and girls for a century, R. M. Ballantyne's *The Coral Island* (1857). Ballantyne thinks his boys are equal to the situation, whether God is helping or not. In his book Jack, age eighteen, is the natural leader who commands with a common sense which validates itself. Ralph, the narrator, is fifteen, but he navigates the schooner back from an exploring trip by dead reckoning; Peterkin is the useful pig-killer. There is danger from visiting savages and from pirates, but the boys are equal to the threat. Written during the full exuberance of Victorian imperialism, the book is a classical "Robinsonade," and Ballantyne never doubts that a public school discipline could subdue a native disturbance, just as easily as Robinson Crusoe built his rustic paradise and rescued Friday. What possible threat could survive the combined attack of Anglo-Saxon ingenuity, a tradition of justice impartially administered, a stiff upper lip, and possibly also a Providence anxious that goodness should win?

Golding replies, "Evil." *Lord of the Flies* is related to *The Coral Island* as Orwell's *Nineteen Eighty-Four* is related to *Rebecca of Sunnybrook Farm*. "Would you like to see what schoolboys are really like?" Golding seems to ask, and we recall that he was for many years a schoolmaster. Vaughan's children come wreathed in light, and Wordsworth's children trail clouds of glory, but Golding's children smell of sulphur and sweaty sneakers and beckon towards Gehenna. They are very like the children in Richard Hughes' novel, *A High Wind in Jamaica* (1929), who are such little fiends that they shock even the pirates! But Golding does not intend us to say, "Children are like that until they grow up." The boys are rescued by adults, but they are in this plight because of a grown-ups' war, and the destroyer which rescues them is itself on a manhunt not unlike that organized by Jack.

The rich concretion of event and character in the novel offers the same possibilities of interpretation that life itself affords. It is inviting, for example, to think of the book as a political allegory. The degeneration of the boys is very like the degeneration of Germany under Adolf Hitler. Trace the gradual demonization of the Third Reich, from the *Urgemütlichkeit* of Bavaria, the waltz, the October fest, the cuckoo clock, to the ovens at Dachau and you will have charted the demonization of Golding's novel. When Jack orders the innocent Wilfred beaten, he seems the quintessential Gestapo agent, beating his pistol butt against the civilized doors of the West.

Or one might read the novel as an attack upon the imperialist ideal. Anticipated by De Foe and luminous in Ballantyne, there was a nineteenth-century conviction that the white man's burden would be easily borne, that the savage corners of the earth would succumb to the attraction of the cult of the gentleman, and that in time the jungles of the world could be ridden in as safely as Regent's Park. But the civilizing dream proved only that. Wild demonries struggled to the surface and erupted as Communism, or Fascism, or a thankless Nationalism that wanted nothing of England. If the structure of order is not ruthlessly preserved, as Shakespeare's Ulysses told his fellow Greeks,

> The rude son should strike his father dead,
> And strength should be lord of imbecility.

Against the resulting convulsive disorder the restraint of English culture is helpless. To expect more of it is to make the mistake of the naval officer who rescues Golding's boys and says, "I should have thought that a pack of English boys . . . would have put up a better show."

Another style of interpretation makes use of the conceptual formulae of the social psychologists. It is tempting to see Freudian depths in several of the incidents, even though Golding has disowned this intention. Writing in the *Spectator* on September 7, 1962, he said that he was surprised when students in creative writing courses in American colleges seemed preoccupied with sex symbolism. He also told a lecture audience that he had read no Freud. But Viennese psychology hangs in the air, and *Lord of the Flies* makes use of several Freudian insights. The episode of the killing of the sow, for instance, is borrowed from Ballantyne, except that Golding describes the kill in terms of sexual fulfillment. And "the Thing" is a Freudian taboo, the forbidden object for which there exists a strong inclination in the unconscious.

The novel also illustrates the theory of play in Freud, namely, that children cut out situations which impress them, and so acquire mastery over them. Their games are examples of "the omnipotence of thought," which is best exemplified in art. The novel also bears out the analysis of play in Johan Huizinga's *Homo Ludens* (1955). Jack and his hunters ritualize the hunting of the pig. According to Huizinga, early play is a deliberate stepping out of life, and is always known to be pretending. Gradually play becomes ritual, and the action which the play represents becomes more and more blurred. Momentary remembrance of the original occasion causes some restraint of the play, and there are times when the mimetic character of the play comes to the fore. Thus when an older boy in Golding's novel throws a stone at a younger boy, "there was a space around Henry, perhaps six yards in diameter, into which he dare not throw. Here, invisible yet strong, was the taboo of the old life. Round the squatting child was the protection of parents and school and policemen and the law." Because game and reality are in the early stages kept distinct, Jack hesitates to plunge his knife into the first pig, just as the boys hesitated in *The Coral Island*.

But the line between play and life becomes faint. The pig hunt had begun as a search for food. Jack and his killers then re-enact the hunting, assigning to one boy the role of the pig. They take up the ritual shout, "Kill the pig. Cut her throat. Bash her in." The chant, like Hitler's brief slogans (or like a college cheer), has the effect of a charm. At the edge of rational discourse, it is more like a scream than a statement, and it moves towards hysteria. "Kill him! kill him!" the boys shout, as once the mob shouted at Golgotha. According to the logic of demagoguery, the spasmodic cries set up a participation mystique, reinforced by the anguish of the dance. The hypnotic incantation, the pulsating dance rhythms, the appeal to subrational violence works with explosive power, and even the horrified Ralph, watching from the sidelines, finds himself stirred. Jack's assassins move imperceptibly from playing children to ritual murderers, and the slaying of Piggy and Simon seems at the end like a fitting prolongation. Whereas at the beginning stage the play imitates life, at the end Jack's convulsive life imitates the game.

A primary Freudian problem lies deeply buried in *Lord of the Flies*. The question has to do with the locus of the disruptive, evil forces that terrify the boys. Are they objective, real in the sense that they exist whether feared by the boys or not? Or are they projections of adolescent fright, bogeymen who people the hovering mountain because the boys put them there? Freud's answer had the dogmatic tone that he always assumed when he was not really sure. "It would be different," he wrote in *Totem and Taboo*, "if demons really existed; but we know that, like gods, they are really only the products of the psychic powers of men."

If the demons were real the problem would indeed be different; but this is precisely what we do not know. Ralph sees the centrality of the problem, and violates the taboo to ask his intellectual friend Piggy about it: "The trouble is: are there ghosts, Piggy? Or beasts?" Piggy, wise for his years, has solved the question along Freudian lines; he has no room in his rational, ordered universe for the absurd. An irrational element, like the notion of a preternatural power, scrambles all the logical equations on which the humanist universe is built. "'Cos things wouldn't make sense," he explains. "Houses, an'—TV— they wouldn't work." This boyish philosopher has gone too far, since it is quite possible to believe both in an orderly universe of law and in the possibility of supernatural revelation; but he is quite right that any notion of the preternatural threatens the inevitable operation of natural laws.

What his rationalist faith does not take into account, and what Ralph's common sense cannot perceive, is that there might be supernatural influences both in the orderly processes of nature and in the miraculous interruptions of those processes, and what both Ralph and Piggy have failed to take into account is the demonic depth which is only partly concealed by nature's repetitions and by the conventions of men. They both underestimate the chthonic power of evil and exaggerate the power of plain truth. When Hitler rose to power the German universities thought that they could overthrow him with the massed power and dignity of thought; when Jack threatened the island with chaos, Piggy thought, "I'm going to him with this conch in my hands. . . . What's right's right." He thinks of the world as a quiet classroom where what is right wins, and so he rashly concludes, "I know there isn't no beast . . . but I know there is no fear, either . . . unless we get frightened of people."

Simon alone faces the terror. In Chapter 5, after the assembly called by Ralph has voted for the belief in ghosts, Simon grants the presence of terror, but thinks that "maybe it's only us." In order to find out the truth, he slips off by himself to climb the magic mountain (for all the world like Moses at Sinai) in order to bring back the news of whatever truth he would find. He comes down from the mountain with the truth about the fallen parachutist; but instead of being hailed as a savior who has dispelled the darkness, he is received exactly as is the man in Plato's allegory of the cave who returns from the daylight to tell the others they are looking at shadows; he is stoned to death.

Ironically, it is the degenerate Jack who knows that the beast exists outside himself. At first his plan is to hunt the thing. When this proves futile ("we wrestle not against flesh and blood," said St. Paul, "but against . . . the rulers of darkness"), he thinks he can drive it out of his thoughts: "We're going to forget the beast," he tells his followers, and "they agree passionately out of the depth of their tormented lives." When the Thing cannot be so simply exorcised, he turns to techniques of propitiation, leaving part of their kill behind for it, and dancing and chanting wildly to placate it. Jack and Roger, simply by knowing themselves, are aware of a depth of evil that is hidden from Ralph and Piggy, with their sentimental confidence in civilized structures. "The theme," said Golding in reply to a recent questionnaire, "is an attempt to trace the defects of society back to the defects of human nature. The moral is that the shape of a society must depend on the ethical nature of the individual and not on any political system however apparently logical or respectable."

It is part of Golding's achievement that like all the great storytellers he enchants his listeners, and they feel themselves involved in what happens to these boys at this place at this time. It is only when he has finished that the reader wonders about the appropriate generalization which is supported by the exemplum he has just read. Perhaps only the professional critic feels called upon not only to respond to the book with pleasure or pain or boredom, but also to explain what the book has said and whether he can approve or not.

When such an effort is made, the reader understands that Golding has made an assertion about evil, which he takes to be part of the data of experience. This evil is not an external power or presence (there are no ghosts), nor is it a defect of political or social structures (no matter what society man constructs, the evil will show itself). But the evil is real, and may be called Beelzebub, Lord of the Flies.

How then shall Beelzebub be chained? Certainly not by social conventions such as culture, education, or systems of law, since the evil can use even these for its obscure purpose. Not by common sense, either, as Ralph, Piggy, and Simon discover; the silken thread of reason cannot bind the raging beast. Nor by ritual propitiation, as Jack and Roger believe, since these gestures serve only to exacerbate the problem, whetting the appetite for blood and power. Where then can help be found? What passing cruiser can rescue not only the boys from their evil, but the adults as well?

Golding does not say. Content to light a signal fire, he warns of disruptive forces that defy the normal disciplinary instruments. He sees rightly with Hobbes that evil is within man, and the rescue by the government cruiser is perhaps his concession to Hobbes' belief that the strong ruler can set matters right. But he does not sufficiently realize that the evil is outside man as well, so that man not only projects evil, but is also sometimes seized by it, as the Nazis undoubtedly were seized by demonic forces in our time. The evil in the world has its intricate power because it takes so many forms, sometimes being projected by man in sheer malice, sometimes seizing men who are helpless before it, and sometimes being imagined by men when there is nothing to fear. Against this supernatural brilliance the cunning of man is not enough.

The missing piece from Golding's puzzle, the denouement which would properly have resolved his plot, is St. Paul's insight that supernatural aid is necessary to do battle with supernatural powers. Had the problem been correctly identified, he would have been led inevitably to the *solutio Christi*, which Milton recognized as the massive answer to Beelzebub:

> *Leader of these Armies bright*
> *Which but the Omnipotent none could have foyld.*

BEING AND WAITING:
THE QUESTION OF GODOT

Frederick J. Hoffman

1

Three things at least are important to the consideration of *Waiting for Godot:* its association with the traditions of the clown and with vaudeville, the question of Godot and his meaning, and the strategies of waiting. As for the first, we need to see it as an existentialist comedy, a genre not ordinarily associated with the philosophies of Sartre *et al.,* but in this case indispensably linked. It is a comedy in its many devices, taken from the reductive and derisive antics of the circus clown, and the vaudeville and the burlesque stage. It owes much to pantomime as well, of which Beckett has elsewhere proved himself a master. John R. Moore, in a wise essay on Godot, has suggested that we may consider "Gogo and Didi as very distant (perhaps the last) descendants of Don Quixote and Sancho Panza."[1] The parallel is justly indicated, but also shrewdly qualified. Estragon and Vladimir are very remote indeed from Don Quixote and Sancho Panza; they are not so much misguided idealist and comic realist, but both existential naturalists. Like the clown or comic, they are often naïve, patient, at times intensely practical and selfish, but durably patient. They exist in Murphy's world of the "nothing new," of continuously disappointed expectations.

There are many tricks which help to make *Godot* one of the greatest adaptations of the clown's skill to the theatre. One of these concerns the lines and curves of stage motion. The linear is indicated again and again by the device of repetition: Simple events, hopelessly trivial in themselves, in repetitive form become metaphysically fearsome. The major repetition is of course that of Act Two, which describes, with variations of some importance, the landscape, the characters, and the motions of Act One. This is to say that life will continue without much change, that expectations of change are generally disappointed, and that the line of time's descent to death is irreversible. The curve

---

[1] "A Farewell to Something," *Tulane Drama Review,* 5 (Sept. 1960), 59.

routines seem to run directly counter to the linear, as they do in Beckett's novels. But in the end they confirm, and even come to resemble, the linear, since they too are made up of repetitive motions. One of the direct effects of the curve in *Godot* is to destroy the notion of teleological purpose. Beckett's characters generally try to escape the straight line of mortality into the curve or sphere, but they are generally disillusioned. In accordance with time-honored suppositions, the curve is supposed to be more aesthetically pleasing as well as metaphysically impressive. But in *Godot* the "regard circulaire" has exactly the opposite effect. In vaudeville and burlesque routines, the cycle is used to define curves, the juggler keeps several spherical objects going in a circle, the spotlight describes a circle on the stage, where the comedian is on center. In *Godot*, however, curves are designed to describe the circular motion of human events; at best they are evasive, and postpone momentarily the line of movement toward mortality. In their most realistic aspect, they are simply forms of repetition—as in the "hat episode" of Act Two, or the "stuck whistle" stammerings of Lucky's "sermon." Most commonly effective is the suggestion of a curve as suggesting "resolution," or a progress of action in drama. *Godot* defies this suggestion. Nothing is resolved in it; there are neither high points nor moments of great passion; there are simply boredom and occasional relief from boredom.

The second comic routine in *Godot* is in the language itself. Beckett's language is "real" in the sense of its being held to commonplace reality. Its realism is indispensable to its critical function; his creatures are victims both of a high degree of expectation sponsored by centuries of rational confidence and of their own sobering recognitions of things as they miserably are. The two languages—that of a metaphysically stimulated confidence, that of an existential limitation—sometimes clash. Always, in *Godot*, the clash is there, though it is often merely implicit. The impact of situational realism is especially strong when it is defined within the limits of "tramps," hobos, the apotheosic "bum." Lawrence E. Harvey has usefully summarized its effects:[2]

> He reduces our gourmet delicacies to carrots, black radishes, and that staple of the starvation time under the German occupation, the lowly turnip. Our sex life leads to venereal disease; our fashionable clothes turn into rags, our lithe youth into stumbling old age, and our busy lives into a solitary waiting for death. We are not free but bound to each other and Godot; we are not equal but exist in a series of compartments in the social hierarchy; even our feelings of charity and fraternity are hesitant and fearful and inspired chiefly by our own selfish needs.

---

[2] "Art and the Existential in *En Attendant Godot*," *PMLA*, 75 (Mar. 1960), 139.

Illustrations of these uses of language are abundant; two of them may be worth reproducing here; the first combines disparagement of our delicate tastes and the uncertainty of our relationship to authority:

> ESTRAGON Give me a carrot. [*Vladimir rummages in his pockets, takes out a turnip and gives it to Estragon who takes a bite out of it. Angrily.*] It's a turnip!
> VLADIMIR Oh pardon! I could have sworn it was a carrot. [*He rummages again in his pockets, finds nothing but turnips.*] All that's turnips. [*He rummages.*] You must have eaten the last. [*He rummages.*] Wait, I have it. [*He brings out a carrot and gives it to Estragon.*] There, dear fellow. [*Estragon wipes the carrot on his sleeve and begins to eat it.*] Make it last, that's the end of them.
> ESTRAGON [*chewing*]. I asked you a question.
> VLADIMIR Ah.
> ESTRAGON Did you reply?
> VLADIMIR How's the carrot?
> ESTRAGON It's a carrot.
> VLADIMIR So much the better, so much the better. [*Pause.*] What was it you wanted to know?
> ESTRAGON I've forgotten. [*Chews.*] That's what annoys me. . . . Ah yes, now I remember.
> VLADIMIR Well?
> ESTRAGON [*his mouth full, vacuously*]. We're not tied?
> VLADIMIR I don't hear a word you're saying.
> ESTRAGON [*chews, swallows*]. I'm asking if we're tied.
> VLADIMIR Tied?
> ESTRAGON Ti—ed.
> VLADIMIR How do you mean tied?
> ESTRAGON Down.
> VLADIMIR But to whom? By whom?
> ESTRAGON To your man.
> VLADIMIR To Godot? Tied to Godot! What an idea! No question of it. [*Pause.*] For the moment.
> ESTRAGON His name is Godot?
> VLADIMIR I think so.
> ESTRAGON Fancy that. [*He raises what remains of the carrot by the stub of leaf, twirls it before his eyes.*] Funny, the more you eat the worse it gets.[3]

The second passage simply points up the confusion of arrangements, of timing, and in general of official calendars. It is akin to many uses of this satiric device, in the plays of Adamov, Genet, and especially Ionesco; in the last named, the cross-purposes technique has often reached the point of great comic drama. Here, Gogo and Didi discuss the time when they may expect Godot to arrive, but they are at a loss to determine the exact time *or* place.

---

[3] *Waiting for Godot*, pp. 14-14a. For some reason, the Evergreen edition numbered only alternate pages. The "a" references are therefore to the pages facing those numbered.

VLADIMIR   A—. What are you insinuating? That we've come to the wrong place?
ESTRAGON   He should be here.
VLADIMIR   He didn't say for sure he'd come.
ESTRAGON   And if he doesn't come?
VLADIMIR   We'll come back to-morrow.

       ✻   ✻   ✻   ✻   ✻   ✻   ✻

ESTRAGON   You're sure it was this evening?
VLADIMIR   What?
ESTRAGON   That we were to wait.
VLADIMIR   He said Saturday. [*Pause.*] I think.
ESTRAGON   You think.
VLADIMIR   I must have made a note of it. [*He fumbles in his pockets, bursting with miscellaneous rubbish.*][4]
ESTRAGON   [*very insidious*]. But what Saturday? And is it Saturday? Is it not rather Sunday? [*Pause.*] Or Monday? Or Friday?
VLADIMIR   [*looking wildly about him, as though the date was inscribed in the landscape*]. It's not possible!
ESTRAGON   Or Thursday?
VLADIMIR   What'll we do? [*10-10a*]

A third comic device of *Godot* is the pratfall, of which there are many variants. It is designed to express unwarranted or at least unexpected pain, and is often useful in the development of reductive satire. It is a comic destruction of cliché sentiments, and is therefore an important agent in maintaining the total effect of grim reality. The pratfall is any disgusting or vulgar defeat or collapse of sentimental expectations. When Estragon asks Vladimir to embrace him, Vladimir obliges, but the effect is anything but sentimental: ". . . (Estragon recoils.) You stink of garlic! Vladimir: It's for the kidneys. (Silence. Estragon looks attentively at the tree.) What do we do now? Estragon: Wait." (*12*) In another scene, when Estragon goes to comfort Lucky, who is weeping because his master has spoken of killing him, he receives a kick in the shins for his pains—this to destroy all pretense of simple human sentiment:

[*Estragon approaches Lucky and makes to wipe his eyes. Lucky kicks him violently in the shins. Estragon drops the handkerchief, recoils, staggers about the stage howling with pain.*] Hanky!
[*Lucky puts down bag and basket, picks up handkerchief and gives it to Pozzo, goes back to his place, picks up bag and basket.*]
ESTRAGON   Oh the swine! [*He pulls up the leg of his trousers.*] He's crippled me!
POZZO   I told you he didn't like strangers. [*21a-22*]

The best example of deflation in *Godot* occurs in Act Two. Pozzo has fallen, writhes, groans, beats the ground with his fists, while Vladimir and Estragon try to decide the wisdom of helping him. Perhaps we

---

[4] Cf. the incident of Edouard's briefcase in Act Two of Ionesco's *The Killer*.

ought first to take advantage of him, "subordinate our good offices to certain conditions?" But Vladimir urges that they help, because "It is not every day that we are needed." (51) The two debate at cross purposes, while Pozzo groans for help. When they finally agree, for two hundred francs, to the deed, Vladimir falls too; then Estragon, trying to help him, stumbles and falls. There follows a melee of fallen bodies and violence, interspersed by cries for pity and charity. (53-53a)

ESTRAGON Suppose we got up to begin with?
VLADIMIR No harm trying.
          They get up.
ESTRAGON Child's play.
VLADIMIR Simple question of will-power.
ESTRAGON And now?
POZZO Help!
ESTRAGON Let's go.
VLADIMIR We can't.
ESTRAGON Why not?
VLADIMIR We're waiting for Godot. [54]

The comic routines are involved crucially in the play's development. Occasionally concerned with the larger questions of time and the prospects of eternity, they are otherwise devoted to the task of collapsing pretensions of any and all kinds. More than any others, they set the play's tone as abjectly low-tempered, with no high-flown rhetoric or hopes. The language and the contradictions, which follow quickly upon one another, serve to undercut all efforts to make the play's meaning somber or "significant" in any but the most strictly factual terms. *Godot* does not tolerate above-level sanctions or celebrations of the human state. And this reductive process applies as well to the Sartrean kind of dramatic emphasis. Edith Kern says[5] of *Godot's* existentialism: "But unlike Sartre, Beckett's characters are never 'en situation.' They are, rather, entirely removed from the more immediate problems of society and, not living within a social world, they do not play a part either in good faith or in bad. . . . They are never 'engagés,' or committed, never the god-like creators of their essence as men."

This point cannot be stressed enough; for, while *Godot* does address itself to some ideas and implies a view of many others, it is concerned above all with men without property and without authority. If it has any generalizing function, it is that the faculty for making generalities is invariably defective. For this reason, the dependence upon comic and burlesque routines is important. The circus clown, for example, often comes upon the scene just after a magnificent display of skill

---

[5] "Drama Stripped for Inaction: Beckett's *Godot,*" *Yale French Studies,* no. 14 (Winter 1954-55), 47.

and grace; and, in the following routine (as a drunk trying the straight line, as a man who disgracefully fails in an elaborately planned demonstration of strength, or succeeds too easily), the clown brings the entire scene down to earth. Beyond this, there is no genuine metaphysical pathos in *Godot*. Estragon and Vladimir are erratically good-tempered and occasionally "helpful," but they have their price and are keenly aware of expedients. They are bumbling fools, but they are not "lovable rascals." In the general move toward the deflation of traditional values noticeable in the modern European theatre, *Godot* has a place. It is at times allied to Ionesco's extravagances (though not in any way to the reliance upon the political and moral assumptions of his *Rhinoceros*), and it occasionally reflects the Manichaean topsy-turvy of Genet and Brecht. But few plays can equal it in skillful employment of the comic for a serious purpose; and nowhere else are the most significant and ponderous issues of our intellectual life so much reduced to scale.

2

The first of these issues is the question of Godot himself. Who is he? And what does he "symbolize"? Estragon and Vladimir are "waiting for Godot," but they do not know who he is, nor when or even if he will come. Ronald Gray insists[6] that Godot *has* arrived, in the image of Pozzo perhaps but it may also be in a number of other manifestations, and that Gogo and Didi haven't recognized him. They are therefore "Christian delinquents," disbelievers, at the very least failing to understand God's manifold ways. This I think as far off the mark as criticism can be, the result of forcing external considerations upon the play.

Godot does not arrive, and he will not arrive. That he exists is at least established as a rumor, but his existence is not according to any theological explanation associated with divinity at all. He exists primarily in the minds and expectations of the two tramps, who therefore feel some necessity to honor an "agreement" to wait for him, according to a schedule dimly and confusedly understood. To Gogo and Didi, he must represent authority or power of some kind; he is not a rational or a consistent or even a likable figure, but he is presumably a man of power. He is "God" in this limited sense, but in any metaphysical sense God does not and cannot exist at all.

This fact is satisfactorily evidenced in the play, and evidence for it of a kind can be found in Beckett's fiction: No Beckett character is seriously interested in God as a metaphysical entity; He is too

---

6 "'Waiting for Godot': A Christian Interpretation," *The Listener*, 57 (Jan. 24, 1957), 160-61.

remote to excite them, and in any case they are almost invariably thrown back on their own resources of imagination and reason for self-definition. Godot is no more God than is the Mr. Knott whom Watt serves. The suggestions of a remote theological being fail to attract the inhabitants of Beckett's world, who choose the metaphors and techniques of transcendence that are to their own liking. As Beckett says of Joyce's, so he might have said of his own work: that his is a world of "vegetation," where people wait, or endure existence, without great expectations beyond mortality. The Christian beliefs are turned to secular metaphors; and the great line of progress in time is toward death rather than either a secular or a theological perfection.

This is not to say that Gogo and Didi are not interested in theological questions. They show on several occasions a lively interest in incidental religious exegesis. In the beginning, the question is raised of the two thieves crucified on either side of Jesus; this is a scene Beckett has explored before, in *The Unnamable,* and in a drastically revisionist style. In *Godot,* Didi brings up the matter: only one of the thieves was supposed to have been saved. Saved from what, asks Gogo; from Hell, says Didi. How is it, he continues, that "of the four Evangelists only one speaks of a thief being saved. The four of them were there—or thereabouts—and only one of them speaks of a thief being saved." (9) But in the ensuing dialogue, it turns out that Didi is not interested in salvation from hell, but only from death. And the theological interests of both are generally limited to life, death, and pain. At another time, Gogo is removing his boots and Didi says, "But you can't go barefoot!"

> ESTRAGON   Christ did.
> VLADIMIR   Christ! What has Christ got to do with it? You're not going to compare yourself to Christ!
> ESTRAGON   All my life I've compared myself to him.
> VLADIMIR   But where he lived it was warm, it was dry!
> ESTRAGON   Yes. And they crucified quick.
> *Silence.* [34a]

In both of these cases, the interest in religion is extremely personal. In the first, it is the matter of justice that interests them, and justice not for Christ but for the thieves; that, and the reliability of evidence interests them. Biblical literature is always so reduced in Beckett's work. There are no heroics, and theological disputation—so interesting and vital to Joyce's Stephen Dedalus—is as effectively deflated as are metaphysical and rational suppositions. The most striking case of this deflationary process is Lucky's "sermon," more properly his "talk," which is viewed as an entertainment in lieu of the dancing

Pozzo would prefer to have him do. Lucky's speech has to do with all pretenses common to an "age of progress," the end result of two and a half centuries of rational confidence. In his *PMLA* article (p. 139), Lawrence Harvey has said of him that, "when he begins to think, he not only deflates the intellectual but at the same time satirizes into non-existence our many specialized professional and avocational categories."[7]

At the urging of Pozzo to "Think!" which is a kind of injected stimulus, Lucky begins, on the question of God's existence: "Given the existence as uttered forth in the public works of Puncher and Wattmann of a personal God . . ." The speech is interrupted by a "quid pro quaqua quaqua" which has the sound of "quack" and in its repetition is a deflationary device. ". . . with white beard quaquaquaqua outside time without extension who from the heights of divine apathia divine athambia divine aphasia loves us dearly with some exceptions for reasons unknown . . ." (28a) His fumbling for words is dramatically suitable, but also a parody of the theological "naming" of concepts. Lucky's qualifications of the truth are also a far-ranging abuse of theological squeamishness; and he proceeds to indicate in his stammer further unwitting irreverence for the "Acacacacademy of Anthropopopometry of Essy-in-Possy," which establishes "beyond all doubt all other doubt than that which clings to the labors of men, . . ." establishes exactly nothing, since other commentaries have hopelessly confused the desire for proof. The tirade proceeds to a parody of the defects of "applied sciences": ". . . the strides of alimentation and defecation wastes and pines wastes and pines and concurrently simultaneously what is more for reasons unknown in spite of the strides of physical culture the practice of sports such as tennis football running cycling swimming flying floating riding gliding conating camogie . . ." and so on. The parody continues, of the view that salvation can be measured exactly in terms of the utilitarian rule: ". . . approximately by and large more or less to the nearest decimal good measure round figures stark naked in the stockinged feet in Connemara . . ." (28a-29) The prevailing and recurrent phrase is "for reasons unknown," there being so many more reasons unknown than reasons known for confidence in rationalist commentaries.

---

[7] The closest link of Beckett to Ionesco is in this "speech." Ionesco has many times lampooned similar pretensions. In *Amédée*, the hero disappears skyward, shouting progressive inanities; Bérenger of *The Killer* is a stickler for the word and ideal of progress, "un possibiliste avant la lettre"; he becomes the "hero" of *Rhinoceros* and thus may be said to have "saved" Ionesco from liberal critics. Pompous and naïve conventions are of course satirized often in Ionesco's plays: *The Chairs*, where the "dearly beloved" old man fulfills his promise of a vital message in the word ANGELFOOD written on the blackboard by a deaf-mute "orator"; the notorious *Bald Soprano*, where the favorite clichés run afoul of absurd cross-purposes; the family scene of *Jack, or the Submission*, etc.

God cannot survive such claptrap, and He does not survive. All theological questions must therefore be brought down to the quizzical personal doubts and definitions of Gogo and Didi. The question whether Godot *is* God or "equals God" should apparently be answered. God is surely one of the integers in Beckett's calculus. The Christian view of God, or definition of Him, is so much a part of moral discussion that tradition must account for it. This is very different, however, from making it directly a part of the speculations of Gogo and Didi. One critic considered *Godot* an "orthodox" Christian work: "The tramps with their rags and their misery represent the fallen state of man. The squalor of their surroundings, their lack of a 'stake in the world,' represents the idea that here in this world we can build no abiding city. The ambiguity of their attitude towards Godot, their mingled hope and fear, the doubtful tone of the boy's messages, represent the state of tension and uncertainty in which the average Christian must live in this world, avoiding presumption and also avoiding despair."[8] This is surely a narrow and a "wishful" interpretation. *Godot* does not argue an orthodox Christian view of doubt and despair; in fact, the doubt and despair are a consequence of the strong reasons for dismissing a personal God who is responsible for a system of moral sanctions and rewards.

Much energy has been spent on the meaning of the word, Godot; it is given in other forms in the play: "Godet," "Godin"; Gogo and Didi are not sure that Pozzo isn't Godot, and Pozzo himself confuses the name in several ways.[9] There is no question that Godot is an eternal "father image," an image of authority deeply wished for and so controlling the imaginations of the two tramps that they consider "waiting for him" a major preoccupation and duty. But the *reliance* upon the existence of an eternal being, to the neglect of personal responsibility for existence, is a major object of Beckett's criticism. The view of Godot is nontheological and untraditional; it is a form of anthropomorphic relationship, if you wish. But *Waiting for Godot* is an existentialist play, and as such it argues against the assumption of an image that drains off the energy of stark human responsibility. If Beckett may be said to be directly criticizing forms of supernatural presumption, it is in terms of the vitiating effects of such diversions of energy. In fact, "waiting" is in itself a meaningless activity, if it is a waiting for a specific supporting force. The two tramps describe again and again the futility of such expectations.

---

[8] *Times Literary Supplement*, Feb. 10, 1956, p. 84.
[9] In his *Perspective* article (p. 136), Hugh Kenner even finds a Godeau, a French cyclist, whose skill links him with Descartes.

3

Near the play's end, Vladimir puts the question of "waiting" quite frankly and eloquently. Waiting equals existing within a time scheme that permits none of the comforts of eternity.

> [*Estragon, having struggled with his boots in vain, is dozing off again. Vladimir looks at him.*] He'll know nothing. He'll tell me about the blows he received and I'll give him a carrot. [*Pause.*] Astride of a grave and a difficult birth. Down in the hole lingeringly, the gravedigger puts on the forceps. We have time to grow old. The air is full of our cries. [*He listens.*] But habit is a great deadener. [*He looks again at Estragon.*] At me too someone is looking, of me too someone is saying, He is sleeping, he knows nothing, let him sleep on. [*Pause.*] I can't go on! [*Pause.*] What have I said? [*58-58a*]

Waiting is the crucial experience of the Beckett character. It involves enduring the world's nonsense, its absurdity, without clear hope of immediate or direct help. The world is charged with mortality: the grave-digger applies the forceps, Death succeeds to life, which succeeds to death. Act Two succeeds Act One as irrevocably and monotonously as Gogo and Didi can predict each other's gestures and eccentricities. In his essay on Proust, Beckett had spoken about the relationship of habit and the act of "suffering" time. Vladimir says, "Habit is a great deadener." The landscape of *Godot* is monotonous and barren. The two tramps are forever asking "What shall we do now?" or seeking diversion. When Pozzo and Lucky leave the first time, the shouting and the crying gone once again, Vladimir says: "That passed the time."

> ESTRAGON   It would have passed in any case.
> VLADIMIR   Yes, but not so rapidly.
> *Pause.*
> ESTRAGON   What do we do now?
> VLADIMIR   I don't know.
> ESTRAGON   Let's go.
> VLADIMIR   We can't.
> ESTRAGON   Why not?
> VLADIMIR   We're waiting for Godot. [*31a*]

The situation of *Godot* is a dreadful void, an emptiness, a wearisome threat of boredom, a desperate need to "fill in the holes of time." The time, moreover, proceeds in a straight line toward death. The directions for Act Two are starkly relevant: Next day. Same time. Same place. The motifs of repetition seal the dreary fate. The round song of the dog in the kitchen is available for endless repetition, and it serves Vladimir to fill in a dread space of loneliness until Estragon arrives on the second day. (*37-37a*) Vladimir spies Lucky's hat, left there from the day before, and then begins a circular hat motion: "Estragon takes Vladimir's hat. Vladimir adjusts Lucky's hat on his head. Estragon puts on Vladimir's hat in place of his own which he hands to Vladimir. Vladimir takes Estragon's hat." (46) And so on. It is an example of the variants and combinations and systems we discover in *Watt* and *Molloy*.

Along with the monotony of *"waiting,"* there is the inevitability of the line moving toward age and death, that "fearful descending line that ends in the grave," as Lawrence Harvey describes it (*PMLA, 141*). The characters change in the time span of the play; they grow weaker. Lucky, who used to dance for Pozzo's entertainment, now can only "think" and talk. (In Act Two he has become mute.) As the play progresses, persons have increasing difficulty in standing up, sustaining themselves. Habit and familiarity grow increasingly boring and irksome.

Waiting has only two possible reliefs and justifications: that it is "for Godot"; that it may either be borne or stopped. Suicide is possible, within the range of human choice. But no one commits suicide; the limb of the tree, for one thing, is too frail, and it would break. In any case, neither Gogo nor Didi has the "strength" to initiate a suicide attempt. Waiting is not susceptible of melodramatic gestures. It is a solemn and a dreadful obligation, and nowhere is that fact more poignantly stated than in the passage at the beginning of Act Two (quoted above). Here, it is the succession of expected events that forms the heart of the experience.

Like all other Beckett characters, Gogo and Didi must not only "fill time" but assert and prove existence, ally themselves forcefully with other existing beings. The dangers of nonexistence forever threaten, and they are even a temptation. *Waiting for Godot,* says Jean Jacques Mayoux, "is on one level a dialectic of suicide, for to wait is to live. Suicide thus appears as a rational decision which should have been undertaken after the very first awareness of the absurdity of life. Once caught up in the 'waiting,' however, no instant of time can ever be decisive again."[10] Waiting is therefore a condition of man; it involves an acceptance both of death and of life.

4

Beckett's other plays are extensions of *Waiting for Godot*. If anything, *Endgame* carries the reductive process even further. The setting reminds us of the spatial limits of *Malone Dies* and *The Unnamable:* it is a room with two small windows high up and no accessible view.

---

[10] "The Theatre of Samuel Beckett," *Perspective,* 11 (Autumn 1959), 1951.

"Bare interior." "Grey light." In the center Hamm sits in a wheel chair, a blood-stained handkerchief over his no-face. Clov pronounces on the ineluctable progress of death: "Finished, it's finished, nearly finished, it must be nearly finished. (Pause.) Grain upon grain, one by one, and one day, suddenly, there's a heap, a little heap, the impossible heap."[11]

The only diversion is for Clov to take Hamm for a "trip around the world," or for him to climb to the window, to see if the world actually exists. Turning about the room in his wheel chair, Hamm is sure that he must be "right in the center." Also in the geometrical economy of the situation is the wall, which Hamm touches with his hand: "Beyond is the . . . other hell." (*p. 26*) At Hamm's request, Clov looks out the window through his telescope:

> Let's see.
> [*He looks, moving the telescope.*]
> Zero . . .
>
> .   .   .   .
>
> HAMM   Nothing stirs. All is—
>
> .   .   .   .
>
> CLOV   Corpsed.
> [*Pause.*]
> Well? Content?
> HAMM   Look at the sea.
> CLOV   It's the same.
> HAMM   Look at the ocean! [*29-30*]

Endgame is a step removed from *Waiting for Godot*, toward death. Both Clov and Hamm await death, and, it would seem, the end of the world. In an outburst of death's-edge rhetoric, Hamm shouts out: "Use your head, can't you, use your head, you're on earth, there's no cure for that!" (*68*) And, a few lines later, begs himself to hold on a little longer: ". . . the stillness. If I can hold my piece, and sit quiet, it will be all over with sound, and motion, all over and done with" (*69*). He goes the whole way, to his death: "Moments for nothing, now as always, time was never and time is over, reckoning closed and story ended" (*83*). There is something curiously static about *Endgame*; it is in Thomas Barbour's view "not so much a short play as a very long metaphysical poem."[12] This impression is a natural consequence of the limitations of the play's movement. It is neither so varied nor so embellished as *Godot*. Nor is it so rich as the novels; the simply stated formulas of *Endgame* are in the novels elaborately spun out, and here on the stage they can offer only a limited development. But the very limitation is in some respects an ad-

---

11 *Endgame,* trans. by the author (New York: Grove Press, 1958), p. 1.
12 "Beckett and Ionesco," *Hudson Review,* 11 (Summer 1958), 272.

vantage. Clov and Hamm describe the arc of a diminished human pretension. They are at the end of life, perhaps near the end of the world. Outside, in "that other hell," there seems no sign of animation; and the father and mother images have disappeared, each in its trash can, no longer to force their lids.

The great difference between the novels and the plays is that the torrent of words diminishes, and in fact—as Beckett's more recent plays testify—may cease altogether. As the words slow down, gesture, look, the simple moves of the body take over. A form of miming has its own poetic effect, and conveys—perhaps in a less complicated way—its own meaning. *Endgame* is less dependent on words than *Waiting for Godot;* it is also less an elaboration of the themes both plays share. "Acts without Words: I" relies upon stage spaces and props, distances and a limited number of actions. Its comedy simplifies the essential idea. The man at center is thrown onto the stage, gets up, dusts himself off, reflects, goes out again, is flung back. Objects are lowered from the flies, offered to him, withdrawn again. Each time he suffers a rebuke, he pauses to reflect, fastidiously attends to his hands, rises to try again. Eventually, he does not move, but simply allows temptations to go unnoticed. He has learned to depend only upon himself, as Barbour says, to "count on nothing but the unvarnished fact of his existence."

Krapp's Last Tape may be said to have two voices—or, rather, one actor who mimes and the tape record of his voice. Again, the themes so elaborated in the novels are here drastically simplified. One may say that they are extracted from the novels, made over for visual representation, and suffer in the transition and immense simplification. Yet this is a form to which Beckett's talent is remarkably suited. Krapp is a perfect specimen of the Beckettian man, reduced in powers of expression to gestures and postures. He is the clown turned meditative. His situation is as desperate as those of Gogo and Didi, and like them he has perceptibly aged. The skull grins beneath the flesh. But there are few details, few props, fewer ideas. He is, in short, in the act of reviewing his past, and he uses a tape-recorder to recapture it.

The description of his few simple actions shows a masterful skill in silent techniques. "He stoops, unlocks first drawer, peers into it, feels about inside it, takes out a reel of tape, peers at it, puts it back, locks drawer, unlocks second drawer, peers into it, feels about inside it, takes out a large banana, peers at it, locks drawer, puts key back in his pocket. He turns, advances to edge of stage, halts, strokes banana, peels it, drops skin at his feet, puts end of banana in his mouth and remains motionless, staring vacuously before him."[13]

The materials are all here borrowed from the tradition of the clown

---

[13] *Krapp's Last Tape* (New York: Grove Press, 1960), pp. 10-11.

BEING AND WAITING: THE QUESTION OF GODOT 389

and the pantomimist. The words are a comic version of *A la recherche du temps perdu.* The tape recorder stutters out a few family-album fragments, to which Krapp attends with the aid of legend and dictionary. "Slight improvement in bowel condition . . . Hm . . . Memorable . . . what? (He peers closer.) Equinox, memorable equinox. (He raises his head, stares blankly front. Puzzled.) Memorable equinox? . . . (Pause. He shrugs his shoulders, peers again at ledger, reads.) Farewell to— (he turns the page) —love." (*p. 13*)

The "last tape" presents him to himself as thirty-nine (a voice "clearly Krapp's at a much earlier time"): ". . . sound as a bell, apart from my old weakness, and intellectually I have now every reason to suspect at the . . . (hesitates) . . . crest of the wave—or thereabouts." (*14*) Krapp "participates in" the life of the tape, laughs appreciatively with it, puzzles occasionally over lost meanings and obscure allusions. "Closing with a— (brief laugh) —yelp to Providence. (Prolonged laugh in which Krapp joins.)" (*17*) But he becomes impatient with the tape's garrulity, winds it forward to the moment he wants to hear: "—my face in her breasts and my hand on her. We lay there without moving. But under us all moved, and moved us, gently, up and down, and from side to side." (*21*) Krapp has obviously reached the past moment he wants to relive, winds the tape back so that it may be repeated (*22-23*). After a few drinks off-stage, he comes back, and to a new running of the recorder denounces "That stupid bastard I took myself for thirty years ago" (*24*). But in the act of denunciation of that "crud," the thirty-year-old memory sticks; and at last he adjusts the tape so that it will repeat it (*27*). As the tape concludes, the voice says, "But I wouldn't want them back. Not with the fire in me now. No, I wouldn't want them back./Krapp motionless staring before him. The tape runs on in silence," as the curtain descends. (*28*)

This is a simplified Proustian exercise, or better a parody of Proust. It is loaded with the sentimentality of the old man caught in a moment of his past, his present a fumbling remnant of it. But even this overly simple rendering of Beckett's conceptions testifies to his skill in using the language of the self.

Some idea of his views of the self may be captured from it; but, more so, from the plays taken together. Their major assumption is that of existential time leading inevitably toward death. Within its passing, there are boredom and desperate strategies to give it significance, or simply to "pass the time." Pozzo, momentarily infuriated by Didi's questions, gives the clue to this blank perspective upon experience: "One day, is that not enough for you, one day he went dumb, one day I went blind, one day we'll go deaf, one day we were born, one day we shall die, the same day, the same second, is that not enough for you? (Calmer.) They give birth astride of a grave, the light gleams an instant, then it's night once more." (*Godot, 57a*)

Within this span of time—this lifetime, this day, this second—the Beckett hero is beset by boredom and pain. Unlike his narrative characters, the heroes of his plays have a limited repertory of devices, whether for passing the time or stopping it. They weave in and out of existence, at once puzzling over its tedium and depressed with their failure to define their actions significantly. When a sentimental note is briefly struck—as in *All That Fall* and *Embers,* two radio plays—it is entertained ironically. The Beckett hero is self-sufficient only when he is starkly alone, has been disabused by the vitality of the Godot image; has brought the world to his level, and is asked uncompromisingly to endure it for what it is. In the plays, the machinery of rationality, the ingenious extensions of consciousness and prolongings of innocence of the novels, are reduced to a minimum. The "man-using-machine" image so prominent in *Molloy* and other fictions is only fitfully and ironically seen; in *Krapp's Last Tape* the machine is a mechanical "memory" to which he addresses his attention. It does nothing to complement what he is, but fixes a part of what he was in his consciousness.

This is the starkest, blankest kind of existential world. The Beckett man is neither existentially curious nor heroically *engagé.* Over all of his meditations there is the awful prospect that (*a*) he can depend only on the world of phenomena (*Godot*) and (*b*) the world of phenomena seems to be disappearing (*Endgame*). In these circumstances, it is difficult to suppose a "Godot" as a god of any kind; he may be a business man or a Cabinet Minister or a Werner von Braun; he is not God.

The alternative choices are extremely limited. As in the novels, they consist of a frantic succession of can't, must, will. To "go on" is to persist in being one's doubting self. The rhetoric of recent works seems to have accelerated the hysteria of *The Unnamable.* In her *Perspective* article (*pp. 127-28*), Ruby Cohn reports Beckett as having said that "*The Unnamable* drove him into an impasse from which his *Textes pour rien* could not extricate him." The *Textes* bear testimony of this impasse; they become, as Miss Cohn says, "epistemological poetry." The "I" is no longer so much concerned with the relationships of selves as with the rhetoric of basic uncertainties. "Est-ce possible [he says in *Texte XIII],* est-ce là enfin la chose possible, que s'éteigne ce noir rien aux ombres impossibles, là enfin la chose faisable, que l'infaisable finisse et se taise le silence, elle se le demande, cette voix qui est silence, ou moi, comment savoir, de mon moi de trois lettres, ce sont là des songes, des silences qui se valent, elle et moi, elle et lui, moi et lui, et tous les nôtres."[14]

---

[14] *Nouvelles et textes pour rien* (Paris: Les Editions de Minuit, 1955), pp. 218-19.

5

Beckett's work brings the "language of the self" to an inescapable impasse. The lines of descent to which it belongs have been described in chapters one through three above. They are chiefly in the Western rational, skeptical tradition beginning with the speculative opportunities offered by Descartes' dualism. Beckett simply takes the self as a starting point, subordinates all of the vast and systematic orders of metaphysical explanation to the position of a cluster of metaphors available to the inquiring self, and proceeds then to a narrative and dramatic series of meditations upon them.

The other line of descent, fully given in chapter one above, is important not so much for its having shifted the ground of observation to the self as for its having reduced its prepossessiveness—the elements of human dignity—within it. The self is not only a skeptical inquirer in this case, but emotionally dispossessed and depressed. It is an important factor in this literature that the "tragic vision" becomes more and more a personal vision, or a nightmare of introspection.

Both the Russian-to-Kafka metaphors and the Descartes-to-Joyce techniques are significantly relevant to a full view of Beckett's world. The Kafka hero is always in danger of becoming vermin, animal, of dying "like a dog" or living like a cockroach; the rationales of respectability risk constantly a deterioration of confidence; and the rhetoric, magnificently though deceptively "realistic," is accelerated in conditions where the self's boundaries are invaded. Dostoevsky's undergroundling always speculates on three levels: that of himself, that of the mirror image of himself (which throws back the self, though with significant refractions), that of the logical equations of reason. All of these are taken up in Beckett, though the third comes natively to him through Descartes and the rationalistic orders of meditation.

Beckett's selves are, to begin with, persons without God, or (Murphy and Watt) persons with God imperfectly within them. As they proceed (chiefly from novel to play to comic interlude or sketch), their deliberations are fixed upon the fragments both of a rational order and of a once well established and defended *amour-propre*. As confidence in either systematic order or self declines, the rhetoric becomes disengaged, runs off on its own. Only in the play does the result come within perceptible scope and order: and this because the requirements of the theatre, however ignored or adapted to his tastes, do make for a more than occasional comprehension of Beckett's dispositions. Yet the theatre also oversimplifies; and, as the *Textes pour rien* prove, the "pure rhetoric" of Beckett's "residual Cartesian" is limited and impeded by dramatic necessities.

The essential "doctrine" of Beckett's work is nevertheless contained within his best play (and one of the best of all contemporary plays),

Waiting for Godot. It is that life consists of "waiting," an individually existential premise which incites no one to an exercise of a Sartrean "dreadful freedom" but has its own agonies and dreads. It is an agony to "wait for Godot" in a place deprived of almost all recognizable natural promise and from a point-of-view all but deprived of confidence. But we "can't go on, we must go on, we will go on": unquestioning, as the Unnamable says, but also unbelieving, in "It, say it, not knowing what" (*Three Novels 401*).

FLANNERY O'CONNOR

Robert Drake

In the essay "The Fiction Writer and His Country," which she contributed to *The Living Novel: A Symposium,* edited by Granville Hicks (Macmillan, 1957), Flannery O'Connor made her Christian commitment as an artist absolutely plain:

> I see from the standpoint of Christian orthodoxy. This means that for me the meaning of life is centered in our Redemption by Christ and that what I see in the world I see in its relation to that. I don't think that this is a position that can be taken halfway or one that is particularly easy in these times to make transparent in fiction.

In the same essay she also observed:

> I have heard it said that belief in Christian dogma is a hindrance to the writer, but I myself have found nothing further from the truth. Actually it forces the storyteller to observe. It is not a set of rules which fixes what he sees in the world. It affects his writing primarily by guaranteeing his respect for mystery.

And, again in the same essay, she concluded:

> The novelist with Christian concerns will find in modern life distortions which are repugnant to him, and his problem will be to make these appear as distortions to an audience which is used to seeing them as natural; and he may well be forced to take ever more violent means to get his vision across to this hostile audience. When you can assume that your audience holds the same beliefs you do, you can relax a little and use more normal ways of talking to it; when you have to assume that it does not, then you have to make your vision apparent by shock—to the hard of hearing you shout, and for the almost blind you draw large and startling figures.

These three statements categorically define Miss O'Connor's conception of her role as a writer with "Christian concerns." Indeed, one might conclude that she throws them down almost like a gauntlet: if this be treason, make the most of it. And treason or heresy it is to many contemporary writers and critics, who, commendably shying away from the concept of literature-as-ideology, assume that the further any writer can get from any kind of dogmatic commitment (unless perhaps to some kind of vague humanitarianism), the better an artist he is apt to be. But these three statements go a long way—in so far as *any* writer can be taken as speaking definitely about his own work— toward explaining Miss O'Connor's "concerns" as an artist, both themati- cally and structurally. For her these opinions were fundamental and in no way "negotiable," and any serious consideration of her work must start there. Indeed, it is principally with these "concerns" that this study proposes to deal.

Unlike some contemporary Christian writers, Miss O'Connor makes no concessions to the non-Christian world: on the whole, she refuses to make her ideology palatable to non-Christian readers by suggesting any alternative philosophical frame of reference other than that of Christian orthodoxy. (And by "Christian orthodoxy" is meant nothing of a narrowly sectarian nature. Perhaps we might define it for our purposes here as those beliefs comprehended and professed in the Nicene Creed.) Today this is an extremely big risk to take: such a theme and such a commitment inevitably deny the Christian writer many readers. Significantly, many of those same readers find Dante and Milton as rewarding as ever. But one suspects that they may be reading *Paradise Lost* and the *Divine Comedy* simply as "poetry" and dis- counting what they believe to be the theological residuum as "history" or perhaps even "mythology"—interesting but no longer relevant in these more enlightened times. After all, Dante and Milton did live a long time ago. . . .

This approach, however, is almost impossible to take with Miss O'Connor. For one thing, she is only recently dead: in a sense, she has not yet passed into history. The settings of her novels and stories are thoroughly contemporary; and more significantly, her overriding strategy is always to shock, embarrass, even outrage rationalist readers —and perhaps most especially those like the sort mentioned above who think Dante and Milton are great poets as long as one doesn't have to take their theology *seriously*. Such readers, significantly, are very quick to defend the King James Bible against the encroachments of more modern translations—not on any theological grounds but rather on literary: here is a literary masterpiece in danger of competition from cheap imitations. T. S. Eliot has pointed out that such a defense assumes of course that the theological content is dead: it's just the "literature" they're interested in.

But Miss O'Connor really seems to believe all that stuff, and she can't be written off for a long time yet as "history." The theology is simply there—as such—and must be reckoned with. In her case, the theology is perhaps even more obtrusive than it is in a Christian writer like Eliot, many of whose poems seem "patient of" a Christian interpretation but not exclusively so. And she has no truck with fashionable existentialist *Angst*—Christian or otherwise. She apprehends man's predicament in terms of classical Christian theology; and she uses the traditional terms without flinching: *sin, grace, redemption, Heaven, Hell,* and all the rest. Furthermore, she often seems to regard her function as prophetic or evangelistic and no bones about it: she *has,* in a sense, come to call the wicked to repentance—and none more so than the modern intellectuals who have no use for Christianity, the Church, or its traditional doctrines. And this may be what does limit her audience: she makes a crucial problem of *belief.* And the fact that she was writing in what has been called the post-Christian world (as Dante or even Milton were not) may have forced her, as she herself intimated, to adopt the violent methods of shock tactics, to draw bolder and bolder *cartoons* rather than representational or realistic sketches.

But by no means is this to say that Miss O'Connor was writing programmatic or propagandistic fiction: if she had been, she would not have written nearly so well. She does not oversimplify either her characters or the dilemmas which confront them, or the conflicts in which they are involved. And she certainly does not offer Christianity as the simple solution or the pat answer to their anguish: if anything, it's quite the reverse—as indeed it is in the Gospels themselves. Miss O'Connor was not writing just tracts for the times, though, in the broadest sense, her fiction is that too. But her vision of man in this world *was* uncompromisingly Christian; she saw all of life in Christian terms; she thought the Gospels were really *true;* and she accepted the historic teachings of the Church. And this intellectual and philosophical position informed everything she wrote. She was not trying to "sell" Christianity; she was—as indeed any writer is—trying to "sell" her particular perception of life in this world as valid.

Though born and bred a devout Roman Catholic, Miss O'Connor rarely wrote about her fellow communicants, largely, one suspects, for geographical and historical reasons. As an almost lifelong resident of rural Georgia, she inevitably knew more—and perhaps more about—Protestants, particularly those in the more fundamentalist and pentecostal sects. But there was nothing narrow or sectarian in her theology: she was *Catholic* in the oldest and widest sense of the term. Indeed, one suspects that Miss O'Connor's hot-gospelers and the Church of Rome have much more in common than not, though of course many of her fictional characters do look on the Pope as the Whore of Babylon. And to them Europe itself is "mysterious and evil, the devil's experiment station." As one of her fundamentalist characters darkly observes, "They never have advanced or reformed. They got the same religion as a thousand years ago. It could only be the devil responsible for that."

Certainly, it does not seem true, as has been once or twice suggested, that Miss O'Connor was a sophisticated Roman making sport with the eccentricities and grotesqueries of her good Southern Baptist brethren. Such a charge is quite wide of the mark. If anything, she seems to take a grim ironic pleasure in siding *with* the Southern fundamentalists against the modern, willful intellectuals and the genteel, self-sufficient schemers who are her greatest villains. The Southern Baptists, the Holy Rollers may be violent or grotesque or at times even ridiculous; but, she implies, they are a whole lot nearer the truth than the more "enlightened" but godless intellectuals or even the respectable do-gooders and church-goers who look on the Church as some sort of glorified social service institution while preferring to ignore its pricklier doctrines. Occasionally, her misguided characters take a more muddled view, falling between these two extremes, like Mrs. Shortley of "The Displaced Person":

> She had never given much thought to the devil for she felt that religion was essentially for those people who didn't have the brains to avoid evil without it. For people like herself, for people of gumption, it was a social occasion providing the opportunity to sing; but if she had ever given it much thought, she would have considered the devil the head of it and God the hanger-on.

Significantly, Mrs. Shortley's son, H. C., "was going to Bible school now and when he finished he was going to start him a church. He had a strong sweet voice for hymns and could sell anything."

In the light of these observations, then, Miss O'Connor's major theme should come as no surprise to us. It is that the Christian religion is a very shocking, indeed a scandalous business ("bidness" some of her characters would say) and that its Savior is an offense and a stumbling block, even a "bleeding stinking mad" grotesque to many. He "upsets the balance around here"; He "puts the bottom rail on top"; He makes the first last and the last first. In short, He revolutionizes the whole Creation and turns the whole world upside down, to the scandal of those who believe that two plus two always equals four (and, with craft, possibly five) or those who believe that they don't need any outside help (a savior) because they're doing all right by themselves. And this Christ comes not lamb-like and meek, as a rule, but in terrifying glory, riding the whirlwind: He is more like Eliot's "Christ the tiger" than gentle Jesus meek and mild. There is nothing sweet or sentimental about Him, and He terrifies before He can bless. Jesus Christ is finally the principal character in all Miss

O'Connor's fiction, whether offstage or, in the words and actions of her characters, very much on. And their encounter with Him is the one story she keeps telling over and over again.

This theme, along with several related subthemes, constitutes the principal burden of Miss O'Connor's work; and, even when it is not obvious, it is usually lurking in the background (like her Christ), ready to spring out to confront her rationalists and do-gooders (and the reader) with its grisly imperative: "Choose you this day whom ye will serve." And it is impossible, implies Miss O'Connor, to blink the issue: there is no place for Laodiceans in her world. For this reason, her fiction, though carefully ordered, even sedate and regular in its narrative progressions, has often the urgent intensity, the ordered ferocity, even, of a dramatic but sober evangelistic sermon. And one feels that, in her continuing insistence on the immediacy and importance of the Four Last Things, she recaptures (as indeed the fundamentalist sects try to do) something of the pentecostal atmosphere of the Primitive Church.

Indeed, the world of Miss O'Connor's fiction seems to wait hourly for Judgment Day—or some new revelation or perhaps a transfiguration, in any case, some sign that the Almighty is still "in charge here." Exactly *what* the event will be is not so important as that her world is subject to the continuous supervision of the Management, who makes itself known sometimes quietly and sedately but, more often here, in a "purifying terror."

With such considerations in mind, it is well now to proceed to an examination of Miss O'Connor's fiction, both thematically and structurally, to see for ourselves this apocalyptic writer at work and to note the strategies she employed (or was forced to employ) to embody her disturbing visions for a largely indifferent or even hostile public. . . .

❊   ❊   ❊

Perhaps Miss O'Connor's most forceful (though not therefore necessarily her best) dramatization of her major theme is to be found in her second novel, The Violent Bear It Away, which incidentally has strong thematic and structural links with "The Lame Shall Enter First," a long story in the posthumous volume. The novel is prefixed with a Biblical quotation (St. Matthew 11:12, Douai version): "From the days of John the Baptist until now, the Kingdom of Heaven suffereth violence, and the violent bear it away." The novel concerns the heroic (or demonic?) struggle of Francis Marion Tarwater to escape the prophetic calling decreed for him by his great-uncle, Mason Tarwater; and it characteristically begins with what is surely one of the most arresting opening sentences in the history of the American novel:

> Francis Marion Tarwater's uncle had been dead for only half a day when the boy got too drunk to finish digging his grave and a Negro named Buford Munson, who had come to get a jug filled, had to finish it and drag the body from the breakfast table where it was sitting and bury it in a decent and Christian way, with the sign of its Saviour at the head of the grave and enough dirt on top to keep the dogs from digging it up.

But this opening sentence is far from being the parody one might first suspect of all Southern "decadent" or Gothic fiction. Rather, it's almost as if Miss O'Connor had shouted "Fire!" or had labeled the novel "Dangerous. Handle with care." And all readers who are unwilling or unable to grant the *donnée*, which she almost never made more explicit, had better leave *now*—perhaps like catechumens in the Early Church.

For Tarwater's soul a titanic battle is waged—between the posthumous influence of the great-uncle (a God-obsessed man, if there ever was one) and a living uncle, Rayber, a psychologist who had years ago thrown off the great-uncle's soul hunger (he thinks) and has now "saved" himself by psychology, technology, and other modern conveniences. In this stern warfare Rayber (is the name as significant as Lucifer's?) is aided by the voice of a "stranger," who later becomes a "friend," speaking to Tarwater's own soul, which offers all the conventional, sophistical arguments against the old man's apostolic "charge." That this is meant to be the voice of the Devil seems fairly obvious, though of course the "friend" tries to persuade Tarwater that the Devil doesn't exist. And his argument is the classic one:

> Jesus or the devil, the boy said.
> No, no, no, the stranger said, there ain't no such thing as a devil. I can tell you that from my own self-experience. I know that for a fact. It ain't Jesus or the devil. It's Jesus or *you*.

The crucial battle rages around Rayber's mentally defective child, Bishop. The old man had instructed Tarwater to baptize Bishop; Rayber is just as determined that Tarwater shall not. Rayber himself had been baptized by the old man when a boy, had found in him also the only real love he had ever known. But he has thrown off those dark atavistic influences now, he thinks, except that sometimes he is overwhelmed by a blind senseless love for his idiot child, whom he is determined to look on as simply "a mistake of nature."

So Rayber, with all his intellectual apparatus, sets out to be Tarwater's "savior," confident that he can lay the old man's ghost—and perhaps the Gospel's too—for the boy. But his grand campaign is frustrated when Tarwater, determined to avoid his calling in his own way, decides to drown Bishop. ("You can't just say NO [as Rayber does] . . . You got to do NO.") But in the very act of drowning him,

Tarwater inadvertently pronounces the words of baptism. For a while longer, Tarwater continues to kick against the pricks, to escape "the bleeding stinking mad shadow of Jesus," Who pursues him, as He does many other O'Connor characters, like the veritable Hound of Heaven. Tarwater is even subjected to the final indignity of rape by the Devil in the guise of a cruising homosexual. But at the end, having returned to his native Powderhead, Tennessee, he has a vision of his great-uncle being fed with the multitude on the loaves and fishes and realizes at last that it is only such food which will satisfy his own insatiable hunger. Then finally he hears *his* charge: "GO WARN THE CHILDREN OF GOD OF THE TERRIBLE SPEED OF MERCY." And having anointed himself with dirt from his great-uncle's grace, he moves onward, "his face set toward the dark city, where the children of God lay sleeping."

The tragic potentialities inherent in Rayber, the man "who wants it all in his head," who has betrayed his past and denied his Lord, are minimized here. They are not so in the case of Sheppard, the City Recreational Director and psychologist-counselor of "The Lame Shall Enter First," who attempts to reform Rufus Florida Johnson, a juvenile delinquent with a club foot, and ironically loses in the process first the affection and finally the very life of his own son, Norton.

Sheppard looks on his counseling job at the reformatory, where he meets Rufus, as something like a priest's—except of course that he does not absolve. "His credentials were less dubious than a priest's; he had been trained for what he was doing." Convinced that Rufus' delinquency is due to a neurosis attributable to his deformed foot, Sheppard has the boy fitted with a corrective shoe, only to have Rufus refuse to wear it. (Similarly, Rayber had tried to replace Tarwater's "filthy hat, the stinking overalls, worn defiantly like a national costume" with clean, more conventional clothes.) And Rufus is "as touchy about the foot as if it were a sacred object"—an attitude that reminds one of Hulga Hopewell's feeling for her wooden leg. Both are the things that, in the Bible salesman's words to Hulga, make them "different" and give them some personal identity, though, appropriately, Hulga's attitude toward her distinguishing affliction seems more idolatrous than Johnson's.

But Rufus is a hell-raiser because, he says, Satan has him in his power. ("I lie and steal because I'm good at it! My foot don't have a thing to do with it!") And, like the Misfit, Rufus poses the real question in non-Laodicean terms: "If I do repent, I'll be a preacher. . . . If you're going to do it, it's no sense doing it half way." (Fittingly, Rufus has a prophet-grandfather who has gone with a saving remnant to the hills, to await an imminent Apocalypse.) Certainly, implies Rufus, salvation is not to be found in Sheppard, "that big tin Jesus

[who] thinks he's God." For Rufus, salvation is not a matter of works: "I don't care if he's [Sheppard] good or not. He ain't *right*." And Sheppard, face to face with Original Sin, that "elemental warping of nature that had happened too long ago to be corrected now," is defeated. But our hearts warm toward him as they do not, on the whole, toward Rayber because the insight that comes to him at the end of the story marks him out as truly tragic.

> He had stuffed his own emptiness with good works like a glutton. He had ignored his own child to feed his vision of himself. He saw the clear-eyed Devil, the sounder of hearts, leering at him from the eyes of Johnson. His image of himself shrivelled until everything was black before him.

There is, finally, no salvation in *works*, whatever form they may take, or in *self*, Miss O'Connor implies again and again; only in that Name which is above every name in earth and heaven—Christ the Lamb, Christ the Tiger, Christ the Lord. In Him alone is salvation to be found. To contradict Him is, finally, to contradict ourselves. And to live without Him is intolerable: it *is* Hell.

Perhaps a final word may be in order here about the lack of tenderness or compassion with which Miss O'Connor has sometimes been charged—especially toward those characters of hers who seem headed for damnation. Miss O'Connor *is* a "tough" writer, but she is not an inhumane one. Nor is she ever just plain bitchy. Her damned characters prepare their own ends: they *do* choose this day whom they will serve. And she refuses to let them off the hook by interfering with the consequences of their actions, which *are* inevitable. (Thomas Hardy, though he did not share Miss O'Connor's Christian persuasion, has often been accused of the same inhumanity simply because he insists, again and again, that, once a choice has been made, the game must be played all the way out.) But, for Miss O'Connor, the wages of sin is *still* death; and she is powerless to intervene in the Hellish consequences which overtake her prideful and self-justified villains.

For her, such "tenderness," very much touted in a modern world that likes to believe there is *always* a second chance and indeed often encourages man to believe that he is a creature more sinned against than sinning, would not only have been unrealistic: it would have been downright sentimental—or even sinister. And at least once she made her views on this sort of modern tenderness very plain— in her introduction to *A Memoir of Mary Ann* (New York, 1961), written by the Dominican Nuns of Our Lady of Perpetual Help Home for cancer patients in Atlanta.

Significantly, this congregation of Dominicans, which now maintains a number of such free homes across the country, was founded late in the nineteenth century by Nathaniel Hawthorne's daughter,

Rose Hawthorne Lathrop, who later became known, in religious life, as Mother Alphonsa. The congregation is called the Servants of Relief for Incurable Cancer. The memoir is an account of the life and death of Mary Ann Long, who entered the Atlanta home when she was nearly four and died there at the age of twelve. In discounting the modern sentimental tenderness which would see in the life and death of such a child a discrediting of the goodness of God and find in it therefore just one more good reason for not believing in Him, Miss O'Connor observed:

> In this popular pity, we mark our gain in sensibility and our loss in vision. If other ages felt less, they saw more, even though they saw with the blind, prophetical, unsentimental eye of acceptance, which is to say, of faith. In the absence of this faith now, we govern by tenderness. It is a tenderness which, long since cut off from the person of Christ, is wrapped in theory. When tenderness is detached from the source of tenderness, its logical outcome is terror. It ends in forced labor camps and in the fumes of the gas chamber.

Not for Miss O'Connor is such tenderness, which, uprooted from a dogmatic rationale, can all too easily become arbitrary and malignant. She holds fast to *charity* and *mercy;* but these of course are, along with Christ, the last things the truly damned want. The gates of her Hell remain locked from the inside.

❋   ❋   ❋

This then is the substance of the scandalous gospel, the harrowing evangel Miss O'Connor proclaims, which is not peace but a sword. But what about the imagery and the forms in which her unsettling visions are embodied?

The discerning reader notices again and again in her works what seems to be almost a predilection for the grotesque as manifested in physical or mental *deformity*. Characters sometimes have one leg or one arm missing, sometimes a club foot or a cast in one eye. Sometimes they are deaf-mutes, lunatics, mental defectives, even hermaphrodites. Frequently, also, Miss O'Connor even manages to suggest physical or mental deformity in her seemingly undeformed characters by comparing them or their appurtenances to that which is inanimate or non-human—for example, the wife in "A Good Man Is Hard to Find," "whose face was as broad and innocent as a cabbage," with her "green head-kerchief that had two points on the top like rabbit's ears." Again, the grandmother in the same story has a "big black valise that looked like the head of a hippopotamus." In the same story, Red Sammy Butts' "stomach hung over [his trousers] like a sack of meal swaying under his shirt." Or again, the old Confederate veteran in "A Late Encounter with the Enemy," who is "as frail as a dried spider," "every year on Confederate Memorial Day . . . was bundled up and lent to the Capitol City Museum where he was displayed from one to four in a musty room full of old photographs, old uniforms, old artillery, and historic documents." The train conductor in "The Artificial Nigger" has "the face of an ancient bloated bulldog"; Ruby Hill in "A Stroke of Good Fortune" is "a short woman, shaped nearly like a funeral urn." And many more such instances might be cited.

But does all this suggest that Miss O'Connor was simply disturbingly (even morbidly) interested in the lunatic, the maimed, and the halt for its own sake? It should certainly be apparent, from the foregoing pages, that she was not. In her view, physical or mental deformity of the outward and visible sort always suggests inner, spiritual deformity. And when she compares man to the non-human, she is suggesting that his efforts to assert his own will, to provide his own "savior," make him into just that—*non-human*, sometimes even *inhuman*. Human beings are most *human* and their personalities as individuals are most nearly fulfilled, she implies, when they remember the Source of all Humanity, the Fountain of all Life and Light Whose creatures they are. And, for Christians, at least one aspect of the Incarnation is God's revelation in Christ of what true *humanity*, true *personality* can be for all of us.

Once when Miss O'Connor was asked why Southern writers showed such a *penchant* for freaks, she replied, perhaps with some irony, that possibly they were the only people left who knew a freak when they saw it. But in a lecture at Notre Dame in the spring of 1957, she went even further:

> I doubt if the texture of Southern life is any more grotesque than that of the rest of the nation, but it does seem evident that the Southern writer is particularly adept at recognizing the grotesque; *and to recognize the grotesque, you have to have some notion of what is not grotesque and why.* . . . [italics mine]

And, for *grotesque* here, we might read *deformity*, which, for Miss O'Connor, always points toward that which is *undeformed*. For her, this undeformed state was to be achieved only when man entered into his "true country," his true life, found only in Christ.

Another aspersion against Miss O'Connor, often made along with the charge of her insistence on deformity, is that her stories have little that is beautiful in them. True it is that Miss O'Connor's characters often have little of physical beauty about them. And often the natural world itself seems ugly, if not downright sinister or hostile, with ominous turnip-shaped clouds lowering overhead and the sun "like a furious white blister in the sky." But more often it is not nature itself which is ugly here but, rather, what man *has made of nature*. In *The Violent Bear It Away*, as Tarwater approaches the city, he sees

> . . . a hill covered with old used-car bodies. In the indistinct darkness, they seemed to be drowning into the ground, to be about half-submerged already. The city hung in front of them on the side of the mountain as if it were a larger part of the same pile, not yet buried so deep.

And at least one critic has noted that the sordid winding streets of Atlanta in "The Artificial Nigger" suggest the labyrinthine circles of Dante's Hell.

One image pattern recurs again and again in Miss O'Connor's fiction, "like a signature," as Robert Fitzgerald has pointed out in his introduction to *Everything That Rises Must Converge*, a quotation which Miss O'Connor appropriated, apparently with some irony, from the works of the French Jesuit, Teilhard de Chardin. It is the recurring "fortress" or "sentinel" line of trees, usually surrounding some bit of pasture—an image which suggests perhaps some fierce spiritual arena where her characters wrestle now with the Devil, now with God. (In "Greenleaf" it *is* a "green arena encircled almost entirely by woods.") But always in such an instance, perhaps by virtue of some form of the pathetic fallacy, it is not the trees themselves—or nature itself—which are sinister or hostile but the spiritual disposition of the "wrestling" characters which makes them so. Surely, Miss O'Connor would have agreed with Pope that all seems infected that the infected spy.

Some of Miss O'Connor's more villainous characters, especially those self-sufficient women, are apt to look on nature as something which can be controlled and mastered, finally perhaps even exploited. To them, it may be just one more *commodity*; it certainly holds no particular *mystery* for them. In "A Circle in the Fire," to the strong-willed Mrs. Cope (surely the name is significant here), "her Negroes were as destructive and impersonal as the nut grass." And this same impiety toward nature may, as the foregoing quotation implies, carry with it an impiety towards others of God's creatures.

A quite different view is represented in the old priest of "The Displaced Person," who marvels at the transfigured beauty of a peacock's raised tail:

> The cock stopped suddenly and curving his neck backwards, he raised his tail and spread it with a shimmering timbrous noise. Tiers of small pregnant suns floated in a green-gold haze over his head. The priest stood transfixed, his jaw slack. Mrs. McIntyre wondered where she had ever seen such an idiotic old man. "Christ will come like that!" he said in a loud gay voice and wiped his hand over his mouth and stood there, gaping.

But to Mrs. McIntyre it's just a peacock; and the sooner the flock dies off, the better she will like it.

Then in "A Temple of the Holy Ghost," the natural order itself seems gone haywire. Two giggling convent-school-girls and their "big dumb Church of God ox" escorts attend a side show at the fair and see a hermaphrodite. But the hermaphrodite's words, spoken in turn to each section of the sexually segregated audience, are, for Miss O'Connor, right on key.

> "God made me thisaway and if you laugh He may strike you the same way. This is the way He wanted me to be and I ain't disputing His way. I'm showing you because I got to make the best of it. I expect you to act like ladies and gentlemen. I never done it to myself nor had a thing to do with it but I'm making the best of it. I don't dispute hit."

It would seem that the hermaphrodite's very existence violates the natural order and presumably calls into question belief in an all-good, all-loving God and His whole Creation, which, we are told, He looked on and found good. But Miss O'Connor doesn't "dispute it" either; she "makes the best of it" too. And the last sentence of the story may be highly significant: "The sun was a huge red ball like an elevated Host drenched in blood and when it sank out of sight, it left a line in the sky like a red clay road hanging over the trees."

The natural world is mysterious and strange, Miss O'Connor implies, sometimes baffling, ugly, even disgusting. In any case, it's surely a "fallen" one. And it is for her very much as it was for Hopkins: bleared and seared by man, wearing his smudge and sharing his smell. But always over this brown bent world there broods the Holy Ghost, with His warm breast and bright wings, blessing and sanctifying our smudged world and lightening our darkness, whether in rest and quietness or in the blinding revelation of the Damascus Road.

Perhaps, to sum it all up, no sentence Miss O'Connor ever wrote better embodies her attitude toward the Creation than one Robert Fitzgerald has pointed out in "A Good Man Is Hard to Find": "The trees were full of silver-white sunlight and the meanest of them sparkled." Surely, surely the operative word here is *meanest*. Miss O'Connor's view then of both man and nature is thoroughly sacramental. If man's body, no matter how warped or deformed, is a temple of the Holy Ghost, the earth also is the Lord's and the fullness thereof. And man violates neither with impunity.

Miss O'Connor's awareness of the ugly, the perverse, and the grotesque is further reflected in her prose style, which at times seems deliberately plain and graceless, sometimes even cacophonous. One might almost say that she had a healthy respect for the ugly—for all that had not been lightened, brightened, and de-odorized by secularism and by de-humanizing "efficiency" and "progress." For her, the Old Adam is *still* a pretty hairy creature. But ugliness, like vulgarity, for which she once observed that she had a "natural talent," is often a sign of vitality, even if it's vitality gone wrong. And, for Miss O'Connor, ugliness was usually preferable to the desiccated decorum of death—and damnation. (Her lady-villains insist particularly, as a rule, on decorum.) But such "decorum" represents not so much a clean, well-lighted soul as it does a whited sepulchre.

Occasionally, also, Miss O'Connor's deliberate awkwardness and cacophony of style remind one of Donne or Hopkins—a stylistic comparison which may suggest a further, thematic resemblance to those two poets of the warped and the skew. They, also, knew a freak when they saw it; and they, also, knew something of the terrible speed of mercy.

Perhaps, finally, it is with such major-minor figures in our literature that Miss O'Connor will be ranked. Her range was narrow, and perhaps she had only one story to tell. (But then didn't Hemingway?) But each time she told it, she told it with renewed imagination and cogency. From some of her remarks in conversation a year before her death, one might have gathered that she had grown tired of her one story, was even perhaps desperately trying to find another one—or perhaps some new way of re-telling the old one. Speculation about what the result of this search might have been is, of course, profitless. But one feels almost certain that, whatever form her possible "new" story might have taken, her fundamental assumptions—and perhaps her methods—would have remained substantially unchanged.

What *is* important is that she remains absolutely unique in American fiction, more skilled perhaps as a short story writer than as a novelist. (She does seem to lose some depth or density of texture in the longer fictional form.) But her vision and her methods were distinctively her own; and her rage for the *holy*—and the *whole*—has left its indelible mark on our literature and our literary consciousness.

❊ ❊ ❊

What then about those readers who do not—or cannot—share Miss O'Connor's "Christian concerns"? How far can they enter into both the substance and the shadow of her work? There *does* seem a point beyond which such readers, even with the best will in the world, finally cannot go: they cannot honestly share the theological assumptions which *are* part of her *donnée*. Some tension in that quarter does seem inevitable, and perhaps finally does deny her the complete acceptance of some very discriminating readers.

And yet, as she herself once indicated, no really good story can be ultimately "accounted for" in terms of a right theology—even for the deeply committed Christian writer or reader. (Such a view as this would certainly set her apart from the programmatic writer with "Christian concerns.") If it's a good story, it's not the theology as such which makes it so, even for the reader who is a professing Christian. Presumably, then, what makes Miss O'Connor's stories good and at times brilliant is that, in her own way, she does seem to have man's number—and the world's. People *are* often as she says; and they *do* often express themselves, in violent words and actions, as she represents them, and not just in darkest Georgia either.

Many non-Christian readers would have finally to agree that Miss O'Connor's diagnosis of the human condition—or predicament—is substantially valid: man does seem "warped" away from *something*, and he does seem to need reconciling with that *something* somehow, perhaps even by violent force. Furthermore, it often does appear in this world that those who are furthest on the way to some sort of reconciliation, nearest to some sort of ruling principle which, after darkness and terror, makes for light and order and peace, seem like extremely unlikely or even unappetizing customers; they truly often seem the least of us all. For such readers, of course, the Good News that this reconciliation is impossible for man to achieve on his own but that it has already been made for him in Christ is literally too good (or illogical? or absurd?) to be true. There they must finally part company with Miss O'Connor. But though they cannot choose here the one thing needful, they find nevertheless that she speaks dark home truths to their hearts, though often in a language which is foreign to them and difficult for them to understand. But Miss O'Connor's Georgia, though often terrible and dark, is no foreign country, finally, for any of us; none of us, finally, is a stranger there. If it *is* foreign, it is foreign only as this world itself is foreign to those of us who feel that our "true country" lies elsewhere.

MORTE D'URBAN: TWO CELEBRATIONS

Thomas Merton

Sooner or later someone will have to write a Ph.D. dissertation to examine the connection between *Morte d'Urban* and *Morte d'Arthur*. A relationship is evident in the "Castle scene on Belleisle—a rather elaborately contrived incident which may disconcert Mr. Powers' clerical readers. (I presume he has some.) It is not easy, in terms of Thomas Malory, to account for the Bishop who bounces the golfball off Fr. Urban's head, or for Mgr. Renton, a man of pungent verbal expressions, who hears the bounce but insists on interpreting it as the sound of a champagne cork popping out of a bottle. But one does not need to account for characters who give such a very good account of themselves, with or without help from Arthurian legend.

The epic of Father Urban begins in the usual Powers style: sustained and withering irony. The first half of the book has an intensity about it that will perhaps discourage those who are disposed to mistrust and fear this seemingly cold, perhaps even clinical satire: it has never been so sharp and so incisive. But is it really cruel? Is it negative? Those who stay with the book will find a change of attitude in the last chapters, and they will discover that Fr. Urban has become a sympathetic, in some ways admirable person. The fact is that the "death" of Fr. Urban is the death of a superficial self leading to the resurrection of a deeper, more noble and more spiritual personality. The novel is more than a ribald satire on the clergy. It is a valid and penetrating study of the psychology of a priest in what is essentially a spiritual conflict. The treatment is of course subtle, and the spiritual element in the story is deliberately understated: but we must clearly recognize not only that it is present but that it is essential to the book. Those who conclude that *Morte d'Urban* is purely negative and hostile to the clergy have not really read the story.

Perfectionists may worry that there are perhaps two Urbans rather than one. There is the more patently Arthurian Urban of the last third of the book: and there is the unmitigated operator, the crass narcissist of the first two thirds. The more earthly Urban becomes suddenly volatile after "Twenty Four Hours in a Strange Diocese," among a choice collection of lay freaks who make him seem very pleasant and

"Morte d'Urban: Two Celebrations." From Worship, XXXVI *(November 1962). Reprinted by permission of the publisher.*

human in contrast. He signs their visitors' book "Pope John XXIII" and takes off into legend in a borrowed sports car.

The presence, in our midst, of such a superb satirist as J. F. Powers is certainly a fact of major importance to American Catholicism. Much has been said, recently, about giving the laity a voice. Mr. Powers is there to prove that the American laity is not altogether passive and mute.

It is perfectly obvious that he speaks not as an embittered critic but as a very serious Catholic, profoundly concerned with the true mystery of the Church, of the priesthood, and of the Catholic faith. It is true that he will certainly appeal more to readers of the *New Yorker* than to those of *Our Sunday Visitor:* but it is a Catholic paradox that, since "Catholic" means universal, a writer who reaches only Catholics proves, by that very fact, that he is not yet Catholic enough. It is true that Mr. Powers may perhaps use his indisputable inside knowledge of the clergy ("How does he know so much about priests anyway?") to their apparent disadvantage. But let us reflect that the mere fact of portraying clerics as they are is not by itself an act of anticlericalism. To think otherwise would surely imply a pretty damaging admission!

Let us grant, then, that the simple frankness of Mr. Powers' satire is balanced by a certain modesty and charity which can make it, if we so desire, most salutary. One seldom finds him either really untrue or totally unkind.

Meanwhile a Council is in session, discussing ways of renewing Catholic life and the Catholic apostolate. It would seem that what Mr. Powers says in *Morte d'Urban* has a very distinct bearing on the need for renewal as it is now experienced in American Catholicism.

Every satirist is by implication a moralist, but as long as he keeps to his art, the morality is never more than an implication. Nor can it be otherwise.

If we are to learn from *Morte d'Urban,* we must take it in its own terms. How does Mr. Powers go to work?

A statement by V. S. Pritchett credits our author with a special "gift for recording natural speech." But there is more to it than that. Mr. Powers is remarkable for the sustained mastery with which he keeps up his sardonic parody of a glib, inexhaustible, semi-rational jargon. It is not natural speech that he records, but all the slogans, the fatuities and the half-truths of which our minds are full. In such rhetoric, the right word is always, of course, the word that just happens to be wrong—the expression that glances off the truth, that just misses having real meaning.

To be more precise, the statements of a Powers character always mean at the same time less and more than they are intended to mean.

The words are not quite accurate in saying what they want to say, and at the same time they speak infinitely damaging volumes by implication, thus confirming the words of Scripture: "A fool's mouth is his ruin, and his lips are a snare to himself" (Prov. 18:7). The dialogue of Powers' characters, then, is always shot through with absurdity, and the cumulative effect of a few pages of it is to leave us convinced of the irrationality and fatuity of their attitudes and folkways.

J. F. Powers handles this instrument with incomparable dexterity, and he has never been so eloquent as in this new book. Evelyn Waugh praised the famous early story, "Prince of Darkness," as a masterly study of sloth. In some of the early chapters of *Morte d'Urban* the author communicates a sense of *acedia* which, if it were not so funny, would border on despair.

He portrays all the horror, all the tedium, all the frenzied inner protest of the extravert who is reduced, in spite of himself, to living a plain religious life of poverty, monotony, and sacrifice.

The importance of *Morte d'Urban*, for a Catholic, is then not only that it is a work of literary genius, but that it makes a specifically religious statement: or at least a statement about religion. I say a statement, not a moral judgment. And this statement is contained principally in the character and the career of Fr. Urban. What kind of priest is he?

If we can extricate ourselves from the ironies of his creator and consider only the "hard facts" (as Fr. Urban himself would surely like us to), we will find him a very energetic and successful priest: one of the few members of the Order of St. Clement (founded by Mr. Powers) who actually amounts to anything.

When he preaches a mission, he has the people sitting on the edge of their pews. When he speaks to a mixed group of Catholics and separated brethren he leaves them all happy, with the feeling that the Church really fits right into our pluralistic society because *he* gets on so well with *them*. When he comes in to St. Monica's parish to help out Fr. Phil (another Powers priest who, like "Prince of Darkness," spends most of his time driving around in his car to get away from claustrophobia), he takes the parish census and gets everything set up for him to build a new church. Is it his fault if the Bishop is not interested? And so on. Fr. Urban, in a word, is the kind people like to call a "good priest" without reservation and without resentment because his zeal is just the kind they have been taught to admire. He is not trying to be holy. He is not trying to encourage crackpot movements. He is not mixed up with radicals, pacifists or integrationists. He is just a great guy with *people*, particularly if they happen to have money.

It is a familiar and not unacceptable picture.

But now if we tune out the other sounds and listen to his thoughts as they are relayed to us by Mr. Powers, we find in him empty gregariousness, not friendship. Verbalism, but not much to say. Cleverness, not talent or intelligence. His clerical zeal, though energetic, is based on an assumed equation between his own enlightened self-interest and the interests of the Church. He owes it to the Church to be a "winner," doesn't he? How else is the Church going to be respected in a competitive and affluent society? In a word, he is a public relations man, an operator, a ham.

It is not surprising, then, that he decides that the best way to put St. Clement's Hill Retreat House on the map is to add a golf course that will "draw the better kind of retreatant."

Fr. Urban is, then, a great priest, if by that you mean he is a clever salesman who can get everybody to buy his image of himself and of the Church as a good, wholesome, worthwhile American package.

Yet it would seem that Mr. Powers does not find this altogether satisfactory. As we watch Fr. Urban at work "with people" (he is not so good when he is not working with people) we become aware of profound religious ambiguities. Just as St. Clement's Hill consists of an old ramshackle retreat house and a fancy new golf course, so Fr. Urban's religion consists of a rather well worn, though effective, road company act, to which he has added an up-to-date public relations routine. There are, with Fr. Urban, two celebrations always in progress: on one level his version of the ritual and the devotions of the Catholic Church, and on another, the profane ritual of marketing and advertisement.

Mr. Powers appears to think that Fr. Urban makes the sacred an occasion for the secular. The celebration of the more profane, monetary exchange seems to be the real basis for communion between Fr. Urban and his clients.

Happily, the story does not end there. And Fr. Urban certainly becomes heroic in the chivalric exploits by which he delivers himself from enslavement to his own commercially successful image. In the end, as a laconic provincial struggling with a brain tumor, he wins our sympathy and admiration.

This book is not a tract for or against anything: yet it can be taken perhaps as a witness and as a warning. The mission of the Church in America is not purely and simply to get itself accepted by wearing an affluent expression and adopting the idiosyncrasies of American business. Preaching the word of God means something more than publicizing an acceptable and popular image of ourselves. We are here to celebrate the mystery of salvation and of our unity in Christ. But this celebration is meaningless unless it manifests itself in an uncompromising Christian concern for man and his society:—the kind of concern expressed in *Mater et Magistra* and in the reiterated papal appeals for world peace.

It would appear that such concern is practically incompatible with the kind of superficiality in thought, in life and in worship so trenchantly satirized in the works of J. F. Powers.

Index

413